THE HOLY SPIRIT

THE OFFICE AND WORK
OF
THE HOLY SPIRIT

JAMES BUCHANAN

THE BANNER OF TRUTH TRUST

THE BANNER OF TRUTH TRUST
3 Murrayfield Road, Edinburgh EH12 6EL
PO Box 621, Carlisle, Pennsylvania 17013, USA

* * *

First published 1843
First Banner of Truth edition 1966
Reprinted 1984
ISBN 0 85151 089 2

* * *

Printed and bound in Great Britain by
Billing & Sons Ltd., Worcester

Contents

PART I

THE SPIRIT'S WORK IN THE CONVERSION OF SINNERS

PART II

ILLUSTRATIVE CASES

PART III

THE SPIRIT'S WORK IN THE EDIFICATION OF HIS PEOPLE AFTER THEIR CONVERSION

PART I

The Spirit's Work in the Conversion of Sinners

I. The Necessity of a Great Spiritual Change

WE have a very solemn statement on this subject from the lips of One whose personal character, as well as his official authority, may well impress our minds with a conviction of its certain and infallible truth. It comes to us from the lips of Jesus – that same Jesus who is the Saviour – the only Saviour of sinners; who pitied us in our lost estate, and entered into a covenant with God on our behalf, and engaged in his own person to render the price of our redemption; and left the throne of heaven, and appeared as a man on earth – a man of sorrows and acquainted with grief, and became obedient unto death, even the death of the cross; – that same Jesus who afterwards ascended up into heaven, and sat down with his Father on his throne – to whom all power is given in heaven and on earth, who, as mediatorial King, is now carrying on the administration of the scheme of grace, and will ere long come in the clouds of heaven to judge the quick and the dead; – that same Jesus declares, and that, too, with the solemnity of a most emphatic asseveration, 'Verily, verily, I say unto thee, Except a man be born again,' or born *from above*,[1] 'he cannot enter into the kingdom of God.' And can we contemplate the character of him who speaks, and his official authority, whether as the Saviour or as the Judge of men; can we consider his love for our souls, and his earnest desire for their salvation – his perfect knowledge of the plan of grace and of every provision which it contains, and his divine commission to declare the will of God, and to decide the case of every soul at the last day, without feeling that the very benevolence of his character, and his almighty power as a Saviour, impart a tremendous force to his words, when 'he that is true, he that hath the key of David, he that openeth and no man shutteth, and shutteth and no man openeth', declares that the door of heaven is barred against every un-regenerate man, and that, notwithstanding all that he suffered on the cross, he will himself decide when he takes his seat on the throne, that 'except a man be born again, he cannot see the kingdom of God'?

In regard to the nature of that change which must be wrought on a sinner before he can see the kingdom of God, I shall only observe at present that it is a *spiritual one*, spiritual in respect alike to its subject, its author, and the

[1] John 3. 3, ἄνωθεν – from *above*, superné.

means by which it is accomplished: *it is wrought on the soul of man by the Word and Spirit of God.* The soul is the *subject* of this change; it is not an external reform merely, but an internal and spiritual renovation, a change of mind and heart, taking effect on the understanding, when it is enlightened, on the conscience, when it is convinced, on the will, when it is subdued, on the affections, when they are refined and purified, on the whole man, when 'he is transformed by the renewing of his mind,' and 'created anew in Christ Jesus unto good works;' so that he is said to be 'a new creature, in whom old things have passed away, all things have become new.' The Spirit of God is the *author* of this change; the soul is born again only when it is 'born of the Spirit,' for 'that which is born of the flesh is flesh, and that which is born of the Spirit is spirit.' It belongs to him to enlighten the darkened understanding, by shining into it and giving it the light of the knowledge of the glory of God; to awaken the slumbering conscience, by convincing it of sin; to subdue our rebellious wills, by 'making us a willing people in the day of his power'; 'to take away the hard and stony hearts out of our flesh, and give us hearts of flesh;' to refine and sanctify our affections; and to 'work in us all the good pleasure of his goodness, and the work of faith with power.' And this spiritual change is wrought by *spiritual means*, for the Word of God, or the truth contained in the Word, is the instrument by which the Spirit acts. 'We are born again, not of corruptible seed, but of incorruptible, even by the Word of God, which liveth and abideth for ever;' and we are saved 'through sanctification of the Spirit, and belief of the truth.'

This change is often preceded by a process of instruction and conviction, and is always followed by a progressive course of sanctification; but it properly consists in our being made willing to comply with the Gospel call, by embracing Christ for salvation, and surrendering ourselves up to him to be taught, and pardoned, and governed, according to his revealed will; and as soon as it is accomplished in the experience of any sinner, his whole relation to God, his prospects for eternity, his views and feelings, his prevailing dispositions and habits, are totally changed; insomuch that he who formerly sat in darkness is introduced into marvellous light; – he who was at a distance from God is brought nigh; – he who was in a state of enmity is translated into a state of peace; – he who was exposed to a sentence of condemnation is forgiven and accepted; – he who was lost is saved.

I need scarcely add, that it is a *great change* which is here spoken of. That is a very great change which is wrought on an infant when it is born into the world, when it is introduced into a new scene, and begins to have a consciousness of its individual existence, and receives a thousand new sensations, and enters on a life of which it had no experience before. So is it with the soul at the time when a new spiritual life is imparted to it; for when our Lord speaks of its conversion under the figure of its being 'born again,' he evidently represents it as a very great change, so great as to bear some resemblance to the first commencement of conscious existence. Many other figures are employed, which are severally descriptive of one or other of its peculiar features, but all equally significant of its greatness. It is called a *renovation* of the soul, or its being made new; a *transformation* of the soul, or its being changed into another likeness; a *translating* of the soul, or its being brought from one position and placed in another, and a very different one; a *quickening* of the soul, or its receiving a new life; a *resurrection* of the soul, or its being raised from the dead; a *new creation* of the soul, or its being created anew by him who made it; the *washing* of the soul, or its purification from defilement; the *healing* of the soul, or its being delivered from disease; the *liberation* of the soul, or its being emancipated from bondage; the *awakening* of the soul, or its being aroused out of sleep; and it is compared to the change which is wrought on the blind when they receive their sight, on the deaf when their hearing is restored, on the lepers when they are cleansed, on the dead when they are raised to life. Now, of this change – so great, so spiritual, so comprehensive – the Saviour himself, who alone can save, declares, 'Except a man be *born from above, he cannot see the kingdom of God.*'

By the kingdom of God in this place, we are to understand, not the external dispensation of the Gospel, or the visible Church of Christ in this world, although it is sometimes used in that sense, but the spiritual and invisible kingdom of God; and the statement here made is designed to warn us that no unconverted man is a member of Christ's spiritual Church on earth, or can by any possibility obtain admission into the Church triumphant in heaven. There is peculiar emphasis in the words; it is not said that he may not, or that he shall not, but that he *cannot;* the impossibility of any unregenerate man being admitted into heaven is declared, and that, too, by him who came to throw the door of heaven open for the reception of sinners, and who holds in his own hands the keys of the kingdom!

That we may arrive at a right conclusion on any subject, two things are necessary – a *sound principle* and a *certain fact*. In the case before us, the principle which our Lord assumes is that a man must be spiritual if he would enter into the kingdom of God; and the fact on which he founds in connection with that principle is that by nature men are not spiritual, but carnal, corrupted, and depraved. If these two things be certain, the conclusion is inevitable, that a great change is indispensably necessary, or, in other words, that 'except a man be born again, he cannot see the kingdom of God.' Let us first of all consider the *fact* which is here assumed, and then, connecting it with the principle which is also assumed, evince the necessity of a great spiritual change.

I. In thus affirming the *necessity* of regeneration, and the impossibility of salvation without it, our Lord proceeds on the supposition, that in our natural state we are fallen and depraved, a supposition which is uniformly assumed in Scripture, and abundantly verified by experience and observation. It is implied in our Lord's words, for unconverted men are there spoken of as being *out of the* kingdom of God,[1] and incapable of entering into it unless they be born again; and it is clearly stated in the 6th verse: 'That which is born of the flesh is flesh, and that which is born of the Spirit is spirit.' In this comprehensive sentence, he places in vivid contrast the two great classes into which all men are divided in Scripture, I mean the regenerate and the unregenerate; but he does so in such a way as to intimate that all men belong naturally to the same class, and that if any have been restored, it was by their being born again. When he speaks of the *flesh*, he does not refer to the body, but to the soul; for, although the term is sometimes used to denote our corporeal frame, as when the apostle speaks of his 'living or abiding in the flesh,' it is more frequently, and always when contradistinguished as it is here from the Spirit, employed to denote *our whole nature*, as naturally *fallen and yet unrenewed*; as when the apostle says, 'So then they that are in the flesh cannot please God; but ye are not in the flesh, but in the Spirit, if so be that the Spirit of God dwell in you.' In this sense it corresponds to 'the *old man*, which is corrupt according to the deceitful lusts,' and to '*the natural man*, which receiveth not the things of the Spirit of God;' and is distinguished from the '*new man*, which after God is created in righteousness and true holiness.' Hence we read of 'sinful flesh,' and 'the fleshly mind,' of which it is said that the 'carnal mind is enmity against God.' When he says, 'That which is born of the flesh is flesh,' he intimates that every human being, as he is born of the flesh or of fallen parents, is himself flesh, fallen, corrupted, and depraved; that is his natural state, his state as he is born, and in which he remains until he is born again; so that *every man*, without any exception, may say with David, 'Behold I was shapen in iniquity, and in sin did my mother conceive me.' And when he adds, 'That which is born of the Spirit is spirit,' he intimates, indeed, that there are now two classes of men in the world, the one natural, the other spiritual, the one regenerate, the other unregenerate; but that this arises not from any original difference, still less from any spontaneous separation, but from a change which has been wrought on some, while the rest remain as they were, a change which is directly ascribed to the

[1] CALVIN – 'Docemur, exsules nos ac prorsus alienos a regno Dei nasci ac perpetuum nobis cum ipso dissidium esse donec,' &c. – *In Evang. Joan.*

regenerating grace of the Spirit of God. But naturally *all* belong to the same class and partake of the same character; and although there may be, and doubtless there are, manifold diversities of disposition and innumerable degrees of guilt among unconverted men, yet in the one, the only point of essential importance, 'there is no difference, for all have sinned and come short of the glory of God.'

Such is the supposition on which our Lord's statement rests, the supposition of the universally fallen and corrupted state of human nature; and did we really believe this truth, did we receive it in its full scriptural import, and in its application to our own souls individually, we should have little difficulty in perceiving the necessity of a great spiritual change, and the impossibility of our being saved without being born again. But this doctrine of natural depravity, although uniformly assumed in the Bible, and frequently asserted in express terms, and abundantly verified by the experience of our own hearts, as well as by the universal history of the world, is so offensive and alarming to every unconverted man, that he is prone, if not to deny its general truth, at least to mitigate and soften its meaning, in so far as it applies to his own case; and hence many a one who admits in general terms, because he cannot decently deny, that he is a sinner, shows by his whole spirit and conversation that he has no idea of what is implied in this confession, and no heartfelt conviction that he needs to be born again. He admits that he has some imperfections, some natural frailties, some human infirmities; he may even charge himself with a few occasional delinquencies, with the omission or careless discharge of duty, and perhaps with certain acts of positive transgression. But while he admits his imperfection to this extent, he is unwilling to believe that he is so utterly fallen as to be unable to restore himself, or to stand in need of so great a change as is implied in being 'born again!' Hence, when his conscience is at any time impressed, he thinks of nothing more than a mere outward reformation, a little more attention to duty, a little more circumspection in his ordinary conduct; and thus 'cleansing the outside of the cup and platter,' he looks for acceptance with God, and admission into his kingdom, although, inwardly, no change has been wrought, none that can, even in his own estimation, correspond with, or deserve to be called, a new spiritual birth. If any such shall read these lines, it should be a very solemn reflection to them, that the Lord Jesus, when he spake to a self-righteous Pharisee, a master in Israel, made no account of his exterior decency, but insisted on the necessity of *his* being born again; and that, too, in terms which declare that this necessity is alike absolute and universal, there being no man of whom it is not true, that he must be converted or condemned. If you imagine, then, that you may enter into the kingdom in some other way, and that you have no need to undergo that great preparatory change, I beseech you to remember that the Lord Jesus is of a different mind, that he makes no exception in your behalf, but affirms, without qualification or reserve, that 'except a man be born again, he cannot enter into the kingdom of God.' That solemn statement rests on the fact of our universal depravity; and even were it more difficult than it is to discover the grounds and reasons on which it is founded, such a declaration, coming from him who is at once the only Saviour and the unerring Judge, should impress our minds with the conviction, that the matter is finally settled and determined by an authority which no power in heaven or on earth can challenge or resist. His authority in this matter is supreme, and one distinct statement of his will should be received as a final and irreversible decision; but the same testimony is often repeated, and in great variety of language. At one time he tells you, 'Except you repent, ye shall all likewise perish;' at another, 'If ye believe not, ye shall die in your sins;' at a third, 'Unless ye be converted, and become as little children, ye shall not enter into the kingdom of God.' But in his words to Nicodemus there is a remarkable peculiarity; he does not merely declare that no unregenerate man *shall* be admitted; he affirms that he *cannot* – that it is *impossible* he should be; and it is to the grounds on which this *impossibility* is affirmed that I now proceed to speak.

II. In the Scriptures, we read of some things that are impossible with men, but which are not impossible with God; and of other things that are impossible both with God and man. Some things that are impossible with men are possible with God, and to these the angel referred, when he said to Mary, 'With God nothing shall be impossible;' and our Lord himself when he said to the disciples, 'With God all things are possible.' But while, in respect to any mere natural difficulty, God's almighty power is more than sufficient to overcome it, there are certain things which may be said to be impossible with God himself – not from any defect of power on his part, but from their repugnance to his essential attributes, and their opposition to his unchangeable will. Hence we read, that 'it is impossible for God to lie,' that he '*cannot* deny himself,' and that 'without faith it is impossible to please him,' the things supposed being in their own nature contrary to the essential character of God, so that he cannot be as he is – he must cease to be God before these things can come to pass. It will be found, that to this class of moral impossibilities, the salvation of an unregenerate man belongs. There is a very remarkable difference betwixt the statement of our Lord to Nicodemus, and the deliverance which he pronounced on another case of great difficulty. In reference to *rich men*, and the difficulty of their entrance into the kingdom, he had said, when the young man mentioned in the gospel 'went away sorrowful, for he had great possessions,' 'I say unto you, that a *rich man* shall *hardly* enter into the kingdom of heaven: and again I say unto you, It is easier for a camel to go through the eye of a needle, than for a *rich man* to enter into the kingdom of God.' But when the disciples said, 'Who then can be saved?' he answered, 'With men this is impossible, but with God all things are possible,' thereby intimating, that although *naturally impossible*, by reason of the manifold obstructions with which a rich man has to contend, it was not impossible for him to remove these obstructions, nor anywise inconsistent with his character to put forth his power for that end; and accordingly, although 'not many rich and not many noble are called,' yet some in every age have been converted, and made signal monuments of the efficacy of his grace. But mark the difference when he speaks of an unregenerate man; he does not say that his entrance into the kingdom, although impossible with men, is possible with God; but he pronounces absolutely, that remaining in that condition, *he cannot see the kingdom of God*, thereby representing it as one of those things which are impossible with God himself, and which would be alike inconsistent with his declared will, opposed to the essential perfections of his nature, and subversive of the unchangeable principles of his government. It is possible, indeed, – oh! it is very possible – that an unconverted man may be converted, that an unregenerate man may be renewed, for this, so far from being opposed to God's will, or character, or government, is in unison with them all, and a fit object for the interposition of his grace and power; but that a sinner remaining unconverted should be saved, that a man 'born of the flesh' should enter the kingdom without being 'born again' of the Spirit, – this is an impossibility, and must be so, so long as God is God.

That it is so will appear from the following considerations.

1. No unregenerate man can see the kingdom of God, because it is impossible for God himself to do what implies a manifest contradiction; and there is a manifest contradiction in the idea that a fleshly mind can, without any radical change of character, become a subject of God's spiritual kingdom. The expression here used to denote the state of safety and happiness into which God brings his people is deeply significant and instructive. It is not spoken of, you will observe, as a state of mere safety – mere exemption from punishment, or immunity from wrath – but as a *kingdom*, a kingdom in which they are safe, because they are protected by his almighty power, and happy, because they are cherished by his infinite love, but still a *kingdom*, in which, besides being safe and happy, they are placed under rule and government, and expected to yield submission and service, as his obedient subjects. And so is it with every one who really enters that kingdom, whether on earth or in heaven; he cannot so much as enter into the outer sanctuary here, and far less obtain admission into the

holy place there, without laying down at its threshold the weapons of rebellion, and returning to his allegiance and duty. There is indeed an external kingdom of grace in which many an unregenerate man may be placed; but the true spiritual kingdom is 'not in word but in power.' 'The kingdom of God,' says Christ himself, 'is within you;' and, says the apostle, 'The kingdom of God is not meat and drink, but righteousness and peace, and joy in the Holy Ghost.' It mainly consists in the setting up of God's throne in the sinner's heart, subduing his will to God's authority, and winning over his affections to God's service; and to say that any man remaining in an unregenerate state can be a member of that kingdom, were to affirm that he might be at one and the same time both an alien and a citizen, a friend and an enemy, alive and dead. Every one must see, that if, when God saves men, he brings them into *his kingdom*, and places them under his own holy government, it is impossible, in the very nature of things, that they can enter it without undergoing a great change; and in this light, there is a self-evident truth and certainty in the words of our Lord, 'Except a man be born again, he cannot see the kingdom of God.'

2. No unregenerate man can see the kingdom of God, because it is impossible for God to lie; and he has expressly said, nay he has *sworn*, that we must be converted or condemned. 'The word of the Lord endureth for ever.' 'Heaven and earth may pass away, but one jot or tittle of that word shall not fail.' 'God is not a man, that he should repent: hath he said, and shall he not do it? hath he spoken, and shall he not make it good?'

It is very true that we read in Scripture of many occasions on which his 'repentings were kindled together,' and he refrained from the execution of his threatened judgments; but if we consider these cases we shall find that they are perfectly consistent with the general doctrine, that he can neither change, nor lie, nor repent, so as to leave his word unfulfilled, or to depart from the principles of his righteous government; and that they afford no ground of hope to an unconverted sinner that he may enter into the kingdom without being born again. God is said to *repent* when, in consequence of the repentance of his people, his *dispensations* towards them are changed; but this change in his dealings with them is only a consistent and suitable manifestation of the *unchangeable* and *eternal principles* on which he conducts his holy administration. Thus, when Rehoboam 'forsook the law of the Lord, and all Israel with him,' the king of Egypt was sent up to Jerusalem with his army to chasten them: and 'the Lord said, Ye have forsaken me, therefore have I also left you in the hand of Shishak. Whereupon the princes of Israel and the king humbled themselves; and they said, The Lord is righteous. And when the Lord saw that they humbled themselves, the word of the Lord came to Shemaiah, saying, They have humbled themselves; therefore I will not destroy them, but I will grant them some deliverance.' Again, when wicked Ahab, of whom it is said, 'There was none like unto Ahab, which did sell himself to work wickedness in the sight of the Lord,' 'rent his clothes, and put sackcloth on his flesh, and fasted, and lay in sackcloth, and went softly: the word of the Lord came to Elijah the Tishbite, saying, Seest thou how Ahab humbleth himself before me? because he humbleth himself before me, I will not bring the evil in his days.' And when the Ninevites repented at the preaching of Jonah, and proclaimed a fast, saying, 'Who can tell if God will turn and repent, and turn away from his fierce anger, that we perish not?', 'God saw their works, that they turned from their evil way, and God repented of the evil that he had said he would do unto them, and he did it not.'

These, and many other instances which might be mentioned, are so many proofs of the precious doctrine, that, under the scheme of grace and redemption, it is perfectly consistent with the truth and faithfulness of God, and the unchangeable principles of his government, to refrain from the infliction of threatened judgments, when 'the sinner forsakes his way, and returns unto the Lord;' but they afford no evidence that a man may be saved without being changed, or that God's threatenings against the impenitent will not be carried into effect. He will repent of the evil only when we repent of the sin; for otherwise, he must falsify his word, and act in direct violation of those eternal principles which make it 'impossible for God to lie.'

3. No unregenerate man can see the kingdom of God, because it is impossible for God to 'deny himself,' or to act in manifest opposition to the infinite perfections of his own nature, in order to save those from suffering who obstinately remain in a state of sin. 'If we believe not,' says the apostle, 'God abideth faithful; he *cannot deny himself.*' Even were God's determination in this matter purely arbitrary, yet being framed by his omniscient wisdom, sanctioned by his supreme authority, supported by his almighty power, and declared by his unchangeable truth, it should command our reverential attention; but it is not arbitrary; it flows, like every other part of his counsel or procedure, from the essential and immutable attributes of his divine nature. There are some things that cannot be otherwise while God is God, and this is one of them: he cannot admit an unregenerate man into his kingdom, for this were to 'deny himself,' and to act in direct opposition to every principle which regulates his procedure as the Governor of the world. The supposition that a sinful man may enter into his kingdom without being born again implies that God must deny himself in three respects: that he must rescind *the law* of his moral government; that he must depart from his *declared design in the scheme of redemption* itself; and,

that he must *reverse the moral constitution of man*, or, in other words, *alter the whole character of his kingdom.*

That a spiritual character is indispensably necessary, in order to our being admitted into the kingdom of God, may be inferred from *the general laws of his moral government.* In one sense, all men, however rebellious, and even devils themselves, are subjects of God's kingdom, that is, they are under his government, as being bound to obey his authority, and responsible to him as their Judge. That we are under a system of government is the intuitive conviction of every thinking mind. We feel that we are subject to checks and restraints which are imposed upon us by some external authority, and which are altogether independent of our own will, insomuch that, although free to act according to our own choice, we cannot alter the constitution under which we live, nor emancipate ourselves from the control of law, nor escape or avert the consequences of our own conduct. That the system of government under which we are placed is essentially a *moral one*, appears alike from the evidence of our own consciousness, and from our experience and observation of the world at large. There is a mysterious law written on the tablets of our own hearts which reveals God as a Lawgiver and a Judge; and our whole experience bears witness to the inseparable connection which he has established betwixt sin and misery on the one hand, and holiness and happiness on the other. This is the general constitution of God's government; and from that government the wicked are not exempted; on the contrary, its reality is evinced by the very experience of those who do most resolutely resist it, just as rebels, when they are punished for their crimes, are still treated as subjects, and become the most signal monuments of public justice.

When our Lord speaks of the 'kingdom of God,' he does not refer to the moral government which is common to all men; but to that kingdom of grace and glory, into which it is his will to gather into one all his redeemed people, a kingdom in which every subject should be alike safe and happy, being delivered from all evil, and defended by his almighty power. He speaks of the state into which, as the Saviour, he brings his people – a state of perfect safety and peace; but still, you will observe, he speaks of it as 'a *kingdom,*' nay, as '*the kingdom* of God,' and this implies, that while in other respects it differs from the universal kingdom, which comprehends under it the righteous and the wicked, the fallen and the unfallen, and extends alike to heaven, earth, and hell, it agrees with it in this, that it implies a system of discipline and government, administered by God himself, according to such rules and principles as are consistent with the perfections of his nature and sanctioned by his unchangeable will. He is represented as the head of this new kingdom, and his people as his subjects there: and although our Lord does not refer to God's general government, but to this new kingdom of grace and glory, we may infer from his language that this kingdom will bear some resemblance to the former, in so far, at least, as to have a moral constitution, such as will make a holy character essential to the enjoyment of its privileges. It must be so, indeed, unless that kingdom be designed to supersede, or rather to reverse the whole moral constitution of the world, and to introduce another and an opposite system, which should make no account of character in the distribution of happiness, and secure exemption from suffering without effecting any deliverance from sin. How far this corresponds with God's actual design as it is revealed in the Gospel will fall to be considered in the sequel; but meanwhile there are two considerations that I would merely suggest as affording a strong presumption that Christ's kingdom cannot materially differ in this respect from the general government of God. The *first* is, that this government is not an arbitrary constitution, arising, like the Jewish ritual, from his mere will, and capable, like that and every other positive ordinance, of being abrogated; but a constitution which, as it derives its authority from his supreme will, is itself derived from the essential and unchangeable perfections of his nature; so that, unless God himself were to change, or the relation betwixt God and his creatures to cease, the leading principles of that government must remain the same under every successive dispensation; – and the *second* is, that it is a government not confined to men, but comprehensive of all orders of his intelligent creatures, applicable to all who are capable of knowing God and serving him, and extending to angels and seraphim, to whose society his people are to be united in the kingdom of glory; so that, unless the redeemed are to be governed by a different law, it is absolutely necessary that they should be spiritual and holy as the angels are in heaven. From these two considerations it is manifest that in setting up a new kingdom God will adhere to those great principles which are involved in his universal moral government; and from its fundamental laws we may infer with certainty, that as they who are saved are said to be brought into a kingdom, nay, into the very kingdom of God, they must be endued with a holy character.

That a spiritual character is indispensably necessary in order to our being admitted into the kingdom of God appears from his declared *design in the scheme of redemption itself*. So far from being intended to reverse or supersede the moral government of God, or to release us from the operation of those laws which connect sin with suffering, the scheme of redemption was designed to secure our happiness by restoring us to a state of holy conformity to God's will. Its design in relation to the law is declared, when our Lord himself said, 'Think not that I am come to destroy the law: I am not come to destroy, but to fulfil;' and the apostle, 'Do we then make void the law through faith? God forbid. Yea, we establish the law.' And its design in relation to ourselves is intimated, when we read that it was alike the purpose of the Father, the Son, and the Holy Spirit, to deliver us from sin as well as from suffering, and to restore us to the image as well as the favour of God. I solicit your attention to the declared purpose of each of the Three Persons in the Godhead, in that scheme of grace and redemption which is the only provision that has been made, or that ever will be made, for your salvation.

The design of God the Father is thus expressed: 'God hath from the beginning chosen you to *salvation through sanctification* of the Spirit and belief of the truth: whereunto he called you by our Gospel, to the obtaining of the glory of our Lord Jesus Christ.' And the design of Christ the Saviour is thus declared: 'Christ also loved the Church, and gave himself for it; *that* he might sanctify and cleanse it with the washing of water by the Word, that he might present it to himself a glorious Church, not having spot or wrinkle, or any such thing; but that it should be holy and without blemish;' 'He gave himself for us, that he might redeem us from all iniquity, and purify unto himself a peculiar people, zealous of good works.' And the design of the Holy Spirit is not only implied in his very office, as the renewer and sanctifier of God's people, and evinced by the whole scope and tendency of the Word, which is the Spirit's message and a declaration of his will; but it is expressly declared, when it is said, 'When he is come, he will reprove the world of sin, and of righteousness, and of judgment;' and that he will 'guide his people into all truth,' so as to fulfil the Lord's prayer on their behalf, 'Sanctify them through thy truth: thy Word is truth.'

From these passages it is manifest that in the scheme of redemption itself God proceeds on the principle that a spiritual character is indispensably necessary in order to our admission into his kingdom. The very salvation which he has provided is *spiritual;* it includes various blessings of unspeakable value, such as the pardon of sin, peace of conscience, assurance of God's love, exemption from hell, and admission into heaven; but these blessings, so necessary to our safety, and so conducive to our happiness, are inseparably connected, by God's appointment, as well as in their own nature, with a new spiritual character, and cannot be enjoyed without it, for the promise runs in these terms: 'Then will I sprinkle clean water upon you, and ye shall be clean: from all your filthiness, and from all your idols, will I cleanse you. A new heart also will I give you, and a new spirit will I put within you; and I will take away the stony heart out of your flesh, and I will give you an heart of flesh. And I will put my Spirit within you, and cause you to walk in my statutes, and ye shall keep my judgments, and do them. And ye shall dwell in the land that I gave to your fathers; and ye shall be my people, and I will be your God.'

If such be God's design in the scheme of redemption – the declared design of the Father, and the Son, and the Holy Spirit – how can you expect to be saved without undergoing a great spiritual change? If you hope to be saved without being born again, your hope must rest, either on the supposition that you are not naturally fallen and depraved, or on the idea that a holy and spiritual character is not indispensably necessary in order to your admission into the kingdom. On one or other of these two suppositions your hope must be built, if you expect salvation without a change of heart; for, if the *fact* be certain, that you are naturally fallen and depraved, and if the *principle* be correct, that 'without holiness no man shall see the Lord,' the absolute necessity of regeneration is at once established. Now, on which-ever of these two suppositions you may take your stand, there is enough in God's declared design in the work of redemption to convince you that they are both alike false and dangerous; for if, on the one hand, you flatter your-selves that you are not so utterly fallen as to require to be renewed, or as to be unable to effect your own restoration, should not your fond confidence in this opinion be shaken, when you find that in the scheme which God himself has revealed for the recovery of men, he proceeds uniformly on the contrary supposition, and makes provision for their regeneration by his own Spirit, and speaks to all in the same language, as sinners that have fallen, and that need to be restored? And if, on the other hand, you flatter your-selves that although you may be partially sinful, you may yet enter into the kingdom without undergoing any great spiritual change, oh! should not this presumptuous expectation be utterly extirpated and destroyed, when you find that it is in direct opposition to *God's whole design*, and cannot be fulfilled without subverting the scheme of grace? For what does your expectation imply? Does it not imply that God will depart from his purpose of saving sinners 'through sanctification of the Spirit,' and save them with-out being sanctified, thereby reversing the constitution of the scheme of grace, and violating the principle on which it is based? In other words, does it not imply that God must set aside the great scheme of redemption, a scheme on which he has already exercised all the riches of his omniscient wisdom, and expended the blood of his Son? that immutable wisdom, and inflexible justice, and unfailing truth, must all bend and bow down before the sinner, and suffer him to enter into the kingdom unrenewed? and do you not see that the whole design of God in the redemption of the world must be abandoned before your hope can be fulfilled? Does it not imply that the Saviour himself must relinquish the object which he had in view, when 'he came to save his people *from their sins;*' that he must adopt a new design, and throw open the door of his kingdom to the unholy and the unclean not to the unholy that they may be renewed, or the unclean that they may be washed, for in that sense the door is always open, and open for all, but to such as seek to remain in their natural state 'dead in trespasses and in sins;' and that he must assume a new character, as the Saviour of those who *refuse* the only salvation he has yet procured, and who are 'neither washed, nor sanctified, nor justified by the Spirit of God?' And does it not imply that the Holy Spirit must relinquish his offices as the Sanctifier and Comforter of his people, or that his functions and operations are unnecessary and superfluous? for why is he revealed as the 'Spirit that quickeneth,' if there be no need of a new birth? why as the Spirit of sanctification, if without sanctification you can enter into the kingdom? and why as the Comforter of the church? Can it be that he is to comfort men while they continue in their natural state, and to pour his blessed consolations into unsanctified hearts, and to make them happy while they remain unholy? All this, and much more, is implied in the presumptuous expectation that any of us can enter into the kingdom without undergoing a great spiritual change: it implies that the scheme of redemption itself must be changed, and that, too, after it has been accomplished by the incarnation, and sufferings, and death of God's own Son; for that scheme proceeds from first to last on the supposition that we are fallen, and that we must be renewed, if we would enter into the kingdom.

That a spiritual character is indispensably necessary in order to our being admitted into the kingdom of God appears *from the actual constitution of our own nature*, which is essentially a moral one, and renders it impossible for us to enjoy heaven, even were we admitted into it, unless our character be brought into conformity with the will of God. We have already seen that the general government of God is a moral government, and that a holy character must be necessary in his kingdom, so long as God is God. We now add, for the purpose of evincing the certainty of this great truth, that the constitution of our own nature is essentially a moral constitution, and that a holy character must be essential to our happiness, so long as man is man. The principles of our own nature, the very constitution of our being, must be reversed, before we could be happy in God's kingdom without a holy and spiritual character. Let me advert to some of these principles; and, viewing them in connection with the character of God's kingdom, you will at once perceive that we must be holy if we would be happy there.

It is a principle of our nature, a law indelibly written on the tablets of our hearts, and by which every one feels that he is a law to himself, that our *character* must be brought into conformity with our *conscience*, otherwise happiness is impossible. Conscience is God's vicegerent in the soul, a secret minister within, which marks the difference betwixt good and evil, and approves of the one but condemns the other; and, while it responds to the unseen Lawgiver, acts sometimes as an accuser preferring a charge, sometimes as a judge pronouncing a verdict, sometimes as an executioner carrying judgment into effect; and, though it slumbers and sleeps, it still awakens with greater strength, and is always present, so that we cannot flee from it, but go where we will, we must carry it along with us; and as a part of our imperishable nature, it will survive death itself, and appear with us at the judgment-seat, and remain with us in eternity. Now, sin and the conscience are opposed the one to the other; and where both meet in the same bosom, there is a fearful conflict, sin struggling against conscience and seeking to stifle it, conscience protesting against sin and appealing to the justice of God. This fearful conflict is, and must be, destructive of happiness. 'There is no peace, saith my God, to the wicked; for the wicked is as a raging sea when it cannot rest.' One or other, therefore, – either sin or the sinner's conscience, must be destroyed before his happiness can be secured. As we cannot get rid of conscience, we must get rid of sin: sin is the disease of our moral nature; conscience is a part of its constitution; and we must not expect that God will alter the structure of our being, in order to make us happy without being renewed. Conscience cannot be destroyed, but *sin may;* and it must be destroyed if you would enter into God's kingdom.

It is a principle of our nature, that, in order to happiness, there must be some correspondence betwixt the *tastes*, the *dispositions*, the *habits* of a man, and the *scene* in which he is placed; the *society* with which he mingles, and the *services* in which he is employed. A coward on the field of battle, a profligate in the house of prayer, a giddy worldling standing by a death-bed, a drunkard in the company of holy men, feel instinctively that they are misplaced; they have no enjoyment there. Now, suppose the scene to be 'the kingdom of God' – a kingdom which is described as consisting in 'righteousness, and peace, and joy in the Holy Ghost' – and that an un-regenerate man were translated into God's immediate presence, and placed among the society and engaged in the services of the upper sanctuary – oh! if he were not thoroughly changed at the instant when he crossed its threshold, can you conceive it to be possible that he could be happy there? Well, then, either our characters must become holy, or the whole style and nature of God's kingdom must be changed. We must be raised to a state of meetness for heaven, or heaven must be lowered and accommodated to our carnal tastes. The latter is impossible; God's kingdom must be holy, and if we would enter into the kingdom, we must be holy too.

From the considerations which have been adduced – from the general laws of God's moral government, from his declared design in the work of redemption, and from the actual constitution of our own nature – it must be evident that a spiritual and holy character is indispensably necessary in order to our entrance into his kingdom; and this principle, thus firmly established, is sufficient to demonstrate the necessity of regeneration, and the impossibility of salvation without it, in the case of all who are naturally fallen or infected with sin. If there be any who can justly plead exemption from this necessity, they are such and such only as can truly say that they are naturally unfallen and spiritual and holy, and as such fit for the kingdom of God. But the Bible proceeds on the supposition that there are none such on earth, that 'all have sinned and come short of the glory of God;' and I believe that every conscience will do the preacher's work, by convincing you of this great truth, provided only it be duly instructed in the things of the kingdom of God. If the spiritual nature of that kingdom, and the holy character of God, and the awful sanctity of his government, and his real design in the work of redemption – if these things be clearly discerned by any man's conscience, as they stand revealed in the light of God's Word – he will intuitively perceive, and instinctively feel, that he must be changed or lost, that he must be born anew, if he would see the kingdom of God.

We learn, however, from the case of Nicodemus, that the doctrine of regeneration is apt to excite surprise and even incredulity, not only in the ignorant and profligate, who make no profession of religion, but in many who belong nominally to the Church of God, who are strict and scrupulous in their attention to its forms, and, to a certain extent, conscientious in acting according to their convictions of duty. The man with whom our Lord held this conversation was a Pharisee; he belonged to a sect which is elsewhere declared to be 'the straitest sect of the law,' and described as 'believing themselves to be righteous, and despising others;' he was 'a ruler of the Jews and a master in Israel,' and as such recognized as fit to teach and direct others in matters of faith and duty; and he seems to have been so far impressed by our Lord's ministry as to be willing to inquire after the truth; for if his coming to Jesus under the cloud of night be a proof that he was still influenced in some degree by the fear of man, his coming at all, and especially his coming with such a confession on his lips – 'Rabbi, we know that thou art a teacher sent from God; for no man can do these miracles which thou doest, except God be with him' – must be considered, if his position in society, his party connections, and his Jewish prejudices be taken into account, as a sufficient proof that he was in some measure impressed, and desirous of obtaining further information. Yet even this man, this conscientious Pharisee, this master in Israel, this timid but honest inquirer, no sooner heard the doctrine of regeneration, and that, too, from the lips of one whom he acknowledged as a teacher sent from God, than he exclaimed, 'How can a man be born when he is old?' and when it was further explained to him, and its absolute necessity declared, he still 'answered and said, How can these things be?' The chief reason of his incredulity doubtless was, that he had no perception of the spirituality and extent of God's law, and no inward and experimental conviction of his own sinfulness – none at least that impressed him with a sense of the necessity of any great change to qualify him for the kingdom of God; and the want of any heartfelt conviction of its necessity left his mind open to the full impression of those little difficulties as to the mode or manner of its production which often occur to those who merely speculate on the subject, but which soon vanish and disappear when the conscience is awakened, and the heart impressed by *the great reality itself*. Perceiving that his mind was perplexing itself with these difficulties, and disposed to question the truth, merely because it could not understand the manner in which so great a change could be wrought, our Lord first of all suggested a beautiful analogy, to show that there were many things whose reality could not be doubted, although the mode of their operation, and many circumstances connected with them, could not be explained. He selected the wind, the vital air by which natural life itself is sustained, which, although it be invisible, is known to us from its effects; he reminded him, that while its operation as an agent in nature was undoubted, there were many circumstances connected with its operation which were shrouded in impenetrable mystery; and left him to infer, that if it were so with that wind which is so essential to the natural life of man, it was not unreasonable to believe that his spiritual life might be produced and sustained by an agency equally real and efficacious, although, like the former, it was also invisible and mysterious: and while he seeks in this way to remove the ground of his incredulity, which was the supposed impossibility of such a change, he at the same time brings before him, and presses on his consideration, another impossibility, as real as the former one was imaginary, – namely, the impossibility of an unregenerate man entering into the kingdom of God. His mind was occupying itself with speculative difficulties as to the way in which so great a change could be wrought; but our Lord tells him, if there be a difficulty on the one hand, there is a much greater on the other, and that it is not so impossible that a man should be born again, as it is that without being born again he should enter into the kingdom of God. It is in this way that we would still deal with the difficulties and objections which are founded on the alleged mysteriousness of the work of the Spirit. We would first of all remind you, that there are many realities which you know and believe in spite of the difficulty of explaining every circumstance concerning them; and then we would press the great reality on your attention, and show that however mysterious the nature and mode of the new birth may be, there is no mystery and no doubt, either as to the fact that you are *fallen*, or as to the *principle* that a spiritual character is indispensable in order to your being members of God's spiritual kingdom; and that, from these two considerations combined, it follows, with demonstrable certainty, that 'except a man be born again, he cannot see the kingdom of God.'

I believe that in most cases the difficulty of convincing men of the necessity of regeneration arises out of the want of a right scriptural apprehension of the *fact* that they are fallen, and corrupted, and depraved; for did they really believe the doctrine of human depravity in its full extent, and in its application to their own souls – were they experimentally convinced of the guilt and demerit of sin, and of their own sinfulness and danger in the sight of God – their own consciences would intuitively discern their need of some great change in order to their entering into his kingdom. A solid work of conviction would, in such cases, be the most effectual argument for the necessity of regeneration. But perhaps this conviction may be wrought in their consciences by simply unfolding and applying the *principle* which our Lord assumes, viz., that a man must be spiritual if he would be a member of God's kingdom; for this principle is evident from the very nature of that kingdom, and every mind which is rightly instructed in regard to it, and which is duly impressed with its spiritual character, its unalterable laws, and its essential and pervading sanctity, must intuitively discern its own unfitness to enjoy it, by the evidence of its own consciousness and in the light of its own experience. For just as one vivid view of God in his true character was enough to draw from the lips of Job that humble confession – 'I have heard of thee by the hearing of the ear, but now mine eye seeth thee, wherefore I abhor myself and repent in dust and ashes;' and just as a view of the glory of Christ had a similar effect on the apostle when he 'fell at his feet as dead;' so may we expect that a correct apprehension of the kingdom of God, and of its awful and unchangeable sanctity, will be accompanied with a profound sense of our own unworthiness, and a conviction that we must undergo some great change before we can be qualified to enjoy, or permitted to enter it.

Let me beseech you individually to weigh well this solemn statement of the Lord, and to consider it in its application to your own souls. You cannot fail to see that he speaks of a very *great* change, since he compares it to your 'being born again,' – of a *very necessary* change, since without it you cannot see the kingdom of God; and when you hear such a statement from the lips of one who is himself the only Saviour of sinners, and who will, ere long, appear as the Judge of all, you cannot fail to be convinced that it is alike your duty and your interest to apply it to your own case, and to improve it for your own salvation. I am aware that some, when they read of the new birth of the soul, contrive to evade the truth which Christ declares, by saying that *his words are figurative*. On this principle they explain away a great part of the Word of God. With them every thing is figurative: we have a figurative fall, a figurative curse, a figurative atonement, a figurative Saviour, a figurative regeneration, a figurative heaven, a figurative hell, in fact, a figurative Gospel. But grant that figurative language is employed on this as on many other subjects, grant that metaphors are used to give us a lively apprehension of its nature; I say *figurative language has a meaning*, nay, it is employed on purpose to *enhance the meaning of plainer words*. What, then, is the meaning of this figure? what is the *reality* which this metaphor describes? Does it not mean some *change* – some *great* change – some *great change of mind and heart* – a change that has some resemblance to a *birth*, a *resurrection*, a *creation*? Why were these *figures* employed, but to declare the *magnitude* of that change, whose necessity is affirmed with a decision and a peremptory plainness which leaves no room for doubt?

II. General View of the Agency of the Spirit

THE first thought that will occur to every reflecting mind, in perusing our Lord's address to his disciples, immediately before his departure, is that *the work of the Spirit is, in its own place, as needful and as important as the work of Christ himself.* We are too apt, in modern times, to overlook the necessity, or to underrate the value of the Spirit's grace; we talk much of the Saviour, but little of the Sanctifier; yet a consideration of the words which Christ addressed to his disciples in the immediate prospect of his leaving them, should teach us that the agency of the Spirit is so essential and so important, that his advent would more than compensate for the departure of the Saviour. 'It is *expedient* for you,' says our Lord, 'that I go away; for if I go not away, the Spirit will not come unto you; but if I go, I will send him unto you.' (John 16. 7). When the disciples heard their Lord utter the first clause of this verse, 'It is *expedient for you* that I go away,' with what wonder must they have listened, and how anxiously must they have waited to hear the reason that could be given for so startling an intimation! Had they been left to their own reflections, and had they consulted together as to what would have been the severest trial they could be called to sustain – the heaviest blow which could be inflicted on their cause – the most dangerous and disastrous event which it was possible for them to conceive, would they not with one consent have agreed in declaring that it would be the departure of their blessed Lord? When it was announced to them, Jesus himself saw the withering effect which it produced on their minds, and he refers to it when he says, 'Because I have said these things unto you, sorrow hath filled your hearts.' And no wonder that they were thus dejected in the prospect of losing the personal presence of him who was their kindest friend, their unwearied benefactor, their patient teacher, – whose wisdom was their guide, his power their defence, his sympathy their consolation, his approval their reward, and his salvation their highest hope. They were attached to him as a personal friend, by the strongest ties of gratitude, and admiration, and love; they had long associated with him on terms of most endearing intimacy; they had often looked with delight on his benignant countenance, 'full of grace and truth;' they had listened to his public preaching and his private conversation, when 'he spake as never man spake;' they had witnessed his miracles of mercy, and his life of unwearied beneficence, 'when he went about continually doing good;' and they had themselves received at his hands every benefit which divine love, combined with the most perfect human kindness, could bestow. And can we deem it wonderful, if the thought of parting with such a friend, whose appearance, and voice, and person were entwined with their fondest affections, filled their hearts with unwonted sadness? But they looked to him in a far higher character; they considered him not merely as their personal friend and benefactor, but as the Messiah that had been promised to the fathers, the hope and consolation of Israel, the Saviour of the world; they knew that he had come on a great public mission, to introduce a new order of things, and to found a kingdom which should never be moved; and although their views of the nature and design of that kingdom were, as yet, in many respects defective or even erroneous, they knew enough to convince them that it was a great, an arduous, and a difficult enterprise, which Christ came to accomplish, that they were destined to be his agents in carrying it on, and that in this capacity they must be exposed to much obloquy and opposition, and even to persecution and death itself, for with that faithfulness which characterized all his intercourse with them, he had himself told them, 'The time cometh, that whosoever killeth you will think that he doeth God service.' Still, these prospects, appalling as they were, might have been braved, and these difficulties surmounted, and these trials endured, by the little band of his devoted followers, had they still been called, as heretofore, to follow Christ's person, and to share with him a common danger; they might have persevered with courage and hope, looking to his wisdom to direct, and his miraculous power to defend them; but now, at this very point, when the object of his mission seemed to be unaccomplished, and when the cloud was thickening around them, and danger lowered over their path, they were to be deprived of their Counsellor, and Protector, and Friend. He was about to leave them and the world in which they dwelt, and to return to his Father in heaven; and therefore, fearing that they should be 'as sheep without a shepherd in the midst of wolves,' 'sorrow filled their hearts.' With what feelings of surprise, then, must they have heard their Lord say, *'It is expedient for you that I go away?'* With what eager curiosity must they have expected an explanation of the reason which should reconcile them to so great, and in their estimation, so irreparable a loss? And when he gave the reason – when he said, 'It is expedient for you that I go away: *for if I go not away, the Spirit will not come unto you; but if I go, I will send him unto you*' – must they not have been impressed with the conviction that the office and work of the Holy Spirit were, in their Lord's estimation, as needful for the establishment and maintenance of his kingdom on earth, as his own office and work had been? And ought *we* not also to feel that we grievously err from Christ's teaching, if we overlook the necessity, or undervalue the operations of that divine agent, whose advent Christ himself declared to be an ample compensation, and more than a compensation for the loss of his visible presence with the Church? For what higher testimony could be given to the necessity and value of the Spirit's agency than what is implied in the words of Christ, 'It is *expedient* for you that I go away; for if I go not away, the Spirit will not come unto you; but if I go, I will send him unto you?'

We learn from the same words, that the gift of the Spirit was *purposely reserved till after the exaltation of Christ, and was then to be dispensed by him,* as the fruit of his purchase, the gift of his grace, and the proof and manifestation of his reward. We are not to suppose, indeed, that when our Lord said, 'If I go not away, the Spirit will not come to you,' he meant to intimate, that the church had heretofore been altogether destitute of the Spirit's grace, or that the disciples to whom he spoke had not yet experienced the benefits of his ordinary influence. We know that long before – not merely before the departure, but before the very advent of Christ – the Spirit's grace had been vouchsafed under the Old Testament dispensation; and that every believer from the beginning had been enlightened, and sanctified, and comforted by his spiritual power. David frequently refers to the Spirit as the author of light, and instruction, and comfort to his own soul: 'Cast me not away from thy presence; take not thy Holy Spirit from me. Restore unto me the joy of thy salvation; and uphold me with thy free Spirit.' To the Jewish Church at large, the Eternal Wisdom of God had said, 'Turn you at my reproof; behold, I will pour out my Spirit upon you, I will make known my words unto you.' And in regard to the apostles, Christ himself had said to Peter, 'Blessed art thou, Simon Barjona; for flesh and blood hath not revealed this unto thee, but my Father which is in heaven.' And again, 'Ye know him; for he dwelleth with you, and shall be in you.' But when he says, 'If I go not away, the Spirit will not come unto you,' he refers to some remarkable manifestation of the Spirit's grace and power, and represents it as being purposely deferred till after his departure. As the advent of Christ was the great promise of the Old Testament, so the advent of the Spirit is the great promise of the New; and just as Christ had executed his offices as prophet, priest, and king, before his manifestation in the flesh, but had a signal coming in the fulness of times; so the Spirit, although given before, 'must have a coming in state, in a solemn and visible manner, accompanied with sensible effects,' as in the appearance of a dove, and in the resemblance of cloven tongues.[1]

[1] Thomas Goodwin, *Works*, (1863) vol. vi. p. 8.

This remarkable effusion of the Spirit had been predicted before in ancient prophecy; and we read both the prediction and its fulfilment in the Acts of the Apostles (chap. 2): 'When the day of Pentecost was fully come, they were all with one accord in one place. And suddenly there came a sound from heaven as of a rushing mighty wind, and it filled all the house where they were sitting. And there appeared unto them cloven tongues, like as of fire, and it sat upon each of them. And they were all filled with the Holy Ghost, and began to speak with other tongues, as the Spirit gave them utterance.' And Peter standing up, said, 'This is that which was spoken by the prophet Joel; And it shall come to pass in the last days, saith God, I will pour out of my Spirit upon all flesh; and your sons and your daughters shall prophesy.' That this is the manifestation of the Spirit to which our Lord referred in his conversation with his disciples, appears from the references which he made to it on other occasions. After his resurrection, and immediately before his ascension to glory, he said to the apostles, 'Behold I send the promise of my Father upon you: but tarry ye in the city of Jerusalem, until ye be endued with power from on high.' 'And, being assembled together with them, he commanded them that they should not depart from Jerusalem, but wait for the promise of the Father, which, saith he, ye have heard of me. For John truly baptized with water; but ye shall be baptized with the Holy Ghost not many days hence.' And 'ye shall receive power after that the Holy Ghost is come upon you; and ye shall be witnesses unto me.' (Luke 24. 49; Acts 1. 4, 8).

From these passages we learn that there was to be a remarkable effusion of the Spirit after our Lord's departure, and that it was purposely deferred, and reserved as a proof and token of his exaltation to the right hand of God. It is expressly said, 'The Holy Ghost was not yet given, because that Jesus was not yet glorified,' (John 7. 39), – so that, for some reason or other, this manifestation was purposely deferred till Christ's humiliation should have closed, and his exaltation commenced. And I think it is very clearly intimated that the gift of the Spirit was reserved as *the crowning evidence*, as the appropriate and peculiar proof of the completion of his work, of its acceptance on the part of God, of its efficacy on behalf of his people, of his having earned and obtained the reward which had been promised, and of his being invested with all power in heaven and on earth to carry into full effect his great design as the Redeemer of the world. Every other fact in his history, every other step in his progress, had its appropriate proof. His incarnation was celebrated by angels, his baptism was accompanied with a voice from heaven, his miracles were witnessed by thousands, his death, his burial, his resurrection, were attested by eye-witnesses. When he arose and appeared among his disciples, they saw and spake with him; and after a season he led them forth to Bethany: 'and it came to pass, while he blessed them, he was parted from them.' They beheld him while he was taken up; but 'a cloud received him out of their sight.' No human eye could penetrate that cloud; they could not follow him, as he entered heaven, and took his seat at God's right hand. But before he ascended he had mentioned the gift of the Spirit as the appointed sign and proof of his exaltation, a token of his power when he should appear in heaven. And, oh! surely it was fitting that some such peculiar evidence should be furnished of a fact which no human witness could attest, but on which depends the certainty of our salvation! For Christ's exaltation is the proof of the completeness of his work, of the acceptance of it by his Father, and of the hopes of all his people. And if his exaltation was to be evinced and certified by the gift of the Holy Ghost, if this was the appointed and pre-signified proof of that glorious truth, then it is to be regarded as the fruit and token of the Redeemer's triumph, and as a pledge that every other blessing which he died to purchase has been won, and will be given to all who believe in his name. When we consider the subject in this light, we may discern the divine wisdom of that arrangement to which our Lord referred, when he said, 'If I go not away, the Spirit will not come to you; but if I go, I will send him unto you;' and see how, when the Spirit actually descended, according to his promise, the apostles must have regarded it as a proof that Christ was exalted; and if exalted, then his mission was divine, his redemption complete, his righteousness accepted, his reward bestowed, his mediatorial authority established; so that when Christ ascended, and the Spirit descended, they might exultingly exclaim, 'Thou hast ascended up on high: thou hast led captivity captive; thou hast received gifts for men, even for the rebellious;' and, turning to the unbelieving Jews, they could say, 'This Jesus hath God raised up, whereof we all are witnesses. Therefore being by the right hand of God exalted, and having received of the Father the promise of the Holy Ghost, he hath shed forth this, which ye now see and hear. Therefore let all the house of Israel know assuredly, that God hath made that same Jesus, whom ye have crucified, both Lord and Christ.'

In the conversation which he held with his disciples, our Lord gives *a comprehensive account of the nature and design of the Spirit's work.*

It is represented as being designed for two very distinct ends, and for two widely different classes of men. It is designed for the conviction of *the world*, and for the confirmation and comfort of *the Church*. The world is spoken of, and also a peculiar people, who have been separated from the world: 'He will reprove or convict *the world*;' but he 'will guide *you* into all truth.' Unbelievers will be convicted by his coming, but believers will be confirmed and edified: 'He shall glorify me, for he shall receive of mine, and shall show it unto you.' So that the gift of the Spirit is designed to have an important influence both on the world and the Church.

In reference to both classes, Christ, in his person, and offices, and work, as the Redeemer, is *the one great subject* which the gift of the Spirit is designed to illustrate; in other words, the Spirit is Christ's witness on earth, affording such evidence of his divine mission and mediatorial authority as is sufficient to convict, if it serve not to convince, unbelievers; and glorifying Christ, by unfolding to his disciples, and enabling them to discern, such views of his glory as serve to confirm them in the faith, and to attach them more closely to his service and cause.

Let us briefly consider the work of the Spirit in reference to each of these two classes of men – believers and unbelievers, or the world and the Church.

Of the former it is said, 'And when he is come, he will reprove the world of sin, and of righteousness, and of judgment: of sin, because they believe not on me; of righteousness, because I go to my Father, and ye see me no more; of judgment, because the prince of this world is judged.' (John 16. 8–11).

The word which is here translated *reprove*,[1] has no exact synonym in our language, and it is difficult to find a term which, like that in the original, is equally applicable to each of the three subjects to which it is here applied. The word *reprove* applies well enough to sin, but not so well to righteousness and judgment; while the word *convince*, which is used in the margin, is ordinarily employed to denote more than is here ascribed to the work of the Spirit, as it implies an actual effect in the way of satisfying the judgment and securing the assent; whereas the original word does not necessarily import any such effect. There is no doubt, however, as to the meaning of the expression. It signifies to *prove upon or against*, to *convict by proof;* or, in other words, to present such evidence as will be sufficient to condemn, if it fail to convince. And that we may understand how the Spirit may be said to convict the world of or concerning sin, and righteousness, and judgment, we should consider separately the *subject*, the *doctrine*, and the *proof*, as they are severally intimated in our Lord's words.

The *subject* on which the gift of the Spirit is designed and fitted to shed a clear and convincing light, is the character and offices of Christ: 'He was despised and rejected of men;' and many among the Jews disbelieved his claims when he professed to be the Messiah that had been promised to their fathers, and accounted him as 'a deceiver of the people.' Now, on *this* subject, the Spirit, when he descended, was to teach three great lessons: He was to *convict the world of sin*, because *they believed not* on Christ – by demonstrating, that he whom they rejected as a deceiver was indeed what

[1] ἐλέγξει

he professed to be, and by giving such a proof of his divine mission as should involve them in aggravated guilt, should they continue to resist, or deny, or question his claims. He was to *convict the world concerning righteousness*, by which I understand the righteousness of Christ, declaring him to be a righteous person whom the Jews had condemned as a malefactor, and not only righteous in his own private character, but in his official relation as the Redeemer of his people, 'the very end of the law for righteousness to every one that believeth.' And he was to *convict the world of judgment* – of judgment in general, as evinced by the whole work of redemption, but more particularly of the judgment that had been executed on Satan, the head of the great apostasy, when he who was the 'seed of the woman bruised the serpent's head,' and when he who ascended up on high 'led captivity captive,' and 'spoiled principalities and powers, and made a show of them openly, triumphing over them in his cross.'

These three lessons or doctrines have reference to one and the same great subject, namely, Christ himself; and they are all taught by one and the same Spirit, and evinced by the same *kind of proof*. The proof in each instance is furnished by *the Spirit*, and by his mere descent, as well as by the revelations which he made. The mere fact of the Spirit's advent after our Lord's ascension was, in the circumstances, sufficient of itself, and apart from any new communication of truth, to prove against the world each of the doctrines or lessons to which I have already referred. It was sufficient to convict the world of the sin of unbelief, since it proved that Christ, whom they rejected, was the Anointed of God; to convict the world of his perfect righteousness, since it proved that Christ, whom they condemned, was accepted as righteous with God; and to convict the world of judgment, since it proved that Christ, whom they had unjustly doomed to die, had been constituted Judge of all, and had executed judgment on the prince of the world himself. So that the mere fact of the Spirit's descent after Christ's ascension, when viewed in connection with his prediction and promise, was of itself a demonstrative proof of his character and office as the Lord's Anointed, and, as such, sufficient to convict if it did not convince, to condemn if it did not convert, those who believed not in his name.

It may appear, at first sight, to be somewhat difficult to connect the proof with the doctrine, or to see the bearing of the one on the other, as they are here stated; but a little reflection will serve to convince you that in reality no demonstration could be more cogent or more conclusive, than what is afforded by the gift of the Spirit in favour of the mediatorial character and offices of the Lord Jesus Christ. For let us only realize the fact as it is set forth in the New Testament; let us bear in mind, that before leaving his disciples, the Lord Jesus had intimated to them that after his ascension to glory, and as a fruit and effect of his exaltation, he would send down upon them the Holy Spirit, and they should be endued with power from on high; and, recollecting this prediction or promise, let us place ourselves in their situation, and endeavour to conceive what must have been their convictions and feelings when that promise was fulfilled: – oh! when they heard the sound of the mighty rushing wind, and when they saw the cloven tongues, like as of fire, resting on every forehead; and when they felt themselves inwardly moved by a new power; and when they began to speak with other tongues, as the Spirit gave them utterance, who can doubt that, in that solemn hour, it would be the first recollection of every disciple that the Lord had spoken of this, and the innermost conviction of every mind that Jesus was indeed exalted, that Jesus was none other than the righteous one, that Jesus was now both Lord and Christ! And what must have been the effect of this manifestation on the minds of believers themselves, we may conceive from the sacred narrative, where it is not only said that 'they were all amazed and marvelled, saying, Are not all these which speak Galileans? and how hear we every man in our own tongue, wherein we were born?' but also, that when Peter explained to them the prophecy which predicted such an effusion of the Spirit, and connected it with the ascension and exaltation of that same Jesus whom they had crucified, they felt instinctively the force of those very considerations which our Lord states; they felt at once that this miraculous manifestation of the Spirit was a sufficient proof that Christ was exalted, and if exalted, then righteous; and if he was righteous, then they were sinful in disbelieving and rejecting him, and accordingly 'they were pricked in their hearts, and exclaimed, Men and brethren, what shall we do?' Christ's exaltation, of which the gift of the Spirit was the predicted proof, is sufficient, when it is duly realized, to carry home the conviction 'of sin, and righteousness, and judgment;' for it was just a vivid view of Christ in his exaltation that disarmed Saul the persecutor, and changed him into a zealous preacher of the cross. These examples may suffice to show that the gift of the Spirit is fitted to *convict the world* by the proof which it affords of Christ's exaltation and of his mediatorial power; to convict the world of 'their sin, because they believe not on him; of his righteousness, because he has gone to the Father; and of judgment, because the prince of this world is judged.'

In reference, again, to God's people, or the Church which he has gathered out of the world, the gift of the Spirit was designed for their instruction, and edification, and comfort. Christ said to his disciples, 'I have yet many things to say unto you, but ye cannot bear them now. Howbeit when he, the Spirit of truth, is come, he will guide you into all truth.' 'He shall

[29]

glorify me; for he shall receive of mine, and shall show it unto you.'

The apostles were to be qualified by the gifts of the Spirit for exercising the office with which the Lord had invested them – for preaching the Gospel among all nations, and for putting on record, for the instruction of the Church in every age, the precious truths of God. They received the gift of tongues on the day of Pentecost, which enabled them to address every man in the language in which he was born; and Christ's promise bore, that along with the gift of tongues, they should obtain such assistance as was needful for recalling the truth to their recollection, and completing the scheme of revelation. The New Testament consists partly of a *narrative*, and the Spirit was promised in these terms: 'He shall bring all things to your remembrance, whatsoever I have said unto you;' it is partly *doctrinal*, and the Spirit was promised in these terms: 'He shall teach you all things, he shall guide you into all truth;' it is partly *prophetical*, and the Spirit was promised in these terms: 'He will show you things to come.' The apostles completed the Gospel, and thus was fulfilled the Lord's intimation, 'I have yet many things to say unto you, but ye cannot bear them now. Howbeit when he, the Spirit of truth, is come, he will guide you into all truth.'

But not the apostles only; all the private members of the Church, and all believers, without exception, were interested in the gift of the Spirit. They were not all inspired, nor were they all endued with miraculous gifts; but they were all partakers of his renewing and sanctifying grace. And to this inward and spiritual work on the soul our Lord refers, as one of the fruits of the Spirit which they should receive. Accordingly we read that on the day of Pentecost there was not only an effusion of miraculous gifts, but also a copious effusion of converting and saving grace: three thousand souls were at once translated out of darkness into marvellous light. We are too apt, in reading the account of this marvellous event, to confine our attention to the miraculous gifts which were then conferred, and to think more of the inspiration by which the apostles were enabled to speak with tongues, than of the renewing, converting, and sanctifying grace which accompanied their preaching, and which turned so many from darkness to light, and from the power of Satan unto God. The former manifestation was more striking to the eye of sense; but the latter is in itself unspeakably more important. The one was a means, an evidence, a sign; the other was the efficient cause of every conversion; and this latter is the ordinary, permanent, and everlasting work of the Spirit in the Church of Christ.

If it be asked how far we are still concerned in the intimation which our Lord made to his apostles of the advent and work of the Spirit after he should leave them, I answer, that from various other passages of Scripture, we learn that we are now placed under a dispensation which is called emphatically 'the ministration of the Spirit,' and under which his people in all nations and ages are left to the Spirit's teaching in the absence of their risen Lord. This is the last, the complete, the crowning dispensation of the scheme of grace. It is true that there are now no miraculous gifts of the Spirit; but the Spirit is still Christ's *witness* in the world, and Christ's *agent* in the Church. He has given such a *testimony* as is sufficient, even in these modern times, to convict the world of sin, and righteousness, and judgment; and he still acts as the Teacher, the Quickener, the Sanctifier, and the Comforter of the Church, 'guiding his people into all truth,' and glorifying Christ, by receiving of his and 'showing it unto them.'

In considering the character of the Gospel dispensation, it is of paramount importance to mark the distinction which is drawn in Scripture betwixt the *external manifestation* of the Spirit on the one hand, and his *internal operations* on the other, and to remember that the 'ministration of the Spirit' includes both. Of the former it is said, 'The *manifestation* of the Spirit is given to every man to profit withal;' that is, the *external exhibition* of the Spirit in his miraculous gifts, for to these the apostle particularly alludes, as is evident from the succeeding verses, was designed and fitted to qualify those on whom such gifts were conferred for public usefulness, both in the way of convincing the world, and edifying the Church. Of the latter it is said, that 'he dwelleth *in us*,' that he 'walketh in us,' that 'he worketh in us both to will and to do,' – that 'he worketh in us all the good pleasure of his goodness, and the work of faith with power;' in fact, as we shall have occasion to show, the exercise of every spiritual grace, and the enjoyment of every spiritual blessing, is ascribed to the direct internal operation of the Spirit on our souls.[1] That the ministration of the Spirit, in the apostolic age, included both the external manifestation and the internal operation above described, cannot be seriously questioned by any candid reader of the New Testament; and that it does so still is evident not only from the fact that the dispensation of the Gospel is expressly called, by way of eminence, 'the ministration of the Spirit,' without any hint being given of any of his essential operations being withdrawn from the Church, but also from the promise of Christ, which is only fulfilled by the presence of his Spirit – 'Lo! I am with you alway, even unto the end of the world' – and from the method in which the Bible appeals, both to the world and the Church, on the subject of the Spirit's *witness* and the Spirit's *agency*. It is true that the miraculous gifts of the Spirit have been withdrawn; but there is still a '*manifestation* of the Spirit' notwithstanding, and such a manifestation as is sufficient to *convict* the world as well as to *edify* the Church. For the Bible – an inspired record in a complete and perfect form – is the Spirit's testimony,

[1] John MacLaurin, *Works*, vol. ii., 110.

the Spirit's witness for Christ in the world, which, more powerfully than any miraculous gift, bespeaks God as its author, and which carries with it such evidence as amounts to 'the demonstration of the Spirit;' insomuch that, as in hearing prophecy of old, so in reading the Bible now, an unbeliever may be 'convinced of all and judged of all; the secrets of his heart are made manifest, and he may be led to worship God, and to feel that God is in it of a truth.' Besides the Bible, there is still in this world the Church, which is the visible body of Christ, a body of which Christ is the head, and the Holy Ghost its quickening and pervading Spirit; and, by its visible presence and wonderful preservation in the world, as well as by its public testimony, the Church is a signal witness for Christ. More particularly, the Holy Spirit still raises up and qualifies men for the work of the holy ministry in the Church, enduing them with such gifts and graces as are needful for them in the various spheres of labour to which they are called.[1] And there is another manifestation of the Spirit still – the *living epistles*, which are known and read of all men, who 'are manifestly declared to be the epistles of Christ, written not with ink, but with the Spirit of the living God; not in tables of stone, but in fleshy tables of the heart.' And if, in addition to these *objective* manifestations of the Spirit,[2] we consider his subjective operations, both in his common influences on the minds of unbelievers, against which 'they strive,' and in his saving influences on the hearts of his people, we shall discover ample reasons for believing that the dispensation of the Gospel is still as really 'the ministration of the Spirit,' as it was in the age of the apostles.

The general view which has been presented of the office and work of the Holy Spirit suggests many practical reflections of great value. Of these I shall only mention the two following: It teaches us how defective and erroneous must be the views of the Gospel which are entertained by those, whether amongst the ministers or members of the Christian Church, who exclude from their creed the doctrine of the Spirit's agency, or at all events habitually overlook its necessity, and neither pray for nor expect his interposition. That any Christian minister, acting under a dispensation which is expressly denominated 'the ministration of the Spirit,' should be jealous of that doctrine which constitutes the very strength of his ministry, and that, too, when he is himself described as 'one that ministereth the Spirit;' that he should regard the active agency of the Spirit in the Church as a foolish or

[1] On this branch of the subject, see the great work by John Owen on the Spirit. *Works* (Goold edition) vol. iii.

[2] The relation which the work of the Spirit bears to the Evidences of Christianity is a subject of profound interest, which has seldom been duly considered, but it does not fall within the design of the present work to expound it.

fanatical notion, when Christ himself declared that the presence of the Spirit there would more than compensate for his personal departure; and that he should treat with ridicule and scorn what constitutes the very substance of Christ's promise, the subject of every believer's prayers, and the object of the Church's hope and expectation; – such views and feelings indicate a lamentable ignorance, not of one doctrine only, but of the whole scheme and constitution of the Gospel; and none can wonder that *his* ministry is not blessed, when he slights the Spirit, who alone can render it effectual.

The view which has been given of the office and work of the Spirit should also address an instructive lesson to those hearers of the Word who imagine that they are now in a less favourable situation than were the earlier followers of Christ. Such men complain that there is now no supernatural manifestation, no visible miracle, no convincing sign of Christ's presence and power in his Church; and are apt to think that had they been permitted to see Jesus the Lord, to hear his voice, and to witness his wonderful works, they would have certainly believed. Now, not to insist on the fact that multitudes who *did* see the Lord in person, who followed him from village to village, and heard his discourses, and saw his miracles, were not only not convinced, but were hardened in unbelief and exasperated into enmity, – I wish you to observe that even his chosen disciples, who companied with him for years, were distinctly told that their future condition would be not worse, but better, when Christ should leave them, and the Spirit descend; and does not this imply that the grace of the Spirit was of more importance to the Church than the personal presence of Christ himself, that it was more than sufficient to compensate for his departure? And what more could be said to convince you of your error, if now, under the final and perfect dispensation of the Gospel, and under 'the very ministration of the Spirit,' you remain in a state of unbelief? It is true you have no miracles; but you have the Spirit's testimony in your hands; and if 'ye believe not Moses and the prophets,' or Christ and his evangelists and apostles, 'neither would ye believe though one rose from the dead.'

For, consider seriously the distinction which is so strongly marked in Scripture betwixt the *miraculous gifts* and the *internal graces* of the Spirit, and ask yourselves which of the two is the more valuable? That they are quite distinct is evident from the fact that they might exist separate and apart from each other. Many, in primitive times, were renewed and sanctified by the Spirit's grace who were not endued with miraculous powers; and some, again, were endued with his miraculous gifts who were not made partakers of his saving grace. This appears from the case of Saul under the Old Testament, who was endued with the gift of prophecy, while his heart was unrenewed, from the case of Judas under the New, and still more from the solemn words of our Lord himself: 'Many shall come to me in that day, saying, Lord, Lord, have we not prophesied in thy name, and in thy name cast out devils, and in thy name done many wonderful works? To whom I will answer, I never knew you; depart from me, ye workers of iniquity.' The miraculous gifts and the internal graces of the Spirit, then, are quite distinct, and might even exist apart. Now, of the two which is the more valuable? Surely that which stands connected with the salvation of the soul; for even were there no express testimony of Scripture on the subject, this inference would be warranted by the simple fact, that his inward grace alone can save the soul. But there *is* an express testimony of Scripture on the subject; for, bringing these two things into direct comparison, the apostle intimates that one saving grace in the heart is of greater value than all miraculous gifts put together. Having spoken (1 Cor. 12. 30) of the gifts of healing, and miracles, and tongues, he says, 'Covet earnestly the best gifts,' an expression which shows that he did not by any means disparage them; but he adds, 'And yet show I unto you a more excellent way.' And what is that? 'Though I speak with the tongues of men and of angels, and have not charity,' or love, 'I am become as sounding brass, or a tinkling cymbal. And though I have the gift of prophecy, and understand all mysteries, and all knowledge; and though I have all faith, so that I could remove mountains, and have not charity,' or love, 'I am nothing.' Here he selects one of the inward graces of the Spirit – for 'the fruit of the Spirit is love' – and declares of it that it is more valuable than all the miraculous gifts of the Spirit combined. Now, these two – the miraculous gifts and the internal graces of the Spirit – being distinct, and capable of existing separately, and the one being so much more valuable than the other, the only question that remains is, Which of the two is the permanent inheritance of the Church? It is evidently the more valuable of the two. The miraculous gifts of the Spirit have long since been withdrawn.[1] They were used for a temporary purpose. They were the scaffolding which God employed for the erection of a spiritual temple. When it was no longer needed, the scaffolding was taken down, but the temple still stands, and is occupied by his indwelling Spirit; for, 'Know ye not that ye are the temple of God, and that the Spirit of God dwelleth in you?' (1 Cor. 3. 16).

---

[1] The fact is admitted by Edward Irving, but is ascribed to the want of faith on the part of the Church. *Homilies on Baptism*, p. 152.

III. General View of the Process of a Sinner's Conversion

IN the last chapter I endeavoured to illustrate the general design of the gift of the Spirit, in reference both to the world and the Church, founding my observations on that comprehensive statement of our Lord, 'It is expedient for you that I go away; for if I go not away, the Spirit will not come unto you; but if I depart, I will send him unto you. And when he is come, he will reprove *the world* of sin, and of righteousness, and of judgment;' and 'he will guide *you* into all truth;' 'he shall glorify me; for he shall receive of mine, and shall show it unto you.' Two classes are here spoken of – the two great classes into which, according to the Scriptures, all mankind are divided – *the world and the Church;* and the gift of the Spirit was designed to have an important bearing on each: it was designed to reprove or convict the one, and to instruct, and guide, and edify the other. It is a mistake to imagine that the gift of the Spirit is so confined to the Church as to have no bearing at all on the unbelieving world. It was expressly intimated by our Lord, that when 'he came, he should reprove the world,' or convict the world by proof, concerning 'sin, and righteousness, and judgment'; and the apostle, referring to one of the miraculous fruits of the Spirit, says, 'Tongues are for a sign, not to them that believe, but to them that believe not; but prophesying' – another gift of the same Spirit – 'serveth not for them that believe not, but for them that believe.' The Spirit, then, affords such proof or evidence to the unbelieving world, as is sufficient either to convince or convict, to convert or to condemn them; while to the believing Church and people of God, he imparts larger and clearer views of divine truth, and enables them to discern 'the light of the knowledge of the glory of God in the face of Jesus Christ.'

But betwixt these two classes, however real the distinction, and however wide the difference which divides the one from the other, there is not now, as there will hereafter be, an impassable barrier of separation. In the state of retribution, believers may say with Abraham, 'Between us and you there is a great gulf fixed, so that they which would pass from hence to you cannot, neither can they pass to us that would come from thence;' but in the present state of grace there is no such barrier; souls are continually passing from the world to the Church, from darkness to light, from death to life; the way is plain, the door is open, the warrant is clear; every believer was once an unbeliever; every saint was once a sinner; and all God's people will gratefully acknowledge, that if they now belong to a peculiar class, and are no longer 'aliens and strangers, but fellow-citizens with the saints, and of the household of God,' this is not to be ascribed to any original difference betwixt them and their fellow-men, for naturally all belong to the same class, and partake of the same character, but solely to that great change which was wrought on their souls, when they 'had their eyes opened, and were turned from darkness unto light, and from the power of Satan unto God.' Now, it is to the case of a soul, while it is *in a state of transition* from the one class into the other, and passing from the world into the Church, that I propose at present to direct your attention; and in doing so I shall endeavour to present a general view of the process of a sinner's conversion, when, being reproved as one of the world, he comes also to be guided and taught as one of Christ's disciples.

In the Holy Scriptures, the origin of the scheme of redemption is ascribed to the love of the Father; and its ultimate issue is declared to be 'the salvation' of his people, or 'their obtaining of the glory of our Lord Jesus Christ;' but betwixt these two there is a middle term, descriptive of a change through which they must pass, a change contemplated and provided for in God's eternal purpose, and essentially necessary as an element in their preparation for the glory that remaineth to be revealed. '*God has chosen you to salvation, through sanctification of the Spirit and belief of the truth.*' This is an integral part of the divine plan, and an essential requisite to our admission into heaven; and it is described in two clauses, the one pointing to the *agent* by whom the change is wrought, the other to the *means* which he employs in accomplishing it: 'through sanctification of the Spirit' – he is the agent; and 'belief of the truth' – that is the means.

We learn from this and many other passages, that our personal and saving interest in the redemption of Christ depends on its being applied to us individually by the grace and power of the Holy Spirit. The Holy Spirit, not less than the Father and the Son, has an important office in the work of our salvation: it belongs to him to apply to individuals the redemption that was purchased by the Saviour. It is through 'sanctification of the Spirit' that any obtain the 'glory of the Lord Jesus Christ.' Christ's salvation can be of no use to any man unless he be made a partaker of it; and he is made a partaker of it only by the work of the Spirit. You may be labouring under a loathsome, inveterate, and fatal disease; a remedy may be provided for you, it may be purchased, it may be offered freely for your acceptance; but if either through insensibility as to your danger, or indifference as to your life, or unbelief as to the skill of the physician, or dislike to his method of cure, you refuse the proffered remedy, it is of no practical use; you disbelieve and die. So is it with your souls; sin is your disease; God has prescribed the cure, Christ has purchased it; it is freely and fully proposed to every sinner in the Gospel; but it is of no saving benefit to any, unless it be applied to them by the Holy Spirit.

It is deeply interesting to observe that in those comprehensive summaries of the Gospel which occur in various parts of Scripture, the agency of each of the three Persons of the Godhead in the work of men's salvation is distinctly stated; and that on the agency of the Spirit the whole practical effect of what was wrought by the Father and the Son is declared to depend. For example, – it is by the Spirit that God approaches to us through Christ; for he draws near to sinners in the Word, which is the Spirit's message, and by the Spirit's grace that Word is rendered effectual: 'He saves us by the washing of regeneration and the renewing of the Holy Ghost, which he sheds on us abundantly through Jesus Christ our Lord.' It is by the Spirit that we have access to God through Christ: 'Through whom we both have access by one Spirit unto the Father.' It is by the Spirit that we become partakers of all the benefits which were purchased by the Son, and are offered by the Father: for 'ye are washed, ye are sanctified, ye are justified in the name of the Lord Jesus, and by the Spirit of our God.'

It is equally true, then, that but for Christ's death, the Spirit would not have been given; and that but for the Spirit's work, Christ's death would have been in vain. This was the view entertained by the divines of the Reformation; and accordingly, you will mark a singular beauty in the arrangement of the Shorter Catechism, where, after a full account is given of Christ's work, both in his state of humiliation and exaltation, the Spirit's agency in the application of redemption to individuals is interposed betwixt the work of Christ and the saving benefits which flow from it to his people. It is the Spirit's work which connects the two, which forms the link betwixt the purchase of salvation on the part of the Redeemer, and the enjoyment of salvation on the part of his people; and never till this great article of our faith is duly understood and acknowledged, shall we either feel as we ought how absolutely we are dependent on free grace from first to last, nor how admirably, at every stage, God has provided for us the grace which we need.

Sanctification is used sometimes in a wider, and at other times in a more restricted sense. In the latter, it is descriptive of the progressive and gradual advancement of believers in the path of faith and holiness and comfort, or, in other words, their spiritual growth after they have been born again; but in the former it includes the new birth itself, as well as the life which flows from it, the first as well as the succeeding steps of that course which begins in conversion, and ends in glory. In this comprehensive sense it denotes a radical change of mind and heart, whereby new views, new principles, new motives, new hopes, and new habits are imparted to them; so that they become 'new creatures: old things pass away; all things become new.' The whole of this change is ascribed to the agency of the Spirit of God: it is 'through sanctification of the Spirit' that a sinner is born again; and it is 'through sanctification of the same Spirit' that he is enabled to die more and more unto sin, and to live unto righteousness.

But while the great change is wrought by the power of the Spirit, this divine agent acts by the use of means such as are adapted to the constitution of the human mind. It is through '*belief of the truth*' that the Spirit fulfils, in the case of adults, our Lord's prayer on behalf of his people 'Sanctify them through thy truth: thy Word is truth.' The Word, or the truth contained in the Word, is the instrument by which the Spirit acts in applying the benefits of Christ's redemption; and it is an instrument admirably adapted to its end. Powerless in itself, it is mighty through God. It is the sword of the Spirit. It is the hammer by which he breaks the rock in pieces. It is the light which he opens the mind to receive. It is the food by which he feeds, and the medicine by which he heals, and the consolation with which he comforts. The Spirit and the Word must not be disjoined; the sanctification of the Spirit and the belief of the truth are inseparably linked together, and are equally essential, the one as an efficient agent, the other as a fit instrument or means. Mark how uniformly they go together in Scripture. Of regeneration it is said, that we are 'born of water and of the Spirit;' he is the agent in that great initial change; but it is also said, we are 'born not of corruptible seed, but of incorruptible, even by *the Word of God;*' that is the instrument by which the change is wrought. Of Lydia it is said, 'The Lord opened the heart of Lydia' – here is divine agency; but the use of means was not superseded, for it is added, 'so that she attended to the things that were spoken of Paul' – here is the instrumentality of the Word. And the Psalmist's prayer, 'Open thou mine eyes,' recognizes the necessity of divine influence; but when he adds, 'that I may see wonderful things out of thy law,' divine truth, as revealed in the Word, is also recognized as the means of his instruction. These two – the sanctification of the Spirit, and belief of the truth – are equally essential, and the one must not be allowed to supersede or exclude the other.

Having premised these general observations, let us now conceive the case of a soul that belongs as yet to the world, or to the class of unbelieving men, and consider the way in which, through the agency of the Spirit of God, he is translated into the other class, and made a living member of his

Church. This transition occurs at the time of his conversion; and the process by which it is effected may differ in different cases, in respect to some of its concomitant circumstances, but essentially and substantially it consists in his being brought to believe the truth, so as to comply with and embrace the method of salvation which is proposed to him in the Gospel. And in order to this, there are *three* distinct steps or stages by which the Spirit of God leads a sinner to the Saviour, which are described and placed in their natural order in the Shorter Catechism, where we read, that 'Effectual calling is the work of God's Spirit, whereby, convincing us of our sin and misery, enlightening our minds in the knowledge of Christ, and renewing our wills, he doth persuade and enable us to embrace Jesus Christ for salvation, as he is freely offered to us in the Gospel.'

The first part of the Spirit's work, in order to a sinner's conversion, is 'to convince him of his sin and misery,' and especially of his *guilt and danger as an unbeliever*, living hitherto without Christ, and therefore without God and without hope in the world. This is expressly declared by the Saviour to be part of the Spirit's work: 'He shall reprove the world of sin: of sin, because they believe not in me.' It does not suit my present purpose to describe the nature of conviction, or to give a detailed account of the sinner's experience under it; that will fall to be considered hereafter. In the meantime, I would only offer an outline of the whole process by which a sinner is translated from the kingdom of darkness into the kingdom of God's dear Son; and show, in regard to each of the stages of that process, the place which it holds, and its indispensable necessity, in order to saving conversion. Conviction occupies the first place; for it is by convicting that the Spirit converts; but when it is thus used, the term must be understood in a large and comprehensive sense, as including a great deal more than is usually implied in mere remorse on account of sin. It is chiefly of their *sin, because they do not believe in Christ*, and of their misery and danger as Christless sinners, that the Spirit convicts transgressors; for the whole work of conviction, as well as the work of illumination and persuasion, has reference to Christ as the great subject of the Spirit's witness. It is important to bear this in mind; for many, under the mere natural operation of conscience, are sensible, at least occasionally, of very bitter and poignant remorse, when they have never seriously thought of Christ or felt their need of a Saviour, whereas the conviction which is spoken of in the Gospel has a direct relation to Christ, and implies not only a sense of guilt on the conscience, but a sense of the sin and misery of remaining in a Christless state. It presupposes, therefore, some general knowledge of Christ and the Gospel, as well as a sense of guilt and a feeling of remorse; and it cannot be produced without an impression being first made on the mind of the certain truth, the awful authority, and the transcendent importance of the Gospel. In this comprehensive sense, conviction presupposes some measure of the enlightening grace of the Spirit, imparting a general view of the truth as it is in Jesus, and enabling the mind to perceive the divine evidence of that truth, so as to feel that it is deeply criminal in slighting or rejecting it; and when it is said, therefore, that in the order of nature and experience, conviction is the first part of the Spirit's work, or the first stage in that process by which he brings a sinner to the Saviour, it is not meant that the Spirit operates directly and only on the conscience, so as to awaken in it a sense of sin, but that he operates on the conscience by imparting such light to the understanding as reaches the conscience, and quickens its perception, and enables it to see and feel that there is sin and danger in not believing in Christ. Such conviction embraces, indeed, the guilt of every sin; and the Spirit recalls to the recollection of the transgressor many sins, both of omission and commission, which he had long overlooked or forgotten; for at that solemn hour God says to him, 'Thou thoughtest that I was altogether such an one as thyself; but I will reprove thee, and set thy sins in order before thy face;' and when his transgressions start up, and pass in dark array before him, he is surprised and startled by the discovery of their number, and magnitude, and manifold aggravations, insomuch that he is ready to exclaim with the Psalmist, 'My transgressions have gone up over mine head, and have become a burden too heavy for me.' Any one sin may thus become the occasion of conviction; and it is by revealing *sin* to the conscience that the Spirit awakens it: but conviction is not complete, nor is it effectual as a means towards conversion, unless it amount to a persuasion, that without Christ our case is desperate, and that we have sinned, as in other respects, so in this especially, because we have not believed in him.

No man ever thinks of going to a physician until he feels that there is disease upon him: he may be diseased, and that mortally, but till he knows and believes that he is so, he seeks not for a remedy. No man cries for a deliverer, until he believes himself to be in danger: he may be in danger, and yet be ignorant of it, and his danger is often greatest when he is least alarmed; but until he knows his danger, he has no desire for deliverance. Just so, the sinner is diseased; but he will never repair to Christ as a physician, till he knows that Christ only is the physician of souls. The sinner is in danger, but never will he flee to Christ for refuge, until he is convinced that without Christ he must perish.

To some this may appear a very easy matter, and one that requires no supernatural agency, since all men will readily admit that they are sinners; and the natural light of conscience itself may seem to be sufficient, especially when combined with the light of the Word, to convince them of their danger. But, easy as it may appear, I apprehend that this is the very stage at which the Divine Spirit meets with the stoutest resistance, and at which the sinner is most resolutely blind to the plainest lessons of the Word. For why is it that so many are found in every congregation, who have listened for years to a faithful ministry, and have become familiar with the joyful sound, while they remain utterly unconcerned about the salvation of their souls, and have never experienced, never even sought after the relief which the gospel offers? – why, but that they have never been convinced of their sin and misery, or at least that they have never been so convinced as to feel that without Christ they must perish? It is indeed an easy thing to say, as many do, that they are weak, frail creatures, or to admit in general terms, what conscience itself forbids them to deny, that they are sinners; but it is no easy and no pleasant thing for any man to open his eyes, and to look fairly and fully on his own condition and character, as it is exhibited in the light of God's Word, or as one day he shall see it at the judgment-seat of Christ. Such a view of himself would mortify his pride and alarm his fears; and hence he takes refuge in certain general confessions, which have little or no meaning, and which leave his pride unmortified and his fears asleep. 'Every one that doeth evil hateth the light, neither cometh to the light, lest his deeds should be reproved.' He shuts his eyes, and thereby contrives to maintain a deceitful security, while he betrays a secret consciousness that the light would disturb or destroy it. Such being the natural tendency and the inveterate habit of every guilty mind, it is not by the mere operation of his own conscience, but by the direct agency of the Spirit of God, that any sinner can be duly convinced of his sin, and misery, and danger. He never sees himself as he really is, until his eyes are opened by the Spirit, and some rays at least of heaven's own light are admitted into the darkened chamber of imagery within. This the Spirit does, partly by revealing to him the essential purity, the unsullied holiness, the awful and infinite perfection of *God's* character, which is no sooner perceived than he marks the contrast betwixt it and his own, and is ready to exclaim: 'I have heard of thee by the hearing of the ear, but now mine eye seeth thee; wherefore I abhor myself, and repent in dust and ashes;' partly by unfolding the spirituality and extent of God's law, and applying it closely to the conscience; which is no sooner felt than he is ready to acknowledge: 'I was alive without the law once, but when the commandment came, sin revived, and I died; partly by recalling to his remembrance many sins long forgotten, or too easily excused, and exhibiting them before his awakened conscience in their true colours; which he no sooner discerns in the light of truth, than he says:' 'I acknowledge my transgressions, and my sin is ever before me;' but chiefly, I apprehend, by directing the sinner's eye to *Christ*, to Christ on the *cross*, suffering for sin, and to Christ on the *throne*, exalted as a Prince and a Saviour, for both in the humiliation and in the exaltation of Christ the sinner perceives, under the teaching of the Spirit, what is fitted power-fully to awaken his conscience, insomuch that it may be safely affirmed that it is by the Spirit's witness to Christ that he is first brought to see the magnitude of his guilt and the certainty of his punishment as a transgressor, and, above all, the hopeless and wretched condition of his soul, so long as it has no interest in such a Saviour. By looking to Christ on the cross, 'he mourns and is in bitterness;' by looking to Christ on the throne, he is 'pricked in his heart, and exclaims, What must I do to be saved?'

It is thus that the Spirit of God, by closely applying the truth to the conscience, *brings a sinner to feel his need of a Saviour;* and the convictions which are thus produced are the first and strongest motives to serious inquiry and earnest prayer. And accordingly, you will generally observe, that when any person in a congregation is benefited by the ministry of the Gospel, the first intimation of this change consists in a deep seriousness of spirit, sometimes in great anxiety and even distress of mind, bordering on despair, the reason of which is, that the Spirit of God is convincing that man of his sin and misery, and applying the truth closely to his conscience, so as to make him feel his need of a Saviour; and he is thus prepared for receiving with all gladness the simple message of grace, as suited to his need; whereas others who say that they are sinners, but without any spiritual perception of the meaning of this confession, easily succeed in quieting their occasional convictions by the opiates of error and self-deceit, and sit for years under the same ministry without making a single step in advance towards salvation, and without being conscious of so much as one earnest desire for its attainment. Conviction of sin, then, and especially conviction of sin and danger, on account of unbelief in Christ, is a *hopeful* symptom, a necessary preparative, a common precursor of a saving change.

When a sinner is thus 'convinced of his sin and misery,' so as to feel his *need of* a Saviour, the next part of the Spirit's work is 'to enlighten his mind in the knowledge of Christ,' as being in all respects *just such a Saviour as he needs.* He may have had some knowledge of Christ before; he may have been well instructed in his earliest years, and the doctrine of salvation may have been long familiar to his mind; but that doctrine now assumes a new aspect, and is studied in a better spirit, when, under the influence of serious conviction, he is brought to feel that his eternity depends upon it. Many parts of the glorious scheme of grace, which, till then, he had regarded as unimportant, or even objectionable, will now appear to his awakened eye to be invested with awful interest and transcendent value; and the more he contemplates it, in connection with his own felt necessities, the more will he be convinced that it is in all respects suitable to his case, and contains neither more than was necessary to meet, nor less than is sufficient to secure, his everlasting welfare. Above all, the *person*, the *character*, the *offices*, and the *work* of Christ, will command his deepest interest; and as he meditates on these, and acquires new and more enlarged views of their glory, his heart will burn within him at every fresh discovery of the power, and grace, and all-sufficiency of the Saviour. The great work of the Spirit is to point the eye of a convinced sinner to Christ, to open up to him the fulness that is in Christ, to unfold his unsearchable riches, to explain the design of his mission, the constitution of his person, the variety of his offices, the nature and the perfection of his work, the certainty and glory of his reward, as our Redeemer; and to this part of the Spirit's testimony for Christ allusion is made, both when it is said that he would reprove or convict the world of *righteousness*, because he has gone to the Father; and also when it is added that he would reprove the world of judgment, because the prince of this world is judged. The Spirit's advent was, in itself, a proof of Christ's exaltation, and, as such, a proof of his righteousness and power, as a Prince and Saviour; and when he comes, the Spirit glorifies Christ, by revealing him to the awakened sinner as the 'Lord his righteousness,' a perfect and accepted 'propitiation,' 'a priest on his throne.' And one vivid view of Christ as *he is*, imparted to the mind in the hour of private meditation or under the preaching of the Gospel, has been sufficient, in many a case, to dispel all the doubts and misgivings of a troubled conscience, insomuch that the man has felt as if on a sudden his eyes had been opened on the light of day, or as if his conscience were relieved from a heavy burden, or as if his whole soul were at once enlarged, liberated from bondage, and intro-duced into the glorious liberty wherewith Christ makes his people free.

And what is very remarkable, *the very same truths* may have been pre-sented to his mind in former times without producing any effect. The truth is the same, but it appears to him in a new light. He has no occasion to alter a single article in his former creed, yet he feels as if he could say: 'One thing I know, that whereas I was blind, now I see.' He knew Christ before, as those knew him of whom it is said, that he was to them 'as a root out of a dry ground, having no form nor comeliness, nor any beauty wherefore they should desire him.' But now every word respecting Christ is sweet, every aspect of his character, and office and work, awakens interest; every thing in Christ is precious, when, under the teaching of the Spirit, he is seen to be 'the fairest among ten thousand, and altogether lovely.' And most sweetly and seasonably does this part of the Spirit's work follow on the conviction of sin. Nor is it unnecessary even in the case of a convinced sinner; for all experience shows that, when overwhelmed with the thought of his own sinfulness, he is prone to doubt or disbelieve the truth as it is in Jesus, or to put a legal construction on the Gospel, or to sink into utter dejection and despair, as if he at least could have no interest in the Gospel, and were too great a sinner to be saved. It belongs to the office of the Spirit to dispel these dark suspicions, and to correct these fatal misapprehensions; and this he does, not by imparting any new information not revealed in the Bible, but by unfolding the truth which the Bible contains, and by simply 'enlightening the mind in the knowledge of Christ.'

Another step remains. It is quite possible that a man may be, to a certain extent, convinced of his sin and misery, and that he may have acquired a considerable degree of knowledge concerning Christ, and yet fall short of conversion. We read that 'Felix trembled,' and of some 'who were once enlightened,' and yet fell away. Indeed, most men in a Christian country have their occasional convictions and fears, and have also some notional acquaintance with the doctrine of salvation; nay, they may seem to 'receive that doctrine with joy,' and yet refuse to undergo the great, the decisive, the saving change. The reason of this is the inveterate depravity of the human heart, and its native aversion or enmity to God. The heart must be renewed, and its enmity slain, before a thorough conversion is accomplished; and the previous process of conviction and instruction is only a means to this end, a means suitable in itself, and sufficient, through the Spirit's grace, but without it utterly ineffectual. Accordingly, the concluding part of the Spirit's work in conversion is, to *renew our wills*, or to *make us willing* to be saved by Christ on Gospel terms. It is not enough to convince a man of his sin and misery; conviction is not conversion. Nor is it enough to instruct him in the doctrine of the Gospel; that doctrine might only inflame his enmity, and exasperate his pride. Conversion implies a *change of heart*. It may seem that the direct agency of the Spirit cannot be necessary here, since all men must be willing to be saved. But it is far, very far from being true that men are willing to be saved, in the Gospel sense of that expression. They *are* willing to escape from misery, simply considered as such, and to secure what they regard as happiness; but they are not anxious – on the contrary, they are averse – to be *saved* as the Gospel proposes to save them. They have no desire to be delivered from sin, and no relish for the spiritual happiness which Christ offers to bestow. Had the Gospel simply proclaimed impunity for sin, or exemption from suffering, and that, live as they might, men should enjoy an eternal happiness suited to their own tastes, then, doubtless, it would have been hailed with one universal acclamation of gratitude and joy; but it makes no such overture. It speaks of a salvation from *sin*, as well as from suffering, and proposes a heaven into which nothing that is unclean or impure shall ever enter; and to say that all men are willing to be saved in that sense, and in this way, were to deny the depravity of human nature, and to affirm that all men are willing to be holy. The great difficulty, then, is, *to make them willing to be saved*, in the Bible sense of that expression, and in the way of God's appointment; and this is effected by the Spirit's grace, 'They are a willing people in the day of his power.'

It is important to mark, that this is the *last* stage in the process, and the completion of the Spirit's work, in converting a sinner. So soon as he is made willing, there remains no barrier betwixt him and the Saviour: he is at perfect liberty, on God's own warrant and invitation, nay, by God's express command, to 'embrace Jesus Christ as he is freely offered to him in the Gospel.' Of every man who reads or hears the Gospel, it may be affirmed that there is nothing betwixt him and salvation, except his own unwillingness to be saved. 'Ye are not willing to come to me, that ye might have life,' – that is the Saviour's charge and complaint. 'Whosoever will, let him take of the water of life freely,' – that is the Saviour's call and invitation. The warrant of every sinner to believe in Christ to the saving of the soul is clear; it is written as with a sunbeam in Scripture; it lies wholly in the Word, which is the Spirit's message, and not at all in the Spirit's witness in the heart. The warrant of the Word is ample; but if any feels that, even with this warrant in his hand, there is something *within* which keeps him back – a depraved heart, a rebellious will, a reluctant spirit – oh! let him acknowledge his own helplessness, and cast himself, with the simplicity of a little child, on the grace of the Spirit of God!

IV. The Work of the Spirit in Enlightening the Mind

HAVING considered the general design of the gift of the Spirit, in reference both to the world and the Church, and described the course or process by which a soul is translated from the kingdom of darkness into the kingdom of God's dear Son, I propose to illustrate separately the various parts of the Spirit's work, or his successive operations on the soul, from the time when it is first taken under his teaching, till it is made 'meet for the inheritance of the saints in light.'

One of his most necessary operations is that by which he conveys *spiritual light into the understanding;* and to this part of his work, which is indeed so important, that it is often put for the whole, the apostle refers, when, speaking of the Holy Ghost as 'the Spirit of wisdom and revelation,' he prays that by the Spirit 'the eyes of our understanding may be enlightened' (Eph. 1. 17, 18), and when he describes true converts as having had their eyes opened, and having been turned from darkness to light; nay, translated out of darkness into God's marvellous light.

The illuminating work of the Holy Spirit may be said to be the groundwork of all his other operations; for it is by the truth known and believed that the Spirit fulfils all the functions of his glorious office.[1] By enlightening the mind in the knowledge of sin, he lays a groundwork for the *conviction* of conscience; by enabling us to see the import and meaning of the Gospel, he proposes motives for *conversion;* by teaching us right views of God and of ourselves, our privileges and prospects, he supplies us with means of *comfort;* by showing us the nature and necessity of Gospel holiness, he carries forward the work of *sanctification;* by disclosing to us scriptural views of our spiritual necessities, he calls forth the *spirit of prayer;* and, generally, he does whatever he is wont to do, by means of the *knowledge* of the truth. Hence it is important to give due consideration to this part of the Spirit's work, that we may be prepared to understand, and rightly to improve,

---

[1] On this important subject, the author refers his readers to a Treatise by Jonathan Edwards, on 'The Reality of Spiritual Light.' *Works*, vol. viii. p. 5? Thomas Halyburton on 'The Nature of Faith;' and John Owen's Discourses on 'The Reason of Faith;' and 'The Causes, Ways and Means of Understanding the Word of God.' *Works*, vol. vi.

whatever we shall find revealed respecting his other operations on the soul.

Such, indeed, is the inseparable connection, or rather the real affinity of all the saving graces of the Spirit, that none of them can exist without being accompanied or followed by all the rest; and hence any one of them may be used to signify the presence of all. Thus, *knowledge, faith, repentance,* and *love* are severally spoken of in Scripture as either comprehending or implying every thing that is essential to a sinner's salvation; and hence a full exposition of any one of these fruits of the Spirit might embrace a description of the whole of the Spirit's work. It is not, then, with the view of separating betwixt them, or assigning the precise order of their production, that we distinguish one part of the Spirit's work from another; but rather with the view of unfolding it, in all the magnitude of its extent, and the variety of its aspects, as it is exhibited in the Gospel.

The Holy Spirit is the *enlightener* of God's people, and imparts *spiritual illumination* to their minds.

This part of the Spirit's work implies a *previous state of spiritual darkness* on the part of those who are the subjects of it; and the natural state of all men is very frequently represented under the figures of darkness, blindness, and ignorance. They are described as 'walking in the vanity of their minds, having the understanding darkened, being alienated from the life of God through the ignorance that is in them, because of the blindness of their heart.' And again, 'The natural man receiveth not the things of the Spirit of God, for they are foolishness unto him; neither can he know them, because they are spiritually discerned.'

Here observe, that this spiritual darkness is *universal*; it is affirmed of all the Gentiles, and we shall find that it is also affirmed of all the unbelieving Jews: it belongs to the 'natural man,' or to every man as he is by nature. It is not dispelled by those common notions of God and divine things, which an unrenewed mind may acquire in the exercise of its own faculties. Nor is its prevailing power disproved by the existence of these notions, any more than the prevailing power of sin is disproved by the existence of some notions of the difference betwixt right and wrong. Nay, as in nature itself there is 'no darkness without a mixture of light,'[1] such light as serves only to make 'the darkness visible,' so is it with the unrenewed soul; its common notions of God are not sufficient to dispel the darkness in which it is shrouded; and hence the apostle, in one place, declares, that when 'men *knew* God, they glorified him not as God;' and, regarding this as a proof that there was some radical defect in their knowledge of him, he speaks of it elsewhere as if it were no knowledge at all; for, says he, 'the world by wisdom *knew not* God.' And may we not apply to these common notions,

[1] Howe, *Works*, viii., 566.

which have nothing in them of the true celestial light, the solemn remark of our Lord himself, 'If the light that is in thee be darkness, how great is that darkness!' This darkness does not consist merely in the absence of outward light, but in the 'blindness of the mind' such blindness as obstructs the entrance of the light, even when it is shining gloriously around us. Thus, of the unbelieving Jews it is said, that they remained in spiritual darkness with the revelation of God in their hands: 'But their minds were *blinded:* for until this day remaineth the same veil untaken away in the reading of the Old Testament; which veil is done away in Christ. But even unto this day, when Moses is read, the veil is upon their heart. Nevertheless, when it shall turn to the Lord, the veil shall be taken away.' (2 Cor. 3. 14–16). A two-fold veil is here spoken of – the one which covered the Old Testament, before the advent of Christ, by whom it was explained as well as fulfilled; and the other which lay upon their own souls, and which prevented them from seeing, even when the first 'veil was done away in Christ.' And so, of multitudes who live in the full blaze of Gospel light, it is said, that they remain inwardly in a state of spiritual darkness; for 'if our gospel be hid, it is hid to them that are lost: in whom the god of this world hath blinded the minds of them which believe not, lest the light of the glorious gospel of Christ, who is the image of God, should shine unto them.' (2 Cor. 4. 3, 4). If this spiritual darkness be natural to all men, and if it may exist notwith-standing the common notions of God and religion which they may acquire by their natural faculties, and notwithstanding the still higher instruction of the written Word; it follows that it can only be removed by an inward operation on the mind itself, and this is expressly ascribed to the enlighten-ing influence of the Spirit. 'The Lord is that Spirit; and where the Spirit of the Lord is there is liberty.' If we would 'with open or unveiled face behold the glory of the Lord,' it must be 'as by the Spirit of the Lord.'

Accordingly, the change which is wrought in the mind at the time of its conversion is compared to a transition from darkness to light, or to the change of night into day. It is said of the Father, that 'he hath delivered us from the power of darkness, and hath translated us into the kingdom of his dear Son;' that 'he hath called us out of darkness into his marvellous light;' and of Christ, that he commissioned Paul 'to open their eyes, to turn them from darkness to light, and from the power of Satan unto God:' but that this was not to be accomplished by mere human teaching appears from that striking passage where God speaks of it as his own peculiar work, and intimates that it could be accomplished by no other than that creative power which, 'when the earth was without form and void, and darkness was upon the face of the deep, and the Spirit of God moved upon the face of the waters,' spoke saying, 'Let there be light, and there was light;' for says the apostle, 'God, who commanded the light to shine out of darkness, hath shined in our hearts, to give the light of the knowledge of the glory of God in the face of Jesus Christ.' And then will the wondering disciple exclaim, 'One thing I know, that whereas I was blind, now I see.'

This great change is ascribed to the immediate agency of the Holy Spirit on the soul. It is ascribed, indeed, to the Father, as 'the fountain of lights, from whom cometh down every good and perfect gift;' and to the Son also, as the anointed Prophet of the Church, 'the light of the world;' but it is the Holy Spirit, who proceedeth from the Father and the Son, by whose immediate personal agency this illumination of the mind is wrought. Our Lord himself promised to send the Spirit as an Enlightener. 'When he, the *Spirit of truth*, is come, he will guide you into all truth.' 'He shall glorify me; for he shall receive of mine, and shall *show* it unto you.' 'The Comforter, which is the Holy Ghost, whom the Father will send in my name, he shall *teach* you all things, and bring all things to your remembrance, whatsoever I have said unto you.' And that this precious promise was not personal to the apostles, nor limited to the primitive Church, appears from the preceding context: 'I will pray the Father, and he shall give you another Comforter, that he may abide with you *for ever;* even the Spirit of truth;' by whose constant presence and continued grace in the Church, he fulfils that other promise, 'Lo, I am with you alway, even unto the end of the world.'

There are various distinct operations of the Holy Spirit as the Enlightener of the soul. (1) As the *revealer* of the truth, by whom it was made known to the prophets, evangelists, and apostles, – for 'holy men of old *spake* as they were moved by the *Holy Ghost.*' 'God hath *revealed* them unto us by his Spirit; for the Spirit searcheth all things, yea, the deep things of God.' (2) As the Author of the Scriptures, inspiring the prophets, evangelists, and apostles to write what should be preserved and recorded for the conviction of the world, and the comfort of the Church, in all ages, for 'all Scripture was given by his inspiration.' So that every individual stands indebted to the Holy Ghost for every ray of light that has ever beamed on his understanding from the page of Scripture. The Bible is the Spirit's message; it is the text-book which he has provided for the Church. (3) But there is, and must be, a more direct operation of the Holy Spirit on every human soul that is enlightened by his truth. It is not enough that he has revealed the truth to his apostles, and that he has embodied and preserved it in an authentic Bible. The *glorious light may shine around us*, without shining *into our hearts*. There is a defective vision that must be cured, a blind eye that must be opened, a veil that must be taken away, a thick darkness within, which must be dispelled by his creative mandate, 'Let there be light.' Notwithstanding all the abundance of Gospel light, it is still true as it ever was, that 'the natural man receiveth not the things of the Spirit of God'; 'that no man knoweth the Son, but the Father; neither knoweth any man the Father, save the Son, and he to whomsoever the Son will reveal him;' and that he is often pleased 'to hide these things from the wise and prudent, and to reveal them unto babes.'

The *Word of God* is the *instrument*, the *Spirit of God* is the *agent*, in this great work of illumination. The Bible is the text-book, but the Spirit is himself the teacher. He is not only the author of that book, but the interpreter of it also, who guides us into a knowledge of its truths. He puts the Bible into our hands, as a 'light unto our feet and a lamp unto our path;' but, knowing that we are naturally blind, and cannot see afar off, he opens our eye and shines into our heart. All the truth which the Spirit ever teaches is *in* the Word; but never would it find *entrance* into our hearts unless he put it there. The Word is a *sword* – a sharp two-edged sword; but its efficacy depends on this – that it is the sword of the Spirit. The Word is a light; but it is 'in *his light* we see light.' 'The entrance of his Word giveth light;' but it obtains entrance only when 'he openeth the heart.' Hence the prayer of the Psalmist, 'Open thou mine eyes, that I may see wondrous things out of thy law;' and the still more remarkable prayer of the apostle, 'For this cause I bow my knees unto the Father of our Lord Jesus Christ, that he would grant you, according to the riches of his glory, to be *strengthened with might* by his Spirit in the inner man.' Here is a powerful work of the Spirit on the soul; it must be strengthened with might. And for what end? 'That ye may be able to comprehend with all saints, what is the breadth, and length, and depth, and height; and to know the love of Christ, which passeth knowledge, that ye may be filled with all the fulness of God.' Here no new truth is said to be revealed; but what is contained in the Word is made known by the inward enlightening of the Holy Spirit.

On the *teaching of the Spirit the efficacy of all the means of grace depends*, and especially the efficacy of the reading and preaching of the Word. Without the Spirit the ministry of the Word would be utterly fruitless for all the ends of saving conversion. It might be a social blessing, as a means of keeping alive a sense of common morality in the world, but never could it be the means of spiritual life to the soul, unless it were accompanied with the enlightening grace of the Spirit. What more powerful than the ministry of the apostles? what reasoning more vigorous, what appeals more overwhelming, what eloquence more lofty, what zeal more urgent, than those of Paul? What love so tender, what tenderness so pathetic, what pathos so touching, what unction so rich and sweet, as those of John? What sacred orator better furnished for his vocation than Apollos, of whom it is written, that 'he was an eloquent man, and mighty in the Scriptures'? Yet even the ministry of inspired men, the preaching of the very apostles of Christ, depended for all its saving efficacy on the grace of the Spirit; for, says the apostle, 'Who then is Paul, and who is Apollos, but ministers by whom ye believed, even as the Lord gave to every man? I have planted, Apollos watered, but God gave the increase. So then neither is he that planteth any thing, neither he that watereth, but God that giveth the increase.' 'We are labourers together with God; but ye are God's husbandry, ye are God's building.' Ministers are often employed as *instruments* in enlightening and converting the soul; and hence they may be said, ministerially, to be the spiritual fathers of their converts. Yet it is not by their own power, but by the power of the Holy Ghost; so that every successful minister might well say with the apostles, 'Ye men of Israel, why marvel ye at this? or why look ye so earnestly upon us, as though by our own power or holiness we had made this man to walk?' This great truth, if it shows the weakness of the minister, will also prove the very strength of his ministry; for never will he feel so deeply impressed either with the greatness of his work, or the dignity of his mission, as when he is most thoroughly convinced that the efficacy of all his preaching depends on the power of the Spirit. This will nerve him with new strength, and inspire him with new hope, when all outward appearances are most unpromising; and in the strength of this simple faith, he will stand prepared to deliver his message, before any audience, savage or civilized, assured that the same Spirit who has brought the truth home to his own soul, can also bring it home, with demonstration and power, both to the obtuse and unlettered peasant, and to the refined, perhaps the sceptical, or the scornful man of science.

Further, the Word, the ministry, and other means of instruction, are adapted to the rational nature of man, and are in their own nature fitted for the purpose for which they are employed; nay, men may, in the use of their natural faculties, be instructed, impressed, and affected by the reading and hearing of the Word; but they cannot be *savingly enlightened* without the teaching of the Spirit.

The Spirit's operations are adapted to the nature of man as a rational and intelligent being; and he works in and by the faculties of the soul. It is the *same mind* which is now in darkness that is to be translated into marvellous light; the same understanding which is now ignorant that is to be informed; the same eye which is now blind that is to be opened and enabled to see. - The Spirit usually exerts his power by the use of *appropriate means*. Omitting from our present consideration the case of infants, who may be sanctified from the womb by the secret operations of the Spirit, it is clear that in the case of adults, the mind is enlightened instrumentally by the truth, which is hence called 'the light of the glorious gospel,' and the 'day-star which rises on the heart.' The Word of God is an *appropriate means of enlightening* the mind; it is an instrument which is in every respect fitted for the purpose for which it is employed. (1 Tim. 3. 14). If any remain in darkness with the Bible in their hands, it is not because there is no light in the Bible, but because there is no spiritual eye to discern it. All the truth which an enlightened believer ever learns under the teaching of the Spirit is really contained in the Bible, although heretofore he had not seen it there: nay, much of it may have been contained in the articles of his professed creed; but it was not known, understood, and believed in its full spiritual meaning as it is now. He is only brought, in many cases, to see what he formerly professed to believe in a new *light*, so as to understand and feel its spiritual import and power, as the truth of God.

Being an appropriate means, adapted to the faculties of the human mind, there can be no reason to doubt that the Bible, like any other book, may convey much instruction to an unrenewed man. When it is affirmed that a natural man cannot know the things of the Spirit of God, it is not implied that the Bible is unintelligibly written, or that he cannot understand the sense and meaning of scriptural propositions, so as to be able to give a rational account of them; for he may investigate the literal meaning of Scripture, and, in doing so, may attach a definite idea to many of its statements – may be able to see their mutual relations – to reason upon them, and even to expound them; and yet, in the scriptural sense, he may be in darkness notwithstanding. There are truths in the Bible which admit of being recognized, and even proved by natural reason, 'for the things of a man may be known by the spirit of man which is in him;' and even 'the things of the Spirit,' when revealed, may be so far understood as to affect and impress the mind which is nevertheless unconverted. The Pharisees had 'the form of knowledge in the law;' they were the great theologians under the Old Testament. Yet our Lord declares, that, studious and instructed as they were, and capable of expounding the writings of Moses, they did not really *know* God, nor understand the writings of Moses. Simon Magus must have had some correct notional acquaintance with the leading truths of the Gospel, and must have been able to put them forth in intelligible propositions, when he made that profession of faith which the apostles themselves regarded as a sufficient ground for his admission to the sacrament of baptism. Yet he had not been spiritually enlightened, for 'he was still in the gall of bitterness and the bond of iniquity.' So our Lord himself speaks of some who hear the Word, and anon with *joy* receive it. They not only have some notion of its meaning, but some impressions of its power; yet they have not the 'light of life.' They are like Herod, 'who feared John, knowing that he was a just man and an holy, and observed him; and when he heard him, he did many things, and heard him gladly.' There is a great difference betwixt the views even of *natural men* on the subject of divine truth, a difference which is strikingly exemplified by the very different language of *the three Roman governors*, Festus, Agrippa, and Felix, in reference to the preaching of Paul. Festus spoke out in the bold language of a natural man, to whom the preaching of the Gospel was *foolishness:* 'Paul, thou art beside thyself: much learning doth make thee mad.' Agrippa was impressed and moved, for he said, 'Almost thou persuadest me to be a Christian;' and Felix was still more deeply moved, for, 'as Paul reasoned of righteousness, temperance, and judgment to come, Felix *trembled.*' The natural man, then, may know something of divine truth, – he may even be impressed and affected by it, without acquiring that *saving knowledge* which our Lord himself declares to be 'eternal life.'

The natural man is capable of acquiring, by the use of his rational faculties, such an acquaintance with the truths of God's Word as is sufficient to *make him responsible for* his treatment of it. Not to enlarge upon other points, let us take the doctrine which affirms the darkness of the human understanding, and the necessity of the enlightening grace of the Holy Spirit, which is often supposed to destroy the grounds of human responsibility in this respect; unless he be taught of God, he cannot have such an experimental knowledge of that doctrine as belongs to the exercised believer, and probably he will not submit to it; but it is stated, nevertheless, in plain intelligible language. He cannot read his Bible without being made aware that it contains this truth, nor can he exercise his understanding upon it, without acquiring some general knowledge of its import; and that knowledge, although neither spiritual nor saving, is amply sufficient as a ground of moral obligation. And farther, he may also learn from the same source, and in the same way, how it is that the enlightening grace of the Spirit is obtained, for he cannot read such passages as these: 'If any man lack wisdom, let him ask of God, who giveth to all men liberally, and upbraideth not, and it shall be given him;' and, 'If ye, being evil, know how to give good gifts unto your children, how much more will your Father in heaven give the Holy Spirit to them that ask him?' – he cannot read such passages as these without forming some notion of prayer as the means by which his natural darkness may be dispelled; and if, notwithstanding his clear natural perception of such doctrines, he either refuses to believe them, or persists in neglecting prayer for the Holy Spirit, he must be dealt with hereafter on a very different principle, and tried by a very different rule of judgment from that which alone is applicable to those who have no Bible to teach them, or no rational mind to be taught. You cannot have sat under a Gospel ministry for years without acquiring such knowledge as is abundantly sufficient to lay you under the most weighty responsibilities. It is a solemn reflection, that this knowledge must either prove 'the savour of life unto life,' or 'the savour of death unto death.' If it be not the means of your *conversion*, it will be the ground of your *condemnation*, 'For this is the condemnation, that light hath come into the world, and that men have loved darkness rather than light, because their deeds were evil. But he that loveth the light cometh to the light;' and he that loveth the light of the Gospel will not shrink from the enlightening work of the Spirit.

Still, it must ever be remembered, that whatever knowledge a natural man may acquire by the exercise of his rational faculties on the Word of God, that knowledge is neither spiritual nor saving, unless he be enlightened by the Spirit. Were I asked to state what is the specific difference betwixt the natural and the spiritual knowledge of divine truth, or how they may best be distinguished from each other, I should feel the difficulty that is usually attendant on a discrimination betwixt two states of mind, which have some common resemblance, and whose difference consists in a quality of which the natural man knows nothing, because he has no experience of it. As it is difficult to convey an idea of colour to the blind, or of music to the deaf, so it is difficult to describe to a natural man the peculiar perceptions of one whose eyes have been opened by the Spirit. And the difficulty is not diminished but increased by the fact, that he has a kind of knowledge which is common to him with the true believer, and which is too apt to be mistaken for that which the Gospel requires. Perhaps the nearest approach that we can make to an explanation may be by asking you to conceive of a man who sees, but has no sense of beauty, or of a man who hears, but has no sense of harmony; just such is the case of a natural man, who sees the truth without perceiving its spiritual excellence, and on whose ear the sound of the Gospel falls without awakening music in his soul. Saving knowledge is not a knowledge of the dead letter or outward form of the Gospel, but a knowledge of the truth in 'the light, and lustre, and glory of it;' 'gustful knowledge,'[1] which has in it a *relish* of the truth as excellent: 'O *taste* and see that the Lord is good.' It is 'the light of the knowledge of the *glory* of God in the face of Jesus Christ.' Just conceive of the different views of Christ which were entertained by those with whom he mingled in Judea, and this will help you to understand the difference, or at least to see that there is one, betwixt the one kind of knowledge and the other. All the Jews who saw Christ had some views concerning him: but to the carnal eye 'he had no form nor comeliness; and when they saw him, there was no beauty that they should desire him;' while to the spiritual eye, he was 'fairer than ten thousand, and altogether lovely;' for, says the

[1] Thomas Halyburton.

apostle, 'He dwelt amongst us, and we beheld his glory, the glory as of the only begotten of the Father, full of grace and truth.' And just as it was then, so is it now: as Christ, the sum and substance of the Gospel, came as the light, 'and the darkness comprehended it not;' as 'he was in the world, and the world was made by him, and the world *knew him not;*' so the Gospel, which is Christ revealed, may be read and heard. Yet 'seeing we may not perceive, and hearing we may not understand,' until the Spirit 'take of the things of Christ and show them unto us,' by 'shining into our hearts.'

Another difference betwixt the two kinds of knowledge consists in this, that true spiritual light carries with it a *self-evidencing power*, and is accompanied with a heartfelt conviction of its certainty, a cordial belief of its truth. When the eye is opened to see the glory of the Gospel, the mind has an intuitive perception of its divine authority; it 'commends itself to the conscience in the sight of God,' and the sinner feels that 'God is in it of a truth.' God has 'magnified his Word above all his name;' it bears upon it a more striking impress of his divine perfections than any other manifestation by which he has ever made himself known; and when the eye is opened to perceive God's glory in the face of Jesus Christ, the mind can no more believe that the Word could be written, than that the world could be framed, by any other than the omniscient One.

But the great discriminating test of the difference betwixt the natural and spiritual knowledge of divine truth is to be found in its practical influence and actual fruits. Spiritual light is accompanied with life and love; it is vital and powerful, transforming, renewing, purifying the soul in which it dwells; for if we behold the glory of God, we are thereby changed into the same image; we love what we discern to be good, we admire what we perceive to be excellent, we imitate and become conformed to what we love and admire. It is not a cold light like that of the moon or stars, but a lively light, accompanied with heat and warmth, vivifying, fructifying; it attunes all the faculties of the soul for the service of God, like the light that fell on the statue of Memnon, and awoke the chords of his sleeping lyre.

The difference betwixt the natural and spiritual knowledge of divine truth is not only real but great. It is as the difference betwixt darkness and light, or betwixt night and day. Every natural man, however educated, is 'alienated from the life of God through the ignorance that is in him.' He may be more learned in the letter of the Scriptures, more thoroughly furnished with all literary erudition, more scientific in his dogmatic orthodoxy, more eloquent in illustration and argument, than many of those who are 'taught of God;' but 'I say unto you, He that is least in the kingdom of heaven is greater than he.' It is not a difference in *degree*, but in *kind*. In that which is common to both, the natural man may have a higher degree of learning than the spiritual; but in that which is peculiar to such as are taught of God, there is no room for comparison; that kind of knowledge, although it, too, admits of degrees as it is possessed by the people of God, belongs to none else, to none but such as are taught by his Spirit. And this difference is great, insomuch that the people of God, whose eyes are opened to understand the Scriptures, are said to have 'a new understanding given to them.' 'The Son of God is come, and hath given us an understanding that we may know him that is true;' not that another faculty is created, but that the old one is thoroughly renewed. And this change is wrought on the understanding itself. It is not enough that the affections be disengaged from sin, so as to remove obstructions to the right operation of a mind supposed to be in itself 'pure, noble, and untainted;' no, the understanding has shared in the ruins of the fall, and is itself perverted; and as such it must be renewed by him who created it, otherwise it will for ever distort the light, however clearly it may shine from the page of Scripture.

As the understanding is the leading faculty of the soul, and plainly designed to influence, control, and govern every other by its light, so darkness here is the prolific cause of much moral and spiritual evil. The understanding, therefore, must be enlightened, if the heart is to be renewed. Spiritual darkness is spoken of in Scripture, not as a mere passive or negative thing, but as a *positive power;* 'the power of darkness' is expressly mentioned, and the apostate angels are represented as kept in 'chains of darkness,' as if it imposed fetters on the soul, and truly none can break those fetters, but he who caused the iron chain to fall from off the hands and feet of his imprisoned disciple.

Our apostasy from God is described as consisting chiefly in our spiritual darkness. The very end of our being was, that we should 'glorify God,' as intelligent creatures might and ought, by perceiving, adoring, and delighting in his glory: this is the highest exercise of angels and seraphim. And if now a dark cloud conceals from us his perfections, if we can have God present to our thoughts without perceiving his glory, this is at once the evidence and essence of our melancholy fall.

This darkness is not only the deadly shade under which our enmity to God finds a shelter and covering, but it is in some sense the cause of that enmity, inasmuch as it gives rise to innumerable prejudices against God, which feed it and keep it alive, and also to multiform delusions, varying from the barest atheism up to the most awful forms of superstition; and if these prejudices and these delusions are to be swept away, and if the enmity which they beget and nourish is to be slain, it must be by him who commanded the light to shine out of darkness, shining into our hearts, to give us the light of the knowledge of the glory of God in the face of Jesus Christ.

This illumination of the Spirit has reference to all Gospel truth, but is given in greater or less degrees, while in every instance it embraces whatever is necessary to be known and believed in order to salvation. 'Ye have an unction from the Holy One, and ye know all things.' 'The anointing which ye have received of him abideth in you; and ye need not that any man teach you: but as the same anointing teacheth you of all things, and is truth, and is no lie, and even as it hath taught you, ye shall abide in him.' From these words it is plain, that every one who is taught of God knows whatever is necessary to be believed in order to salvation, and that he is not left absolutely to depend on mere human teaching; but it is equally clear from the context, that this anointing does not supersede the use of such helps and such means of information as God has graciously provided for his Church; on the contrary, the same apostle says, 'I write unto you, fathers, because ye have known him that is from the beginning; I write unto you, little children, because ye have known the Father;' 'I have not written unto you because ye know not the truth, but because ye know it.' The apostle's letter was designed and fitted for their instruction, and was useful, not only in 'stirring up their pure minds by way of remembrance,' but also in helping them to apply the truth to the exigencies of their condition, as one that exposed them to the seductions of false teachers, and in enabling them to grow in the knowledge of God; for among Christians there are degrees of spiritual light, as among natural men there are degrees of secular knowledge; and the one kind of knowledge admits of growth and increase, and depends on the use of ordinary means, not less than the other. We may know the Lord, like Apollos; yet we may be brought, like him, to 'know the way of the Lord more perfectly.' As the knowledge which is common to all who are taught of God embraces whatever is necessary to be known and believed in order to salvation, while, being imparted in greater or less degrees, there may be a diversity of opinion even amongst true Christians on points of minor importance, we see at once the origin and the nature of that wonderful uniformity of sentiment amongst them which marks the unity of Christian faith in regard to all the fundamental truths of God's Word, while we may reasonably expect to find a variety of opinions, arising from different degrees of light, even amongst such as are in the main and substantially at one. And this consideration ought to be improved as a lesson of universal charity and of mutual forbearance among the disciples of Christ.

It is a precious Bible truth, that the enlightening grace of the Holy Spirit, although it be specially promised to the Gospel ministry as that by which alone their peculiar functions can be successfully exercised, is not confined to them, nor to any one class or order of men, but it is common to all believers. Every private person, – every humble man, who takes his Bible in his hand, and retires to his closet to read and meditate on it there, is privileged to ask and to expect the teaching of the Spirit of God. 'If any man lack wisdom, let him ask of God, who giveth to all men liberally, and upbraideth not; and it shall be given him.' The direct communication of every soul with God as 'the Father of lights,' with Christ as 'the light of the world,' and with the Holy Ghost as 'the Spirit of truth,' shows what standing the Christian people have in the Christian Church; and that, although God has graciously provided for them ministerial helps and spiritual guides, he has not left them absolutely dependent on any order of men; still less has he subjected them to mere human authority in matters of faith: 'their faith must stand not in the wisdom of men, but in the power of God.'

V. The Work of the Spirit in Convincing the Conscience

IT is part of the Spirit's work to convince the soul of its sinfulness.

I. There is, indeed, a conscience in man, which fulfils alike the functions of a law, by prescribing the path of duty, and the functions of a judge, in pronouncing sentence against transgression, a conscience which impresses every man with a sense of right and wrong, and which often visits the sinner with the inward pangs of conviction and remorse.

But *conscience*, while it exists, and while it serves many useful purposes, is not sufficient in its present state to awaken the soul to a full sense of its real condition, although it be amply sufficient to render it responsible to God as a Judge, and to make it a fit subject for the convincing operations of his Spirit.

That in its present state it is not sufficient of itself, nor even when it is surrounded with the outward light of the Gospel, to awaken the soul to a due sense of its own sinfulness, appears from various considerations. 1. It is manifest that conscience has shared, like every other faculty of our nature, in the ruinous effects of the fall; and the natural darkness of the soul prevents it from seeing its own corruption. It must be so, indeed, if by the fall we have lost the perception of *God's glory*, or can no longer discern the excellency of his holiness; for our views of sin stand connected with, and must be affected by our views of God, one vivid view of his glorious character being sufficient to make the sinner tremble at the sight of his own vileness, and to exclaim with Job, 'I have heard of thee by the hearing of the ear; but now mine eye seeth thee: wherefore I abhor myself, and repent in dust and ashes.' In as far, then, as the fall has 'alienated us from the life of God through the ignorance that was in us, because of the blindness of our hearts,' in the same proportion must it have weakened that power of moral perception, or that principle of conscience, which should convince the soul of its own sinfulness; and never, till it is restored to a spiritual acquaintance with God, will it come to see its guilt in all its loathsomeness and aggravations. 2. That natural conscience, unaided by the Spirit of God, is not sufficient of itself to bring a man to a right sense of his own sinfulness appears further from the tendency of habitual sin to sear and deaden the conscience, whereby it comes to pass, according to the sovereign appointment of God, that conscience becomes weaker in proportion as sin grows stronger in the soul, till the sinner may arrive at a point of degeneracy at which he is wholly given over to a reprobate mind, and so far from being condemned by his conscience, he may dare to justify his wickedness by 'calling good evil, and evil good.' Instead of being ashamed of his guilt, he may even 'glory in his shame.' We read of some whose 'mind and conscience is defiled;' and of others 'having their conscience seared with a hot iron,' the habitual practice of sin having a deadening influence over that principle by which alone sin is checked or condemned. This natural provision is in accordance with the great law of moral retribution which is laid down in Scripture, a law which ensures the progressive improvement of those who make a right use of the imperfect light they have, and the rapid degeneracy of those who corrupt or abuse it; 'for whosoever hath, to him shall be given; and whosoever hath not, from him shall be taken even that which he seemeth to have' (or thinketh that he hath). Now, if this be the natural law of conscience, that its moral perceptions become dead, and its condemning power weak, in proportion as the power of sin becomes habitual and inveterate; it follows that the more need there is for a thorough work of conviction, the less is it to be expected from the mere operation of natural conscience, and that, if the Spirit of God do not interpose, the case of such a soul is hopeless. 3. But lest it should be thought that this second proof applies only to the case of gross and hardened transgressors of the divine law, let me observe further, that the experience of the more decent members of society, and even of many formal members of the church, affords ample evidence that natural conscience, unenlightened by the Spirit of God, is not sufficient to convince the soul of its sinfulness; for of many such it may be said with truth, that they have no just idea of *sin* as in its own nature, and in all its manifestations, an odious and hateful thing. Natural conscience in such men takes cognisance chiefly of gross outward transgressions, and of these, too, mainly as they stand connected with the peace and order of society, or with the decencies and proprieties of social life; it is a mere prudential reason; but of sin as it appears in the sight of God it thinks little, and still less of those heart-sins and that radical depravity from which all actual transgressions proceed. It condemns murder, but does it equally condemn pride? It condemns filial ingratitude and disobedience to an earthly parent, but does it equally condemn ungodliness, which is the natural element of every unrenewed mind, and which implies filial ingratitude and disobedience to our Father in heaven? How can it discern the inherent turpitude of sin, unless it be taught the inherent loveliness of what is spiritual and divine? and whence can this be learned but from the teaching of the Spirit? In fact, the work of *conviction* implies a work of *illumination*, and is based upon it. It is by enlightening the mind to discern the truth that the Spirit quickens the conscience; and so long as the mind remains in darkness, the conscience is prone to sleep. It is when the light of God shines into the heart that his vicegerent there starts from his slumbers, and lifts a responsive voice to the call of his Master. And hence it is that we read of an *enlightened conscience*, a conscience that pronounces truly when it is rightly informed.

4. The necessity of a convincing work of the Spirit further appears from the fact, that it is the most difficult of all things to fix the mind of any man on a *due consideration of sin*. Try to fix your own mind for any length of time on a steady consideration of sin, or endeavour to fix the mind of any child, or servant, or friend you have on this exercise, and you will at once find that it is all but impossible to succeed. The mind recoils from it. It will dwell on the sins of others, especially if they have provoked its resentment by a sense of wrong done to itself; but on sin in its own nature, and especially on its own sins, it cannot dwell; it flies off to some other and more inviting subject; or, instead of seeking to know the real state of the case, it busies itself in devising plausible excuses, and in putting blinds, as it were, on its own eyes. And so is it even when the subject is forced on its attention, and the ear is compelled to listen to a full exposition of it. The most searching sermon fails to convince, unless it be carried home with demonstration of the Spirit and with power. How often does the sinner hear that 'every sin deserveth the wrath and curse of God,' that it is 'an abominable thing which the Lord hateth,' that it is a 'great wickedness,' a loathsome disease, a hell-deserving crime? and yet, either attaching no definite meaning to the plainest language that can be employed, or shifting the charge away from himself to others, or inwardly deceiving himself by some plausible pretext or other, he sits unawed, unmoved, and rises and retires to his home without one salutary conviction on his conscience, without one impression deep enough to trouble his peace. And hence the free proclamation of a free salvation passes unheeded, because as yet he feels no need of a Saviour, and has no concern for his soul. If any sinner, then, is to be brought to such real heart concern about the state of his soul as is necessary for his thorough conversion, he must be convinced of sin by a power above that of mere natural conscience, even by the power of the Spirit of God.

II. In convincing of sin, the Spirit of God, acting agreeably to the moral constitution of our nature, takes the conscience as the subject of his operations, and seeks to *enlighten*, *quicken*, and *invigorate* it by the light and power of divine *truth*.

It is the conscience that is the *subject* of his operations. It is the moral faculty, the faculty of discriminating betwixt right and wrong, which makes us fit subjects for the convincing work of the Spirit. Had we no conscience, we should be incapable of moral convictions, as are the living but irresponsible beasts of the field and fowls of the air. But under the ashes of our ruined nature there are certain 'sparks of celestial fire,' the lights of conscience, which, dim and decayed, are yet not extinguished, and which render us responsible on the one hand, and susceptible of being renewed on the other. And just as natural reason is capable of discerning spiritual things when it is enlightened by the Spirit; so natural conscience is capable of discerning the evil of sin when it is rectified and strengthened by the Spirit.

But while conscience is the subject of true conviction, the Spirit of God is the author of it. He works in and by the conscience; so that while the Spirit reproves and convicts the sinner, the sinner is self-reproved and self-condemned. The conscience is quickened by the Spirit out of that lethargy into which it had fallen, through the benumbing influence of sin; it is invigorated and reinforced with new energy by the Spirit, having fresh life and power infused into it; it is called into action on its appropriate objects by the Spirit, and enabled steadily to view the sins with which the transgressor is chargeable; and, above all, it is enlightened by the Spirit, so as to discern sin in the light of truth. Thus conscience, once darkened and inert and powerless, acquires prodigious energy, and becomes one of the most active and powerful principles of the soul, prescribing the law, and pronouncing the sentence of judgment in that inner chamber of judicature from which there lies no appeal but to God himself. Conscience, once awakened by a ray of spiritual light, is an awful thing; and what tremendous power it may acquire when it is quickened by the Spirit may be inferred from the energy which it puts forth when it is called into action by the reproofs of mere human faithfulness. Let a man commit a secret sin, and so long as no human eye was supposed to be privy to his guilt he may contrive to lull his conscience to sleep; but let a friend charge him with the fact, or even hint a suspicion of it, and the mantling cheek, the agitated look, the trembling frame, will at once evince how one's conscience may be quickened into tremendous action by a ray of light passing to it from another mind; and, successful as he may have been in quelling his own remorseful thoughts by devising palliations of his guilt, he will no longer attempt to deny the sinfulness of the fact, but try to disprove the fact itself, as the only possible way of escaping from the sure decision of another man's conscience on his case. This instructive and familiar example shows that all along conscience is alive in the sinner's breast – not dead, but asleep – and how easily it may be awakened into vigorous conviction by a single ray of heaven's light piercing through the veil of nature's darkness, by the power of the Spirit of God.

The Spirit of God thus quickens the conscience by the light and power of *divine truth*. The truth is the instrument by which this change is wrought. He reproves by enlightening. He reaches the conscience through the medium of the understanding. It is not a mere physical change, or a change wrought out in a way that is contrary to the laws of our moral nature; but a moral change accomplished by moral means, adapted to that nature, and fitted for the purpose for which they are employed. He finds entrance for the light of truth. and the conscience once enlightened acts its appropriate part, and pronounces its unerring sentence.

The truths of God's Word are the means of conviction, and almost every one of these truths may be employed for this end. The principal means of conviction is the *law*, the *law* of God in its purity, spirituality, and power; for 'by the law is the knowledge of sin,' and 'the law is our schoolmaster to bring us to Christ.' The law in its holy commandment, the law in its awful curse, the law in its spiritual nature, as reaching to the heart, and in all its length and breadth as extending over every department of human life, the law in its condemning power, whereby 'every mouth must be stopped, and all the world must become guilty before God' – this law is unfolded to the understanding and applied to the conscience by the Holy Spirit, and immediately, by its own self-evidencing light, it convinces; the conscience is constrained to do homage to the law, and to acknowledge that 'the law is holy, and the commandment holy, and just, and good;' while, self-convicted and self-condemned, the sinner exclaims, 'But I am carnal, sold under sin.' And yet it is not a new law, nor one of which the sinner had heretofore been entirely ignorant, that becomes the means of his conviction; he may have read and repeated the ten commandments a hundred times, and may be familiar with the letter of God's requirements, and yet some one of these very commandments may now become as an arrow in his conscience, the very sword of the Spirit. A notional acquaintance with the law is one thing, a spiritual experience of its power is another. Witness the case of the apostle Paul, an educated man, brought up at the feet of Gamaliel, walking from his youth upwards according to the straitest sect of the law, a Pharisee; who can doubt that he was familiar with the letter of God's law? yet, being destitute of any spiritual experience of its power, he regarded himself as having been without any due knowledge of the law till he was taught by the Spirit of God; for, says he, 'I was alive without the law once; but when the commandment came, sin revived, and I died.' Previously he had only that notional and common knowledge which he elsewhere describes as 'the form of knowledge, and of the truth in the law.' And what was it that converted the form into sub-stance? It was one of those very commandments which he had often read and repeated without perceiving its spiritual import or feeling its convict-ing power: 'I had not known sin but by the law, for I had not known lust, except the law had said, Thou shalt not *covet*.' He seizes the tenth command-ment, a commandment which directly refers to the state of a man's heart, and finding that his heart cannot stand the test of a law so pure and spiritual, he is inwardly convinced of sin, as well as made conscious of its power; and so every sinner who obtains a glimpse of the real nature of the divine law, which, like its heart-searching Author, is heart-searching too, must on the instant feel, that if this law be the rule of judgment, then, by the deeds of the law shall no flesh living be justified; for 'all have sinned and come short of the glory of God.'

But when it is said that *the law* is the principal means by which the Spirit of God convinces the conscience of a sinner, that term must be understood in an enlarged sense, as including under it every principle which has any relation or affinity to the conscience, and every fact in which any such principle is involved. It is not the bare law, as it stands declared in the Ten Commandments, that is the sole instrument of conviction, but the moral principle of that law, whether as it is displayed in the retributions of a righteous Providence, or illustrated by the afflictions of human life, or exemplified in the conduct of believers and the perfect pattern of Christ, or as unfolded in the parables, or as embodied in the Gospel and shining forth in the cross. The law is a schoolmaster that brings the sinner to Christ; but Christ is a teacher that brings the sinner to know the law as he never knew it before. The law points the eye of a convinced sinner to the cross; but the cross throws in upon his conscience a flood of light which sheds a reflex lustre on the law. Hence we believe that the Gospel of Christ, and especially the doctrine of the cross of Christ, is the most powerful instrument for im-pressing the conscience of a sinner, and for turning his convictions into genuine contrition of heart. And this because the Gospel, and especially the doctrine of the cross, contains in it the spirit and essence of the law; it recognizes and proceeds upon the moral principles of God's government, and affords a new and most impressive manifestation of the holiness of the Lawgiver, and the turpitude of sin; while, at the same time, it unfolds such a proof of the compassion and love of God as is peculiarly fitted to melt and subdue the heart, which the mere terrors of the law might only turn into a more hardened and unrelenting obduracy. Let the sinner who makes light of sin turn his eye to the cross of Christ, and he will see *there*, as well as amidst the thunderings and the lightnings of Sinai, that the Lord is a jealous God, that sin is the abominable thing which he hates, and that he is resolved, at all hazards, and notwithstanding whatever suffering it may occasion, to visit it with condign punishment; let him look to the cross, and behold there, suspended on that accursed tree, the Son of God himself; let him listen to the words which fell from that illustrious sufferer in the midst of his agony and passion, 'My God, my God, why hast thou forsaken me?' and let him then inquire, why was it that he, of whom it had been once and again proclaimed from the highest heavens, 'This is my beloved Son, in whom I am well pleased,' and of whom it is recorded, that once and again, on his bended knees, and with all the earnestness of importunate supplication, he had prayed in the garden, 'O my Father, if it be possible, let this cup pass from me' – why was it that he, who was thus affectionately spoken as of God's beloved Son, and who, as a Son, so submissively poured out his heart into a Father's ear, was nevertheless subjected to the agony and death of the cross? And when, in reply to all his inquiries, the Bible declares, that the Son of God suffered because he had consented to become chargeable with sin; that he 'who knew no sin was made sin for us,' and that, therefore, 'it pleased the Lord to bruise him, and to put him to grief;' that 'he was wounded for our transgressions, and bruised for our iniquities;' and that *he* died, because the wages of sin is death: – oh! does not the sinner now feel in his inmost soul, that if Sinai be dreadful, Calvary has its terrors too; that if 'by the law is the knowledge of sin,' the Gospel adds its sublime and harmonious commentary; that the cross of Christ is the most awful monument of Heaven's justice, the most solemn memorial of the sinner's danger; and does he not infer, with all the quickness of intuition, that if sin was not *spared*, nor left *unpunished*, but visited with condemnation and death, when it was imputed to his own, his only, his well-beloved Son, much less will sin, unexpiated and unforgiven, be spared, or left unpunished, when, after this solemn work of atonement, God will arise to plead with those who cleave to that accursed thing which nailed the Saviour to the tree? The cross, – the cross of a crucified Saviour – is the most powerful, the most impressive demonstration of sin, and righteousness, and judgment. The cross may well alarm every sleeping sinner, and awaken every slumbering conscience, and stir into agitation and tumult every listless and impenitent heart. It is the law by which we obtain the knowledge of sin; but the law is magnified in the cross; and it is the *law in the cross* that carries home to every awakened conscience the most alarming convictions of guilt. Can I hope to be spared, may one say, when 'God *spared not* his own Son?' Are my sins venial, or light? These sins of mine were enough, when transferred to the Son of God, to nail him to the tree! May I venture into eternity in the hope that my sins may be forgotten there? And why were they remembered here, when God's Son ascended the hill of Calvary? May not the strictness of God's law be relaxed in my favour? But why, oh! why was it not relaxed in favour of Christ? No; that *one* fact, that awful cross which was erected on the hill beside Jerusalem, annihilates every ground of careless security, tears from me every rag by which I would seek to cover my shame, drives me from every refuge to which I would repair; – that one fact, that Christ died for sin, shuts me up to the conviction, that as a sinner I stand exposed to the wrath and curse of an offended God, and that the outraged law must receive a full and final vindication. But must it be by my personal and ever-lasting punishment? Yes, assuredly, if I stand on the footing of law; for 'the soul that sinneth, it shall die.' But look again to that mysterious cross: amidst the darkness which surrounds it, and the awful manifestations of God's wrath which the sufferer felt, there breaks forth a light, glorious as the sun shining in its strength, unlike the lightnings which flashed around Sinai; this is the Sun of Righteousness rising with healing in its beams, the effulgent light of God's love, the glorious manifestation of God's grace and mercy; for 'God *so loved* the world as to give his Son.' Look once more; for the same cross which wounds will also heal; the same conscience which is pierced by the arrows of conviction may be pacified by the Gospel of peace; and thus all that is terrible in the cross, when combined with the tenderness of God's mercy, and the amazing, the self-denying, the self-sacrificing love of the Saviour, will then only awaken convictions in the conscience, to melt and change them into sweet contrition of heart.

It is thus that, under the Gospel dispensation, the Spirit of God convinces the conscience by pressing home the eternal and unchangeable principles of the law, as these are embodied, illustrated, and displayed in a new and better dispensation. It is not the naked law, but the law in all its forms and manifestations, and especially the law in the facts and truths of the Gospel, which is thus used. For the Spirit reproves *the world of sin* – why? because they believe not on me; of righteousness, because I go to my Father; of judgment, because the prince of this world is judged – all having reference to Christ and his cross.

III. The work of conviction, of which the conscience is the subject, the Spirit the author, and the light of truth the means, consists in impressing the soul with a sense of its own sinfulness, and exciting in it some suitable feelings of fear, and shame, and self-condemnation.

Sin, when presented to the mind in the light of conscience, and especially in the light of God's truth unfolded and applied by the Spirit, is discerned to be a vile and odious thing; and in order to this a principal part of the Spirit's work in conviction is to set before the sinner's mind a discovery of *sin* in its own nature, and to fix him on a *due consideration* of it. This, as we have already seen, is an exercise in which every sinner is very unwilling to be engaged; he shrinks from the subject would willingly forget it, and even when it is presented to his mind, is prone to take partial views of it and especially to excuse and exculpate himself. But God is often pleased to take the sinner into his own hands, and to press him with 'line upon line, and precept upon precept,' until he is made to see sin in its true character, and especially to see his own sinfulness. He brings his sins before him, and presses them on his attention. 'These things hast thou done, and I kept silence; thou thoughtest that I was altogether such an one as thyself; but I will reprove thee, and set them in order before thine eyes.' 'Now consider this, ye that forget God; lest I tear you in pieces, and there be none to deliver.' Formerly he thought seldom of sin; now he might say with David, 'My sin is ever before me.' There are many different ways in which the mind may thus be awakened to a sense of its guilt. Sometimes it is occasioned, in the first instance, by some *gross outward sin*, too flagrant to pass altogether unreproved by the most sluggish conscience, and which may lead the sinner to reflect what must be the state of his heart, and what his desert at the hand of God; sometimes by a growing sense of his inherent depravity, strengthened every day by his experience of the instability of his best resolutions, and the weakness of his highest efforts after amendment; sometimes by a faithful reproof from a friend, which conveys to his conscience the startling intimation that his character is not so highly esteemed by others as it is by himself, which sets it on inquiry, and awakens self-distrust; sometimes by a searching sermon, an awakening providence, by the judgments which God executes on others, or by distress sent into his own family, or by his being brought himself to the borders of the grave, and when, in spite of himself, he is compelled to think of God, and sin, and judgment to come. In short, almost any text in the Bible, and almost any event in life, may be the *occasion* of calling the conscience into action, and pressing his own sinfulness home upon his attention; and the Spirit of God arrests and fixes it, till he makes such *a discovery of sin* as is suited to his case. In the quaint, but striking and comprehensive words of an eminent commentator[1], 'The Spirit convinceth of the *fact* of sin, that we have done so and so; of the *fault* of sin, that we have done ill in doing so; of the *folly* of sin, that we have acted against right reason and our true interest; of the *filth* of sin, that by it we are become odious to God; of the *fountain* of sin, the corrupt nature; and lastly, of the *fruit* of sin, that the end thereof is death.'

Sin, thus presented to the mind, and discovered in somewhat of its native deformity, is applied to the conscience so as to excite some suitable feelings of fear, and shame, and self-condemnation.

[1] Matthew Henry (See John 16. 9).

No such feelings can be awakened until the sinner has some sight of the evil of sin, and some conviction of his own sinfulness. All the thunders of Sinai, and all the threatenings of the law, and all the curses that are written in this book, and all the terrors of a judgment to come, may fall upon his ear without awakening any serious concern, until conscience is roused within, and responds to the voice of God above. An unconvinced conscience is utterly insensible: blinded by sin, it cannot see; and hardened by sin, it cannot feel. This deep insensibility, this stupid lethargy, this deadness of the conscience to all sense of fear and shame, arises from ignorance of God's character and law, or from unbelief, which, in spite of all testimonies to the contrary, refuses to acknowledge God as a righteous Governor and Judge who will assuredly bring every sinner to judgment, and punish every sin; or self-delusion, by which many a sinner flatters himself, that however it may fare with others, he has no reason to fear; or some false persuasion in religion, which acts as an opiate to all conviction, such as the persuasion that God is too merciful to punish, or too great to mark a commission of sin; or that an orthodox profession, a correct exterior, or a regular attendance on ordinances will secure his safety. Alas! how is many a conscience lulled to sleep by such mere delusions; and how often do these delusions serve, like so many shields, to ward off and repel the sharpest arrows of the Spirit! Under their fatal influence, the conscience may remain insensible till the sinner's dying hour; nay, death itself will not arouse it, nor will it feel its own guilt and danger, till the realities of eternity are disclosed. Hence you hear of the calm and unruffled indifference with which many a wicked man meets his death, the apathy and unconcern with which he can look back on a life of sin, even when he stands on the brink of the grave; and you may often wonder at this, and be ready to exclaim, How comes it that 'the wicked have no bands in their death,' if there be a Judge above, and a living conscience within? I answer, that here in this very spectacle, in this very insensibility, this deathlike apathy of the sinner's conscience at that solemn hour, you have just one of the most affecting manifestations of the righteous retribution of God, the manifest effect of that great law of conscience, whereby it is ordained that one who has long resisted the light shall be left in darkness, and that, by stifling his conscience, 'he is given over to a reprobate mind.' He has no sight of his own sin, no shame, no fear, just because his conscience has been blinded or stifled, or because he is deceiving himself with some false persuasion of his safety. Oh! let it not be said that a hardened conscience, which is insensible alike to the fear and the shame of guilt, is an enviable thing, or that it may not be the worst, the last stage of man's degeneracy. For the loss of shame is the crowning proof of long-continued sin. Mark, I pray you, the course of a wicked man. Behold him first as an infant, clinging fondly to a mother's breast, and gladly returning a mother's smile; behold him as a boy, in all the buoyancy of youthful health, with a heart as yet unscathed by the habits of sin, and alive to every generous impulse, and so sensitive to praise or blame, that a word, a look, will elevate or deject them: follow him onwards for a few years, when, yielding to the current of this world's wickedness, he plunges into its deadly waters: see him when he returns from the haunts of vice to his once happy hearth. Now, instead of being touched with a mother's love, or awed by a father's look, the sternest reproof falls unheeded on his ear, and his whole bearing shows that he is beyond the strongest of all influences – the influence of home. Still he is alive, it may be, to the opinion of others, and especially would he stand well in the estimation of his companions, if not for temperance, and chastity, and religion, yet for truth, and honour, and kindness of heart; but as he advances in the fatal path, truth, and honour, and kindness of heart, are all sacrificed on the shrine of self-indulgence; he is separated by his own vices from the companionship of equals; and now, descending rapidly, he loses all regard for God and man, and becomes utterly reckless. And when, urged by want or passion, he commits some fatal crime, he feels perhaps less compunction for shedding the blood of man, than he felt in other days for a youthful folly; and when charged, convicted, and condemned, he may enter his cell, and walk to the gibbet, amidst crowds of awe-struck spectators, with no other feeling than the mere shrinking of the flesh from suffering, with neither shame, nor fear, nor self-condemnation in his heart of stone!

But when the sinner obtains a sight of the evil of sin, and especially of his own sinfulness, his convictions are attended with some suitable feelings or emotions, such as fear, shame, and self-condemnation. These feelings are the suitable, and, in one sense, the natural attendants of conviction. When sin stands disclosed, especially in the light of God's truth, it throws a dark shadow in upon the sinner's soul, which overawes, and agitates, and terrifies him. Conviction produces shame: for sin is seen to be a vile and loathsome thing; and the soul, which is covered with sin, is felt to be vile and loathsome too. Conviction produces fear: for a sense of guilt is inseparably connected, through conscience, with a sense of danger. And conviction produces self-condemnation: for it is not in the reproof of another, not even the reproof of God himself, but such reproof so applied as to become his own decision upon his own case, that conviction for sin consists.

Now, these feelings, in a greater or less degree, are the appropriate and natural concomitants of conviction, by whatever means the conscience may come to be convinced. Let the conscience, whether acting by its own energy, or as quickened by the Spirit of God, obtain a realizing conviction of sin, and forthwith it pronounces a condemning sentence, and awakens shame and fear; and that, too, when the sinner's personal habits, and his known opinions, and general circumstances in the world, would seem to make such a visitation the most unlikely. Take a few familiar but striking illustrations from the Word of God.

Fear and shame were alike unknown in a state of conscious innocency; but our first parents sinned, and immediately conscience called forth into action these latent feelings of their souls: 'The eyes of them both were opened, and they knew that they were naked;' there was shame the first-fruit of sin. 'And they heard the voice of the Lord God walking in the garden in the cool of the day; and Adam and his wife hid themselves from the presence of the Lord God amongst the trees of the garden. And the Lord God called unto Adam, and said unto him, Where art thou? And he said, I heard thy voice in the garden, and I was *afraid*, because I was naked; and I hid myself;' – there was shame mingled with fear.

The Scribes and Pharisees brought an adulterous woman to Christ, demanding to know what sentence should be pronounced against her. Jesus answered, 'He that is without sin among you, let him first cast a stone at her;' and immediately they which heard it, the self-righteous Pharisees, 'being convicted by *their own conscience*, went out, one by one, beginning at the eldest even unto the last; and Jesus was left alone, and the woman standing in the midst.' Here we see conscience breaking through all the fences of self-righteous security, and compelling the guilty to retire in self-confusion from the presence of the Lord.

A lawyer came to Christ, and 'stood up and tempted him, saying, Master, what shall I do to inherit eternal life?' Jesus answered, 'What is written in the law? how readest thou?' And when he had given his own account of the law, and in his own words, Jesus said, 'Thou hast answered right; this do and thou shalt live.' But, it is added, he, not content with this sentence of approbation, was *willing to justify himself* – Why, but that while Christ pronounced an approving sentence on the law which he had explained, conscience pronounced another, a condemning sentence on himself, as a conscious transgressor of that law? and his seeking to *justify* himself when Christ had brought no charge against him, nay, when Christ had expressly said, 'Thou hast answered right; this do and thou shalt live,' proves that every sinner, however self-righteous, carries about with him an inward witness, which no sooner sees the pure light of God's law than it becomes an *accuser;* and, in spite of all the sophistry of self-deceit, forces him at least to excuse, exculpate, and extenuate his guilt, if he would ward off or escape from a sentence of self-condemnation!

Herod the Tetrarch belonged to the family party or sect of Herodians who were opposed to the Pharisees in many respects, and in religious matters seem to have been associated with the sceptical Sadducees, who believed neither in angel, nor spirit, nor the resurrection from the dead; yet no sooner did he hear of the miracles of Jesus, than his guilty conscience, bursting the flimsy covering of unbelief, forced him to exclaim, 'It is John whom I beheaded: he is risen from the dead;' 'John the Baptist is risen from the dead, and therefore mighty works do show forth themselves in him.' Mark the power of conscience, how it starts from its sleep and fastens on the guilty sinner, and raises up around him imaginary terrors, and makes him believe, against his professed creed, in the reappearance and resurrection of that faithful messenger, whose head he had severed from his body, but whose holy form still haunted his presence and scared his peace!

'A band of men and officers,' with lanterns, and torches, and weapons, came to the garden of Gethsemane by night for the purpose of apprehending Jesus. 'Whom seek ye?' said the meek and lowly Saviour. 'Jesus of Nazareth,' was the reply. 'I am he,' answered the same calm voice; but it was a voice of power, that spoke like thunder to their consciences; for 'as soon as he had said unto them, I am he, they went backward, and fell to the ground.' Behold the power of conscience, awakening fear, and agitation, and awe, and casting a band of officers and armed men to the ground before a defenceless and unresisting captive!

Judas was with the band of soldiers on that fearful night Judas, who had associated with the Lord for years, who had covenanted with his persecutors to betray him for money, who now marked him out by the preconcerted sign, Hail, Master, and kissed him. Oh! it might be thought that a conscience which had for years resisted the light of the Saviour's teaching, and witnessed the blessed example of his holy life, and stood firm against the melting tenderness of his love, that a conscience which left him free to form his unhallowed purpose, and to plan the mode of its execution, and to take the price of blood, and to kiss the Saviour in Gethsemane, that a conscience so steeped in guilt might have acquired an obduracy which no subsequent reflection could overcome, and that, if it troubled him not now in the act of treachery, it might never trouble him more; but even in the breast of Judas conscience was not dead, but asleep, and it awoke with terrific power when his purpose had been safely carried into effect. And if you would see the self-condemning power of God's vicegerent in the guiltiest heart, look at that traitor and apostate, who, when the eyes were now sealed in death whose mild look of reproof might have withered his soul within him, when the tongue which spake as never man spake was silent as the grave, felt a new power rising within his own bosom which condemned him, and under the burden of his own remorse, and shame, and fear, 'he repented himself, and brought again the thirty pieces of silver, and said, I have sinned in that I have betrayed innocent blood. And he cast down the pieces of silver in the temple, and departed, and went and hanged himself.'

I have referred to these scriptural examples of conviction, for the purpose of showing that fear, shame, and self-condemnation are its appropriate and suitable attendants, and that these harrowing feelings are immediately produced in the soul, when at any time, and by any means, it obtains a view of its own sinfulness. There may be no sense of sin, and then there will be no sense of fear, or shame, or self-condemnation; but let a sense of sin be awakened, and these emotions will spring up instantaneously along with it. Now, this sight and sense of his own sinfulness may be awakened at any time; it may be awakened suddenly, and when it is least expected. A single text of Scripture, a faithful sermon, an awakening providence, a vivid view of God's justice, a solemn thought of eternity – any one of these may break up the false security of a sinner, while the Spirit of God has at all times access to his conscience, and can disturb, and trouble, and arouse it. The unbeliever has really no security for one hour's continuance in peace; thoughtless and unconcerned as he is, unawed either by the rebukes of conscience, or the authority of God, or the terrors of a judgment to come, he may at any time be made to feel a power rising up within, a power long dormant, but now roused into tremendous action, a power which troubles his soul, and brings over it a horror of thick darkness and a cloud of appalling terrors, which overwhelms him now with shame under a sense of his vileness, and now with fear, under a sense of his danger; a power which gives to every long-forgotten sin a new place in his memory, and brings the whole train of his sins to pass in dark array before him, and imparts to each of them a scorpion's sting; a power from whose presence he cannot flee, for it is within him, and go where he will he must carry it along with him; and which has this mysterious prerogative that, while it asserts a supremacy over every other faculty of his nature, and a right to judge and condemn every violation of its authority, it makes him to feel that he is not dealing with himself only, but with God, the Judge of all. Willingly would he make light of sin as before, but now sin has become a burden too heavy for him to bear; he would laugh at his fears as the phantoms of superstition, but something within tells him they are too real to be scorned; he would brave it out as formerly amongst his gay companions, and show no touch of shame, but his soul sinks in the effort, and loathes itself and every thing it once loved. 'A wounded spirit who can bear?' The intolerable anguish of conviction, when an awakened conscience rages unpacified within, no tongue of man can utter, no heart of man conceive. What must it be with the conscience of an unbeliever, when from the lips of God's own people, while they lay under a passing cloud of conviction, such words as these were extorted by its power: 'When I kept silence, my bones waxed old through my roaring all the day long. For day and night thy hand was heavy upon me; my moisture is turned into the drought of summer.' 'O Lord, rebuke me not in thy wrath, neither chasten me in thy hot displeasure; for thine arrows stick fast in me, and thy hand presseth me sore: there is no soundness in my flesh, because of thine anger, neither is there any rest in my bones, because of my sin. For mine iniquities are gone over mine head: as an heavy burden they are too heavy for me.' 'I am troubled, I am bowed down greatly, I go mourning all the day long.' 'I am feeble and sore broken: I have roared by reason of the disquietness of my heart.' On another occasion: 'I remembered God and was troubled, I complained and my spirit was overwhelmed. Thou holdest mine eyes waking; I am so troubled that I cannot speak.' 'Will the Lord cast off for ever? and will he be favourable no more? Is his mercy clean gone for ever, doth his promise fail for evermore? hath God forgotten to be gracious, hath he in anger shut up his tender mercies?' And so Job in a like case: 'The arrows of the Almighty are within me, the poison whereof drinketh up my spirit; the terrors of God do set themselves in array against me. For thou writest bitter things against me, and makest me to possess the iniquities of my youth.' If conscience have power to awaken such feelings of shame, and dread, and self-condemnation in the case even of righteous men when visited with a temporary withdrawment of the light of God's countenance, oh! what must its power be when it is awakened in the case of impenitent and unpardoned sinners. And awakened it must be, sooner or later; and if not sooner, certainly not later than the hour when, leaving this world, and entering into the world of spirits, the realities of eternity will burst at once on their view.

Even in the case of men who are never savingly converted, conviction of sin may not be the mere fruit of natural conscience, but the effect of a common work of the Spirit on their minds. Many seem to suppose that the Spirit of God never operates except where he accomplishes the whole work of conversion; but there are not a few passages in Scripture which seem to imply that souls which are never converted may nevertheless be the subjects of his convincing power. They are convinced and reproved, not only by the light of natural conscience, nor only by the outward light of God's Word, but by the inward application of that truth to their consciences by the power of the Spirit of God. It is surely not unreasonable to believe that the Spirit of God may operate on their minds in the same way and to the same extent, although for a very different end, as Satan does, the spirit that now worketh in the children of disobedience – presenting the truth even as Satan presents falsehood, applying the motives of conversion even as Satan urges the allurements of sin, while the sinner's mind is left to make its choice. Accordingly, we read of unrenewed men, who, under a common work of the Spirit, were once 'enlightened, and tasted of the heavenly gift, and were made partakers of the Holy Ghost,' who, nevertheless, were not renewed unto repentance, or thoroughly converted to God, of some 'who sin wilfully after they have received the knowledge of the truth,' and who, on that account, are described as 'doing despite unto the Spirit of grace.' Such persons were not savingly converted, for none who have been renewed and sanctified by the grace of the Spirit will ever fall away or come into condemnation; but they did share, notwithstanding, in that work of the Spirit which is ordinarily preparatory to conversion. They may have had some knowledge, some conviction, some impressions from the Spirit of grace, and these are in their own nature good and useful, having a tendency and fitness as a means to prepare their minds for a greater change; and if they fail to subdue their wills to the obedience of Christ, they will serve, at least, to make it manifest that nothing but their own unwillingness stood in the way of their being saved. When such convictions decay and die without saving fruit, it is because they are not suitably improved or submissively followed; for it is the law of Christ's kingdom, that one talent suitably improved procures another, while the neglect of it incurs its forfeiture: 'To him that hath shall be given, and he shall have more abundantly; but from him that hath not shall be taken away that which he hath.' 'For the earth which drinketh in the rain that cometh oft upon it, and bringeth forth herbs meet for them by whom it is dressed, receiveth blessing from God: but that which beareth thorns and briers is rejected, and is nigh unto cursing, whose end is to be burned.'

It appears, then, that the minds of unconverted men may be the subjects of conviction, of which the Spirit of God himself is the author; and that they are responsible, not only for the light of natural conscience, nor only for the light of God's Word, but for the light and those convictions which the Spirit may awaken in their souls. And if this common operation of the Spirit stops short of conversion, it is not because the same motives are not presented to their minds as to those of other men who are savingly changed, but from their own stubbornness in resisting these motives, and because their *will* stands out against the work of the Spirit. Here lies the radical difference betwixt the converted and the unconverted: both may be the subjects of a convincing work of the Spirit; but in the one the will is stubborn and refuses to yield, while in the other the will is by God's sovereign grace effectually subdued, so as to concur with his holy design; so that a real willingness to be renewed and sanctified is the characteristic mark of a new creature. Hence those in whom the conscience is convinced, while the will is unsubdued, are thus described: 'But they rebelled, and vexed his Holy Spirit; therefore he was turned to be their enemy, and he fought against them.' 'Ye stiff-necked, and uncircumcised in heart and ears, ye do always resist the Holy Ghost.' And the apostle warns even the professing followers of Christ in these solemn words: 'Grieve not the Holy Spirit of God'; 'Quench not the Spirit.'

IV. The work of conviction may be carried on in various ways, and may differ greatly in different cases, but in some degree it is necessary in all to a saving work of conversion. It may be commenced and carried on in various ways. Sometimes it comes on a hardened sinner in advanced life like a sudden flash of lightning from heaven; sometimes it is implanted, like a seed, in the soul of a child, which grows with his growth, and strengthens with his strength. Sometimes it is occasioned by one gross actual sin, which overwhelms the mind with a sense of its guilt and danger; at other times, by a calm review of the whole of a man's experience, which impresses his mind with a sense of the radical corruption of his nature. Sometimes the sins of youth are recalled and set in order before him; at other times his neglect of Gospel grace, his forgetfulness of prayer, his misimprovement of privileges, his frequent declensions, his broken resolutions, his unfulfilled engagements, his unsanctified Sabbaths, his ingratitude for mercies, his inattention to the voice of judgment or of mercy, a fit of sickness, or the dangerous illness of a wife or friend, or the thought of death, or a vivid view of God's justice or of the Saviour's love – in any one or all of these various ways, sound conviction may be wrought in the conscience.

It differs, too, in its degree and duration in different cases. Some are brought through deep waters, others are more gently conducted to the Saviour. Fear, and shame, and self-condemnation, are inseparable from deep conviction, where it exists by itself and without a knowledge of the Saviour; but they may be wrought in a greater or less degree, and in some cases they are immediately swallowed up in a sense of redeeming love.

I mention these diversities in the experience of different men, with the view of removing a stumbling-block which has often given uneasiness, a mistake which has often been injurious to the sincere believer. Many, when they hear that conviction is essential to conversion, and when they further hear or read of the sharp convictions, the deep distress of mind, the fearful terrors which some have experienced, have been ready to question the soundness, or at least the sufficiency of their own convictions, because they find nothing corresponding to it in their own experience. For their relief and comfort let me assure them, that if they be really convinced and humbled on account of sin, it matters little whether their experience corresponds in all respects with the experience of other men or no; nay, that so various are the operations of the same Spirit, 'who divideth to every man severally as he will,' that it is impossible their experience can correspond with that of all other believers. God's Spirit deals with each according to his own necessities, and the work to which he is called. Sometimes he leads a sinner to heaven by the very gates of hell, to strong faith through the fiery furnace of unbelief,[1] to the heights of holy love through the depths of wrath. At other times, conviction is no sooner awakened than it is allayed, at least in its painful agitations and fears, by the healing voice of mercy. You may think, indeed, that your convictions ought to be much deeper, your fears more alarming, your sorrow more intense, your self-reproof more severe; but be it remembered, that mere fear and sorrow 'belong not to the precept, but to the curse,' and are not so much 'required as inflicted on the sinner;' and if you have a deliberate and abiding conviction of your own sinfulness, accompanied with a persuasion that you are thereby worthy of punishment, and capable of being saved only through the mercy of God, you have the substance of true conviction, and need not perplex yourselves about its mode or form.

But some such conviction of sin is *essential*, and cannot be dispensed with. The very nature of conversion presupposes it. No sinner will ever receive Christ as a Saviour until he is convinced that he needs to be saved; and this implies a conviction of his guilt, a sense of his danger, and a persuasion of the absolute impossibility of saving himself.

V. The *result* or *issue* of this work of conviction, while in some respects it is the same in all, is in others, and these of the highest importance, different in different men.

In some respects it produces similar effects in all who are the subjects of it. Of these we may mention the feelings of fear, shame, and self-condemnation, formerly noticed, which in some degree, greater or less, are experienced by every convinced sinner, and which correspond with 'the spirit of bondage unto fear' spoken of by the apostle, and which are the effect of the law applied by the Spirit, and the utmost that the mere law can produce. Besides this there is an *inward conflict* betwixt *sin* and the *conscience*, a conflict which is widely different, and must be carefully distinguished from that other conflict of which the apostle speaks as being carried on in the soul of the true believer, and which is a warfare, not betwixt *sin and the conscience*, but *betwixt sin and the will*. Of this latter conflict, the unconverted man may have little or no experience; but of the former, every convinced

[1] Thomas Halyburton.

sinner is conscious; he feels that conscience and sin are at war within him; that while sin enrages and exasperates the conscience, conscience denounces and condemns sin; so that he is torn and rent by two antagonist forces, and his inward peace is destroyed. All this may consist with the prevailing love and power of sin; the will may still be on its side, while conscience stands opposed to it. Remorse and even sorrow may also be felt, that remorse which has no affinity with true repentance, that sorrow of the world which worketh death. Nay, under the influence of conviction, many an unconverted man may form the resolution, and make some efforts after amendment of life, which, being based on a spirit of self-sufficiency, and having no dependence on the sanctifying grace of God, and unaccompanied with earnest prayer for the Spirit, quickly come to nought; and he returns 'like a dog to his vomit, and like a sow that was washed to his wallowing in the mire.'

Now, at this point, the one stem or stock of conviction divides into two great branches, – one which brings forth the fruit of repentance, and another which ends in the production of final reprobacy. Both may be covered with the buds and blossom of a fair profession; but the fruit is widely different. The contrast betwixt the two is finely exemplified by the opposite effects of the same truth, as declared by Peter and Stephen respectively. When Peter preached, the Jews were '*pricked* in their hearts,' and began to inquire in earnest, *What must we do to be saved?* But when Stephen preached, they were '*cut* to the heart,' yet they only *gnashed on him with their teeth*. (Acts 2. 37; 7. 54).

With one class, conviction of sin stops short of thorough conversion. Such conviction was salutary in itself, and had a tendency to lead the sinner onward to a happy change; but its power is resisted, its suggestions stifled, its voice drowned by the clamour of unruly passions. Such convictions are like the startling of a man in sleep, who quickly turns himself back on his pillow, and sinks again into lethargy; or like a sudden flash of lightning, exciting momentary awe and terror, but quickly passing, and leaving all in darkness as before. They may continue for a longer or a shorter period, and may recur at intervals through a long life, but they are ever treated in the same way, and produce no greater effect; they arouse the conscience, but do not conquer the will; they alarm the fears, but do not subdue the heart; they make sin dreadful, but they do not make it hateful to the soul. It loves sin, and hates its convictions; and, therefore, the former is cherished, while the latter are suppressed. Oh! it is a fearful case when God comes so near to the heart, and the heart is thus wilfully closed against him! – for such convictions can neither be resisted without incurring guilt, nor stifled without leaving behind them, like a fire that has been kindled and quenched, the black traces of their power, in their withering and hardening influence on the heart.

With another class, conviction works towards conversion, and, under the influence of evangelical motives, issues in true and lasting repentance. The soul, convinced of its guilt, and impressed with a sense of its danger, is prompted to ask, What must I do to be saved? How shall I flee from the wrath to come? Sensible of its vileness, and loathing itself on account of it, it begins to inquire, How may I be cleansed from the pollution of my nature, and the foulness of my sin? If, when the soul is thus convinced and anxious, the glorious scheme of grace and redemption is unfolded to its view; if it be enabled to look to the cross, and to Christ as the Lamb of God that taketh away the sin of the world; and if it be penetrated with a lively sense of the love of Christ to sinners, and of God's mercy through him—then stern conviction will be melted into tender contrition, and the most harrowing remorse into kindly repentance. The heart which trembled, and was perhaps hardened under the ice-cold fetters of conviction, is subdued by the beams of the Sun of Righteousness. The soul, under the horror of darkness, may have been a scene of inward agony; but one ray of heaven's light, piercing through the gloom, converts it into a scene of peace. In the greatest tumult of conviction, a single word of Gospel comfort may produce inward quiet, when it is spoken by Him who said to the raging sea, 'Peace, be still, and immediately there was a great calm.' The convinced sinner, thus apprehending the love of Christ, and the glorious design of his Gospel, is thoroughly changed by means of it; his stubborn will is subdued, and he is made willing in the day of divine power; in a word, he undergoes a change of mind and heart, which is called evangelical repentance, and, in this its largest sense, is the same with being born again. Then legal conviction becomes evangelical contrition. In this there is *sorrow*, but not the sorrow of the world which worketh death; *shame*, but such as humbles without depressing the soul; and *fear*, but not the fear which hath torment, not the fear that is associated with the Spirit of bondage, but filial fear, having respect to the majesty of God, and even to his warnings and threatenings; yet not the servile fear of a condemned malefactor, but the ingenuous fear of a forgiven child.

AN ADDRESS TO CONVINCED SINNERS

As there may be some who have already passed, or are now passing through the various stages of conviction, and as their present situation is one of a very critical nature, on the due improvement of which their eternal welfare depends, I would earnestly solicit their attention to a special statement of the duties of *convinced sinners*.

1. Beware how you deal by your convictions, and remember that you are responsible to God for your treatment of them. Whether they have been produced by the unaided exercise of conscience, or by the natural influence of the Word of God, or by the direct agency of the Holy Spirit applying the truth to yourselves individually, there they are in your bosom, and they will either prove a blessing or a curse. They cannot leave you as they found you; they will subdue or harden every soul in which they have found a place. You cannot rid yourself of them without doing violence to your conscience and despite to the Spirit of grace. You may try to allay them; you may seek, by hurrying into the world, and by mixing with thoughtless companions, and perhaps by having recourse to the soothing opiate, or the intemperate draught, to forget the fears which haunt you; you may even succeed in regaining a temporary security; but so far from diminishing, you are only adding to your guilt, and while you shun fear, you rush into greater danger. If there be one thing for which a man is responsible to God, it must be the manner in which he deals with the convictions of his own conscience. And even in the present world, although it be not a state of strict retribution, there is going on in the experience of every sinner, a process of judicial equity, which proceeds on the principle of aiding every attempt, however feeble, to improve the light he has, and of withdrawing that light from those by whom it is neglected or despised. The same convictions, improved by one man and stifled by another, will issue in results as opposite as light and darkness, or heaven and hell!

2. Instead of stifling your convictions, seek to know more and more of the evil nature of sin, and of your own vileness in particular. Beware of dismissing them as idle, or imaginary, or exaggerated terrors; and rest assured, that as yet you know comparatively nothing, either of the nature of sin, or of your own characters as they appear in the sight of a holy God. That you may know more of it, fix your minds on a serious consideration of sin, place it in the light of God's Word, look on it as it appears in the cross of Christ, consider it in connection with the curse of the law, the sufferings of life, the agonies of death, and the realities of a coming judgment; and that you may feel as well as know what it is, seek to be suitably affected by a sense of sin, till the conviction be thoroughly inwrought into the very frame of your minds, that you cannot justify nor even excuse it.

However deep and painful your convictions may be, you may well believe that you are infinitely more sinful and vile in God's sight than in your own: first, because of the natural darkness, depravity, and deceitfulness of your hearts, which prevent you from seeing yourselves as God sees you; and secondly, because of God's essential, infinite, and unsullied purity, of whom it is said, that 'the heavens are not clean in his sight; that he chargeth his angels with folly;' 'that he is of purer eyes than to behold iniquity, and that he cannot look upon sin.' And that this solemn thought may be impressed on your mind, dwell much on the contemplation of God's character, contrasting it with your own; endeavour to realize the thought of God as the omnipotent and omniscient Searcher of hearts, the pure, and holy, and just Governor and Judge, till you are ready to exclaim with Job, 'I have heard of thee by the hearing of the ear; but now mine eye seeth thee: wherefore I abhor myself, and repent in dust and ashes;' or with Isaiah, 'Woe is me! for I am undone; because I am a man of unclean lips, and I dwell amongst a people of unclean lips; for mine eyes have seen the King, the Lord of hosts.'

3. Having acquired a sight and sense of your own sinfulness, listen with submission to the sentence of God's law. Apply that sentence to yourselves, and beware of any disposition that may spring up within you, either to quarrel with it as too severe, or to imagine that God cannot or will not enforce it. God's sentence must be a just one, and cannot be reversed, however it may be questioned, by man. It stands revealed in the Bible; and although conscience may not immediately respond to it when it is first announced, yet the serious and frequent consideration of it will gradually impress and affect the conscience, till in the end you will be constrained to acknowledge that sin *deserves* God's wrath and curse. The sentence of the law, duly reflected on in connection with your present experience of the curse that follows on sin, and with your future prospect of a judgment to come, will strengthen the self-condemning power of conscience, and shut you up to the conviction that you are 'without excuse,' and that every 'mouth must be stopped, and all the world become guilty before God.' And then, like David, you will be ready to justify God, and to condemn yourselves, saying, in the language of sincere confession, 'I acknowledge my transgression; that thou mightest be justified when thou speakest, and be clear when thou judgest.'

We should resist every tendency to question either the equity of God in pronouncing, or the willingness of God to execute this sentence, by such reflections as these: (1) That this sentence is plainly revealed in his Word. (2) That being the sentence of God, it must be just and righteous; for, 'will not the Judge of all the earth do right?' (3) That, however it may be questioned, it cannot be reversed by man; it may be disputed or denied, but cannot be disannulled or expunged from the statute-book of heaven. (4) That God is really the only competent Judge of what punishment is due on account of sin, and what penalties are needful for the ends of his universal government; and, (5) That as he has unquestionably the power, so he has shown that he has the will to carry that sentence into effect, by the expulsion of the apostate angels, by the universal prevalence of death, and, above all, by the sufferings of Christ on the cross.

4. Beware of having recourse to false grounds of confidence, or unscriptural means of relief. Under the pressure of conviction, the mind is prone to seek rest wherever it can find it, and too frequently it is found in some refuge of lies. Some false doctrine, or some superstitious practice, is often embraced, which serves to lull rather than to pacify the conscience, instead of that pure truth, and that Gospel holiness, which alone can restore it to spiritual life and health. Like the diseased, and feverish, and sleepless patient, who, instead of seeking to remove his distemper and to recruit his health by wholesome diet, has recourse to the soothing draught or the exciting stimulant, which allays the symptoms, while it aggravates the disease; thus false doctrine, or partial and erroneous views of divine truth, may minister temporary relief to an awakened conscience, as when the sinner eagerly grasps at the doctrine of the ultimate salvation of all men, or of God's mercy as exercised without respect to justice, or of the impossibility, or great unlikelihood of everlasting punishment, or of the power of mere moral amendment to obliterate the stain of guilt, and restore him to the favour of God, or of the efficacy of some external ordinance, or some ecclesiastical privilege, to secure his safety. And so, some superstitious observance, grafted on one or other of these false doctrines, is made the opiate of conviction, as when the poor Papist has recourse to confession, and trusts to the absolution of a priest; or the uninstructed Protestant fancies that by a decent life and regular attendance at church and sacrament his salvation may be secured. Thus it is that many say to themselves, 'Peace, peace, when there is no peace;' while others seek relief by rushing into the world, and, by endless change of scene, and society, and employment, contrive to forget convictions which they cannot endure. But let it be your inmost persuasion that there is no stable ground of confidence, and no safe means of relief, except such as can bear the light of truth, and stand the test of God's infallible Word; and that nothing ought to pacify a sinner's conscience, except that which alone can propitiate and satisfy an offended God. Conscience is God's vicegerent in the soul, and it can only be surely and permanently satisfied by that which God himself regards as a satisfaction for sin.

5. Beware of the temptations which are peculiar to your present state, and steadfastly resist them. Every state has its peculiar snares: when convictions are weak we are tempted to indifference in regard to salvation; when consolations abound, we are too prone to fall into spiritual pride; and when consolations are withheld, and convictions strong, we are apt to sink into despair. This is the temptation to which strong convictions tend.

The mind is apt to take a false and exaggerated view of its own sins; for although we can never think too ill of sin, we may charge ourselves unjustly, and make a really false application of Scripture, by regarding every infirmity as a wilful sin, and every wilful sin as a token of utter reprobation.[1] It is apt also to question whether its sins be pardonable, and its salvation possible, thereby limiting the efficacy of God's grace and the Saviour's sacrifice, and excluding itself from the means of Gospel consolation; nay, like a diseased stomach, it turns the most wholesome food into poison, extracting nothing from the most precious promises, from the freest invitations, from the richest privileges of the Gospel, but a soul-withering sense of its own wretchedness in having no interest in them; and, penetrated with the unwarranted idea of its own hopeless condition, it first believes in this fiction of its own fancy, and then raises out of it a thousand imaginary terrors, and dark phantoms of evil.

I know that in such cases reasoning can do little, and reproof still less; and that none but God himself can bind up and heal this wound. But while we look to earnest and persevering prayer as the most effectual means of ultimate relief, I may humbly represent what appears to me to be the duty of a convinced sinner in such a case. And I have no hesitation in saying that the convictions of an awakened conscience are good and useful in themselves, and ought to be cherished and yielded to *in so far as they tend to humble us;* they ought not to be yielded to, but resisted, when they go beyond this their legitimate object, and *threaten to plunge us into despair.* It is not the conviction of your own sinfulness that you resist in such a case, but a misapplication of conviction, a false inference from it, a fatal error growing out of it, which has no warrant in the Word of God. Repentance, deep humility, and self-abasement, are the lawful and proper effects of conviction, and these are warranted by Scripture; but hopelessness, despondency, or despair, are not warranted by Scripture, and ought therefore to be resisted as an unscriptural error. The Gospel is glad tidings, tidings of great joy to every, even the chief of sinners; and you can have no warrant from the Gospel to cherish that frame of mind. It is true that the Gospel speaks of the sin against the Holy Ghost; but it is spoken of in general terms, and so as to give no divine warrant to any sinner to believe that he has incurred it; and therefore this conviction of your having been guilty of that sin is a mere conclusion or inference of your own understanding, unsupported by express Scripture, unsanctioned by divine authority, and not capable, therefore, of being pled with justice in opposition to the uniform tenor of the Gospel, which, speaking to you as a sinner, nay, as the very chief of sinners – calls, and invites, and entreats you to believe and be saved.

[1] Robert Bolton's *Comforting of Afflicted Consciences,* pp. 56, 62.

And therefore, I say, cherish conviction of sin so long as it tends to humble you, but so soon as it verges on the border of despair, resist it. God's truth is then converted by Satan into a strong temptation: resist the devil, and he will flee from you. This gloomy apprehension it may not be in your own power to remove, 'yet it is your duty to oppose it to the uttermost. When God clothes the heavens with darkness, and makes sackcloth their covering, and shuts up in the prison-house where no light can be perceived, it is natural to take a kind of pleasure in yielding to despondency, and in defending it by many arguments. But to *resist* this tendency requires self-denial, and is the path of duty, however difficult.' 'Therefore, when the cloud appears blackest and most impenetrable, and when conscience or imagination are mustering up their heaviest charges and forebodings, endeavour to believe that there is *One* behind and above the cloud, whose beams of grace will at length break through it, and shine in upon you with a sweeter lustre than ever.'[1]

6. Let the convinced sinner acquaint himself more fully with *the complete remedy* that is proposed to him in the Gospel for *all* that is really evil in his present condition. He may have read the Bible before, and may have acquired a cold, intellectual notion of its leading truths; but never was he so well prepared for entering into its spirit, and feeling the suitableness of its provisions, and the power of its consolations, as he is now. Every sentence will now appear to have a new meaning, every truth a freshness, every encouraging word a sweetness, unperceived before. When the heart is interested when the conscience is seriously impressed, the mind will be awake, and active, and quick to discern what otherwise might escape his notice. The convinced sinner cannot read his Bible without feeling that it is in all respects suited to his condition, and that it proposes a complete remedy for all its evils. There are just two comprehensive objects which an awakened conscience demands; the first is, the pardon of sin; and the second, the purification of the sinner; and the more thoroughly awakened any conscience may be, the more impossible is it to satisfy it on these points by any expedient of mere human origin, while it will all the more certainly respond to the method prescribed in the Gospel by God himself. For there he finds both the great objects of his anxiety inseparably linked together, and each proposed in its greatest fulness, and on principles which satisfy the conscience, as well as relieve its fears. Does he inquire after pardon, and does his conscience suggest that, as sin deserves punishment, and as God is a righteous Judge, pardon cannot be indiscriminately bestowed, nor granted without some sufficient ground or reason? The gospel proposes a free pardon so free that the chief of sinners may take it freely; but a pardon not

[1] John Love's *Letters*, p. 284.

granted without a sufficient ground or reason; for it is a pardon founded on atonement, a pardon not bestowed until divine justice was satisfied, a pardon which exhibits God as the just God and the Saviour, a pardon which, as it depends on principles which satisfied the demands of God's justice, may well be regarded as sufficient to meet the demands of a sinner's conscience. The sacrifice of Christ that one sacrifice is the complete remedy for all guilt. Yet sin, sin still strong in the heart, the power of that loathsome thing which makes a sinner vile in his own eyes, this also must be taken away; for, free as the pardoned sinner may be of all the guilt of his past transgressions, every conscience feels instinctively that sin still reigning must be a constant disturber of its peace; but here, too, the gospel provides a remedy; it proposes the Holy Spirit as the sanctifier, by whose agency the principle of a new spiritual life is implanted in the soul, and gradually strengthened and matured, until, after a progressive sanctification, he shall be made 'meet for the inheritance of the saints in light.' Look at the whole remedy in all its fulness, and every convinced sinner will see, that it is not only suitable, but that it is adequate to all the exigencies of his case.

7. Let the convinced sinner seek a sure personal interest in that remedy by closing with the free offer of the Gospel. Every sinner to whom the Gospel is preached may be said to have a certain interest in it, as it is presented, exhibited, offered to all, without exception. But a saving personal interest in it depends on its being embraced, accepted, received. The general interest which every sinner has in it, and of which no man can deprive him – for it is given by God himself – is a sufficient warrant for his seeking this more peculiar and saving interest; in other words, every sinner who is invited to believe, is warranted and encouraged to believe to the saving of his soul. And he who can so far trust God as to take him at his word, and to rest in the assurance of his faithfulness and sincerity in making this offer, need not fear that when he embraces it, it will be withdrawn, or left unfulfilled. But let him not rest in this general persuasion – let him act upon it; and, by a deliberate exercise of mind, and in the most resolute manner, let him take Christ as his own Saviour, and give up his soul into Christ's hands; and, 'emboldened by the free invitation which warrants him to take the waters of life freely, let him put in his claim to take Christ home, in his person, merit, power, and love, as his own.' This explicit and distinct closing with Christ, by which the sinner takes him in all the fulness of his offices and benefits, and gives himself to Christ, soul, body, and spirit, to be pardoned, sanctified, and saved by him, is the decisive act by which a convinced sinner may secure his safety, and arrive at peace and joy in believing.

8. The convinced sinner should give utterance to his convictions in the

language of confession, and to his desires in the language of earnest prayer. Confession relieves the mind of much that is painful in conviction while it is pent up and restrained in the sinner's heart, and, at the same time, deepens the humility which ought to be produced by it, by bringing the sinner into immediate converse with a holy God. And these effects will the more surely follow, in proportion as confession is specific and full: 'He that confesseth his sin, and forsaketh it, shall find mercy.' But real conviction produces inward desire; and that desire, expressed before God, is prayer. Let the sinner pour it out before the Lord, nothing doubting that 'his ear is not heavy that it cannot hear, neither his arm shortened that it cannot save.' Let him pray in the assurance that he is warranted and encouraged to do so, and that God will fulfil his own promise by granting his request. Yea, though he be kept long at a distance, and may be tempted to retire under a feeling of disappointment, let him persevere, and wait, and seek; let him knock loud and long at heaven's gate and take no denial; but wait until God himself open the door, and a flood of heaven's light bursts on his astonished eye: let him pray as fervently as the greatness of his interest demands; and let him pray on until that interest is secured. For never should a sinner leave off the exercise of prayer while the throne of grace is standing, and God, seated on the throne, is waiting to be gracious there!

When we address ourselves to sinners who are labouring under a conviction of sin, there are two classes of men, of very different characters, who may feel as if they had no interest in our message, and who may be in danger of applying it, although in different ways, to the injury of their own souls.

There are some of God's people who, when they hear of the convincing work of the Spirit, and of the deep convictions which others have experienced, may be unable to discover, in their present state of mind, any thing that corresponds to what they think ought to be the experience of every true Christian, who are not conscious of that deep sorrow, and those alarming fears, which a sense of sin might be expected to inspire, and who may, therefore, be ready to question whether they have yet undergone the great change which is essential to salvation. They complain of their coldness, and apathy, and unconcern, of the hardness of their hearts, the insensibility of their consciences, and the want or weakness of that deep heartfelt contrition which they ought to feel. Now to such I would say, distress of mind is not the substance of true repentance, although it may be its frequent attendant, and that there may be true conviction, and genuine humility of heart, where there is no anguish or sensible remorse. Indeed, contrition is often most genuine, and humility most profound, when all that is painful and alarming in conviction has been removed by a view of the grace and mercy of a forgiving God, and an all-sufficient Saviour. All that is terrible in conviction of sin and wrath may be, and often is, prevented, or immediately dispelled by a clear view of the scheme of redemption; and it is enough that you be really humbled, however little you may be distressed; it is enough if you be emptied of all self-righteous dependence, and convinced that you are 'wretched, and miserable, and poor, and blind, and naked.' Now your very complaints of the want of due humiliation on account of sin may be an evidence that you are one of those of whom our Lord speaks when he says, 'Blessed are the poor in spirit: Blessed are they that hunger and thirst after righteousness, for they shall be filled: Blessed are they that mourn, for they shall be comforted.' It has been truly said, 'that hardness of heart deeply felt and lamented, is real softness. A stony-ground hearer, and one seriously afraid of remaining such, are two different characters.'

There is, however, another class of men, who, when they hear of deep conviction of sin, are conscious of nothing in themselves which bears the least resemblance to it; and who may, therefore, be ready to conclude that the exhortations which are addressed to such as have experienced it are not applicable to them. They may even suppose that, because sin has given them little or no uneasiness, they need give no heed to the remedy which is proposed in the Gospel, and continue, as they have been, indifferent to the whole subject. These men differ from the former, in that they cherish their impenitence, and even glory in it. But let them beware: the very indifference the very absence of all concern about repentance, is the most alarming symptom in their spiritual condition. For just as in some cases of disease, the utter want of pain is the very worst symptom, and the surest precursor of natural death, so this insensibility of the conscience, this utter recklessness in regard to sin, is the worst symptom, and the surest precursor of death eternal. If they were concerned about their impenitence, if the hardness of their hearts grieved them, if they were humbled because they saw so little, and felt so little, of the evil of sin, these were hopeful symptoms: but utter unconcern, death-like indifference, accompanied with no sense of its sinfulness, and no desire for its removal, this is the characteristic of a 'hard and impenitent heart,' which is alike proud and presumptuous in its obstinate resistance to all the truths of the Bible and the teachings of the Spirit.

VI. The Work of the Spirit in Renewing the Heart

WE come now to consider that great change which is so frequently spoken of in Scripture under the various names of conversion, repentance, and regeneration; and which is described by the expressive figures of passing from darkness to light, and of rising from death to life.

And that we may clearly understand wherein it properly consists, and perceive its relation to the truths which have already been illustrated, it is important to observe: 1. That this great change is usually preceded by a preparatory work of instruction and conviction, which differs in different cases in respect to its *extent*, *duration*, and *result;* but which, in some degree, is necessarily implied, or presupposed, in every case of real conversion in adult age.

There is often a preparation of mind going before conversion, by which the mind is fitted for its great change, just as wood, by being dried, becomes ready for catching fire when the torch is applied to it. This preparatory work consists chiefly in the instruction of the understanding, and conviction of the conscience, and is promoted gradually, and often for a long time before conversion, by the reading of the Word, by the lessons of a gospel ministry, by Christian society and conversation; while it is often more rapidly advanced by those dispensations of Providence which impress the mind with a sense of the unsatisfying and uncertain nature of all earthly good, and which bring before it the realities of death, and judgment, and eternity. By such means the mind is often instructed, and the conscience awakened, long before that change is wrought upon it which is described as real, saving conversion.

This preparatory work may be more or less extensive. Sometimes it amounts to little more than a few occasional thoughts of God and eternity, by which the mind of a sinner is haunted when he least expects or wishes to be troubled by them; but which have not sufficient power over him to attract his serious attention to the things which concern his peace. Sometimes, again, the sinner is so situated, that, by the daily reading of the Word, and by regular attendance on ordinances, he acquires, before his conversion, a clear and comprehensive acquaintance with all the leading doctrines of divine truth; so that he may be apt to suppose that little remains to be added to his knowledge until, by the teaching of the Spirit, he sees that the light which was in him has been but darkness, and that he knew nothing yet as he ought; and so conviction of sin may be occasional or constant, and more or less intense, while as yet he remains in an unconverted state.

This preparatory work may be more or less protracted. With some it issues in immediate conversion, as in the case of the thief on the cross; with others it tends gradually and slowly to the same result, as in the case of those who stay long at the 'place of the breaking forth of children;' while, with not a few it stops short of conversion, and leaves them, at the end of life, as doubting and undecided as it found them.

For this preparatory work of instruction and conviction may issue in very different results. Whether it be considered as the fruit of a man's natural faculties exercised on the truths of God's Word, or as the fruit of a common work of the Spirit on his mind, it is clear that, while it is good and useful in itself, as having a tendency, a fitness as a means in order to conversion, it does nevertheless fall frequently short of it, and terminates without effecting a saving change. It may be the work of the Spirit of God notwithstanding. The grace of the Holy Spirit has usually been considered and treated of under distinct heads, 'as preparing, preventing, working, co-working, and confirming.'[1] And difficult as it may be to assign the reason why the Spirit's grace is more effectual in some than in others, there can be no difficulty in understanding the causes which render his grace ineffectual in the case of many who are convinced without being converted. Such persons have been instructed in the knowledge of divine truth, and they have been visited with occasional, and sometimes with deep convictions of conscience; but they fall short of conversion – why? *first*, because, in the spirit of un-belief, they slight the testimony of God and the warnings of their own consciences, resisting the light, or refusing to apply the truth to their own case; *secondly*, because, in the spirit of carnal security, they love a false peace, and refuse to be disturbed out of their pleasant dreams, and would willingly be let alone to enjoy their fatal slumber; *thirdly*, because in the spirit of rebellion against God, they cleave to that accursed thing which he denounces, their heart's love being given to some sin, even while, perhaps, their conscience condemns it; *fourthly*, because, in the spirit of the world, which is enmity against God, they allow other influences, even 'the lust of the eye, or the lust of the flesh, or the pride of life,' to wear out and obliterate from their minds the impression of God's Word and Spirit; and the gay counsel of ungodly companions, or the taunts and sneers of mere

[1] John Owen.

formalists in religion, or the easy doctrines of false teachers, who say, Peace, peace, when there is no peace, have greater power over them than the combined testimony of their own consciences, of God's faithful ministers, and of His Holy Spirit of truth; and *lastly*, because the 'prince of the power of the air, the spirit that now worketh in the children of disobedience,' leads their will captive to his sway, even when it is urged by all the motives of the gospel to repent and be saved. Oh! it is a fearful case, the case of a man thus enlightened in his understanding, thus convinced in his conscience, thus far brought on in the way which leads to conversion, and yet deliberately stopping short, wilfully turning aside, resolutely resisting all the teaching of God's Word and Spirit; but it is one which will make it plain on the last day, that, if he perish, it is not because he had no knowledge, and no conviction, but because he has stifled both. To that man may God himself say, 'What more could I have done for my vine that I have not done for it? Wherefore, when I looked that it should bring forth grapes, brought it forth wild grapes?' Even as now, the same God is saying to every such sinner, 'As I live, saith the Lord God, I have no pleasure in the death of the wicked, but that he turn from his way and live: turn ye, turn ye; why will ye die, O house of Israel?'

But while, from these and similar causes, the preparatory work of instruction and conviction may come short of saving conversion, some such work is necessarily presupposed in that great change of heart. Not that we hold any natural or moral qualification to be indispensable for the efficacy of the Spirit's work. No! 'the wind bloweth where it listeth,' and the Spirit may come suddenly to a heart which, till then, was wholly unprepared to receive him. His gifts were bestowed on Saul, without any moral qualification, when he prophesied; and on Amos, without any natural qualification, when the Lord took him as he followed the flock, and said to him, Go, prophesy; and so, in his converting grace, he called the thief on the cross suddenly, and he converted three thousand murderers of the Lord at once on the day of Pentecost. Such unexpected and sudden conversions he is often pleased to effect, for the purpose of impressing us with the reality and the power of his gracious operations on the hearts of men, and with the certainty of his continued agency in the Church of God. But in other cases, previous instruction and education are employed as a preparatory means, so that every faculty is filled; like pipes laid under ground with the gaseous fluid, there is no light, but there is a real preparation for light; and when the Spirit applies the torch, the fluid is converted into flame. And, universally, without excepting the most sudden conversions, this change implies and presupposes some knowledge in the understanding, and some conviction in the conscience; they may be suddenly produced, and simultaneously there may be a change of heart, but, in the order of nature, that change presupposes these things: for it is a change of will, which implies a motive; it consists in embracing Christ as a Saviour, and this implies a sense of danger; it is called repentance, and this implies a sense of sin. So that even in the case of the most sudden conversion, the understanding must be to some extent enlightened, and the conscience convinced, before that decisive change is wrought in which conversion properly consists. Take the remarkable case of the malefactor on the cross; and even here you will see a preparatory work, of short continuance no doubt, but still real, and implying both instruction and conviction. Suppose that this sinner came to the cross with no more knowledge of the Saviour than the other who reviled him, still on the cross there was presented to his mind as much truth as was necessary to convince and convert him. From the words of the blasphemers who stood around him, who said in mockery, but with truth, 'He saved others,' from the inscription on Christ's cross, 'This is Jesus of Nazareth, the King of the Jews,' and from the prayer of Christ, 'Father, forgive them, for they know not what they do,' – from these sources proceeded to the soul of this malefactor as much truth as was necessary for his conversion; it enlightened his mind, it convinced his conscience; it had power, when applied by the Spirit, to make him believe and pray, 'Lord, remember me when thou comest into thy kingdom.' And so in other cases of sudden conversion, such as that of Paul, of the Philippian jailer, and of the three thousand on the day of Pentecost; although there was no moral qualification of any kind beforehand, the understanding was enlightened, and the conscience convinced by such truth as was then presented, and this issued in thorough conversion to God.

II. Conversion is not a partial work on any one faculty, but a change on every faculty of the mind, whereby the sinner is renewed really, though not perfectly, in the whole man after the image of God.

It takes effect on the understanding, when the understanding is enlightened by the Spirit; on the conscience, when the conscience is convinced by the Spirit; on the will, when the will is subdued by the Spirit; on the affections, when the affections are purified, and refined, and elevated by the Spirit; and on the life, when the life is regulated by the Spirit, and conformed to the rule of God's law.

As in conversion all the faculties of the soul are renewed, and restored to their proper uses and ends, so no one of them can be renewed without a renewal of every other; and hence the change that is wrought in any one of them is often used in Scripture to denote the whole of this great work. The terms which are employed to describe this change are relative, and have each of them a reference to the previous state of the soul in that respect wherein it is changed. Thus, *illumination* has respect to the soul as *darkened; regeneration* to the soul as *dead; repentance* to the soul as *convinced* of its sinfulness; *conversion* to the soul as *turned* from the error of its ways; *renovation* to the soul as *renewed* after the image which it had lost. And these are so inseparably linked together, that any one of them is often used to describe the whole change which is wrought in the soul by the Spirit of God; as when the apostle describes it by saying, 'God hath shined into our hearts;' and again, 'You hath he quickened;' and again, 'Repent and be converted;' and again, 'Whosoever believeth shall not perish, but shall have everlasting life.' Such, it would seem, is the saving grace of the Spirit, that it takes effect alike on the understanding, the conscience, the will, the affections, and the practical habits, leaving no part of our nature in its original state, but renewing every part, and restoring it to healthful exercise. And hence all 'old things pass away, and all things become new;' the understanding obtains new light, the conscience new power, the will a new bias, the affections a new object, the life a new rule and end; so that the whole man is renewed, and a new impress and image stamped upon it. But that image is yet imperfect, and far from resembling, in all respects, the likeness of Him after whom it is formed. No faculty of our nature is left unchanged; but neither is any faculty changed at once into a state of perfection. The understanding, the conscience, the will, the affections, the habits of a true convert, are all brought under the influence of the Holy Ghost; but he does not restore them at once to full health and vigour; he renews, but does not perfect them at the time of conversion.

These views may serve to guard against two errors, the one consisting in the supposition, which is too apt to be entertained by nominal professors, that a few notions infused into the understanding, a few convictions awakened in the conscience, a few emotions excited in the heart, amount to the whole of that change which is implied in conversion; the other is the apprehension incident to true Christians, that because they have reason to mourn over the imperfection of every grace that is the fruit of the Spirit, they cannot have been converted or renewed after the image of God. These errors lie at the two opposite extremes, the one of carnal and unwarranted security, the other of Christian doubt and fear.

III. Conversion properly consists in a sinner being brought actually, intelligently, and cordially, to close and comply with God's revealed will on the subject of his salvation.

Some conviction of sin being wrought in the conscience, and some knowledge of God's truth imparted to the understanding, the sinner is, at the time of his conversion, brought to the point; he comes to a final decision, a decision which implies at once a firm assent of the understanding in an act of faith, and a full consent of the will in an act of deliberate choice. He surrenders himself to the power of God's truth. He submits to God's revealed will in the matter of his salvation. Convinced that he is a great sinner, and that Christ is a great Saviour, a Saviour appointed by God himself, qualified alike by the dignity of his divine nature, the tenderness of his human sympathies, and the efficacy of his meritorious work, to save unto the very uttermost all that come unto God by him, a Saviour exhibited and proposed to every sinner in the general doctrine of the Gospel, and declaring his own free and unutterable love in its universal calls and invitations – the sinner, taking that Gospel as his warrant, comes to Christ, closes with him, embraces him in all the fulness of his offices, and surrenders himself without reserve into the Saviour's hands, to be washed, and justified and sanctified according to the terms of the everlasting covenant. This is conversion; this will secure the salvation of the sinner, and nothing short of this can. There must be a decisive closing with the Gospel call, a final determination, first on the part of the understanding; and, secondly, on the part of the will. We must come to a decision; and believing it to be infallibly certain that Jesus is the Christ, the only, but an all-sufficient Saviour, we must close with him as he is revealed to us in the Gospel, and choose him as 'all our salvation and all our desire.' It is not enough that we are visited with occasional convictions of sin; so was Cain, and so was Herod, and so was Judas; nor is it enough that we acquire some speculative knowledge of divine truth; so did Agrippa, who was almost persuaded to be a Christian, and so also did Simon Magus, who made such a profession as was sufficient for his baptism, and who yet remained 'in the gall of bitterness, and the bond of iniquity.' Conversion implies much more; it implies an actual, deliberate, and cordial closing with Christ in his revealed character, and a surrender of our souls into his hands. It is a radical heart-change, by which the sinner is brought to close in right earnest with the Saviour. He may have been troubled in his conscience before, and moved in his affections, and, to a certain extent, instructed in the truths of God; but till now, he hesitated, and delayed, and doubted; the bargain was not struck, the covenant was not subscribed, the decisive act was not done; but now he is brought to a point; the business, long in negotiation, is about to be finally settled; he sees the magnitude of impending ruin, the fearful hazard of an hour's delay; and hearing that Christ, and Christ only, can save him, he believes, and he comes to Christ, deliberately and solemnly, to commit his soul into his hands, and to embrace him as his own Saviour.

This decisive act of closing with Christ, and complying with God's revealed will in the matter of our salvation, although it may at first sight appear a very simple and easy process, includes in it, I apprehend, every thing that is essential to saving conversion, or that is declared in Scripture to accompany or flow from it. Let the sinner close with Christ in his scriptural character; in other words, let him have a correct apprehension of Christ as he is revealed in the Gospel, and cordially believe on him, and choose him as his own Saviour, in all the fulness of his offices, and he is really from that time a converted man, however defective his knowledge and his experience in many other respects may be; he has already experienced all that is essentially involved in that great change, and every other consequence which properly flows from conversion will ensue.

This decisive act implies: 1. That he believes Jesus to be the Christ; in other words, that he believes the same Jesus who was crucified on the hill of Calvary to be the Son of God, manifested in human nature, as the Saviour of sinners; and, as such, executing the will of God, acting by his authority, bearing his commission; nay, anointed with the Holy Ghost, as a Prophet to declare God's infallible truth, as a Priest to satisfy God's inflexible justice, and as a King to subject the world to God's rule; a Christ once crucified, but now exalted, invested with almighty power, and able to save unto the very uttermost all that come unto God by him. 2. This decisive act of closing with Christ in his revealed character implies that the man feels himself to be a sinner, and, as such, condemned by God's law, exposed to God's threatenings, and in imminent danger of eternal ruin; while he has no means and no power to save himself, but must be indebted to a Saviour. 3. It implies that he is willing, or rather that he has been made willing, to receive, own, and submit to Christ as God's Anointed One, and in respect to every one of his offices, as the Redeemer of God's people; that he willingly submits his understanding to Christ's teaching, receiving the truth from his lips, and on his authority, as the infallible truth of God; that he willingly acquiesces in the method of being justified, not by his own righteousness, but by the righteousness of Christ, seeking to be pardoned only through the merit of his blood shed on the cross, and accepted only through the efficacy of his meritorious obedience; and that he willingly subjects his heart and life to Christ's royal authority, that his heart may be renewed and sanctified by Christ's Spirit, and that his life may be governed and regulated by Christ's law; in a word, that he is willing to receive and embrace a whole Christ and a whole salvation; and to surrender himself unreservedly, soul, body, and spirit, into Christ's hands, to be saved and sanctified, governed and dealt with, now and eternally, according to the terms of the everlasting covenant.

Here we have a real thorough conversion, which consists mainly and essentially in repentance and faith, two gifts of the Spirit which are often used together, or even separately, to denote the whole of this great change, repentance indicating what the sinner turns *from*, faith, what he turns *unto*. Conversion is the turning point at which he turns out of the broad way which leads to destruction, and into the strait, the narrow way which leads unto life. He then flees from the wrath to come, and flees to Christ as his refuge; he forsakes the service of sin, and follows Christ as his Master; he shuns perdition, and seeks salvation in Christ as his Saviour. Now repentance describes his conversion with reference chiefly to what he turns from, and faith describes his conversion with reference chiefly to what he turns to; and each implies the other, there being no true repentance where there is no faith, and no true faith where there is no repentance; while both are wrought in the soul, at the time of its conversion, by the power of the Holy Ghost applying the truth as it is in Jesus. From this radical change of heart there flows an outward change of life, reformation of life proceeding from a renewed mind; first, 'the tree is made good, and the fruit becomes good also;' the fountain is purified, and the stream that flows from it is also pure.

The production of true faith is often spoken of in Scripture as amounting to the whole work of regeneration: 'Whoso believeth that Jesus is the Christ, is born of God.' And again, 'To as many as received him, to them gave he power to become the sons of God, even to as many as believe on his name; which were born, not of blood, nor of the will of the flesh, nor of the will of man, but of God.' Here every one who really believes is said to be born of God; and as every true believer is a converted man, it follows that the production of saving faith is equivalent to the work of regeneration.

But then it must be a real scriptural faith such as is required in the Gospel; not the faith which the apostle James declares to be dead, but that living faith which is described in Scripture as a well-grounded belief resting on the sure testimony of God; a positive belief, not a mere negation, or absence of disbelief, nor a doubtful and wavering opinion, but a thorough conviction of mind; an intelligent belief, such as is inconsistent with blind ignorance, and implies a perception of the meaning of God's truth; a full and comprehensive belief, embracing all that is essential to be known in regard to the method of salvation; this belief implying scriptural apprehensions of God in his true character, of Christ in his person, as Immanuel, in the fulness of his offices as Mediator, his great design and his finished work, and of ourselves, as guilty, depraved, and exposed to a sentence of righteous condemnation. This belief, thus founded on God's testimony, and implying spiritual apprehensions of his truth, is a vital, active, and operative principle, bending the will to a compliance with God's call, awakening suitable emotions of reverence, fear, complacency, delight, love, and joy, renewing, transforming, purifying the soul, and effecting a complete change on all our practical habits. The production of this real, living, and sanctifying faith, is the great work of the Spirit in conversion, a work which implies or produces a universal change on all the faculties of our nature; so that as soon as this faith is implanted in his soul, the sinner becomes a new man, the truth of God, received by faith, renewing his understanding, his conscience, his will, his desires, his affections; 'old things pass away, and all things become new.'

Every believer, then, in the Gospel sense of that term, is born again; in other words, no one is a believer who is not regenerated, nor is any adult regenerated who is not a believer. The production of saving faith is that wherein regeneration properly consists. But then it must be such a faith as the Gospel requires and describes; and that faith, although it may have its seat in the understanding, implies a change in our whole moral nature, and especially a renewal of the will. The understanding is, in the order of nature, the leading and governing faculty of the soul, and it is by means of truth cordially believed that the great change is accomplished. But the truth is either not duly understood, or not really believed, where it works no change on the heart and habits of the sinner. He may read, and speak, and speculate about it, he may even embrace some fragments of it, and hold them tenaciously as the shibboleth of his party; but the substantial truth of Christ's Gospel cannot be really understood and believed by any man who remains unconverted. He is an unbeliever, if he be unregenerate. An un-regenerated believer, or a regenerated unbeliever, are expressions which have no counterpart in the Word of God. And if it be so, then is it certain that the production of true Gospel faith is equivalent to being born again. It is true that many an unregenerate man may suppose that he believes, he may never have questioned the general truth of God's Word, he may even have ranged himself on the side of the Gospel, and by a public pro-fession, or in private conversation, he may have often defended and maintained it; nay, he may have had many thoughts passing through his mind, many convictions awakened in his conscience, which show that he is not altogether ignorant or unimpressed; and sometimes under a Gospel ministry, he may, like the stony-ground hearers, have heard the message with emotions of delight and joy, and, like Herod, he may have gone forth and done many things in compliance with the preacher's call; and in such a case, it may seem to be a hard saying to affirm, that after all his reading, and hearing, and doing, he is, or may be, an unbeliever still. Yet I apprehend that nothing can be plainer from the Word of God than that these transient impressions may often be experienced by an unconverted man, and that the man who is not regenerated and transformed by his faith has no true faith at all. He may not question the truth, but neither does he fully understand and firmly believe it; he may embrace a part of it, but the substance of Gospel truth he excludes from his thoughts; instead of yielding his mind up wholly and unreservedly to its subduing and transforming power, he holds down or suppresses the truth in unrighteousness; and by a thousand shifts and expedients, the man who is unwilling to be brought wholly under its influence contrives to shut it out, while at the same time he may make a profession of a general faith. The mind which is unwilling to be thoroughly renewed manifests its unwillingness, not by refusing to obey the truth after it has been firmly believed, but at an earlier stage, by shutting its eyes to whatever in that truth is offensive to its taste.

IV. One characteristic difference betwixt the preparatory work of instruction and conviction which is often experienced by unconverted men, and the effectual work of saving conversion, consists in this, that, in the latter case, all voluntary resistance to God's gracious will is overcome, and the sinner is made willing to close with the Gospel call.

Every sinner's heart offers resistance to God's truth. There is a resistance arising from unbelief, which refuses to receive his testimony; there is a resistance arising from pride, which repels his charges and accusations; there is a resistance arising from the natural enmity of the carnal mind, which opposes itself to his authority; there is a resistance arising from the prevailing love of sin, which recoils from the purity and spirituality of his service. Hence many a man who has experienced much of a common work of conviction, and who has acquired some clear knowledge of the scheme of divine truth, is nevertheless found to stop short, and stand still, or turn aside, when he seems to be in a promising way towards conversion, just because, when it comes to the point, he cannot make up his mind to a full and cordial reception of the Gospel. Convinced as he is, and perhaps troubled with his convictions of sin and danger, and enlightened as he is in the knowledge of that way of salvation which the Gospel reveals, he would willingly grasp at some of those blessings which it holds out to him; willingly, most willingly, would he secure the pardon of his sins, and exemption from the wrath to come, and some good hope of a happy, or at least a safe eternity; but when he looks into the Gospel, and finds that, if he would close with Christ, he must close with him out and out; that if he would obtain pardon, he must take a new heart along with it; that if he would be saved from hell, he must consent to be made meet for heaven; that he must receive the Holy Spirit into his heart, and live under the power of faith, and walk in the path of humility and self-denial and devotedness to God, that he must deny himself, and take up his cross, and follow Christ, and that he must submit *to be saved from his sins* – oh! then he finds that there is much in the Gospel which he most earnestly desires to secure, but much also in the same Gospel, and inseparable from it, which he is most anxious to shun; he hesitates; he would take a free pardon, but he will not take a full Gospel salvation; his heart recoils from it; and at this point, this critical, this decisive point, when he is choosing for eternity, choosing betwixt life and death, betwixt heaven and hell – at this decisive point, when the full salvation is freely offered, and placed at his acceptance, and his eternal welfare might be secured by his willingly taking it, here, when nothing but his own unwillingness stands in the way, he pauses, he stops, he will not yield, he falls short of conversion.

Such is the case of a man half convinced, half persuaded to be a Christian; and it affords a melancholy confirmation of the Scripture doctrine that it is the sinner's unwillingness that constitutes the only bar to his conversion, the sure and equitable ground of his future condemnation. And if this be the great characteristic difference betwixt such a man and a true convert, it follows that a real willingness to close with Christ, and to receive a full salvation, that this, although a simple, is a strong and sure evidence of conversion to God. It is this, indeed, which is everywhere set forth in Scripture as the turning point, the crisis, the decisive change. Every man that is really willing to be saved in the full Gospel sense, to be saved out and out without exception and without reserve, has really undergone a change such as no human power could accomplish. No man who is really willing, in this sense, to come to Christ, and to close with him, has ever been, or ever will be, sent empty away. It is the will on which all depends. If the will be ranged on the side of God and Christ, it was the Spirit that placed it there; if the will be changed, all is changed; if the will be won over to the Gospel, the Gospel is won over, with all its blessings and promises, to the sinner's side.

V. This decisive change admits of no degrees, and is substantially the same in all cases, while it is circumstantially different. Conversion may be preceded by certain preparatory means which have a fitness and tendency towards it; and it may be followed by an after-growth; but, in itself, it is a quickening of the soul, by which it passes from death unto life, and a decisive change, by which it is translated from the kingdom of darkness, and brought into the kingdom of God's dear Son.

There is no one point in its history at which it can be said of any soul, that it is neither converted nor unconverted. Conversion *admits of no degrees*. A man may be more or less wicked in his natural state, and he may be more or less holy in his regenerate state; but he cannot be more or less converted; he must either be converted or unconverted, regenerate or unregenerate, alive or dead. There is no middle way. Every man who is not converted is a mere natural, unregenerate man, however rational, moral, and amiable he may be in the common relations of life.

This decisive change is, in substance, the same in all, while it admits of endless diversity in the circumstances by which it is accompanied. The varieties that may occur in the experience of true converts are almost infinite. Some are suddenly converted as soon as their thoughts are arrested and fixed on divine truth; others are carried on, gradually, along a protracted course of preparatory instruction; some are visited with deep convictions of sin, and terrible alarm of conscience; others no sooner see their sins than they are enabled to rejoice in the remedy; some are excited and agitated, even to the disturbing of the bodily functions; others meekly receive the ingrafted Word, and drink in the dew of heaven quietly, as the silent flower. All these varieties may occur, and it is important to mark them; because we are thus guarded against the error of seeking in our experience all the circumstantials which we have heard or read of as accompanying the conversion of others. The experience of others is not, in these respects, a rule to us; the Spirit acts how he will, and exercises a sovereignty in this matter; it is enough if we have the substance of true conversion. Now that substance is the same in all: it consists in true faith, such faith as subdues the will, and closes with Christ according to the terms of the covenant; in other words, it consists in a change of mind and heart, by which it turns from sin unto God through Jesus Christ; and he who can find the evidence of this change in himself need feel no alarm about the absence of mere circumstantial and non-essential accompaniments.

VI. This decisive change is wrought by the truths of God's Word, applied and rendered effectual by the Holy Ghost. The Spirit of God is the agent by whom this work is wrought. It is everywhere ascribed to him in Scripture. He opens the eye; He enlightens the mind; He works in us both to will and to do of his good pleasure. The truths of God's Word are the means by which the Spirit effects this change in the case of adult persons.

We are 'born again, not of corruptible seed, but of incorruptible, by the Word of God, which liveth and abideth for ever.' 'The law of the Lord is perfect, converting the soul: the testimony of the Lord is sure, making wise the simple. The statutes of the Lord are right, rejoicing the heart: the commandment of the Lord is pure, enlightening the eyes.' 'I have begotten you by the Gospel.' These and similar expressions clearly show that the Word, or the truth contained in the Word, is the instrument by which the Spirit of God accomplishes the great change of mind and heart which is implied in saving conversion. Many questions have been raised upon this point, and agitated with great keenness, as whether the Spirit's influence is exerted mediately or immediately on the mind by a direct physical impulse or by intermediate moral means; and whether, in the order of nature, the illumination of the mind be prior or subsequent to the production of a spiritual principle in the heart: but for my present purpose it is unnecessary to discuss these questions, – it being acknowledged on all hands, that the truth contained in the Word is instrumentally useful as a means in the hand of the Spirit. And even were it impossible to explain the mode of his operation, we shall find no difficulty in admitting its reality notwithstanding, if we bear in mind that it is 'a new creation' of which we speak, a supernatural change, such as cannot in all respects be explained any more than the creation of the world itself; for 'the wind bloweth where it listeth, and we cannot tell whence it cometh, or whither it goeth; and so is every one that is born of the Spirit.'

The truth is so applied by the Spirit as to be made *effectual* for conversion. It accomplishes the design for which it is fitted and intended; it convinces the understanding, it carries the will along with it. The call of the Gospel takes effect, and becomes effectual calling, when the sinner is thus enabled and disposed to close with it. The work of the Spirit includes moral suasion; but it is also 'a work of power.' (Eph. 1. 19).We are made a 'willing people in the day of his power.' On this point also a question has been raised – whether the grace of the Spirit be irresistible or not? It is clear that unconverted men are charged with 'resisting the Holy Ghost;' for 'God strives with them, and they strive against God:' but that grace which they resist is rendered effectual in the case of all who believe, not by virtue of any power in themselves, but by God's power, 'who worketh in them both to will and to do of his good pleasure.' And to those who are inclined to deny the efficacy of the Spirit's grace, I would only suggest the question: What do you pray for when you implore God to enlighten, to sanctify, and comfort you? Is it merely that he would give you the means of instruction, and sanctification, and comfort? or is it not rather that he would make these means effectual in your experience, by dispelling your darkness and subduing your corruptions, and saving you by his mighty power? All your speculative doubts on this point will vanish, if you will only consider the import of your own prayers.

VII. Regeneration implies a great deal more than mere moral amendment, or external reformation of life. It is a change of heart. 'The tree must be made good before the fruit can be good.' A new birth is essential to a new life. There is no real holiness, except what springs from a renewed heart. 'That which is born of the flesh is flesh: that which is born of the Spirit is spirit.'

This decisive change is so important that our eternal welfare depends upon it, our state and relation to God here, and our everlasting destiny hereafter. Converted or unconverted, that is the great question. If converted, then pardoned, safe, sanctified, interested in all the privileges and in all the promises of the Gospel. If unconverted, then unforgiven, unsafe, unsanctified, destitute of all interest in any one privilege or promise of the Gospel.

Were the question asked, Are you converted? various answers might be returned to it, if every reader would only express what is passing in his own mind. Some might answer at once: No! we have no hesitation, no difficulty in coming to a decision: the inmost feelings of our hearts, and the whole habits of our lives, testify, with sufficient plainness, that we have not been converted: we see no need, and feel no desire for so great a change! Some others might say: Yes! we believe ourselves to be converted. But of these there may be two very different classes, the one, who really are what they profess themselves to be; the other, who have a name to live, while they are dead. Many more might say, We are in doubt as to this matter; we cannot fully determine whether we have yet undergone so great a change; we fluctuate betwixt assurance and doubt – betwixt hope and fear. And of these also there may be two distinct classes, the one really converted, although they know it not; the other as really unconverted, although they fancy that they have some reason to think they may have undergone some slight change.

Now it belongs not to man to decide as to the condition of individuals; every one must decide for himself. But the transcendent importance of the subject, as one on which the eternity of every soul depends, affords a strong reason why we should come to some decisive determination.

In regard to those who are in doubt as to their spiritual condition, I admit at once that a man may be really converted, and yet may not be so fully aware of the change that has been wrought upon him as to be able to use the strong language of the full assurance of hope; but they ought to be reminded that it is their duty to 'give all diligence to make their calling and election sure,' and not to sink into indifference and security when, according to their own confession, every thing that most nearly concerns them in time and in eternity is in doubt. Mere doubt as to the fact of a saving change having been already wrought may not be a sufficient evidence of their being unconverted; but indifference, sloth, and security, existing along with such doubts, and cherished while the soul is yet at this awful uncertainty – these are evil symptoms, and should be seriously considered. Pray that you may be converted, and that your calling and election may be made sure.

But may a man who is in doubt as to his being yet converted, or who has reason to think that as yet he is unregenerate – may such a man pray? I answer, unquestionably; nay, a really unregenerate person may be exhorted to pray for regenerating grace. Witness the apostle's words to Simon Magus, words which proceed on a great general principle, viz., that whatever God requires in a way of duty, we should do, in dependence on his grace to help us. The unregenerate man has duties that are required of him; and it cannot be thought that his present condition, however depraved and helpless, releases him from the obligation. The danger of his present state should urge him to pray, and seek, and knock; while the gracious promise of the Holy Spirit should encourage him. That promise is indefinite, and is exhibited and proposed in the general doctrines, and calls, and invitations of the Gospel, so as to afford a sufficient warrant for faith to every sinner in drawing near to God.

VII. The Result of the Spirit's Work in Conversion

THE grand result of the Spirit's work in conversion is described by the apostle, when he says, 'Therefore if any man be in Christ, he is a new creature: old things are passed away; behold, all things are become new.' (2 Cor. 5. 17).

I. When a sinner is converted to God, he is said in Scripture to be united to Christ. He becomes a living member of that spiritual body of which Christ is the Head; and it is from his union with Christ that he derives all those blessings which he enjoys now, or hopes to enjoy hereafter. In virtue of this union, he is identified, as it were, with Christ, and Christ with him; insomuch that he is represented as having died with Christ when he died, and as having risen with Christ when he arose from the dead; his sins are reckoned to Christ's account, and Christ's righteousness is imputed to him; so that, as Christ suffered his punishment, he will share in Christ's reward: he is 'a joint heir with Christ,' and has an interest in every privilege or promise which God has given to his Son on behalf of his people. The legal or judicial effect of this union is his entire justification, the pardon of his sins, the acceptance of his person, his adoption into God's family, and his final admission into heaven. And to this effect of his union with Christ the apostle refers, when he says, 'Yea doubtless, and I count all things but loss for the excellency of the knowledge of Christ Jesus my Lord; for whom I have suffered the loss of all things, and do count them but dung, that I may win Christ, and be found *in him*, not having mine own righteousness, which is of the law, but that which is through the faith of Christ, the righteousness which is of God by faith: that I may know him, and the power of his resurrection, and the fellowship of his sufferings, being made conformable unto his death; if by any means I might attain unto the resurrection of the dead.' But there is another effect of this union which is equally important. By being united to Christ as a member of his spiritual body, he comes to be animated by that Spirit which pervades it, the Spirit of Christ, which is, as it were, the vital power of his body, and which actuates every member belonging to it, the Spirit with which the Head was anointed, and by reason of which he was called the Christ of God, being like the ointment which was poured on the head of Aaron, and which went down to the skirts of his garments. Every member of his body shares in this anointing, and the spiritual effect of this vital union is, that 'from Christ the Head, the whole body fitly joined together, and compacted by that which every joint supplieth, according to the effectual working in the measure of every part, maketh increase of the body unto the edifying of itself in love.' Or, as the same truth is elsewhere represented under another figure, every believer is a branch in Christ, the true vine, and from Christ derives that sap and nourishment which renders him fruitful: 'Abide in me, and I in you. As the branch cannot bear fruit of itself, except it abide in the vine; no more can ye, except ye abide in me. I am the vine, ye are the branches: he that abideth in me, and I in him, the same bringeth forth much fruit; for without,' or out of, 'me ye can do nothing.'

Such is the union which is declared to subsist between Christ and his people, and in virtue of which every converted man is said to be 'in Christ.' If we inquire by what means this union is effected, or how it is that we may be grafted into the vine, we shall find that it is by faith. Faith is the bond which unites the sinner with the Saviour. No unbeliever is in Christ, no believer is out of Christ. Nominal and formal professors may be said, indeed, to be in Christ externally or apparently, by reason of their connection with his visible body, the Church; and to their case our Lord seems to refer when he says, 'Every branch in me that beareth not fruit he taketh away,' referring to fruitless and faithless professors, who are as withered branches that receive no vital sap or nourishment from the vine to which they seem to belong; but the reason is, that they have no faith; his Word does not abide in them, nor does his Spirit animate them. That which constitutes the vital union is FAITH. The Jews, the natural branches, were broken off because of unbelief; and, says the apostle, 'Thou standest by faith. Thou wert cut out of the olive tree which is wild by nature, and wert graffed contrary to nature into a good olive tree.' The Jews, the natural branches, were in this tree as members of God's visible Church, but through unbelief they were broken off; the Gentiles, who were branches of a wild olive, and had no connection at all with the true vine, were grafted in by faith: so that in both cases, faith is the bond of union.

II. Now of every man who is thus united to Christ, it is said he is a new creature, or, that there is a new creation. And if we would understand the import of this statement, or what is meant by the new creation here spoken of, we may derive much instruction from a comparison of two other passages (Gal. 6. 15 and 5. 6), where the same expression occurs, and which throw much light on each other, and also on the text. In the first the apostle says, 'In Christ Jesus neither circumcision availeth any thing, nor un-circumcision, but *a new creature;*' and, in the second, he says, 'In Jesus Christ, neither circumcision availeth any thing, nor uncircumcision; but *faith which worketh by love';* and from a comparison of the two we may infer that by a new creature in the one, he means the same thing as is described by 'faith which worketh by love' in the other; or, that 'faith working by love' is the new creation which is wrought in the soul of a sinner when he is converted to God and united to Christ.

The production of true faith is often spoken of in Scripture as equivalent to the whole work of regeneration: 'Whoso believeth that Jesus is the Christ is born of God;' and 'He that believeth shall not come into con-demnation; but is passed from death unto life;' 'He that believeth on the Son hath everlasting life;' and, 'Being justified by faith, we have peace with God through our Lord Jesus Christ, by whom also we have access by faith into this grace where we stand, and rejoice in hope of the glory of God.' But then it must be a vital faith, such as is required in the Gospel, a living and active principle, serving at once to connect us with Christ, and to constrain us to live no longer to ourselves, but to him that died for us, and that rose again. In a word, it must be 'the faith which worketh by love.' LOVE is the sum of God's law, and the spring of all acceptable obedience; for, said our Lord himself, 'Thou shalt love the Lord thy God with all thine heart: this is the first and great commandment. And the second is like unto it, Thou shalt love thy neighbour as thyself. On these two commandments hang all the law and the prophets;' and, says the apostle, 'Love is the ful-filling of the law.' Now love is the spring which faith touches, and through which it brings into play every faculty of soul and body in the service of God. The Gospel, being a message of love from God, cannot be believed without awakening a responsive love in our own bosoms: we will, we must love him, because he first loved us; and loving him, we will love one another for his sake; and if it be true that 'whosoever believeth that Jesus is the Christ is born of God,' it is equally true that every child of God must love his Father in heaven, and that 'every one that loveth *him that begat,* loveth those also that *are begotten of him.*' The Gospel message is fitted to call this powerful principle into operation; and wherever it does so, we see the Gospel fulfilling the very end of the law; we see faith producing that love which is the bond of perfectness, and through love all the peaceable fruits of righteousness. And thus, and thus only, is the whole character changed, and changed so thoroughly as to justify the strong language of the apostle, when he says, 'Therefore if any man be in Christ, he is a new creature: old things are passed away; behold, all things are become new.'

You cannot fail to see the connection between the two clauses of the passage, when they are thus explained: we are united to Christ by faith, and the new creation consists in 'faith which worketh by love;' so that it follows, 'if any man be in Christ, he is a new creature; old things are passed away; behold, all things are become new.'

It is of considerable practical importance to view the subject in this light, not only because it affords a clear and definite explanation, in a few comprehensive words, of all that is essentially implied in the new creation, but also because it may serve to guard us against two very opposite errors, into one or other of which many hearers of the Gospel are apt to fall. Some, when they read of the great change which must be wrought on a sinner before he can enter into the kingdom of God, and are visited with some remorseful reflections on the carelessness or delinquencies of their past life, are so far impressed with God's truth as to resolve on breaking off some of their former habits, and may actually begin a work of outward reformation, – forsaking the tavern and the haunts of profligacy, and the company of the careless and profane; and repairing to church, and sacrament, and assuming the outward observances of a religious life. Far be it from us to discourage or despise these practical reforms; they are included in the duty which you owe to God and your own souls; and they will materially promote your present comfort, as well as bring you more frequently and more hopefully into contact with the means of grace. Persevere, then, in the course of outward amendment, and in the practical work of self-reform. But oh! remember, lest even your amendment should become a snare to you, that a *new creation is God's work;* that it consists, not in an amendment of life merely, although that will assuredly flow from it, but in a change of mind and heart, and that the only root on which the fruits of true righteousness will grow is 'faith that worketh by love.' Mere civil virtue may spring from many roots – from law, from policy, from prudence, from education, from example; but Christian virtue is the fruit and product of Christian faith. The nature of the fruit depends on the nature of the tree: first make the tree good, says our Lord, and the fruit will be good also: let the heart be changed, and the life will be reformed. But if you rest in mere outward reformation, while you are destitute of the 'faith that worketh by love,' you are only 'cleansing the outside of the cup and platter,' and you will resemble whited sepulchres, which are outwardly beautiful, while they inclose a mass of putrid corruption. It is by faith that you must be justified; it is by the same faith, working by love, that you must be sanctified; and any external reformation that is grafted on another stock, although it may have the semblance of sanctification, has nothing in it of its substance, and will neither suffice for your safety now, nor for your welfare hereafter. This is the first great error against which you should be warned by the doctrine of the apostle, when he declares that in Christ Jesus nothing that is merely external or ceremonial will avail you, but 'a new creation;' and when he tells you that this new creation consists mainly in the production of 'faith that worketh by love.'

But there is another error, at the opposite extreme from the former, which is equally dangerous, and which, it is to be feared, not a few are prone to embrace. Some, when they read of the privileges and promises which are given to faith, – when they hear that 'whoso believeth that Jesus is the Christ is born of God,' and that 'he that believeth shall not perish, but shall have everlasting life,' immediately conclude, that because they have never questioned the truth of the Gospel, and have, on the contrary, acquired a good measure of speculative knowledge, and ranged themselves on the side of those who profess the faith of Christ, they need give themselves no uneasiness; their creed is sound, their orthodoxy is unquestionable; and they flatter themselves, therefore, that their souls are safe. Oh! would to God that a sound creed were always combined with a new heart, and that an orthodox profession were never separated from a holy and spiritual character; but God's Word, as well as our own experience, testifies the reverse. And hence the necessity of urging the great principle, that 'faith without works is dead,' that speculative knowledge if nothing if it have no spiritual fruits, and, that, if any man be in Christ, 'he is a new creature: old things are passed away; behold, all things are become new.'

When a man believes so as to be united to Christ, his faith works by love so as to change his whole character; and for this reason he is said to be a *new creature*, and to have 'put off the old man with his deeds, and to put on the new man, which is renewed in knowledge after the image of him that created him.' And that we may understand the nature and extent of that change which is wrought on a sinner at the time of his conversion to God and union with Christ, I observe—

1. He is a new creature, because he is brought into a *new state;* or, in other words, because his relation to God is entirely changed. Formerly he was in a state of wrath; for the 'wrath of God is revealed from heaven against all ungodliness and unrighteousness of men;' now he is in a state of peace; for 'being justified by faith, we have peace with God through our Lord Jesus Christ.' Formerly he was in a state of enmity, for 'the carnal mind is enmity against God;' now he is in a state of reconciliation, for 'them that were some time alienated, and enemies in their minds by wicked works, yet now hath Christ reconciled.' Formerly he was in a state of imminent danger, 'without Christ, without God, and without hope in the world;' but now he is in a state of perfect safety; for 'if God be for us, who can be against us?' 'All things are yours; and ye are Christ's, and Christ is

God's.' Thus thoroughly is the state and condition of a sinner changed when he is united to Christ: he is brought, as it were, into a new world, every thing assumes a new aspect, he has passed from death unto life, and exchanged the bondage of Satan for the liberty of a child of God.

2. He is a new creature, because, under the teaching of the Spirit, he has acquired *new views*, new views of himself, his nature, his character, his sins, his duties, his trials, his proper business, his everlasting prospects; new views of life, its vanity, its shortness, its uncertainty, its real nature and momentous importance, as the only season of preparation for eternity; new views of the world, its gorgeous pageantry and broken cisterns, its deceitful and ensnaring pleasures, its destructive lusts, its utter repugnance and opposition to God; new views of the truth, that same truth with which he may have long been familiar as it is presented in the letter of Scripture, or in the terms of an orthodox catechism or creed, but to which he now attaches a new meaning, his eye being opened to see, and his heart to feel, its spirituality, its certainty, its awful magnitude and importance with relation to his own soul. God hath shined into his heart, to give him the light of this knowledge, and he feels as if a veil had been removed from before his eyes; so that, although he may still see only as 'through a glass darkly,' and perhaps at first more confusedly still, as did the man who 'saw men as trees walking,' still he is ready to exclaim, 'One thing I know, that whereas I was blind, now I see.' He has now new views *of God*, his infinite nature, his perfect character, his wonderful works, his ways in Providence, his purpose and plan of grace; these things, which were formerly dark and doubtful, or which had no power to arrest and fix his thoughts, or which flitted before his fancy as shadowy and unsubstantial forms, have now acquired a reality, and a power, and a magnitude which render them the most frequent objects of his contemplation, and leave a sense of awe on his spirit, insomuch that whereas formerly 'God was not in all his thoughts,' he 'now sets the Lord continually before him.' He has new views *of sin*, of sin in its relation to God, as opposed to every perfection of his character, to every precept of his law, and every principle of his government, 'the abominable thing which the Lord hateth;' and of sin in its relation to his own soul, exposing it to the wrath and curse of God, polluting and defiling it, so that it becomes utterly vile; infecting it with loathsome spiritual disease, like an overspreading leprosy, disturbing, or rather destroying, its inward peace; perverting and depraving every one of its faculties, and binding them down by an intolerable tyranny, in a state of self-imposed bondage. Thus conceiving of sin, he sees its heinousness, its demerit, and the justice of that sentence which God has denounced against it; and instead of making light of it, as he once did, he feels it to be a heavy

burden; instead of rolling it as a sweet morsel under his tongue, he feels it to be a root of bitterness; and instead of excusing it, he condemns himself on account of it, saying, 'The law is holy, and the commandment holy, and just, and good;' 'but I am carnal, sold under sin.' He has new views of *salvation*, of its absolute necessity, of its infinite value as 'the one thing needful,' the pearl of great price, for which he is willing to bear the loss of all things, and to count them but dung; 'for what is a man profited if he should gain the whole world and lose his soul; or what can a man give in exchange for his soul?' – of its difficulty, or rather its impossibility, in so far as his own resources or efforts are concerned; for his new views of God, and of his government, of sin, and its demerit, teach him to entertain new thoughts also of the conditions on which salvation depends, and he is prepared to acquiesce with admiration and gratitude in that scheme of grace and redemption which formerly appeared foolishness to him, but which now, to his awakened conscience, commends itself as 'the wisdom of God, and the power of God.' 'The natural man receiveth not the things of the Spirit of God, for they are foolishness to him; neither can he know them, because they are spiritually discerned;' but when he is converted by the teaching of the Spirit, all his views are changed: doctrines which he was at first disposed to ridicule or dispute, come to be regarded as first truths, or self-evident principles, which carry their own evidence along with them to an awakened conscience, and he is as a man awaking out of sleep, and exchanging the dreams of night for the realities of day – 'old things have passed away; all things have become new.'

3. He is a new creature, because he has been endued with *new affections*, or rather his affections have been directed to *new and worthier objects*. Formerly they were withdrawn from God, and as they must have some object, they were centered on some worldly thing – power, or pleasure, or wealth, or fame – and hence he was ungodly, as having no supreme affection for God, and subject to worldly lusts, 'the lust of the eye, the lust of the flesh, and the pride of life.' These lusts are not eradicated by conversion; they may long continue to be to the believer what the Canaanites were to the people of Israel: 'They shall be as thorns in your sides, and their gods shall be a snare unto you; that through them I may prove Israel, whether they will keep the way of the Lord or not.' But their power is broken, when, under the teaching of the Spirit, the mind is turned from lying vanities to the living God, and new, and holier, and better objects are embraced by the heart's affections. Faith worketh by love – love to God as a reconciled and forgiving Father, which, springing from a lively sense of his mercy in the scheme of redemption, is evermore nourished and strengthened by new instances and tokens of his goodness, and rises at

length into a complacent esteem and profound adoration of his essential character, so that he is loved the more in proportion as he is better known; and every new discovery of his boundless perfections, every new manifestation of his wisdom, and faithfulness, and power, adds fuel to the flame of this holy affection: love to Christ, as God and man, uniting in his own person the perfections of the divine with the sympathies of the human nature; and endeared by the recollection of what he did and suffered, the humiliation to which he submitted, the agony which he endured, the lovely graces which he exercised, the precious benefits which he purchased, and the freeness with which they are conferred. Christ is precious to the believer, and 'the love of Christ constraineth him;' and love to God as his Father, and to Christ as his elder brother, is combined with, and tends to nourish a disinterested love towards his people as brethren, and towards all men as God's offspring; so that he will be ready to 'do good to all men as he has opportunity, but especially,' as being more closely related to them by the most sacred bonds, 'to such as are of the household of faith.'

4. As the objects of his affections are new, so also are his *desires and aims*. Formerly, these were directed solely to the world; he knew of nothing better, and cared for nothing more than its fleeting vanities; but now they are raised above the world to God as his chief good; and extend beyond the world to heaven as his everlasting home. His supreme desire is to know and enjoy God, to maintain communion with him, to acquire larger views of his perfections, and a sweeter sense of his presence, to become conformed to his will, and to be transformed into his image. 'There be many that say, Who will show us any good? Lord, lift thou up the light of thy countenance upon me. Thou hast put gladness into my heart more than in the time that their corn and wine increased.' 'My soul followeth hard after God; early will I seek thee: my soul thirsteth for thee, my flesh longeth for thee in a dry and parched land, to see thy power and thy glory as I have seen thee in the sanctuary.' This being his chief end and chosen good, his desires will be set on every thing that has a tendency as a means to lead towards it; and hence his deep concern as to his saving interest in Christ, his earnest prayers for pardoning mercy and sanctifying grace, his patient waiting upon God in the way of his own appointment, and his spiritual appetite when, 'like a new-born babe, he desires the sincere milk of the word, that he may grow thereby.' For spiritual life has its instincts as well as natural; and just as surely as a new-born child will crave the food which nourishes the body, so will a soul that has been born again desire and seek after its congenial aliment. And seeing that here every thing is imperfect, and that in its present state he cannot enjoy God as he would, he will look beyond the world for the full satisfaction of his desires. The world

was once his all; but now another world, infinitely greater and more glorious, has been brought into view; and, by its surpassing worth and loveliness, has attracted his affections towards it; so that, in some measure he feels that his citizenship is in heaven, that his home is there, and that it is alike his duty and and his privilege to 'set his affections on things above, and not on things which are on the earth; for the things which are seen are temporal, but the things which are not seen are eternal.'

5. He is a new creature, because he has *new enjoyments*, enjoyments springing from the exercise of his gracious affections, from the enlarged and elevated views which have been imparted to his mind, from the blessed privileges of which he has been made a partaker, from the sweetness of that inward peace which passeth all understanding, from the comfortable communion which he holds with God, and the new aspect in which every thing within and around, above and before him, appears to one who has been reconciled to his God. He may have enjoyed nature before, and may have looked with rapt admiration on its smiling landscapes, and swelling seas, and peaceful lakes; but a new element of joy mingles with his thoughts, when, looking on all these in the light which religion sheds on them, he can say, 'My Father made them all.' He may have delighted in the exercise of his faculties before, and may have felt a conscious elevation when engaged in some lofty study; but a new element of joy is infused into his spirit, when, raising his thoughts from things terrestrial to things celestial and divine, he contemplates them in the light which God himself has shed upon them in his Word, and in the delightful assurance that 'what he knows not now he shall know hereafter.' And so he enjoys what he never knew before, peace of conscience, even the very peace of God, which passeth all understanding, and the blessedness of him whose iniquity is forgiven, 'whom God chooseth and maketh to approach unto him;' and finds that 'in the very keeping of his commandments, there is a great reward,' that 'wisdom's ways are ways of pleasantness, and all her paths are peace.'

6. He is a new creature, because his *habits* are totally changed, in so far as they were previously inconsistent with the will of God. He leaves the broad way, and walks in the narrow path. Whatever in his previous course of life was at variance with God's law is at once abandoned; whatever duty he had formerly neglected, whether religious, personal, or relative, he now honestly seeks to discharge. His own will is no longer his guide, but God's will; by that unerring rule his whole life is regulated: 'Lord, what wilt thou have me to do?' is the language of his heart. If he had previously been intemperate, or dishonest, or profane, or profligate, inattentive to the Word, and sacraments, and prayer, the change which has been wrought on his spirit will appear in his altered habits; and if, as is sometimes the case,

he had been always decent in his external deportment, and regular even in his religious observances, although the change will not be so visible to his fellow-men, he will be conscious of it in his own bosom, inasmuch as he will now be actuated by new motives, and will really feel that he is leading a new life; that what was once form has become power; and that 'old things have passed away, and all things have become new.'

7. He is a new creature, because he has now *new expectations and hopes*. He does not merely desire, he also hopes to obtain the unspeakable things which God has prepared for them that love him. Seeing that life and immortality have been brought to light in the Gospel, and that, besides being certified as infallibly true, the way to reach them has been revealed, and a gracious invitation given to betake himself to that way, and a promise of all needful grace vouchsafed, he conceives the possibility of his being admitted to the glory which remains to be revealed; and although his hope may for a time be feeble, and often well-nigh extinguished by his remaining corruptions, still it is within him, and if not sufficiently lively to assure, it may be strong enough to sustain him in the posture of waiting patiently for God. This hope is an anchor to his soul, 'both sure and steadfast, entering into that which is within the vail;' and it is altogether a new thing: the unconverted sinner may have no sense of danger, and may cherish a false security, but he has no such hope: this is one of the fruits of the Spirit, for 'the fruit of the Spirit is hope.'

8. He is a new creature, because he has now *a new experience*, and especially *a new conflict* in his soul, even that same conflict to which the apostle refers in Romans 7, betwixt the law in his members and the law of his mind. There is a conflict of which an unconverted man may be conscious; I mean the conflict betwixt sin and the conscience; but a new conflict begins when he is born again, and that is a conflict betwixt sin and the will. The difference betwixt the two consists entirely in the position of the will. In the former, the will is on the side of sin, and both are opposed to the conscience; in the other, the will is on the side of conscience, and both are opposed to sin. This may be said to be the characteristic difference betwixt the converted and the unconverted; both are subject to an inward conflict, but the one is willing to side with conscience, the other is willing to side with sin. When the will is made to change its position, when it is brought off from its alliance with sin, and ranges itself on the same side with conscience and God, the great change is wrought; there may be, there will be a conflict still; for, 'there is a law in the members warring against the law of the mind,' and our whole life must be a warfare; and this conflict may be severe, and arduous, and protracted, insomuch that often the believer may be ready to exclaim, 'O wretched man that I am! who shall deliver me?

But the very existence of such a conflict, in which the prevailing bent and disposition of the will is on the side of God and holiness, is a proof that 'we have been renewed in the Spirit of our minds,' and that God has begun that good work in us which he will carry on unto perfection.

This experience of a spiritual conflict is really one of the new things which belong to the new creature; and I have thus briefly adverted to it, with the view of obviating an injurious misapprehension which is too apt to be entertained by those who, considering the description which is here given of the new creature, in whom 'old things have passed away, and all things have become new,' and contrasting it with their own manifold imperfections and remaining corruptions, are ready to question whether it can be applicable to them. Now you will carefully observe, that while it is said that 'all things become new,' it is not said that any thing is yet made perfect; there is a great change, a change so great that it is called, and fitly called, 'a new creation,' a change in the sinner's state, and views, and affections, and desires, and enjoyments, and habits, and hopes, and experience, such as God only can effect, and such as makes the sinner a new man, and to live, as it were, in a new world, and to lead a new life; but not only is the new creature like a new-born child, weak and feeble, and destined to grow and gather strength by degrees; it is also surrounded and closely connected with a body of sin and death; nay, sin still dwells, although it no longer reigns, in the believer's heart: it is there, not now as a tyrant, but as a traitor; not as a sovereign, but as a watchful spy; and he is called to watch against it, and to pray against it, and to fight against it, until the Lord shall release him from his warfare by calling him to his everlasting reward.

The most serious question that any man can put to himself is, Am I in Christ? To be in Christ is to be safe in life and death, in time and in eternity; to be out of Christ is to stand exposed every hour to the most appalling danger. To be in Christ is to be in a hiding-place from the wind, and a covert from the tempest; to be out of Christ is to stand defenceless before that storm which will, ere long, burst forth to consume his adversaries, and to sweep away every refuge of lies; to be in Christ is to be reconciled to God, pardoned and accepted; to be out of Christ is to be at enmity with God, guilty and condemned; to be in Christ is to be adopted into God's family as children, and if children, then heirs, heirs of God, and joint heirs with Jesus Christ; to be out of Christ is to be aliens from the commonwealth of Israel, and strangers to the covenants of promise, without Christ, and therefore without God, and without hope in the world; to be in Christ is to be a new creature, renewed, sanctified, and made meet for glory; to be out of Christ is to be dead in trespasses and sins, polluted in our own blood;

to be in Christ is to be prepared for death, and judgment, and eternity; to be out of Christ is to have nothing but a certain fearful looking for of judgment and fiery indignation.

Would you come to a safe decision as to your present state, so as to be able to answer the question, Am I in Christ or no? Permit me to suggest another question, Are you a new creature? 'If any man be in Christ,' says the apostle, 'he is a new creature;' he is converted and changed, 'so that old things pass away, and all things become new.' It is by faith that we are united to Christ; and wherever that faith exists, it works; it works by love, and thereby produces the peaceable fruits of righteousness. The particulars which have been illustrated may aid you in arriving at a safe and satisfactory answer to this inquiry, if, in the exercise of serious self-examination, and with fervent prayer for the guidance of the Spirit, you apply them closely each to his own soul. Are you conscious of having undergone any such change as has been described, any change in your views, any change in the object of your affections, any change in the prevailing bent of your desires, any change in the sources of your most cherished enjoyments, any change in your outward habits or in your inward experience, such as corresponds with the account given in Scripture of the 'new creation,' or 'the second birth?' In prosecuting this momentous inquiry, permit me to caution you against the danger of either *requiring more*, or being *satisfied with less*, than the Bible declares to be implied in this great change. Nothing short of a new birth, a radical heart change, will suffice; for 'except a man be born again, and born of the Spirit, he cannot see the kingdom of God;' and this should be a solemn thought to the careless, and to mere nominal Christians, to those who are at ease in Zion, having a name to live while they are dead. But on the other hand, in seeking to ascertain the state of your soul, you must not insist on finding more than what is, in your experience or character, essentially implied in conversion, for thus you may unwarrantably deprive yourselves of the comfort which God has provided for you in the Word.

VIII. The Regeneration of Infants

IT is a doctrine of the Confession of Faith, that 'elect infants, dying in infancy, are regenerated and saved by Christ through the Spirit, who worketh when, and where, and how he pleaseth;' and again, 'That baptism is a sacrament of the New Testament, ordained by Jesus Christ, not only for the solemn admission of the party baptized into the visible Church, but also to be unto him a sign and seal of the covenant of grace, of his ingrafting into Christ, of regeneration, of remission of sins, and of his giving up unto God through Jesus Christ, to walk in newness of life;' that 'not only those that do actually profess faith in and obedience unto Christ, but also the infants of one or both believing parents are to be baptized;' that 'although it be a great sin to contemn or neglect this ordinance, yet grace and salvation are not so inseparably annexed unto it, as that no person can be regenerated or saved without it, or that all that are baptized are undoubtedly regenerated;' and that 'the efficacy of baptism is not tied to that moment of time wherein it is administered; yet notwithstanding, by the right use of this ordinance, the grace promised is not only offered, but really exhibited and conferred by the Holy Ghost, to such (whether of age or infants) as that grace belongeth unto, according to the counsel of God's own will, in his appointed time.' And in the Articles of the Church of England we read, 'Baptism is not only a sign of profession and mark of difference, whereby Christian men are discerned from others that be not christened; but it is also a sign of regeneration or new birth, whereby, as by an instrument, they that receive baptism rightly are grafted into the Church, the promises of forgiveness of sin, and of our adoption to be the sons of God by the Holy Ghost, are visibly signed and sealed, faith is confirmed, and grace increased by virtue of prayer unto God.' And 'the baptism of young children is in any wise to be retained in the Church, as most agreeable with the institution of Christ.'

Such is the doctrine of the Churches of England and Scotland, and indeed of the Reformed Churches generally,[1] on the subject of regeneration in the case of infants. The importance of the subject is apparent at once, when we reflect that one-half of all the children that are born into the world die in

[1] See the Helvetic, Belgic, and French Confessions.

early life, and before they have reached the full standing of members in the Christian Church. No reflecting mind can contemplate this fact without being prompted to inquire, whether any, and what provision has been made for the spiritual life and eternal welfare of these children, and without being impressed by the vast interests which that question involves. And its importance is not diminished, but rather enhanced, by the errors, both doctrinal and practical, which prevail to a lamentable extent on this subject at the present day.

It is evident, that if any provision has been made for the spiritual welfare of infants, and if that provision be included in the covenant of grace, they must be dealt with substantially on the same principles which are applicable to other sinners, and yet there is a peculiarity in the case which renders it worthy of distinct consideration. Let us review the points both of resemblance and of diversity betwixt the two. They resemble each other, in that children as well as adults are fallen, guilty, and depraved. This is expressly declared by our Lord, when he affirms, 'That which is born of the flesh is flesh;' by David, when he confesses, 'I was shapen in iniquity, and in sin did my mother conceive me;' by Paul also, when he says, 'By one man sin entered into the world, and death by sin; and so death passed upon all men, for that all have sinned.' 'Death reigned even over them that had not sinned after the similitude of Adam's transgression;' and it is significantly implied in the ordinances of circumcision and baptism, for why were children circumcised on the eighth day, in token of their spiritual separation from the corrupt mass, if they needed no separation? and why are children baptized, in token of their spiritual cleansing, if they be not naturally defiled? If children resemble adults in respect of that natural corruption, from which, as a polluted fountain, all actual sin proceeds, then are they also placed in such a relation to God, and so subjected to his curse, as to stand in need of salvation. Another point of resemblance betwixt the two cases consists in the oneness of the salvation which is common to both; they must be saved substantially in the same way, there being one only method of salvation for all sinners; they must be saved according to the terms of the covenant of grace, through the redemption of Christ, and the regeneration of the Holy Ghost. It is equally true of young and old, that 'there is no other name given under heaven whereby they can be saved, but the name of Jesus;' and that 'except a man be born again, he cannot see the kingdom of God.' This also is expressly declared in the doctrine of Scripture, and is significantly intimated in the ordinances of the Church, for when a child is baptized, it is 'baptized in the name of the Father, and of the Son, and of the Holy Ghost; it is baptised *into*[1] the name of each person in the Godhead,

[1] εἰς τὸ ὄνομα, not '*in nomine*,' as in the Vulgate.

and not simply as they are distinct subsistences in the undivided Trinity, but as they are officially concerned in the recovery of lost souls; in other words, it is baptized into the name of 'God in Christ,' the Father, the Saviour, the Sanctifier. And thus is significantly represented to us the identity of that salvation which is common to the infant and the adult members of his spiritual Church.

But, on the other hand, there is a marked peculiarity in the case of infants, and a difference betwixt their case and that of adults, which cannot be overlooked. For not only is there, in the case of infants, no actual sin, such as has been contracted by every one who has reached the age of distinct personal responsibility, but there is at first no capacity of thought or understanding, such as could render them fit subjects for the operation of that truth which is, in the case of adults, the instrument by which the Spirit of God carries on his work in the heart; and hence some, supposing the Spirit's grace to be inseparably connected with the belief of the truth, have been led to question whether infants be capable of regeneration at all; while others have been content to leave them to God's general mercy, perhaps with an unavowed, and, it may be, an unconscious feeling, that it would be unjust in him to cast them off. But this is no proper subject for indifference: it involves the question of their salvation; for if saved at all, they must be born again; and unless they be capable of the Spirit's grace, they are incapable of the Gospel salvation. And seeing that they are not yet capable of forming a correct apprehension of the truth, nor of being enlightened and sanctified by its instrumentality, as adults are, it becomes us to inquire, with reverence indeed, and deep humility, but still with that ardent and tender interest which natural affection itself might prompt, whether they be, in any sense, capable of the Spirit's grace, and admissible into the kingdom of God?

1. *That children, however young, even infants in their mothers' arms, are fit and capable subjects of divine grace*, may be evinced by various considerations. Several of these considerations afford a presumption in favour of the expectation that some provision would be made in the scheme of grace on their behalf; while others of them afford a positive proof that such a provision exists, and is available for their benefit.

The presumptive proofs are such as these. When we examine the constitution of the human race, we find that it differs materially from that of the angelic race, of whom it is written, 'that they neither marry, nor are given in marriage,' each of these being created distinctly, and standing on his own personal and independent responsibility from first to last; whereas in the case of men, the family institute has been adopted, in virtue of which every human being comes into the world closely connected with others, liable to be affected for good or evil by the influence of their opinions and habits, and left, during the years of infancy, as in trust in their hands. He is not, in the first instance, independent, nor able to think or to act for himself, but grows up gradually into a state of personal responsibility. Now to this, which is the actual constitution of human nature, the scheme of revealed truth adapts itself. It reveals God not merely as the God of individuals, but as the 'God of families,' 'the God of ages and generations,' and in all his dealings with men, as having respect to the hereditary constitution which he has given to the human race, 'visiting the iniquities of the fathers upon the children, unto the third and fourth generation of them that hate him, and showing mercy unto thousands of them that love him and keep his commandments.' Distinct from this family institute, yet admirably adapted to it, as the scheme of revelation is in all other respects to the constitution and course of nature, is the *federal system*, by which men are placed under Adam as the head of the legal, and under Christ as the head of the evangelical dispensation; so that, as from the one they inherit the fruits of revolt, from the other they receive the fruits of redemption. Now, as God has constituted two distinct heads, the first and the second Adam, and as, in fact, children are found to be included along with their parents in the one, and share, in consequence, in the ruinous effects of the fall, a strong presumption arises hence, that children may be included also along with their parents in the other, and so included as to share in the blessed effects of the redemption. And as to their being incapable at their tender years, and while their minds are yet immature, of any participation of the divine nature which is imparted by the Spirit, surely it cannot be thought that they are less capable of this than they were of being infected by the virus of original sin.

These are presumptions, I admit, and nothing more; but they may have their use in clearing away those unfounded and injurious prejudices with which too many come to the study of the question, and in preparing them for giving to it a dispassionate and impartial consideration. And if they be sufficient for this end, they serve the chief purpose for which they are adduced, while the positive proof on the subject will be found to afford ample evidence for affirming, that in the actual scheme of grace provision has been made for the case of infants, and that they are fit and capable subjects of the Gospel salvation.

That proof consists chiefly (1) in express doctrinal statements on the subject; (2) in recorded instances of sanctified infancy; (3) in the analogy of the typical dispensation; and (4) in the ordinance of baptism, as applicable to infants in the Christian Church.

Of the express doctrinal statements on this subject, I shall only select one, which being accompanied with a most significant action, performed by Christ himself on little children, appears to me to be sufficient of itself to determine, not the question of infant baptism, but the prior and more important question of their interest in the kingdom of God. We read (Luke 18. 15) that 'they brought unto him also infants, that he would touch them,' or, as it is in the parallel passage of another Gospel, 'that he would put his hands on them and pray;' but when his disciples saw it, they rebuked them. But Jesus called them (the infants[1]), and said, 'Suffer little children to come unto me, and forbid them not, for of such is the kingdom of heaven.' It is added (Mark 10. 16), 'And he took them up in his arms, put his hands upon them, and blessed them.' Now, be it remembered that these words were uttered, and this act was done, not as a mere expression of personal tenderness, such as every benevolent mind must feel towards these helpless, and, just because they were helpless, these most interesting children; the words were uttered, and the act was done, by him in his official character as Redeemer, and in the exercise of his public ministry as the Prophet of the Church; and while the former declare that *of such* (of such in point of age as well as of disposition) is the kingdom of God, that is, his own church, whether on earth or in heaven, is in a great measure composed, the latter (I mean his act when he put his hands on them, and blessed them) implies that they are the objects of a Saviour's love, and capable of receiving a Saviour's blessing; nay, that they are fit subjects of the Spirit's grace, for the imposition or the laying on of hands was the usual sign by which the communication of the Spirit was shadowed forth. And can we doubt, then, that infants, however young, who are fallen in Adam, may be saved by Christ? How his blessing operated we know not; but is there any parent whose mind is so sceptical, or his heart so cold, as to imagine that the putting on of the Saviour's hands, and the pronouncing of that blessing on these little children, could have no efficacy, or that it was an idle ceremony, a mere empty form?

Of the *recorded instances* of infants who were the subjects of the Spirit's grace, I might mention, first of all, 'the Holy Child,' the infant Jesus himself, whose body was prepared, and his human soul filled with the Holy Ghost, so as to be wholly 'without sin;' but as this is a peculiar and unparalleled instance, seeing that he descended not from Adam by ordinary generation, but was conceived of a virgin by the power of the Holy Ghost, I shall not dwell upon it here, although it is fraught with profound instruction to all,[2] but shall select the case of his illustrious forerunner, of whom it was predicted by the angel, that 'he should be filled with the Holy Ghost even from his mother's womb;' and the case of Jeremiah under the Old Testament, of whom it is written, 'Before I formed thee in the belly

---

[1] βρέφη – αὐτά.

[2] See John Owen's 'Work of the Holy Spirit on the Person of Christ.' *Works*, vol. iii.

I knew thee, and before thou camest forth out of the womb I sanctified thee; and I ordained thee a prophet unto the nations.'

The *analogy of the typical dispensation* affords another proof. The ordinance of circumcision, which was given to Abraham, and continued under Moses and the prophets, was in itself, considered as a sacrament of that dispensation of the scheme of grace, an evidence that the children of believers had then an interest in God's covenant; for it was appointed to be observed on the eighth day, and it was to Abraham and his seed a 'seal of the righteousness which is of faith.' But when that dispensation is regarded in its typical aspect, as designed to prefigure or foreshadow the better things which were still in reserve for the Church under 'the ministration of the Spirit,' the argument is so strong as to be altogether irresistible in favour of the interest of infants in the scheme of grace and redemption.

And, finally, the proof is completed by the ordinance of baptism in the Christian Church, if that ordinance be applicable to children; I say, if it be applicable to children; for there are some who deny that it ought to be administered to them, and to such the argument derived from the rite of baptism, in favour of the interest of children in the provisions and promises of the covenant of grace, will appear to have no force or validity, until it is first proved that the ordinance was intended for them. On the proof of this it is not my present purpose to enter;[1] we can forego the use of this proof when speaking to those who object on this ground, seeing that the interest of infants in the covenant of grace is established on other and independent considerations; and instead of arguing from the institution of baptism to the interest of children in the covenant, I would rather argue from the latter to the former, and seek to impress their minds, in the first instance, with the precious truth that infants have an interest in the covenant, and that they are fit and capable subjects of divine grace; whence it would naturally follow that they are capable also of receiving the sign and seal, and ought to receive it, if there be the slightest reason to believe that they have not been excluded by divine authority from all participation in that holy ordinance.

On these grounds, I think it must be evident that infant children are *fit and capable subjects* of divine grace, and that they are included in the covenant of redemption. It may be difficult for us to understand in what way the Spirit of God operates on their minds, or through what medium they obtain a participation of the blessings of salvation, which are said to be 'by faith.' The regeneration of infants may be ascribed to a direct operation of the Spirit on their minds, and in this respect may be said to resemble what is

[1] See Ralph Wardlaw on *Infant Baptism* for the Scriptural argument, and Wall's *History for the Historical*.

supposed by some to be in every case the primary influence of the Spirit, under which the soul is passive, and by which, without the intervention of any instrumentality, he effects a permanent change, 'predisposing it to receive, and love, and obey the truth.' By this direct operation he may implant that principle of grace which is the germ of the new creature, that incorruptible seed, which may lie long under the furrow, but will sooner or later spring up, and produce the peaceable fruits of righteousness. Our older divines were wont to distinguish between the principle or habit of grace, and the exercise of grace,[1] and to maintain that the principle might exist in children who were as yet incapable of the exercise, and that grace in such was real and saving.[2] It may be generally connected, too, with the faith of the parent, in whom, during the period of nonage, the infant is federally included.[3] But is sufficient to say, in the language of the Westminster Confession, that 'they are regenerated and saved by Christ through the Spirit, who worketh when, and where, and how he pleaseth,' – for 'the wind bloweth where it listeth, and thou canst not tell whence it cometh, and whither it goeth: so is every one that is born of the Spirit.' And to him who objects to the regeneration of infants on the ground of its mysteriousness, may we not say that the natural birth of a child is full of mystery: 'I am fearfully and wonderfully made: marvellous are thy works, and that my soul knoweth right well. My substance was not hid from thee when I was made in secret, and curiously wrought in the lowest parts of the earth. Thine eyes did see my substance, yet being imperfect; and in thy book all my members were written, which in continuance were fashioned, when as yet there was none of them;' and in the preacher's words, 'As thou knowest not what is the way of the Spirit, nor how the bones do grow in the womb of her that is with child, even so thou knowest not the works of God who maketh all.'

But there is another explanation of the subject which has obtained extensive currency; I refer to the doctrine of *baptismal regeneration*. If baptism be designed, as we have no doubt it is, for the benefit of infant children, it has appeared to many that this precious ordinance affords the readiest explanation of the means by which the Spirit of grace executes his gracious work, by imparting to them the germ of a new spiritual life, and engrafting them into the Church of Christ. On no subject is it more necessary to speak with caution, and to think with accuracy, especially in the present day, when the most opposite errors are current respecting it;

---

[1] John Owen, ii. 283, 482, 492.
[2] Ibid. ii. 413.
[3] *Homilies on Baptism*, Edward Irving, 346, 349.

some representing baptism as a mere ceremony, a naked sign, or an empty form; while others are strenuously contending that in every case in which it is administered, it necessarily implies regeneration, and that no other regeneration is to be looked for. The language of the Westminster Confession is equally opposed to each of these pernicious errors; and while it unfolds the spiritual import of baptism in all its fulness, by the use of scriptural terms, which may almost seem at first sight to imply all that the advocates for baptismal regeneration contend for, it singles out with the strictest discrimination, and condemns with the utmost explicitness, the groundless opinions which have been mixed up with that doctrine, so as at once to confirm the truth and to correct the error.

Let us briefly unfold the doctrine of the Confession on this subject.

1. It proceeds on the supposition that children are fit and capable subjects of divine grace, and that they have an interest in the covenant prior to their baptism. They do not acquire an interest in the covenant by being baptized; they are baptized because they have an interest in the covenant. This distinction is of great practical value in many points of view; it utterly subverts the doctrine, that none are regenerated who have not been baptized, and thus serves to comfort the heart of many a bereaved parent, whose child may have died before that sacred rite could be administered, and enables us to say with the utmost freedom, that while we contend for infant baptism, we are under no necessity of unchristianising the children of our Baptist brethren, who from conscientious conviction refrain from the use of that ordinance. It will be found also to throw considerable light on the proper nature and use of baptism itself. Now that an interest in the covenant of grace is presupposed in baptism must be evident to every one who inquires into the ground of his warrant to apply for that ordinance on behalf of his children, as yet unbaptized. Abraham had first an interest in the covenant, and then circumcision was added as a sign and seal of his interest in it; for it was 'the seal of the righteousness of faith which he had, being yet uncircumcised;' and so, in like manner, the children of believing parents have an interest in the covenant, and they receive baptism as the sign and seal of that interest which they had, being yet unbaptized.[1] Their prior interest in the covenant lies in the terms of the promise, – 'the promise which is unto us and to our children' – 'I will be a God unto thee, and to thy seed after thee,' and depends on the relation in which they stand to believing parents; for if either father or mother be a believer, the children are recognized as having a title to baptism, and that, too, by virtue of their having an interest in the covenant, according to the expressive words of the apostle (1 Cor. 7. 14): 'For the unbelieving husband is sanctified by the wife, and the unbelieving wife is sanctified by the husband; else were your

children unclean, but now are they holy.' For 'if the root be holy, so are the branches.' (Rom. 11. 16).

2. The children of believing parents having a prior interest in the covenant, receive baptism as a sign and seal of their engrafting into Christ, – of regeneration, of remission of sins, and of their engagement to be the Lord's. That all this is included in that sacred ordinance will be evident, if we simply read over those passages of Scripture which have an express bearing on the doctrine of baptism: 'Know ye not that so many of us as were baptized into Jesus Christ were baptized into his death? Therefore we are buried with him by baptism into death: that like as Christ was raised up from the dead by the glory of the Father, even so we also should walk in newness of life.' (Rom. 6. 3). 'In the days of Noah, eight souls were saved by water. The like figure whereunto even baptism doth also now save us (not the putting away of the filth of the flesh, but the answer of a good conscience toward God.') (1 Pet. 3. 20, 21) 'By one Spirit are we all baptized into one body, whether we be Jews or Gentiles, whether we be bond or free; and have been all made to drink into one Spirit.' (1 Cor. 12. 13). 'In whom also ye are circumcised with the circumcision made without hands, in putting off the body of the sins of the flesh by the circumcision of Christ: buried with him in baptism, wherein also ye are risen with him through the faith of the operation of God, who hath raised him from the dead.' (Col. 2. 11, 12). 'Then Peter said unto them, Repent, and be baptized every one of you in the name of Jesus Christ for the remission of sins, and ye shall receive the gift of the Holy Ghost. For the promise is unto you, and to your children, and to all that are afar off, even as many as the Lord our God shall call.' (Acts 2. 38, 39). These passages are sufficient to show that there is a profound significancy in baptism; and that it is neither a naked sign nor an empty form, but a true sacrament, and real channel of grace. And in interpreting this symbolical institution, we are free to present it in all the fulness of its meaning to the faith of the church, and to show what efficacy is in it when it is made effectual. But you will observe that the apostles, when they used these expressions, were speaking of baptized men, who had been admitted into the Church on the profession of their faith in Christ, and that they thus spoke of the efficacy of their baptism on the supposition that their profession had been sincere, and that their faith was real. In such a case, there can be no doubt that baptism was both a sign and a seal of saving grace, any more than that, if such persons had died after their conversion, and before their baptism, they would have entered into glory, like the poor unbaptized malefactor on the cross. But having been spared to receive that external sign and seal of the covenant, the apostle refers to it as the token and pledge of their salvation. And so, had he spoken of the

children of these same men, but still on the supposition that the parents were true believers, he would have used the same language in regard to them, seeing that the children are included with, or rather in, their parents, in the provisions and promises of the covenant, and had an interest in it, being yet unbaptized.

Viewed in this light, the ordinance of baptism is fraught with the richest instruction and encouragement. It embodies all the fundamental principles of the Gospel, and exhibits every truth that is necessary to salvation. In baptism, the name of each person in the Trinity is pronounced over us, not merely to mark the distinction of these persons, but to intimate their harmonious co-operation in the scheme of grace, and the official relation in which they stand to us in the covenant of redemption. We are baptized into the name of each, into the name of the Father, as our Father, into the name of the Son, as our Saviour, into the name of the Holy Ghost, as our Sanctifier; we are washed, and thereby declared to be naturally unclean; we are washed with water, as a sign of the blood of Christ, which cleanseth away the guilt of sin, and as a sign also of 'the washing of regeneration and the renewing of the Holy Ghost;' and thereby we are taught at once the possibility of God's entering into covenant with an unclean thing, and the means by which its uncleanness may be taken away. And when a child is thus baptized on the strength of a parent's faith, we see the federal principle which pervades the scheme of grace as well as the covenant of works, and the parent is impressively reminded of his responsibility, as being answerable to God for his child, at least during its infancy or nonage. Whether, therefore, we consider baptism as a sign of grace, or as a seal of the covenant, or as a visible witness for the truth, or as an intelligible symbol of spiritual blessings, it is fraught with profound instruction; and not less fraught with encouragement to faith, since it is a true sign and a real seal, and ought to be regarded by every parent as a pledge of his child's interest in the covenant of grace, and as a motive and stimulus to hope, and pray, and labour for its everlasting salvation.

In what respects does this view of the nature and efficacy of baptism differ from the doctrine of *baptismal regeneration*, as it is taught so generally in modern times? It may seem, at first sight, to differ from it chiefly in two respects. The latter doctrine is understood to mean, that *every one is regenerated who is regularly baptized, and that no one is regenerated who is not baptized.* The Westminster Confession, while it unfolds the doctrine of baptism in all its fulness, carefully guards against these inferences from it; and declares, 'that although it be a great sin to contemn or neglect this ordinance, yet grace and salvation are not so inseparably annexed to it, as that *no person* can be regenerated or saved without it, or that *all* that are

[123]

baptized are undoubtedly regenerated.' But I apprehend that there is a far more important difference betwixt the two systems of doctrine: the one represents regeneration as an inward spiritual change, wrought in the mind and heart by the power of the Spirit of God; while the other speaks of it as a mere external or relative change, which has no necessary and no uniform connection with any degree of spiritual renovation.[1] The latter system speaks of every baptized person as regenerated, while it admits that many of them may be and are unrenewed. Did the question relate only to the right use of a term, or to a distinction betwixt one term and another, it might be of little consequence in most cases, though not in this, where the sense attached to regeneration would go far to nullify the import of many precious texts of Scripture; but the evil is greatly increased when, having attached this meaning to the term, it is contended that no other regeneration is to be sought or hoped for,[2] and that all are alike regenerated, whether elect or non-elect, and whether ultimately they be saved or lost. Considered in this light, our divines have generally opposed the doctrine of baptismal regeneration. 'Regeneration does not consist,' says Owen, 'in a participation of the ordinance of baptism, and a profession of the doctrine of repentance. This is all that some will allow unto it, to the utter rejection and over-throw of the grace of our Lord Jesus Christ. For the dispute in this matter is not whether the ordinances of the Gospel, as baptism, do really com-municate internal grace unto them that are, as to the outward manner of their administration, duly made partakers of them, whether *ex opere operato*, as the Papists speak, or as the federal means of the conveyance and com-munication of that grace which they betoken and are the pledges of; but whether the outward susception of the ordinance, joined with a profession of repentance in them that are adult, be not the whole of what is called regeneration? The vanity of this presumptuous folly, destructive of all the grace of the Gospel, invented to countenance men in their sins, and to hide from them the necessity of being born again, and therein of living unto God, will be laid open in our declaration of the work itself.'[3] 'The error

---

[1] 'If regeneration takes place in baptism, it cannot, upon principles of common sense, be an entire change of mind: if it is an *entire change of mind* – a radical change of heart and soul – upon principles of common sense and experience, it cannot take place in baptism.' – Bishop Bethell on *Regeneration in Baptism*, p. xiii.

The same writer refers to Bishop Mant, Waterland, Wall, and others, as founding on the distinction betwixt regeneration and conversion, or spiritual renewal, and illustrates the distinction by the case of Paul, 'who, though converted, was not regenerate, till he had washed away his sins in baptism!'

[2] Molesworth says, 'The only subsequent regeneration is the regeneration of the corruptible to the incorruptible in the resurrection to life eternal!' – p. 110.

[3] Owen's *Works*, ii. 247; see also p. 513.

of baptismal regeneration,' says Irving, whose ideas of the spiritual import of baptism were sufficiently high, 'consisteth not in holding that the true children of God are regenerated at their baptism, and from thence should date their admission into the household of faith, – which, with all my orthodox fathers in the Church, I hold to be the only true doctrine, – but in holding that every person who is baptized doth virtually thereby become regenerate, and possessed with the Holy Spirit; or, to speak the language of theologians, that the inward grace is so connected with, or bound to, the outward ordinance, that whosoever receiveth the one doth necessarily become partaker of the other. This is an error of the most hideous kind, bringing in justification by works, or rather by ceremonies, destroying the election of the Father, the salvation of the Son, and the sanctification of the Holy Ghost, – and exalting the priest and the ceremony into the place of the Trinity.'[1] And the judicious Scott sums up the received doctrine in these five propositions: – '1. Baptism is truly the sacramental sign and seal of regeneration, as circumcision was under the Old Testament, and not regeneration itself, nor inseparably connected with it. 2. Adults, sincerely professing repentance and faith, are already regenerate, and in baptism receive the sign and seal of the righteousness of faith which they had, yet being unbaptized. 3. The event, as to each baptized infant, must determine whether it was, or was not, regenerated in baptism. 4. Baptism is not universally and indispensably necessary to salvation, but regeneration is. 5. Ungodly and wicked persons, who have been baptized, need regeneration, even as all wicked Israelites needed the circumcision of the heart, and the Jews, in our Lord's days, needed regeneration.'[2]

But while we guard against extreme opinions on the one hand, it is equally necessary to guard against extreme opinions on the other; and there is reason to fear, that if by some the efficacy of baptism is unduly magnified, it is by many more unduly depreciated, or altogether disbelieved. We have seen that children are fit and capable subjects of the Spirit's grace, and that the ordinance of baptism is a sign and seal of 'engrafting into Christ.' In the case of an adult, where there is no faith, it is devoid of efficacy; and in the case of a child, where there is no faith on the part of the parent, through whom alone the child has a claim to this ordinance, it may be equally ineffectual; but this hinders not that in either instance it may be a real channel, as well as a visible symbol of grace, where faith is exercised in the covenant promise. And I cannot help thinking that the administration of baptism to an infant child is fraught with rich encouragement to the parent, and with profound instruction to the child himself when he arrives at a riper age; for

[1] Irving's *Homilies on Baptisim*, 387.

[2] Thomas Scott's 'Remarks on Bishop Tomline's *Refutation of Calvinism*.'

in baptism there is, as it were, a visible application made to that child individually of the sign and seal of all the grace which the covenant contains, such an application as gives a special and personal direction to all the invitations, and calls, and promises of the Gospel; and it is alike fitted to nourish the faith and hope of the parent, and to call forth, at a later period, the grateful acknowledgments of his offspring, or to impress them with a very solemn sense of the responsibility under which they lie. And although I cannot agree with those who seem to argue that there would be no ground for Christian education, unless regeneration were included in baptism,[1] yet it seems very clear that education may be stimulated, and conducted too, on a better principle, by reason of the truths which baptism unquestionably implies. The parents knowing that, on the ground of *his* faith, his children are declared to be 'holy,' and, as such, have been admitted to the privilege of baptism, should feel that he is thereby encouraged to regard them as fit and capable subjects of the Spirit's grace, and as having such an interest in all the privileges and promises of that covenant as affords ample warrant for the exercise of faith, and hope, and prayer; and the children, as they grow up, should be frequently reminded that they were dedicated to God, that they were baptized into the name of the Father, and of the Son, and of the Holy Ghost, and they received baptism as a privilege for which they must give in an account. And when, at any time, in after-life, they have any doubt as to their interest in the covenant, they may look back to the personal application of the seal of the covenant to themselves individually, while as yet they were unconscious infants, and draw from it a precious assurance of the perfect freeness of the Gospel. To believing parents, again, who have lost their children in infancy, the truths which have been illustrated are fitted to impart a consolation such as the world can neither give nor take away.

We have purposely reserved the case of infants for distinct consideration. To some it may appear that it would have been a more natural course to consider the effect of baptism in the first instance, and thereafter to develop the course of the Spirit's operation, when children grow up to a capacity for knowing and believing the truth. But as the work of the Spirit is spoken of in Scripture chiefly with reference to adult persons, and as in their case only can we trace it in its visible manifestations and actual fruits, we have

---

[1] *Christian Morals,* by William Sewell, Professor of Moral Philosophy at Oxford. This book proceeds on the assumption of baptismal regeneration, and represents that doctrine as the groundwork of Christian Ethics. With much that is objectionable, it presents some fine views of the improvement which should be made of baptism, and of the connection, too often overlooked, betwixt Christianity and Education.

drawn our illustrations from their experience. And it deserves to be remarked, that even those who hold the highest views of baptismal regeneration, should not on that account object to a detailed illustration of His subsequent operations on the mind and heart, since they admit that whatever grace may be imparted at baptism, there must be an internal and spiritual change of mind and heart, a change wrought by the agency of the Spirit and the instrumentality of the truth in riper years, before any man can enter the kingdom of God.

PART II
Illustrative Cases

I. The Philippian Gaoler : Acts 16.19-34

THE nature of a sinner's conversion to God is illustrated in Scripture in various ways. Sometimes in the way of doctrinal statement; as when it is represented in general terms as a change of mind and heart, wrought by the Spirit of God applying the truths of his Word, whereby the sinner is led to turn from sin unto God; sometimes by the use of figurative or metaphorical expressions descriptive of the various aspects in which it may be viewed; as when it is denominated a *resurrection*, a *new birth*, an *enlightening*, a *transformation*, a *renewing*, a *cleansing*, a *cure*, an *awakening* of the soul sometimes by the help of parables, or stories derived from ordinary life, and employed to illustrate spiritual truth; as when the apostasy, and ruin, and wretchedness of the natural man, and the commencement, progress, and consummation of his conversion are represented in the history of the Prodigal Son; and, lastly, by the account of many instances of genuine conversion which the Spirit of God has recorded in the Word, and which afford a practical illustration of the truth, such as is admirably fitted at once to awaken our interest in it, to impart a clear idea of its nature, and to impress our minds with a sense of its reality, as matter of personal experience.

I propose to consider some of these scriptural cases of conversion, such as that of the Philippian Gaoler, the Ethiopian Treasurer, Cornelius the Roman Centurion, Saul the Persecutor, Lydia of Thyatira, the Malefactor on the Cross, and the three thousand on the day of Pentecost, viewing them as so many illustrative specimens of that great change which must be wrought on ourselves individually, if we would enter into the kingdom of God. And I do the rather prefer such cases of conversion as are to be found in Scripture, before all others that have been reported in the diaries of private Christians or the more recent history of the Church,[1] because, being recorded by the Spirit of God, they are of standard authority, and exhibit the truth without any admixture of error or enthusiasm, but in connection with the personal history and actual experience of individuals of various views, and dispositions, and habits, so as to enable us at once to

[1] John Owen selects the case of Augustine. In 1833, the Rev. J. K. Craig, published a work in 2 volumes on *Conversion*, in a series of all the cases recorded in the New Testament, defective, doubtful, real; intended as a help to self-examination.

discover, by a simple comparison, what was common to all, and what is essential in every case of conversion, and to separate from each the mere circumstantial accompaniments. And in reviewing these cases, I trust we shall be impressed with a solemn sense of the greatness of conversion, when we reflect that God himself has not deemed it unworthy of his own infinite mind to mark and to record in his Word the commencement, and progress, and completion of this change in the bosoms of *individual men and women;* the mere fact that such cases are recorded being a sufficient proof at once that God regards the conversion of a soul with profound interest, and that as 'there is joy in heaven among the angels of God when one sinner repenteth,' so the Holy Spirit is near him, watching his progress, aiding his efforts, and rejoicing in his success.

The first case which I select is that of the Philippian Gaoler, which affords an interesting and instructive example of real conversion to God. And in illustrating the words in which it is recorded, I shall, 1st, Consider what is said of the state of his mind before his conversion; 2nd, The circumstances which accompanied, and the means which effected, this great change; and, 3rd, The true nature of it, or wherein it properly consisted, and the practical results which followed it.

1. In respect to the state of his mind before the time of his conversion, you will observe, on a careful review of the narrative, that there are two distinct descriptions of it, or rather he was successively in two different states of mind, first, as a *careless sinner*, and then as a *convinced sinner*, before he became a *converted man*.

It is evident that, down to the time when the earthquake occurred, he had been a careless, unregenerate, worldly man. This appears, not so much from his having imprisoned the apostles and made their feet fast in the stocks, for that might be thought to be his duty in the subordinate situation which he filled; and the guilt of persecution properly rested on the people who accused, and the magistrates who condemned them, of whom it is said that (ver. 19) when the masters of the damsel, who had been possessed with a spirit of divination, and who had been miraculously cured, – when they 'saw that the hope of their gains was gone, they caught Paul and Silas, and drew them into the market-place unto the rulers, and brought them to the magistrates, saying, These men, being Jews, do exceedingly trouble our city, and teach customs which are not lawful for us to receive, neither to observe, being Romans. And the multitude rose up together against them; and the magistrates rent off their clothes, and commanded to beat them. And when they had laid many stripes upon them, they cast them into prison, charging the gaoler to keep them safely: who, *having received such a charge,* thrust them into the inner prison, and made their feet fast in the stocks.' The guilt of this persecution rested mainly on the magistrates and the multitude, and the gaoler was no farther responsible for it than as he was their agent in carrying it on; but that he was a careless sinner appears with conclusive evidence from his conduct afterwards, when (ver. 26) 'suddenly there was a great earthquake, so that the foundations of the prison were shaken; and immediately all the doors were opened, and every one's bands were loosed. And the keeper of the prison, awaking out of his sleep, and seeing the prison-doors open, he drew out his sword and would have killed himself, supposing that the prisoners had been fled.' We have here a lively delineation of a worldly, careless, godless man, distracted and driven to desperation by a sudden and unexpected temporal calamity. He supposed that his prisoners had escaped, and that he would be called to account by his earthly superiors, and condemned to forfeit the situation which he held; and immediately, under the influence of 'that sorrow of the world which worketh death,' 'he drew out his sword, and would have killed himself.' The thought of suicide was an indication of utter practical atheism; for it showed that he had *no fear of God*, since he was more afraid of 'them that could kill the body, than of Him that could cast both soul and body into hell;' that he had no *care for his soul*, since he was ready to peril its salvation, merely because he apprehended the loss of his situation on earth; and that he had no concern, or rather was utterly *reckless about eternity*, since, to escape from the misery of the present hour, he was about to rush, unprepared and unsummoned, into the presence of his Judge. The idea of suicide is one that could not have occurred to any man, however severe the trials, and however heavy the disappointments which he was called to endure, unless he were utterly ignorant and careless in regard alike to God and his own everlasting prospects; and from the fact that 'he drew out his sword, and would have killed himself,' we infer that down to the time when the earthquake occurred, he was a mere worldling, – an indifferent, careless, and un-awakened sinner.

But a change was wrought on his state of mind *before* his conversion, and which was only preparatory to that still greater change: from being a *careless*, he became a *convinced* sinner. This preliminary change consisted in strong convictions of conscience and lively apprehensions of danger; and these, although suddenly produced, were alike sincere and profound, insomuch that it is said (ver. 29), 'He called for a light, and sprang in, and came trembling, and fell down before Paul and Silas, and brought them out, and said, Sirs, what must I do to be saved?' Here is a great change, a change from total apathy to real concern, from utter recklessness to sincere and anxious inquiry. He appears to have been suddenly seized with an agonizing sense of his guilt and danger. And there is an affecting contrast betwixt his present convictions and his former carelessness; for the same danger existed then as now: his sins were as many and great; God was as just, and holy, and terrible, eternity was as vast and awful, when he thought not at all of these things, as now, when, in agitation and alarm, he could think of nothing else; his danger was not created by his convictions, it was only realized and impressed on his conscience: his state was as perilous before, when, in the recklessness of unbelief, he drew a sword, and would have killed himself, as now, when, with a newly awakened anxiety and earnestness, he was inquiring what he should do to be saved. But now he was brought under deep concern as to the state and prospects of his *soul*. He was convinced of his danger, and of the need of salvation; for his question was understood and answered by the apostles as having reference to his spiritual state and everlasting prospects. And this conviction, although suddenly awakened in the bosom of one who had heretofore been a careless sinner, may be accounted for by what he had seen and heard since the apostles had appeared at Philippi. We find that the apostles had been certain days in that city; that Paul had preached by the river side, 'where prayer was wont to be made;' that Lydia had been converted, and, along with her household, had been baptized; and that a miracle had been wrought on the damsel possessed with a spirit of divination. These things had occurred before that memorable night; and although the gaoler might not have been personally present, he could hardly fail to hear the report of what had happened, as we find that the whole city was thrown into an uproar, and 'the multitude rose up together against the apostles, and the magistrates rent off their clothes, and commanded to beat them.' And besides the report of these things, the *conduct* of the apostles in prison was fitted to impart much instruction; lacerated with stripes, loaded perhaps with chains, and with their feet fast in the stocks, 'at midnight Paul and Silas prayed and sang praises unto God; and the prisoners heard them.' That song of praise at the dead of night, and within the walls of a public prison, bespoke a sustaining power which no prosecution could crush, a peace which the world could neither give nor take away; and when the song ceased, and the prayer was ended, 'suddenly there was a great earthquake, so that the foundations of the prison were shaken, and all the doors were opened, and every one's bands were loosed.' These events, whether witnessed by the gaoler, or reported to him when he awoke out of sleep, must have impressed his mind with the conviction that there was some unearthly greatness in these men, and some unseen power working in their behalf, especially when, in the midst of that awful scene, in which the earth had opened, and the foundations of the prison were shaken, and when, in utter distraction and terror, the gaoler drew his sword, and would have killed himself, he heard Paul's voice rising calm and clear above the confusion, and saying, 'Do thyself no harm, for we are all here.' Such seem to have been the circumstances which awakened the conscience of this careless sinner, and brought it under the power of strong convictions, for 'immediately he called for a light, and sprang in, and came trembling, and fell down before Paul and Silas, and brought them out, saying, Sirs, what must I do to be saved?'

But while a marked change had been wrought on his views and feelings, inasmuch as, from being a very careless, he had become a deeply convinced sinner, you will carefully observe that he was not yet a *converted man*. He was only at the stage of conviction, which precedes conversion, but which is not always followed by it. He had strong remorse; but remorse is not repentance; he had a deep sense of fear; but fear is not faith; he had an awful apprehension of danger; but danger may be apprehended while the method of deliverance is unknown. These convictions were useful as preparatory means, as motives to serious inquiry and earnest attention; at the most, they were but *hopeful symptoms;* they neither amounted to conversion, nor did they afford any certain ground to expect that this great change would follow; for such convictions, however profound, may be and often are stifled, resisted, and overcome. The careless sinner may be startled for a time in his slumber, and the transient alarm passing away, he may fall back again into the sleep of spiritual death, and the latter end of that man is worse than the beginning.

That the gaoler was not yet converted is evident from the question which he put to the apostles, a question which implies, indeed, that he was now convinced of his danger, and concerned for his soul, and impressed with the necessity of salvation, and willing to inquire after it, but which also implies, that as yet he was ignorant of the method of salvation, and the ground of a sinner's hope; nay, his question seems to imply that besides being ignorant as yet of the only ground of acceptance with God, he was still, notwithstanding all his convictions, disposed to look to something that he *might himself do* as the means of effecting his deliverance; for it is very remarkable, that even when, under an agonising sense of guilt and danger, *he came trembling* to the apostles, his question to them was not, How can I be saved? but, What must I *do* to be saved? and this accords with the disposition and tendency of every natural mind. However deep his convictions may be, and however alarming his fears, the first impulse of every convinced sinner, before he is savingly converted, is to look to some efforts or doings of his own as the means of his deliverance, and to betake himself to a reformation of life, or to deeds of charity, or to penance and self-mortification, or some other outward observance, in the vain hope that he may thereby construct for himself a ground of hope, and secure the forgiveness and favour of God. Down to the time, then, that he put this question to the apostles, he was an unconverted man, although he had been so far changed as from a careless to have become a convinced sinner.

2. Let us now consider the *means* by which his conversion was effected, as distinct from the circumstances by which it was preceded or accompanied. It is of considerable practical importance to separate these two, and to consider what is essential to conversion, apart from the mere circumstantial accompaniments which were peculiar to this individual's case. Of the latter we may mention the earthquake, the opening of the prison-doors, the bursting of the prisoners' bands, and other such circumstances, which in this particular case were employed as means of awakening the conscience and impressing the mind of a careless sinner; whereas, in other cases God brings about the same change without any such manifestation of miraculous power, sometimes by the ordinary dispensations of his providence, and at other times by the simple operation of his truth. It matters little by what circumstances a sinner is first awakened to inquire, whether by the earthquake, or the still small voice, provided only that he is convinced of his sin and danger, and led to inquire in earnest after the salvation of his soul. But while the circumstances which may accompany this change are very various in different cases, the *means* of conversion – that by which it is properly effected, are one and the same in all: it is nothing else than the truth as it is in Jesus, or the full and free Gospel of the grace of God. The gaoler was not converted by the earthquake, and the shaking of the prison, and the opening of the prison-doors; on the contrary, the *immediate* effect of these miraculous events was such a terror and distraction of mind, that 'he drew out his sword, and would have killed himself;' and even when they were made the means of awakening his conscience, and impressing him with a sense of danger, they only served the preparatory purpose of exciting him to earnest inquiry: but what the earthquake and the other miraculous events of that memorable night could not do was done by the simple proclamation of the Gospel message. For when he came to the apostles, and, trembling under a sense of his guilt and danger, asked them, saying, 'Sirs, what must I do to be saved?' they immediately replied, 'Believe on the Lord Jesus Christ, and thou shalt be saved.' And this word was the instrument of his conversion, the means by which the convinced sinner became a converted man!

In this short but comprehensive passage, we have only, as it were, the text of Paul's discourse; for it is evident that he unfolded its meaning, and instructed the gaoler fully in the truth, since it is added, 'They spake unto him the word of the Lord, and to all that were in his house.' The whole discourse is not recorded; but the substance of it is preserved in that precious answer which was given to the gaoler's question, and which contains in a few pregnant words a summary of the Gospel, a complete directory to every anxious inquirer after the way of peace. They directed him to look out of himself *to Christ*, to relinquish all hope of salvation by works, and to seek salvation by faith, and to depend not at all on his own righteousness, but on another righteousness which God had provided, and which Christ had wrought out for him. They exhorted him to believe on *the Lord Jesus Christ*, which implies, *first*, that he should believe the truth concerning Christ which is involved in the names which are here given to him, and which, doubtless, was more fully explained in the subsequent address: as that Jesus of Nazareth was the Son of God, and the Saviour of sinners; that he was anointed by the Father with the Holy Ghost, and therefore to be received as the Christ of God, the Messiah that had been promised to the fathers; – that he was anointed for the discharge of his various offices, as God's Prophet, to declare his mind and will, as God's High Priest, to make atonement for sin and intercession for sinners, and as God's King, to whom all power was given in heaven and on earth; that once humbled, he was now exalted, so that every tongue should confess that he is Lord, to the glory of God the Father. All this is implied in the names which are here given to him: he is called '*Jesus*,' 'because he should *save* his people from their sins;' and '*Christ*,' because he is the Lord's Anointed, to whom the Spirit was given without measure, in token of his designation, by divine appointment, to the offices which he sustained, as well as to qualify him for effecting his great redemption; – and '*Lord*,' because he is highly exalted, not only in respect of the original dignity of his nature, but also in respect to the reward which he should earn, and the glory which should follow his humiliation, on the completion of his work. And the gaoler was called, in the first instance, to believe these truths concerning Christ, because they constitute the means by which sinners are savingly converted, there being enough of Gospel truth in the very name of Jesus to be an adequate object of saving faith, and to work that great change; for 'whoso believeth that Jesus is the Christ, is born of God,' and there is 'no other name given under heaven among men, whereby we must be saved,' but the name of Jesus.

The apostle's exhortation further implies that, believing the truth concerning Christ, the gaoler should place his own personal trust and reliance on Christ alone, that he should come to him, and commit his soul into Christ's hands as one who was able to save unto the very uttermost, and receive and embrace him as his own Saviour in all the fulness of his offices, as he is freely offered in the Gospel. In other words, that he should believe the truth concerning Christ, with a special application of it to the

[137]

case of *his own soul*, not resting in vague generalities, nor contenting himself with speculative inquiry, but closing with Christ as his own Saviour, and resting on him as all his salvation and all his desire. For the apostle speaks pointedly to him, and says to him individually, 'Believe on the Lord Jesus Christ, and THOU shalt be saved.' Many precious lessons are taught by the apostle's answer, which are applicable for the direction and encouragement of convinced sinners in all ages of the Church; but omitting these for the present, and confining our attention to the case of the individual before us, I shall only observe, that the general truth which he was called to believe concerning Christ as the Anointed Saviour of sinners, afforded a sufficient warrant and reason for his immediately relying on Christ as his own Saviour; and that, when he was exhorted to believe on the Lord Jesus Christ, and encouraged to hope that he should be saved, he had presented to him the sum and substance of the Gospel message, which is glad tidings of great joy, even to the chief of sinners.

The Gospel thus proposed was the means of his conversion: and, considered as a means, it was alike suitable and sufficient; suitable as prescribing a remedy in all respects adapted to the evils which he felt or feared; and sufficient, as containing every thing that was needed to instruct, or encourage, or persuade him. The Gospel is the only, and it is an adequate means; but it is a means and nothing more. It is an instrument whose efficacy depends on its being applied by the Spirit. It is not said, indeed, of the Philippian gaoler, as it is of Lydia in the same city, that 'the Lord opened his heart;' but it is manifest that the Spirit must have concurred with the Word: the mere Word will not do it. If you doubt this, the same words are now, and have often been, addressed to you, and with a special application to each of your souls: 'Believe on the Lord Jesus Christ, and thou shalt be saved.' You have read these words, and you have often heard them before; and even thus much of God's truth is sufficient to convert a sinner, and to bring about a sudden and universal change, but only when it is applied with power by the Holy Ghost; for your own experience may serve to convince you, that the same words which converted the gaoler may be repeated often, and pressed with earnestness, and fully unfolded and explained, and yet leave you as unconcerned and unconverted as before. So the gaoler might have been in danger, and yet have cherished his former security, or he might have been visited with convictions of conscience, and yet have stifled them, or he might have been alarmed, without inquiring after salvation, or he might have inquired, without discovering the truth, or he might have heard the truth, without believing it, had not the Spirit of God convinced him of his danger, and awakened a spirit of earnest inquiry, and made known to him the Gospel, and disposed and enabled him to receive and rest upon Christ as all his salvation and all his desire.

3. We are now to consider the nature of that great change which was thus wrought on his mind, or wherein it properly consisted, and the practical fruits which followed it.

It is clear that his conversion properly consisted in his complying with the apostle's exhortation – by '*believing on the Lord Jesus Christ.*' Until he believed he was unconverted; but, so soon as he believed, he became a converted man. The production of *true faith* is a *new creation*; it is not a mere change of opinion, but a radical and thorough renovation of mind, in virtue of which it may be said, that from the same hour in which he 'believed on the Lord Jesus Christ,' he became 'a new creature: old things passed away; all things became new.' Not that it is a small matter to be born again, but it is a great thing to believe. Many who have never questioned their own faith in Christianity, and who presume that they are believers, merely because they have not opposed it, may be totally unconscious of any thing in their own experience which bears any resemblance to that of the Philippian gaoler, when, under deep convictions of conscience, and with earnest desire after salvation, he was first taught the truth concerning Christ, and enabled to form a vivid and realizing conception of his office and power, as the real, only, and all-sufficient Saviour of sinners; but every one who, like him, has been really awakened to a sense of his sin and danger, and who has been led to contemplate Christ in his true character, and really to believe on him for salvation, will acknowledge that on the instant when he acquired the first inward conviction of the truth, he passed, as it were, from darkness into marvellous light, that he then experienced a very great change in all his views and feelings, that a new mind was given to him, and a new life seemed to have begun, insomuch that he felt as did the blind man when he was restored to sight: 'One thing I know, that whereas I was blind, now I see.'

A *real, simple, and scriptural faith* is that essential element, without which there can be no conversion, and in which it properly consists; but this faith has uniformly certain accompaniments and effects, which are so many proofs of its genuineness and tokens of its efficacy. The 'faith which is without works is dead, being alone;' but living faith *worketh* by love, and it is deeply interesting to mark, in the short and simple narrative of the gaoler's conversion, how soon and how surely the faith of the Gospel is followed by the peaceable fruits of righteousness. For that narrative bears, – 1st, That he thirsted for more instruction; that he hungered for the bread of life; and was solicitous to know more of divine truth. For, after hearing the answer which the apostles gave to his question, it is said (ver. 32), 'They spake unto

him the word of the Lord;' just as it is said that they who, on the day of
Pentecost, 'gladly received the word,' 'continued steadfastly in the apostles'
doctrine and fellowship, and in breaking of bread, and in prayers. 2*nd*, That
he was concerned, not only for his own soul, but also for the souls of his
family; for 'all that were in his house' were brought together to hear the
word. 3*rd*, That his faith wrought by love, producing gratitude and kindness to his instructors; for 'he took them the same hour of the night, and
washed their stripes,' 'and when he had brought them out, he set meat before
them.' 4*th*, That he had peace and joy in believing: his fears were removed,
and in their stead a new happiness sprang up in his bosom; for 'he rejoiced,
believing in God with all his house.' And, finally, he made an open profession of his faith, and evinced an entire submission to the authority of
Christ, by consenting to be baptized with all his family, and thereby
declared that, even in the midst of a city where magistrates and people were
alike opposed to the religion he professed, he was not 'ashamed of the
gospel of Christ,' since he had felt it to be 'the power of God unto salvation
to every one that believeth.'

In this narrative we have an interesting example of true scriptural conversion; and we may deduce from it several instructive lessons, which are
applicable for the benefit of the Church in all ages.

We learn from it such lessons as these:—

1. That men, in their unconverted state, are often utterly careless, and
destitute alike of all fear of God, of all concern for their souls, and of all
solicitude about death, and judgment, and eternity. This was the character
of the gaoler when he was about to rush unprepared into the presence of his
Judge; and it is the character of many amongst ourselves, who have never
felt that religion was a great reality, nor experienced any deep impressions
of its awful truths, nor spent a single hour in the serious consideration of the
state of their souls, the relation in which they stand to God, and their future
prospects in eternity; and who, 'having no fear of God before their eyes,'
have no sympathy with such as are in earnest on the subject of religion, but
are disposed to ridicule their exercises and their experience as the dreams of
fanaticism. This utter insensibility, this deathlike apathy, is one of the
worst symptomo sf a man's spiritual state.

2. While they are thus careless, God is often pleased to make use of some
solemn and awakening dispensation of providence to arouse and alarm
them, as the earthquake was employed in the case before us, and the un-
loosing of the prisoners, which threatened the gaoler with temporal ruin.
So God brings a careless sinner into sudden and imminent danger, or visits
him with affliction, with disease of body, or bereavement in his family, or
embarrassment in his wordly affairs – and this, because 'when they have

no changes, the men of the world fear not God;' but when smitten by the rod of his providence, they may be awakened to serious thought. These afflictive dispensations are often useful as preparatory means; and many a Christian may trace his first serious impressions to a season of personal or domestic trial; but they are not effectual of themselves for thorough conversion, and do often, in point of fact, fall far short of it, as is evident in the case of Israel of old, of whom it is said, 'When he slew them, then they sought him; and they returned and inquired early after God: and they remembered that God was their Rock, and the high God their Redeemer. Nevertheless they did flatter him with their mouth, and they lied unto him with their tongues. For their heart was not right with him, neither were they steadfast in his covenant.'

3. Sometimes the trials and disappointments of careless sinners only serve to exasperate their natural enmity; and, instead of producing a meek, and quiet, and broken spirit, issue in the 'sorrow of the world which worketh death,' as was the case of the gaoler, when, under the pressure of unexpected calamity, his first impulse was to draw his sword and kill himself; and of Ahithophel, who, 'when he saw that his counsel was not followed, saddled his ass, and arose, and gat him home to his house, to his city, and put his household in order, and hanged himself, and died, and was buried in the sepulchre of his father.'

4. But in other cases a *work of conviction* is wrought in the conscience, which may be more or less intense, and of longer or shorter duration, but is in some degree essential to saving conversion; such conviction of *guilt and danger* as impressed the mind of the gaoler when he came trembling and said, 'What must I do to be saved?' This is a hopeful symptom, but it is not a decisive proof of a saving change; on the contrary, such convictions are often stifled and suppressed, and, instead of subduing, they exasperate, as in the case of Felix, who trembled while Paul preached, but was not converted; and of those in the Acts, who were 'cut to the heart' by Stephen's doctrine, but only 'gnashed on him with their teeth;' and of others 'who were *cut* to the heart,' and only 'took counsel to slay them.' Convictions are useful only when they produce an earnest spirit of thoughtfulness, and lead the sinner to inquire, 'What must I do to be saved?'

5. The Gospel, which is mainly designed to reveal an answer to that question of an awakened conscience, is the only effectual instrument of conversion. Other means may concur in carrying forward the preparatory process, but this alone can work the great, the saving change. All other expedients are worse than useless, they are pernicious and fatal to the soul. The only answer that ought in any case, or in any circumstances, to be given to the question, 'What must I do to be saved?' is the answer that was

returned to the Philippian gaoler, – 'Believe on the Lord Jesus Christ, and thou shalt be saved.'

And the circumstances in which that answer was given throw an interesting light both on the perfect freeness of the Gospel and the certainty of salvation to every one that believeth; – on its *freeness*, as being proposed even to the chief of sinners; for Paul, you will observe, had no scruple in proposing the *full* Gospel to the gaoler on the instant when he came to him, although he had hitherto been a careless, unconverted man. He did not say to him, 'You have been a great sinner, I have no Gospel for you; a little while ago you drew your sword, and were about to commit suicide; how can you hope to be saved?' No! but to this trembling sinner he said on the instant, and without any qualification or reserve, 'Believe on the Lord Jesus Christ;' and that answer is the sinner's warrant at the present hour. And it throws an interesting light on the *certainty* of salvation; for he did not say, Believe, and you *may* be saved; but, Believe, and thou SHALT be saved. There is no doubt, no uncertainty, no cautious reserve, but an absolute assurance; and that assurance is the sinner's encouragement at the present hour. To every sinner, however careless, and however deeply convinced of sin, we are warranted by the apostle's example in saying, *fully* and *freely*, without any conditions or exceptions, 'Believe on the Lord Jesus Christ, and *thou* shalt be saved.'

6. *Conviction* ends in *conversion* only when a true sense of sin is combined with a belief of the Gospel, or an apprehension of the mercy of God in Christ. The careless sinner may become a convinced sinner by the operation of natural conscience, or by the power of the law, aided by the awakening dispensations of Providence; but he does not become a converted man until he believes the truth as it is in Jesus, and realizes the fact that Jesus is the Christ. Conversion properly consists in the production of repentance and faith; and a new birth is followed by a new life. Conversion by the Word produces conformity to the will of God, and faith is fruitful of works. All these truths are exemplified in the case of the gaoler at Philippi, and are confirmed by the experience of every believer at the present day.

II. The Dying Malefactor: Luke 23.32-43

THE crucifixion of the Lord Jesus was so ordered as to furnish a striking illustration, at once of the depth of his abasement, and the certainty of his reward. To enhance the agony and the shame of his death, he was crucified between two thieves, being numbered with transgressors, placed on the same level, in the public view, with men whose lives had been justly forfeited by their crimes, and subjected, in his last moments, to the painful spectacle of their sufferings; but, to evince the certainty of his reward, to make it manifest that the joy which was set before him, and for which he endured the cross, despising the shame, would be realized, and to give him as it were a pledge in hand, that 'he should see of the travail of his soul, and be satisfied,' one of the thieves who suffered along with him was suddenly converted; and, in the lowest depths of the Redeemer's humiliation, in the darkest hour of the power of darkness, when Satan's policy seemed to be crowned with complete success, this immortal soul was snatched as a brand from the burning, and given to Christ as a pledge of his triumph, and the first fruits of a glorious harvest. While others mocked and reviled him, and when his chosen disciples stood aloof, the dying malefactor relented, his conscience awoke, his heart was touched; and, amidst the ridicule, and the execrations, and the blasphemies of that awful hour, one solitary voice was heard, issuing from the cross beside him, which called him 'Lord,' and which spake of his 'kingdom' in accents of faith, and penitence, and prayer. And how must that voice have gladdened the Saviour's heart! and imparted to him, in the midst of his bitterest agony, a foretaste as it were of the 'joy that was set before him,' exhibiting, as it did, a proof of the efficacy of his death, the faithfulness of God's covenant-promise, and the certainty of his reward! For it, even now on the cross, and before his work was finished, this stricken spirit fled to him for refuge, and was quickened into spiritual life in the very hour of death. Was it not a sure pledge and earnest that he should yet bring many sons and daughters to glory, when, being by God's right hand exalted to the throne, he should receive the promise of the Father, and shed forth the Spirit from on high?

I. In reference to the state of this man's mind before the time of his conversion, nothing is recorded that would lead us to suppose that he had ever thought seriously of religion, or acquired any knowledge of the Gospel, until he was brought to Calvary. He is described as a malefactor, and more specifically as a *thief* or robber – a desperate character, fearing neither God nor man – whose crimes exposed him to the highest penalties of the law; and his own confession admits the justice of the sentence under which he suffered: 'We receive the due reward of our deeds.' On a comparison of the parallel passages in the Gospels of Matthew and Mark, it would seem that at first he had joined with the other malefactor in reviling the Saviour; for in the one it is said, 'The thieves also, which were crucified with him, cast the same in his teeth;' and in the other, 'They that were crucified with him reviled him,' expressions which may, indeed, be interpreted generally, as descriptive of Christ's extreme humiliation in being subjected to reproach from such a quarter, this class of men being spoken of as partaking in the crime of embittering his last moments, just as the soldiers are said to have filled a sponge with vinegar, because one or more of them did so; but if they be understood as applying specifically to each of the two, they are sufficient to show that, at first, the one who was converted was as ungodly and as guilty as the other.

But immediately before his conversion, and preparatory to it, a change seems to have been wrought in the state of his mind, a change which consisted in a deep conviction of sin, and a just sense of his own demerit on account of it. For when one of the malefactors railed on Jesus, 'the other, answering, rebuked him, saying, Dost not thou fear God, seeing that thou art in the same condemnation? And we indeed justly; for we receive the due reward of our deeds.' The whole process was so suddenly accomplished in this case, that it is difficult to say whether, in the order of time, the convictions which are expressed in this remarkable confession preceded, by any perceptible interval, his cordial reception of the truth; but as, in the order of nature, conviction precedes conversion, we may consider it as part of his experience, while as yet he was in a state of transition from darkness to light. The words of his confession imply that his conscience, which, by the commission of crime, might have been seared as with a hot iron, was now deeply impressed with a sense of sin; and it was a true sense of sin, not the mere 'sorrow of the world which worketh death,' but godly sorrow, working towards genuine repentance; for although the condemnation of which he speaks might be the temporal sentence of death, pronounced and executed by his fellowmen, his language shows that he viewed his guilt with reference not to men merely, but to God also – to God, as the supreme Lawgiver and the final Judge. As a resident at Jerusalem, or at least in Judea, the seat of true religion, he had probably enjoyed some of the advantages of

early religious instruction, and had been taught some of the elementary
truths of Scripture; for he speaks of God, the only living and true God,
whose name he knew and feared, although he had lived in the violation of
his law. The thought of God as a Lawgiver and Judge was now vividly
present to his mind; and the conception of God's character, combined with
the inherent power of conscience, which, even in the breasts of the most
depraved, is never altogether extinguished, produced that conviction of
sin which is invariably accompanied with the fear of God, and of a judgment
to come. So long as God can be kept out of view, there may be a secret
consciousness of guilt, without any sensible alarm or apprehension of
danger; and hence the malefactor's question to his hardened fellow-
sufferer – 'Dost not thou fear God?' but so soon as God is present to the
mind, every conscience intuitively connects guilt with danger, and awakens
fear of the wrath to come, for conscience instinctively points to God as a
Judge, to God as an avenger.

But, in the case before us, as in every other where there is a commencement of a work of grace in the heart, conviction of sin was accompanied,
not only with the fear of danger, but with such a sense of demerit, as led to
the acknowledgement that punishment was *justly deserved*. This is not
always implied in the mere terrors of an awakened conscience, and would
be altogether repudiated by a conscience still asleep. The malefactor who
railed at Jesus might not be able to deny his guilt, and he might yield himself
as a passive and unresisting victim to the arm of public justice, merely
because he could not, by any resistance, escape from the punishment of his
crimes; but had he been asked to acknowledge that he justly merited the
bitter death which he was called to endure, he would, too probably, have
denied that he was so guilty as to deserve such a punishment, and complained of the hardship and severity of his case. In reference to God, the
supreme Judge, and the retributions of an eternal world, he seems to have
had no fear; for he could join, even at that solemn hour, and in spite of his
own sufferings, in the insults and blasphemies which were poured out on the
meek and lowly Saviour: but even had his conscience been so far awakened
as to impress him with the fear of God and eternity, he might still have been
utterly destitute of that deep sense of the evil nature of sin which led his
fellow-sufferer to acknowledge that he was receiving only the due reward
of his deeds. A convinced sinner may tremble, as Felix did when he heard of
temperance, and righteousness, and judgment to come; and he may be
conscious of a deep horror when he hears of 'the worm that shall never die,
and the fire that cannot be quenched;' yet the omniscient eye of him who
can analyse the confused emotions of a sinner's heart might not discern
there any one element of genuine contrition; on the contrary, he might find

the fear of wrath, and the dread of hell, combined with an invincible spirit of opposition to God's authority, an undying reluctance to condemn his own sin, and an unyielding determination to deny the rectitude and reasonableness of its penalty. And when, therefore, the poor malefactor was so far convinced of his sin as not only to be impressed with a sense of his danger but also with a sense of his demerit and of God's justice, we see the commencement of a great change, which affords the best and most hopeful symptom of his ultimate and entire conversion.

II. While he was thus changed so as to have become a convinced sinner, he was not yet a converted man, but his conversion immediately followed; and it will be interesting now to inquire into the circumstances which accompanied, and the means which, under God's blessing, effected that great change. It was alike complete and sudden, it was wrought, like the conversion of the gaoler, in a short space of time, and yet it amounted to an entire revolution in all his views and habits, insomuch that he became a new man, and, born on the cross, he passed into heaven. Now, what was there in the circumstances in which he was placed, and in the means which were brought to bear upon him, that could account for so great a change?

If we place ourselves in his circumstances; if, by a strong mental effort, we bring ourselves to look on the scene which he saw, and to realize, by the eye of faith, what then passed before the eye of sense; if, joining the crowd which throned the judgment-hall of Pilate, we listen with the same personal interest which the poor thief must have felt when Pilate made the proposal to release one or other of the condemned; did we then join the tumultuous procession, and follow the meek Sufferer as he slowly walked along with the thieves, 'followed by a great company of people, and of women, who lamented and bewailed him; did we hear the words of warning and consolation which he spake to the daughters of Jerusalem, – did we stand beside him on the hill, when the cross which Simeon was honoured to bear was firmly planted in the ground; did we see 'the man of sorrows' carried by violence, and nailed to the accursed tree; did we look on his benignant countenance, and listen to his awful words; did we behold the sudden darkening of the sky, and the rending of the rocks, which gave a deep impressiveness to the scene; then, with *our* knowledge of the personal dignity of the sufferer, the causes, design, and end of his death, and the fulness of all gospel truth which is embodied in his cross, we could have no difficulty in conceiving how such a scene, so witnessed and so understood, might have converted any sinner unto God. It is, indeed, nothing else than a spiritual view of the scene then witnessed on Calvary which is the chief means of every conversion, the cross of Christ being to every instructed disciple the power of God and the wisdom of God unto salvation, insomuch that every believer will say with the apostle, 'God forbid that I should glory, save in the cross of the Lord Jesus Christ.' Looking back to that scene with the eye of faith, the Christian derives from it all his sublimest views and his holiest impressions of the truth; he delights to contemplate what the poor malefactor was then privileged to witness; and as often as he reviews the events of that awful hour he is filled with awe and wonder, with admiration and gratitude and joy.

But while the scene at Calvary must appear to every instructed mind the most solemnly interesting and the most profoundly instructive scene which was ever witnessed on earth, it was quite possible that, to an unenlightened mind, it might fail to impart any spiritual or salutary impression; and we are to put ourselves into the place of this poor malefactor, and inquire what were the means of his conversion, when it is clear he came to Calvary in a state of great ignorance and guilt, and yet was suddenly brought out of darkness into marvellous light.

We have already seen that he had been brought under convictions of sin such as are sufficient to show that, depraved and guilty as he had been, he had still a conscience in his breast, and some notion, however obscure and feeble, of God as a Lawgiver, Governor, and Judge. He was a man, a poor, wretched, and degraded man; but still a man, and therefore a fit and capable subject of conversion; and partly from the light of nature, which is never altogether extinguished, and partly from his early education in a country where the knowledge and worship of the true God were established, he had acquired the knowledge of some elementary truths, such as the being and providence of God, the difference betwixt right and wrong, the demerit and sure punishment of sin, which was sufficient to awaken remorse and apprehension, but had no power to effect his conversion. Real conversion to God depends on the knowledge and belief of the truth as it is in Jesus; how, then, was this poor malefactor converted, and whence did he derive his acquaintance with that truth which alone maketh wise unto salvation? Oh! it is deeply interesting to mark how a heart that has been opened by the Spirit of God, and awakened to earnest and serious inquiry, will pick up the fragments of Gospel truth in whatever form they may be presented to it, and will find nourishment in the very crumbs which fall from the Master's table! for, in the case before us, there was no formal discourse, no full disclosure of doctrine, no systematic instruction; but his eye was opened to observe, and his ear to hear, and his heart to receive the truth as it was presented incidentally during his progress from Pilate's hall to the hill of Calvary, and exhibited before his crucifixion there; and there are just three sources from which he derived those simple lessons which sufficed for his conversion:—

The first was, *the testimony of Christ's friends;* not only the testimony of Pilate, who declared that 'he had found no fault in him,' but that of many others who bore witness to his spotless character, and of whom it is said (Luke 23. 27), that 'there followed him a great company of people, and of women, which also bewailed and lamented him.' The innocence of Christ was thus impressed on the malefactor's mind, and is pointedly referred to in his confession, 'We receive the due reward of our deeds, but this man hath done nothing amiss.'

The second was, *the deportment of Christ,* the meek majesty of that suffering Saviour, the words he uttered, breathing a spirit so different from that of this world; these seem to have deepened the impression of his innocence and worth. His address to the daughters of Jerusalem, so solemn, yet so tender; and still more, the prayer for his murderers, 'Father, forgive them, for they know not what they do;' – that address, and this prayer, pronounced at such an hour, the one exhibiting a prophet's faithfulness, the other a Saviour's love, and both breathing a spirit of meek submission to God's will, and intimating the guilt of sin, the certainty of future judgment, and the necessity of forgiveness – these few words, uttered in such circumstances, might reveal to the poor malefactor such a view of Christ as would irresistibly impress him with the conviction that he was no common sufferer, and that his was no ordinary death; and constrain him to believe that he was none other than the Son of God and the Saviour of men; the Son of God, for he calls him Father, and the Saviour of men, for he prayed for the forgiveness of his very murderers.

But there was a third: he was not left to ponder on the scene without a commentary, and that commentary was furnished *by the Saviour's enemies;* first of all, in the sneers and blasphemies which they uttered; and secondly, in the inscription which was put on the cross. They meant it not; but in these they gave such a testimony to the Saviour as sufficed for the conversion of his fellow-sufferer. 'The rulers,' we read, 'derided him, saying, *He saved others.*' Yes, he saved others; he had healed the sick, and given eyes to the blind, and ears to the deaf, and life to the dead; and that testimony to Christ's miraculous power sank deep into the heart of the dying man beside him. But who was this to whom his very enemies gave witness, that 'he saved others,' or what did he profess to be? This also the dying malefactor learned from their lips: 'Let him save himself, *if he be the Christ, the chosen of God;*' If thou be the king of the Jews, save thyself;' and they put a superscription over him, 'This is *the King of the Jews.*' These words used in, ridicule or rancorous hatred, conveyed to the mind of the malefactor the idea of what Christ claimed and professed to be; and when combined with what he had seen and heard, with the testimony which had been given to his miraculous powers, now confirmed by the preternatural darkness of the sky, and the rending of the rocks, with what he had witnessed of his God-like bearing, 'full of grace and truth,' and with the words which had fallen from his lips, they carried to his heart the conviction that the illustrious sufferer was indeed the Son of God, the Christ, the Messiah that had been promised to the fathers; that, although suspended on the cross, he was *the King;* and if a king, then he had a kingdom; and immediately the prayer of faith broke from his quivering lips, 'Lord, remember me when thou comest into thy kingdom!'

III. If we now consider the nature of the great change which was thus suddenly produced, or wherein it properly consisted, and the results which flowed from it, we shall find that the turning point of his conversion was his believing that *Jesus was the Christ.* This was precisely the point in question, both with the scornful multitude and the subdued malefactor. They doubted, he believed. They required another kind of evidence, 'Let him come down from the cross, and we will believe on him:' he did not come down from the cross, but having died there, he arose from the dead, and their unbelief remained; but the dying malefactor, satisfied with the evidence already given, saw his glory through the veil of his humiliation, and embracing him in his true character as the Christ, the chosen of God, he believed to the saving of his soul.

It was simply by faith and by faith in the simple truth that Jesus is the Christ, that this man passed from death unto life; but here was *great faith* indeed. For consider the circumstances in which Christ was then placed. He was in the lowest depths of his humiliation, in the extremest hour of his agony on the accursed tree, suffering the sentence of death as a public criminal, surrounded by multitudes who ridiculed and reviled him, forsaken by his chosen disciples, and complaining that he had been forsaken of God himself; yet, in these circumstances of humiliation, and sorrow, and shame, the dying malefactor called him *Lord,* and spake of his *kingdom,* and addressed him in the *language of prayer!* Yes; when Jesus was slowly dying on the cross, and had no prospect of life, still less of a kingdom on earth, the poor malefactor showed at once the greatness of his faith and his correct apprehension of the nature of Christ's kingdom, by uttering a prayer which implied in it the hope of his own immortality and of a spiritual and eternal kingdom in heaven. Here was a manifestation of faith to which we can find no parallel in the history of the apostles themselves. They called him Lord *after* his resurrection; but this man calls him Lord on the very cross; they spake of his kingdom, but doubtfully, and with many gross earthly anticipations: 'We *trusted* that it had been he which should have redeemed Israel;' and, 'Lord, wilt thou at this time restore the kingdom to Israel?', but this man speaks of his kingdom as a future inheritance, whose certainty was not affected by his shameful and ignominious death. And believing in Christ as the Lord's Anointed the Messiah which had been promised unto the fathers, he embraced him as his own Saviour. Encouraged, doubtless, by the grace which he had witnessed, and by that most merciful prayer for his murderers, he felt that he could confide and trust in such a friend; and therefore he addressed him in the language of believing *prayer*: 'Lord, remember me when thou comest into thy kingdom.'

This prayer is alike touching from its simplicity, and remarkable for its comprehensive brevity. He seemed to ask little, yet he asked every thing that was necessary for his everlasting welfare: 'Lord, remember me,' was his simple and modest request; but it included much; it cast him on the Saviour's care, it put his soul into the Saviour's hands, it expressed his faith, his dependence, his desire, his hope: as if he had said, I am a poor dying sinner; thou are a king going to thy kingdom; thou canst save me. I leave myself in thy hands; I lean on thy love: Lord! remember me!

The circumstances of the case did not admit of that full exhibition of the practical fruits of conversion which adorn the life and conversation of every true believer; for he was converted at the eleventh hour, and was no sooner converted than he died and entered into glory. We have, however, even in this brief narrative, some precious indications of the great moral change which had been wrought on his mind and heart. He evinced a true sense of sin, a thorough conviction of its demerit, a just apprehension of the punishment that was due to it; an awful fear of God, a lively trust and confidence in the Saviour, a serious thoughtfulness in regard to the future, a disposition to pray, and a new-born but honest zeal for righteousness and truth, which prompted him to rebuke his fellow-sufferer in these remarkable words, 'Dost not thou fear God, seeing thou art in the same condemnation? And we indeed justly; for we receive the due reward of our deeds;' and these new principles and feelings would no doubt have evinced their power, by altering all his habits and his whole course of life, had life been prolonged. It is true that, in many cases, serious thoughts of God and judgment and eternity are often awakened in the souls of unconverted men when they have the near prospect of death, and that in many cases when health is restored and life prolonged, they 'vanish like the morning cloud, and the early dew.' So that in the case of most late conversions, there is a painful feeling of doubt as to the genuineness and stability of those good resolutions which are awakened in the mere prospect of death, such as must prevent any very certain deliverance on the actual state and eternal prospects of such as are not spared to verify their profession by a consistent Christian life. But in the instance before us there is no room for doubt; we have the infallible testimony of Christ himself sealing this man's conversion and assuring him of eternal glory. The grand result of the change that was wrought upon him on the cross is declared in these words: 'Verily I say unto thee, To-day shalt thou be with me in paradise.' No sooner was the prayer uttered than the promise was given; and that promise was to be immediately fulfilled. The Lord gives more than was asked: the malefactor's request was, 'Lord, remember me!' but the answer far exceeded the demand; it spake to him of paradise, and of Christ's presence there, and of his admission that very day. What a sudden transition, what a glorious change! A malefactor, condemned for his crimes to die, led to Calvary that he might be nailed to a cross, converted there, as he hung between life and death, on the brink of eternity, and on the self-same day born again, justified, adopted, saved; translated from earth to heaven, from Calvary to paradise, from a cross of shame to a throne of glory!

On a review of the interesting narrative to which our attention has been directed, we may derive from it many *instructive lessons* which are applicable to all sinners at the present day.

1. It exhibits a remarkable proof of the Saviour's power. That this malefactor was a great sinner only serves to show that He by whom he was delivered was a great Saviour; that he had reached the extreme point of guilt, and the very end of life, only serves to make it clear that 'Christ is able to save unto the uttermost.' The power of Christ to *subdue* the most hardened sinner, and his power to *cancel* the most aggravated guilt, and his power to open the gate of heaven, and secure our admission there – all this is evinced with undeniable certainty by the fact that, even in the lowest depths of his humiliation, before his work was finished, or his reward secured, he snatched this brand from the burning, and rescued this captive from the power of Satan, and carried him as a trophy from the cross, when he entered within the veil. And oh! if such was Christ's power then, who should *now* despair, who knows that Jesus, then on the cross, is now upon the throne, exalted as a Prince and Saviour, to give repentance and remission of sins?

2. It exhibits a precious proof of the perfect freeness of his grace. Loaded with crime, and standing on the very verge of an eternal world, what could have been of any avail to this poor sinner but *grace*, and *grace* that was perfectly free? Righteousness he had none; good works he had none; he was self-convicted and self-condemned; and he had nothing before him but the certain fearful looking for of judgment, unless God had *grace*, and that *grace* were free. But when he heard the Saviour pray for his murderers, when he heard him pray for *their* forgiveness, the idea of *free grace* to pardon sin seems to have entered into his inmost soul, and he ventured to ask that the

Lord would remember him; and immediately, such was the grace of Christ, he required no previous qualifications, demanded no acquired merit, imposed no conditions, made no stipulations of any kind; but gave him at once an answer in peace, and a full and irreversible promise of admission into glory – and this, too, while he was in such agony as might have been expected to concentrate all his care upon himself; yet even then he had room in his heart for the sorrows of this poor sinner.

3. It has been remarked, that in the Bible this is a solitary example of a man being converted at the hour of death; there being *one* such instance that none may *despair*, and only one, that none may *presume*. Presumption and despair are the two great rocks on which we are ever in danger of making shipwreck; and this narrative may well serve to guard us against both. Against despair, for why should any man *despair* who reads of the thief who was converted on the cross? and against presumption, for who dare *presume* when he reads that there was another thief on another cross who died unconverted there? The hoariest sinner that lives may be encouraged by the one, but the boldest sinner may be deterred by the other. 'The one was taken, and the other left.'

4. We learn from this narrative how little of God's truth may serve for conversion, if it be suitably improved by the hearer, and savingly applied by the Spirit. The penitent on the cross was saved by means of mere fragments of truth, and these presented to him in the blasphemies of Christ's accusers and the inscription on his cross. This is a delightful thought, when it is viewed in connection with the case of the poor and ignorant, and of others who live under a dark or defective dispensation of truth; but it is unutterably solemn when viewed in connection with our own case, for how shall we escape if we die unconverted, after the light we have received, the many sermons we have heard, the much truth which we have slighted and despised!

5. We learn, that on the instant of his conversion, a sinner acquires all the rights and privileges of a child of God, and that if he die immediately thereafter, he will immediately pass into glory. No sooner was this malefactor converted, than he was assured by the Lord himself, that on the selfsame day he should be with him in paradise. Had he lived on earth, he would have been capable of growth and increase in grace; but the new creature, although but as a new-born babe, is entire in all its members, and capable of entering into the kingdom, however short its earthly span.

III. Paul: Acts 9. 1-22

THIS case of conversion is, in many respects, the most remarkable of all the examples which the Spirit of God has recorded for the instruction of the Church. Saul of Tarsus, the Jewish persecutor, was suddenly converted into Paul, the Christian philanthropist, the zealous apostle of the Gentiles. And whether we consider the masculine talents, the education, the learning, the morals of the man; or the suddenness and magnitude of the change which was wrought upon him; or the rich and varied fruits of personal holiness and public usefulness which sprang from it, we shall discover ample reason for regarding him as one of the most signal monuments of the riches and efficacy of divine grace. It is peculiarly fortunate, too, that, in this instance, our materials are so abundant, that there can be no difficulty in forming a correct conception, both of his state of mind before his conversion, and of his experience afterwards; for not only have we three distinct accounts of his conversion in the Acts of the Apostles (Acts 9. 1-22; 22. 1-21; 26. 4-19), but several instructive references to it in some of his epistles (as Gal. 1. 13; 1 Cor. 15. 9), while every part of his writings teems with illustrations of the magnitude and extent of that great spiritual change by which the persecutor became a preacher of the faith he had despised.

I. In reference to the state of his mind before his conversion, we derive much interesting information from various parts of his writings. It is evident, I think, that, *in point of intellectual culture and attainment*, as well as natural vigour and energy of mind, he was superior, not only to most of the primitive converts, but to all his fellow-apostles. It appears that, from his infancy, he had shared in the rich advantages of a liberal education; and that, as he advanced in years, he was introduced to lettered and cultivated society, which his capacious mind was qualified at once to appreciate and to improve. In a notice which is incidentally given of his early life, we read that he was born in Tarsus, the chief city of Cilicia, a capital long distinguished for a university, where Grecian learning was taught with eminent success. Whether he attended that university or not is uncertain; but, from the frequent and appropriate quotations which he makes in several of his speeches and epistles from the poets and philosophers of Greece, it is certain that there, or elsewhere, he had acquired a knowledge of polite literature, and a taste for the pursuits of learning. He could speak to the polished Athenians, on Mars's hill, in their own exquisite tongue. (Acts 17. 22). During his abode at Tarsus, indeed, he had, in part, followed the occupation of his father, as a *tent-maker*, for it was the custom of good families among the Jews to bring up their children to a trade, even though they should be destined to the more liberal pursuits of learning; and the advantage of this early training was afterwards exemplified in the experience of this remarkable man. We find that, while he was yet young, he left Tarsus, and repaired to Jerusalem, the chief seat at once of Jewish learning and religion, probably with the view of pursuing his scriptural studies, and qualifying himself for the sacred office of scribe, or doctor of the law; and he there enjoyed the privilege of studying under Gamaliel, who is described 'as a member of the council, and doctor of the law, had in reputation among all the people.' He had enjoyed, then, the best opportunities which his age afforded for becoming acquainted both with Greek and Jewish literature. And that he had genius to relish, and industry to profit by these advantages, appears from his wonderful writings and labours in after life, as well as from his own testimony: 'I am verily a Jew, born in Tarsus, a city in Cilicia, yet brought up in this city at the feet of Gamaliel, and taught according to the perfect manner of the law of the fathers;' 'And I profited in the Jews' religion above many my equals,' or contemporaries, 'in mine own nation.'

In respect, again, to his *religious opinions and moral habits*, it is clear that he was by conviction, as well as in profession, a Jew, holding the faith of the Old Testament, and observing the worship of the one living and true God, in opposition to all the false but seductive forms of polytheistic superstition which prevailed among the other nations, and which had been adorned with all the attractions of poetry and painting and sculpture, by the genius of Greece and Rome. And not a Jew only, but a *Pharisee*, a strict professor of the Jewish faith, maintaining, in opposition to the Sadducees, who were, both in their principles and habits, the libertines of the age, those grand doctrines which they had discarded, such as the immortality of the soul, the resurrection of the body, and the certainty of a judgment to come; and exhibiting, in his outward deportment, a fair, and even a strict example, both of ceremonial observance and of civil virtue. His own account of his early life shows that he was never, either in his own estimation or in that of his fellow-men, irreligious or immoral; on the contrary he says, 'My manner of life from my youth, which was at the first among mine own nation at Jerusalem, know all the Jews; who knew me from the beginning, if they would testify, that after *the most straitest sect of our religion, I lived a Pharisee.*' (Acts 26. 4). 'And I profited in the Jews' religion above many my equals in mine own nation, being more exceedingly zealous of the traditions of my fathers.' – (Gal. 1. 14). 'Though I might also have confidence in the flesh. If any other man thinketh that he hath whereof he might trust in the flesh, I more: circumcised the eighth day, of the stock of Israel, of the tribe of Benjamin, an Hebrew of the Hebrews; as touching the law, a Pharisee; concerning zeal, persecuting the church; touching the righteousness which is in the law, blameless.' (Phil. 3. 4). Such is the account which he gives us of his character before his conversion – an account which may, at first sight, appear to be inconsistent with those humbling confessions and those deep penitential feelings which he uttered in other parts of his writings, where he speaks of himself as 'less than the least of all saints,' and as the very 'chief of sinners;' but, on further reflection, these expressions, when compared together, will only serve to show that the fairest exterior may conceal an unsanctified heart; and that a correct creed, and a moral life, may well consist with the absolute necessity of regeneration. It is not said that he was any thing more than a Pharisee; and our Lord himself declared to his disciples, 'Except your righteousness exceed the righteousness of the scribes and Pharisees, ye shall in nowise enter into the kingdom of God.' He knew the law *in its letter*, and yet was ignorant of its *spirit and power;* for, at a subsequent period, he made this acknowledgment – 'I was alive without the law once; but when the commandment came, sin revived, and I died.' By the law is the knowledge of sin: but it is by the law spiritually understood; and hence he was destitute of any true sense of sin, till he was impressed with the spirituality of the law. 'I had not known sin, unless the law had said, Thou shalt not covet.' In this state of mind he was neither more nor less than a zealous formalist, resting in the correctness of his creed, and the decency of his life, and the strictness of his religious observances, while his heart was far from being right with God; and shared largely in the character which is ascribed to the sect to which he belonged, when it is said of them, that 'they trusted in themselves that they were righteous, and despised others.'

In respect, again, to *his views of Christ and the Gospel*, he was not only an *unbeliever, but a violent persecutor of the Christian Church.* Here is a melancholy combination of apparently opposite and incompatible qualities of character: a learned, religious, moral, and self-righteous man, evincing a disposition to oppress and exterminate the followers of the meek and lowly Jesus. We read that, at Stephen's martyrdom, 'the witnesses laid down their clothes at a young man's feet, whose name was Saul;' and 'that Saul was consenting unto his death.' And during the great persecution which followed, it is said, 'As for Saul, he made havoc of the church, entering into every house, and haling men and women, committed them to prison.' Nay, not content with this, his zeal urged him to proceed further: 'And Saul, yet breathing out threatenings and slaughter against the disciples of the Lord, went unto the high priest, and desired of him letters to Damascus to the synagogues, that if he found any of this way, whether they were men or women, he might bring them bound unto Jerusalem.' On this subject he often expressed, after his conversion, the deepest and most penitential sorrow; and it is clear that herein he acted in opposition to the advice of his great master, Gamaliel (Acts v. 34); yet I apprehend that we are not entitled to regard it as a proof, either that he was naturally cruel in his disposition, or insincere in the profession of his former faith. It is true, indeed, that persecution for conscience' sake can, in no case, be defended, and this was afterwards acknowledged by the apostle himself; but then it ought to be remembered that the principle of toleration was not recognized in the age in which he lived, and never exemplified – whatever may be said of the 'mild spirit of Paganism'[1] – where there was any thing that opposed, and would not coalesce with its polytheism. We are too apt, in judging of Paul's conduct to the primitive Christians, to carry with us all our modern ideas of liberality and mutual toleration, and, by applying these to his case, to draw from it a very harsh and injurious reflection against his character. But it is a well-known historical fact, that some of the most violent persecutors of the Church have been, in their private character, not only devoutly attached to their own religion, but tenderly affectionate to their friends: such, for example, was Marcus Aurelius, in ancient Rome; and Charles the First, and Sir Thomas More, in our own country. They resembled the 'devout and honourable women,' of whom we read in Acts 'that they were stirred up, with the chief men of the city, to raise persecution against Paul and Barnabas, and expelled them out of their coasts.' It was zeal, blended with deplorable ignorance, rather than any ferocious or savage disposition, which in these, and similar cases, led to persecution; and, considering the tenderness of heart and warmth of affection which were subsequently manifested by the apostle of the Gentiles, I cannot help believing that it was the perfect sincerity of his attachment to the law of Moses which prompted him to oppose what he then conceived to be an impious innovation, and that it was his very zeal for what he thought to be the cause of God, which stirred him up to persecute what he no doubt believed to be a dangerous heresy. In most cases of controversy, and especially in those in which controversy ends in persecution, it will generally be found that there is at least an *image* of right and justice for which each party contends; and that zeal for what they conceive to be truth and justice gives them a consciousness of sincerity even in an unholy cause. We might find many illustrations of this remark in the

[1] Edward Gibbon.

controversies of modern times. But in the case before us, I think it is clear that Saul had 'a zeal for God, but not according to knowledge,' that he was ignorantly opposing the same authority which he professed to revere, that the very sincerity of his attachment to the traditions of his fathers made him unapt to entertain the thought, that, in persecuting the followers of Christ, he might probably be found to fight against God; for such is the account which he gave of his present state of mind after his conversion, when, penetrated with a conviction of his guilt, and deeply humbled on account of it, he could still say, 'I verily thought that I *ought*' – a false sense of duty is clearly implied – 'to do many things contrary to the name of Jesus of Nazareth; and many of the saints did I shut up in prison, having received authority of the chief priests; and when they were put to death, I gave my voice against them. And I punished them oft in every synagogue, and compelled them to blaspheme: and being exceedingly mad against them, I persecuted them even unto strange cities.' (Acts 26. 9). And again, 'I was before a blasphemer, and a persecutor, and injurious; but I obtained mercy, because I did it ignorantly, and in unbelief.' (1 Tim. 1. 13).

Such seems to have been the character of Saul; and there is enough in it both to account for his opposition to the Gospel, and to show that he needed, not less than the reckless gaoler at Philippi, or the poor malefactor on the cross, to undergo a great spiritual change before he could enter into the kingdom. His character was, indeed, so respectable, that some, looking only to the fair exterior, may be at a loss to discover in this learned, religious, moral, and self-righteous man, any thing else than his violent opposition to the Gospel, in persecuting its first professors, that called for any change; but, on deeper reflection, they will find cause to believe that his vehement zeal 'in breathing out threatenings and slaughter against the disciples of the Lord,' if it did not necessarily imply a cruel and bloodthirsty disposition, did at least indicate a frame of mind in all respects opposed to the spiritual and benign genius of the Gospel, and that it is to be regarded as the natural fruit and the outward manifestation of a rancorous aversion to the truth as it is in Jesus. It showed that in his heart he was an enemy to Christ and his cause; and there was enough of enmity in his bosom to render regeneration absolutely needful, as well as to account for his zeal in the work of persecution. Learned as he was, his very learning made him look down with contempt and scorn on the illiterate fishermen who had appeared in opposition to the doctrine of the Scribes and Pharisees; religious as he was, his very religion prompted him to oppose a system of doctrine at variance with all his preconceived opinions; moral as he was, his very morality fostered a spirit of self-righteous confidence, which rendered the humbling doctrine of the cross utterly offensive to him; and patriltic as he was, so patriotic that his heart seems to swell when he speaks of 'the Israelites, to whom pertained the adoption, and the glory, and the covenants, and the giving of the law, and the service of God, and the promises,' his personal convictions, his national pride, and his party spirit all combined to exasperate his hatred and excite his contempt for those who represented Jesus of Nazareth as the Messiah that had been promised to the fathers, the Messiah whom he, like most of his countrymen, probably expected as a temporal prince to deliver them from the Roman yoke and establish a powerful monarchy in Judea; and hence, when Jesus appeared, claiming this august character, he might conceive that he was justly condemned, and that his followers might also be put to death as deceivers of the people. In those very features of his character, then, which at first sight seem the most amiable, and the least likely to lead to such a result, we find the very strength and source of his opposition to the Gospel, just as, in modern times, none are more bitter and inveterate against the doctrines of free grace and a life of spiritual religion, than those moral, decent, and self-righteous men, who have a form, while they deny the power of godliness.

But I apprehend that Saul's violent opposition to the truth is to be ascribed, in no small measure, to certain convictions which had been awakened in his conscience by what he had seen and heard of the Gospel, and the conduct of its professors, *convictions* which were not effectual to subdue, but were abundantly sufficient to stir up and exasperate his enmity. It does not appear that he had been present at the crucifixion of Christ; but he was present, as an interested and active spectator, at the death of Stephen, the first martyr for the truth; he had heard his sublime discourse, and looked on his countenance when 'his face seemed as it had been the face of and angel,' and witnessed his triumphant death, when he fell asleep, saying, 'Lord Jesus, receive my Spirit,' and 'Lord, lay not this sin to their charge;' and on a mind like Paul's such a scene must have made some impression. If it did not disarm and subdue, it would excite and exasperate. It might, and probably did, awaken some inward misgiving, some secret suspicion that possibly there might be truth in that Gospel which Stephen sealed with his blood, and some feeling of uneasiness, amounting even to pain, for such is often the effect of conviction awakened in the conscience of unbelieving men, as is remarkably evinced when it is said of those who surrounded Stephen on that memorable occasion, 'When they heard these things, they were cut to the heart, and gnashed on him with their teeth;' and again, of those who listened to the faithful testimony of Peter and the other apostles, 'When they heard that, they were cut to the heart, and took counsel to slay them.' The arrow of conviction, where it fails to bring the sinner bleeding to Christ, saying, 'What must I do to be saved?' seldom fails to exasperate his natural enmity, so as to rouse his violent opposition to Christ and his cause; insomuch that, when at any time we see a man breathing out violence and threatenings against the ministers and people of God, we are ready to think that at one time that sinner must have had an arrow sticking fast in his conscience, and that he is uneasy, and restless, and wretched within, in consequence of its rankling and festering sore. And that Paul had experienced some such convictions, appears, I think, from the language of our Lord,' when he said to him, 'It is hard for thee to kick against the pricks.' It is as if he had been pricked in his heart, and as if he was goaded on to violence and bloodshed by convictions which he was determined to kick against and resist, in so far as they tended to subdue his haughty spirit to the faith and obedience of the Gospel; just as king Saul's persecution of David was stimulated by a secret consciousness of his own guilt, and a lurking suspicion that David was the Lord's Anointed.

II. If we now consider the circumstances which accompanied, and the means which effected his conversion, we shall find that, while it was brought about in a miraculous way, it was the *result of the truth* which was made known to him by the *vision* and the *voice* of the Saviour, and which was carried home to his heart by demonstration of the Spirit and by power from on high. It is said, that 'as he journeyed, he came near Damascus: and suddenly there shined round about him a light from heaven: and he fell to the earth, and heard a voice saying unto him, Saul, Saul, why persecutest thou me?' The miraculous accompaniments of his conversion were the shining light, a 'light above the brightness of the sun,' the supernatural voice, and the sudden infliction of blindness, which was afterwards miraculously cured, when there 'fell from his eyes as it had been scales;' but while these and similar circumstances were useful as subordinate means, in the way of arresting his attention and impressing his conscience and affording evidence for the truth, it was the truth itself, the simple truth as it is in Jesus, which effected the conversion of Paul; and herein it resembles the case of every other sinner.

That truth was presented to him in three distinct *ways:*— 1. It was embodies, as it were, and exhibited in *the vision of Christ*. And that you may understand the suitableness of this manifestation, and what a flood of light it was fitted to pour into his mind, I request you to remember, that as Saul did not at that time believe in Jesus, he must have regarded him as an impostor, who had been justly condemned and put to death; and that his unbelief, which had probably been founded on the extreme humiliation of Christ when he appeared as a 'man of sorrows and acquainted with grief,' was doubtless confirmed by his death and burial, when his enemies seemed to have triumphed over him. And what, then, could be better fitted to un-

deceive him – to convince him of his former error, and to unfold to him the
glorious truth – than the personal appearance of the same Man of Sorrows,
after he had been crucified, in the brightness of his resurrection glory, and
in the dignity of his exaltation? The mere appearance of the Saviour in such
a form contained in it the whole Gospel; it proved as well as exhibited the
truth: it showed that he had risen from the dead, that he had ascended up
on high, that he had been exalted by the right hand of God, and if exalted,
then he was what he professed to be, the Son of God, the Christ, the
Messiah that had been promised to the fathers; nay, that he had finished the
work which the Father had given him to do, that his work had been
accepted, and his reward earned, insomuch that now 'all power was given
to him in heaven and on earth;' and from the cross he had passed to the
throne! All this must have flashed at once on the mind of Saul, as soon as he
was made acquainted with the person who spake to him from amidst that
shining light!

2. While the truth was embodied and exhibited in the vision of Christ,
it was further explained by his *voice*. We find no formal discourse, no full
exposition, no systematic statement of the truth, but a few intimations,
which, when combined with what he then witnessed, and what he afterwards learned, were enough to produce in his mind the faith which is unto
salvation. When he said, 'Who art thou, Lord?' the Lord said, 'I am Jesus
whom thou persecutest: it is hard for thee to kick against the pricks. And he,
trembling and astonished, said, Lord, what wilt thou have me to do? And
the Lord said unto him, Arise, go into the city, and it shall be told thee what
thou must do.' When the voice asked him, 'Saul, Saul, why persecutest
thou me?' he must have had some indistinct impression that it was Jesus who
spoke to him, for he knew in his conscience that he was persecuting his
disciples, and the miraculous vision convinced him that he was in the Divine
presence, for he called him LORD; but when, in answer to his question,
'Who art thou?' he received that express declaration, 'I am Jesus' – or as it is
in the 22nd chapter, 'I am Jesus of Nazareth,' – 'oh! what deep convictions
and emotions must at that instant have rushed into his soul! If Jesus was
indeed alive; if he had really risen from the dead; if he had ascended into
heaven; and if he now stood in his immediate presence, then Saul must
have felt, with all the quickness and certainty of intuition, that in opposing
the Gospel, he was fighting *against God;* and no wonder that he lay on the
earth '*trembling and astonished*,' when he knew that the same Jesus who was
crucified in weakness had been raised in power, and had now come down –
might it not be to judge and destroy? There was, indeed, no word of
threatening, but a pointed question, a touching expostulation, demanding
the reason of his present conduct, in such a way as must have awakened his

conscience to *reprove him of sin.* That he felt the reproof, and was alarmed on account of his guilt and danger, appears from his 'trembling;' but fear is not faith; remorse is not repentance; nor is there sufficient power in mere terror to effect the conversion of the heart. The heart is turned by the attraction of the Saviour's love; and if, on the one hand, the words of Christ served to impress his mind with a very awful sense of his guilt, seeing that they represented his persecution of the Church as equivalent to the per-secution of Christ himself, they were also fitted, on the other hand, to convey to his mind a very vivid idea of the tenderness of his compassion and the riches of his grace. For when the Saviour said, 'I am Jesus whom thou persecutest,' what a discovery was made of his love to his own people ! Saul was not consciously persecuting Christ, he was only pursuing his poor followers; he was in quest of certain *men* and *women* at Damascus, that he might bring them bound to Jerusalem; but when Jesus met him by the way, he did not say to him, Saul, Saul, why persecutest thou *them,* but, Why persecutest thou *me,* intimating thereby that he identifies himself with his people, that in all their affliction he is afflicted, that they were 'members of his body, of his flesh, and of his bones,' that if any one member suffered, the Head sympathized and suffered too, according to his own language in another place: 'Inasmuch as ye did it unto one of the least of these my brethren, ye did it unto me!' But full as it was of love for his people, this language might have only terrified the trembling persecutor, and driven him to the verge of despair, had there been no manifestation of tenderness and compassion to himself: he might have thought, if, in pursuing these men and women, I have been persecuting Christ, the Lord of Glory, there is no hope for me; but immediately Jesus drops a word of kindness, which was as a cordial to his sinking spirit; his very expostulation breathes a spirit of tenderness, and shows that the persecutor had a place in the Saviour's heart; for mark the gracious words, 'It is hard for *thee* to kick against the pricks:' it is hard, not for *me,* whom thou persecutest, not for my poor followers, the men and women whom thou art haling to prison; but, 'it *is* hard for *thee.*' Oh! then, the Saviour had a sympathy even for this sinner; the Prince of Peace was concerned for this persecutor, and spake of the hardship the injury he was doing to himself. And how must this tender-ness have touched his heart, at a time when he was self-convicted, and self-condemned, especially if, by 'kicking against the pricks,' he understood the Lord to mean his resisting the convictions of his conscience, and setting himself in opposition to the truths which he had now been taught. By such means he was at once convinced of his sin and danger, and satisfied of the truth of the Gospel, and instructed in the relation which Christ bears to his people, and the compassion which he felt for himself; and to these means he refers afterwards as having been instrumental in God's hand in bringing him to a knowledge of the truth: 'I certify you, brethren, that the Gospel which was preached of me is not after man. For I neither received it of man, neither was I taught it, but by *the revelation of Jesus Christ.*'

3. While Saul was first brought to the knowledge and belief of the truth by the *vision* and *voice* of the Saviour himself, God was pleased, even in this remarkable case, to put honour on his own ordinance, by employing *the ministry of Ananias* to instruct and confirm him in the faith: Ver. 6, 'The Lord said unto him, Arise and go into the city, and it shall be told thee what thou must do.' Ver. 10, 'And there was a certain disciple, named Ananias, and to him said the Lord in a vision, Ananias! And he said, Behold, I am here, Lord. And the Lord said unto him, Arise, and go into the street which is called Straight, and inquire in the house of Judas for one called Saul of Tarsus: for, behold, he prayeth, and hath seen in a vision a man named Ananias coming in, and putting his hand on him, that he might receive his sight. Then Ananias answered, Lord, I have heard by many of this man, how much evil he hath done to thy saints at Jerusalem: and here he hath authority from the chief priests to bind all that call on thy name. But the Lord said unto him, Go thy way: for he is a chosen vessel unto me, to bear my name before the Gentiles, and kings, and the children of Israel; for I will show him how great things he must suffer for my name's sake. And Ananias went his way, and entered into the house; and putting his hands on him, said, Brother Saul, the Lord, even Jesus, that appeared unto thee in the way as thou camest, hath sent me, that thou mightest receive thy sight, and be filled with the Holy Ghost. And immediately there fell from his eyes as it had been scales: and he received sight forthwith, and arose, and was baptized.'

The words of Ananias, and his very mission to him at such a time, must have enlarged his views, and strengthened his belief of the truth: for he had been taught to expect such a visit from one who should tell him what he ought to do; and when he came, and spoke to him of Jesus who had appeared to him by the way, and wrought a miraculous cure of his blindness, and imparted to him the gift of the Holy Ghost, and accosted him as a brother, and exhorted him to 'arise, and be baptized, and wash away his sins, calling on the name of the Lord,' he could not fail to regard these events as at once a signal proof of divine interposition, and a manifest fulfilment of Christ's promise; and, what was much better fitted at once to subdue and comfort him, as so many precious tokens of the Saviour's care and kindness for himself individually, such as might well awaken the liveliest gratitude, and afford a ground of confidence and hope. For mark the minute knowledge, the personal kindness, the pastoral care of the Lord

Jesus Christ; he keeps his eye on this spirit-stricken penitent as he enters into the crowded city; he marks the street; he singles out the very house in which he takes up his abode, and comes to another disciple, whom he also names, and says, Go, for behold he prayeth!

By these means – by the vision of Christ, by the words he spake, and by the ministry of Ananias – the truth was presented, along with its appropriate evidence, to the mind of Saul; but it is of importance to observe, especially with a view to account for his being immediately employed in the work of preaching the Gospel, that as soon as he was convinced of Jesus being the Messiah, *all his Old Testament knowledge became at once available;* he had now obtained possession of the key which unlocks that storehouse of typical and prophetic instruction; and his previous familiarity with the writings of Moses and the prophets must have qualified him, in no ordinary degree, for understanding, and expounding, and vindicating the Gospel, as soon as he was brought to believe that 'the testimony of Jesus is the spirit of prophecy.'

But neither the *vision* nor the *voice* of Christ, neither the ministry of Ananias nor Saul's familiar acquaintance with the writings of Moses and the prophets, would have availed for effecting his conversion, without the grace of the Holy Spirit. We read that he received *the Holy Ghost;* and if this is to be understood of his supernatural gifts, it is equally certain he must have received his spiritual grace; for he himself testifies, 'By the grace of God I am what I am.' 'It pleased God to reveal his Son in me.' 'God, who commanded the light to shine out of darkness, hath shined in our hearts, giving us the light of the knowledge of the glory of God in the face of Jesus Christ.'

III. If we now inquire into the nature of this great change, or wherein it properly consisted, and the practical results in which it terminated, we shall find that his whole conversion hinged on one point; it depended on his believing that '*Jesus was the Christ.*' A single thought is often the key to a great discovery, and so a single event may be the occasion of a total revolution in the whole opinions, and feelings, and habits of a man. Thus it was with Paul. The single thought that now took possession of his mind, and threw a clear and steady light on the whole scheme of revealed truth, was that Jesus was the Christ of God; and the single event that carried home to his heart a conviction which revolutionized his whole creed, and character, and conduct was the personal appearance of Jesus, once crucified but now exalted, as he journeyed towards Damascus. He saw Jesus – Jesus was then alive; he saw Jesus shining in light above the brightness of the sun, – Jesus was then glorified, and if glorified, his work was accepted, his Gospel true, his authority divine, his power almighty; and that one thought was enough to convert the Pharisee into a penitent, the persecutor into a preacher, the Jewish bigot into a Christian philanthropist. The change was sudden, indeed, but it was also complete; for Christ was above, and the Spirit within him. From that hour he became a 'new creature; old things passed away; all things became new.'

Oh! it is deeply instructive to mark the contrast, in every point of view in which it can be contemplated, betwixt his former and his future character. His life was now turned, as it were, into a new channel. And if his change was sudden, it was also permanent. He had now *new views*, new views of *himself:* 'I was alive without the law once: but when the commandment came, sin revived, and I died.' Once he was a Pharisee, believing himself to be righteous, and despising others; now he is a penitent, confessing himself to be the 'chief of sinners,' and 'less than the least of all saints;' once he was built up in the fond conceit of his own worth, now he accounts it but as filthy rags: 'Though I might also have confidence in the flesh. If any other man thinketh that he hath whereof he might trust in the flesh, I more: circumcised the eighth day, of the stock of Israel, of the tribe of Benjamin, an Hebrew of the Hebrews; as touching the law, a Pharisee.' 'But what things were gain to me, those I counted loss for Christ. Yea, doubtless, and I count all things but loss for the excellency of the knowledge of Christ Jesus my Lord: for whom I have suffered the loss of all things, and do count them but dung, that I may win Christ, and be found in him, not having mine own righteousness, which is of the law, but that which is through the faith of Christ, the righteousness which is of God by faith.' He had new views *of God;* he now saw 'the light of the knowledge of the glory of God in the face of Jesus Christ;' new views of *the law;* he saw it now in its true character, as a ministration of death, a covenant gendering to bondage, a schoolmaster to bring him to Christ; he had new views of the *Gospel,* as God's truth, of Jesus as God's Christ, of his Church as God's people, of the Jews and their fearful guilt, of the Gentiles and their predicted privileges; and his views being thus changed, his affections and aims, his pursuits and pleasures, his habits and his hopes were all alike new, insomuch that the bigoted Jew became the universal philanthropist, exclaiming, 'Is he the God of the Jews only? is he not also of the Gentiles?' and the fierce persecutor became the fervent preacher, exclaiming, 'The weapons of our warfare are not carnal, but spiritual, and mighty through God to the pulling down of strongholds;' and he who breathed out 'threatenings and slaughter, and was exceedingly mad against the people of God,' devoted his life to their service, taking upon him 'the care of all the churches,' 'making himself all things to all men if possibly he might gain some;' and nothing moved by peril and persecution, nor 'counting his life dear unto himself, that he might finish his course with joy, and fulfil the ministry which he had received of the Lord Jesus, to testify the Gospel of the grace of God.'

Need I dwell on the moral and spiritual fruits of his conversion? Read his matchless epistles, study the simple but sublime narrative of his life, and see how brightly and how steadily the fire of divine love, which was first kindled in his breast on his way to Damascus, burned there, and how it continued to brighten and to burn more strongly in the face of all obloquy and opposition and danger, till his warfare was ended, and his soul was joined to the kindred society of seraphic spirits in the sanctuary above. And let those especially who declaim against conversion as a fanatical or enthusiastic dream, and suspect it the more if it be suddenly wrought, behold in the life of Paul the *reality and the practical fruits* of this great change; for the *new life* which he led flowed from his *new birth* on the way to Damascus; this was the fountain, that was the pure and fertilizing stream. His conduct, indeed, had been decent and regular, and in many respects exemplary before; but still his life was changed as well as his heart; it was regulated by new principles, and conversant with other objects, and devoted to higher and better ends, insomuch that now he could say, 'The life which I live in the flesh, I live by the faith of Christ, who loved me, and gave himself for me.'

Many practical lessons might be deduced from this case, as that,

1. A man may be *learned, decent,* and *exemplary* in many things, and yet be destitute of spiritual life, so as to require, not less than the irreligious and immoral, to be converted and renewed. 2. A form of godliness, where its power is absent, is a grievous snare to the soul. 3. A zeal for God may exist which is not according to knowledge, and a man may be sincere in following a course which is leading him down to the chambers of death. 4. Ignorance of the Gospel, combined with the form of religion and a decent moral life, is often observed to issue in inveterate opposition to Christ and his cause, especially where the conscience is weary and restless, by reason of its unappeased convictions. 5. The one truth, that 'Jesus is the Christ,' is sufficient, when it is really believed, at once to lay a solid ground of hope for the sinner, and to change him into a new man. 6. *Faith* works by love, so as to constrain the believer no longer to live unto himself, but unto Him that died for him, and that rose again; and prompts him to make known to others the truth which has brought peace and comfort to his own soul. 7. The *conversion* of Paul is a striking evidence, and *the life* of Paul is a striking illustration, of the power of truth.

IV. The Ethiopian Treasurer: Acts 8.26-40

THE case of the Ethiopian Treasurer affords a beautiful example of the way in which an ignorant, but sincere and devout inquirer, is often led, under the guidance of the Spirit of God, and notwithstanding many unfavourable circumstances in his condition, to a clear and saving knowledge of the truth as it is in Jesus. It belongs to a different class of cases from that to which the Philippian Gaoler, the Dying Malefactor, and Saul the Persecutor, are to be referred, since these memorable characters, while they differ from each other in many respects, agree in this, that each of the three was chargeable with some specific crime of a very aggravated nature – the Gaoler with intentional suicide, the Malefactor with robbery, and Saul with persecution and bloodshed – while nothing is recorded of the Ethiopian that is criminal, and much that is creditable to his character, his main defect being his ignorance of divine truth, and even that he was devoutly seeking to remove. His experience, therefore, is fitted to illustrate the case of such as have long been seeking the truth, but are still 'walking in darkness and having no light;' and it cannot fail, when rightly understood and duly considered, to impart to them a very large measure both of instruction and encouragement.

I. In his *previous state* there were many unfavourable circumstances which might seem to render his conversion a very difficult undertaking, while there were, at the same time, some very hopeful symptoms.

Among the unfavourable circumstances which might seem to present an obstacle to his conversion, and which probably retarded his progress in acquiring a knowledge of the truth, I may mention his *birth and residence* in Ethopia, a land of heathen darkness – at a great distance, probably not less than one thousand miles from Jerusalem, the seat of the true religion; his wordly *wealth*, which is often a snare to the soul (for 'how hardly,' says our Lord himself, 'shall a rich man enter into the kingdom of God;' and again, 'I say unto you, it is easier for a camel to go through the eye of a needle than for a rich man to enter into the kingdom of God;' for not only the cares of the world, but the deceitfulness of riches also, and other lusts, choke the Word and render it unfruitful); and his elevated *rank and extensive influence*, as 'an eunuch of great authority under Candace, queen

[166]

of the Ethiopians.' He belonged to a class of men who exercised almost unlimited power in some of the Eastern nations, and who were notoriously
addicted to intrigue and the other arts of courtly ambition; and this might
be a bar in the way of his spiritual progress (for 'ye see your calling,
brethren, how that not many wise men after the flesh, not many mighty,
not many noble are called; but God hath chosen the foolish things of the
world to confound the wise, and God hath chosen the weak things of the
world to confound the things which are mighty, and base things of the
world, and things which are despised, hath God chosen; yea, and things
which are not, to bring to nought things that are, that no flesh should glory
in his presence.') It is manifest that these, or some other circumstances of a
like nature in his condition, had exerted an injurious influence over him,
and had retarded his progress in the acquisition of religious knowledge; for
he was, as we shall immediately see, lamentably ignorant, notwithstanding
all the efforts he had made; and looking on him as he returned in his chariot
to his native land, we might be ready, in a spirit of hopelessness, to exclaim,
'Can this Ethiopian change his skin?'

But while many circumstances in his outward condition were unfavourable, we cannot read the narrative without discovering some hopeful
symptoms in the state of his mind. For while he was by birth and residence
an Ethiopian Gentile, he was, notwithstanding, both in his creed and in his
profession, a proselyte to the Jewish faith, and a believer in the one only, the
living and the true God. Although surrounded by the forms of polytheistic
superstition, and living in a land of gross spiritual darkness, he had in some
way, not described, become acquainted with the revelation of divine truth
in the Old Testament Scriptures, and his eye had been opened to discern the
true light, so far as to satisfy him that it was the light of heaven. Thus much
is implied in the fact that 'he had come to Jerusalem to worship,' and that on
his return he was engaged in reading the Old Testament Scriptures. And
this instance affords an exemplification and proof of a very delightful truth,
– I mean the extensive influence which was exerted by the Jewish dispensation on the surrounding nations. While it was in some respects
limited and local, as being specially designed for the children of Israel, and
established in the land of Judea, it was nevertheless fitted to instruct other
nations in the grand principles of religious truth, and all the great nations of
antiquity were successively brought into such near contact, and such
familiar intercourse with the Jews, as could not fail to impart to many a
thinking mind amongst them the knowledge of the one living and true
God. In the earlier part of their history, the Jews were connected with the
Egyptians who were the wisest, the Canaanites who were the most war-
like; and the Phœnicians, the most commercial of these nations; and at a

later period, partly by their long captivity, partly by their dispersion and their residence in almost every city, they were intermingled with the Assyrians, the Persians, the Greeks, and the Romans, insomuch that not only was the Old Testament translated into Greek for the use of the Hellenic Jews, but heathenism itself derived from it many useful hints, as well as the materials of many a fable, as is clear in the case of Zoroaster and others. And as the Old Testament dispensation was fitted to exert such an influence over the surrounding nations, so provision was made for the admission of *proselytes* to some, at least, of the privileges and services of the Jewish Church. These proselytes have been divided into two classes, called respectively the proselytes of righteousness and the proselytes of the gate; and these were in the habit of coming up to Jerusalem at the stated festivals as well as the Jews that were scattered abroad; of whom it is said, that on the day of Pentecost, which occurred after the crucifixion of the Saviour, there were then assembled 'Parthians, and Medes, and Elamites, and the dwellers in Mesopotamia, and in Judea, and Cappadocia, in Pontus, and Asia, Phrygia, and Pamphylia, in Egypt, and in the parts of Libya about Cyrene, and strangers of Rome, *Jews* and *proselytes*, Cretes and Arabians,' speaking different languages, but worshipping the same God. The Ethiopian Treasurer was one of these; and his coming out of Ethiopia, and repairing to Jerusalem, was a virtual declaration that his mind could not rest in the popular mythology of his own country, that he saw the error of polytheism, and admitted the cardinal principle of the divine unity, and was in itself a solemn and public testimony to the supremacy of the God of Israel.

While he was, both by conviction and profession, a believer in the one only, the living and the true God, and a proselyte to the Jewish faith, he was also a devout worshipper, and an attendant on the services of the Jewish Church. It is said of him, that 'he had come to Jerusalem to *worship*,' not to inquire merely, still less to speculate or dispute, but to engage in the solemn exercises of public religious worship at one of the greatest festivals of the Jewish Church. It is important to mark this, for it shows that he was already imbued with a *spirit of prayer*, a hopeful symptom in any case, and one of the first in all; for of Paul, Jesus said to Ananias, 'Behold, he prayeth;' – and of Lydia, that 'she attended the apostle's ministry by the water side, where prayer was wont to be made;' and of Cornelius, that 'as he prayed at the ninth hour, the angel of the Lord appeared to him.' True prayer is *never lost;* the cry of an earnest spirit comes in unto God in his holy temple, and in due time will bring down an answer in peace. But 'whoso cometh unto God must believe that he is, and that he is the rewarder of them that diligently seek him;' and what encouragement, then, had this Ethiopian to pray, or what was the ground and warrant of his faith? He was not by birth a Jew; he was 'an alien from the commonwealth of Israel, and a stranger to the covenants of promise;' he had no natural or civil connection with those 'to whom,' (and, as they themselves supposed, to them alone), 'pertained the adoption, and the glory, and the covenants, and the giving of the law, and the service of God, and the promises.' He was a foreigner, an African, a negro, a Gentile, an eunuch, and how, then, could he hope to associate himself with the people of God, and dare to approach his temple? Oh, mark how a simple faith, and a devout spirit, and an earnest mind will surmount a thousand difficulties, and bring a sinner into the way of peace. He *had* a warrant for his faith and hope, – a warrant in the Old Testament Scriptures, which was enough to embolden him to draw nigh. For besides the prayer which was uttered at the dedication of Solomon's temple, in the very book of the prophet Isaiah (56. 3) which he read in his chariot he found this precious word of promise, 'Neither let the son of the stranger, that hath joined himself to the Lord, speak, saying, The Lord hath utterly separated me from his people: neither let the eunuch say, Behold, I am a dry tree. For thus saith the Lord unto the eunuchs that keep my Sabbaths, and choose the things that please me, and take hold of my covenant; even unto them will I give in mine house and within my walls a place and a name better than of sons and of daughters: I will give them an everlasting name, that shall not be cut off. Also the sons of the stranger, that join themselves to the Lord, to serve him, and to love the name of the Lord, to be his servants, every one that keepeth the Sabbath from polluting it, and taketh hold of my covenant; even them will I bring to my holy mountain, and make them joyful in my house of prayer: their burnt-offerings and their sacrifices shall be accepted upon mine altar; for mine house shall be called an house of prayer for all people.' This man was both an eunuch and a stranger; and, being such, he knew that this promise comprehended him; and in the faith of it he came to Jerusalem, and worshipped the God of Israel there.

Besides a spirit of prayer, he had also a spirit of *diligent inquiry*, combined with that humility and teachableness which may be justly regarded as the most hopeful symptoms of a great and blessed change. That he had an inquiring and docile mind appears not only from his going up from Ethiopia to Jerusalem, a distance of about a thousand miles, passing from Africa to Asia, and leaving for a time the cares of his honourable and re-sponsible office, that he might be present at the Feast of Pentecost, but still more strikingly from the manner in which he was occupied on his return from Jerusalem: instead of casting aside his religion when the festival was over, or allowing his mind to be diverted to other objects, 'he sat in his chariot reading the prophet Isaiah.' Probably he read aloud, for the benefit of his attendants; at all events he had his Bible in his hand, and was engaged in reading its sacred contents; so that he had himself procured a copy of the Scriptures for his own use – a roll which must have been written by himself, or obtained at great expense, – and which he carried with him as his companion by the way. But even this is not so remarkable as the humility and teachableness with which he received Philip, a stranger, and one who, perhaps, was neither in point of dress nor manners likely to attract the regard of a man of rank and station. Yet, when he joined himself to the chariot, and ventured to ask the question, 'Understandest thou what thou readest?' instead of spurning the question, he replied with child-like humility, 'How can I, except some man should guide me,' and he requested Philip that 'he would come up and sit with him.'

While there were several hopeful symptoms in this state of mind, it was manifest that he was still extremely *ignorant of the truth*. He was not only destitute of all knowledge of Christ and the Gospel, but he had no correct apprehension of the spiritual meaning of the Old Testament in which he professed to believe, and which, in the midst of much remaining darkness, he still continued to read. For when, after reading a part of the 53d chapter of Isaiah, he put the question, 'I pray thee, of whom speaketh the prophet this? of himself, or of some other man?', his language, if it indicate a spirit of sincere inquiry, betrays also a lamentable degree of ignorance, and makes it manifest that he was still in a condition like that of the Jews themselves, of whom it is said by the apostle, 'Their minds were blinded: for until this day remaineth the same veil untaken away in the reading of the Old Testament; which veil is done away in Christ. But even unto this day, when Moses is read, the veil is upon their heart.' His language seems to indicate that he had no acquaintance with the spiritual import of the Old Testament, and that, if he was attached to the Jewish faith, he adhered to it chiefly as a sublime system of religion which taught his duty to the one living and true God, but without any intelligent apprehension of its connection with the scheme of grace and redemption, or the work of Messiah who had been promised to the fathers.

II. If we now consider the manner in which he was brought to a saving knowledge of the truth, we shall find an interesting and encouraging exemplification of the care with which God provides for the instruction of a sincere inquirer, although he may be placed in circumstances apparently the most unpromising. The Ethiopian had just been at Jerusalem, where the mighty moral movement had already begun which was destined to revolutionize the world. He had been at Jerusalem, where Immanuel, God manifest in the flesh, had preached, and suffered, and died, and risen again from the dead. And he had been at Jerusalem at the Feast of Pentecost, when the promise of the Father was fulfilled by the descent of the Holy Spirit in the miraculous gift of tongues, and three thousand souls were converted in a single day. It cannot be supposed that a stranger of rank and influence, possessing, as he no doubt did, many facilities of intercourse with the leading men at Jerusalem, could fail to hear, during his sojourn in that city, the numerous reports about Jesus which were then circulating in the country, and especially in the capital, of Judea. It is evident, however, from the narrative before us, that he had left Jerusalem without acquiring a knowledge of the truth as it is in Jesus. He had been in the holy city where Christ himself had ministered, and where his apostles were now proclaiming the Gospel of the kingdom, and had left it, perhaps for ever, and now he was on his way back again to that land of spiritual darkness, where he could have no reasonable prospect of enjoying such opportunities of grace as Jerusalem afforded. But God himself had given him a spirit of inquiry and a spirit of prayer; and although his journey to Jerusalem had not led him to find what he was seeking, God, whose ways are not as man's ways, sent it to him in the midst of a desert, when his back was turned on Jerusalem, and he was returning to a land of darkness. God met him in the desert of Gaza, and he was converted there! And there is much in the narrative that is fitted to impress our minds with a sense of the lively interest and the tender solicitude with which God regards and provides for the instruction of a single soul. First of all, there is the ministry of an angel: 'The angel of the Lord spake unto Philip;' 'For there is joy in the presence of the angels of God over one sinner that repenteth;' and 'are they not all ministering spirits sent forth to minister to them that are the heirs of salvation?' *2nd*, There is the ministry of an evangelist, specially commissioned to attend to this individual; and it is very remarkable, as evincing God's watchful solicitude for a single soul, that Philip was commanded to leave his work at Jerusalem and in the villages of Samaria, and to go unto the desert, at a time when multitudes were attending his ministry, and when his labours there appeared to be remarkably blessed, for it is said, 'Then Philip went down to the city of Samaria, and preached Christ unto them. And the people with one accord gave heed unto those things which Philip spake, hearing and seeing the miracles which he did; and there was great joy in that city.' And afterwards 'they returned to Jerusalem, and preached the Gospel in many cities of the Samaritans.' Yet, for the sake of one humble inquirer, who had come to Jerusalem to worship, and was returning through the desert to a land of darkness, but reading his Bible by the way, an angel was sent from heaven; and Philip was taken away from the crowd who listened to him at Jerusalem and Samaria, that he might minister the word of life to one benighted soul! And, lastly, the Spirit of God was there, in that dreary desert, watching over this prayerful man, even that blessed Spirit who 'leadeth the blind by a way that they know not, and maketh darkness light before them, and crooked things straight.' The Spirit directed Philip: 'Go near, and join thyself to this chariot.' The Spirit enabled him to speak a word in season, and the Spirit gave the hearing ear and the understanding heart; and then, when the work was done, he withdrew the human agent to follow his Master's service in another place. Such was the agency employed for the instruction of the Ethiopian eunuch. And can we consider it in connection with the circumstances which have been described without regarding it as a very affecting proof of the solicitude with which God cares for every inquiring soul, and a most encouraging fulfilment of God's promise, 'Then shall ye know, if ye follow on to know the Lord?'

But while the ministry both of an angel and an evangelist, and the agency of the Holy Spirit, are expressly declared to have been employed on this occasion, you will observe that the means by which his conversion was effected was simply the truth as it is in Jesus. And herein it resembles the conversion of every other sinner. Having mentioned that the place of the Scriptures which he read was the 53rd chapter of Isaiah, the narrative adds (ver. 35), 'Then Philip opened his mouth and began at the same Scripture, *and preached unto him Jesus.*' It were easy to show, by an analysis of that chapter, that it afforded ample materials for a full exposition of the Gospel; for it is an eminent prediction of Christ, a prediction so full, indeed, and yet so minute and circumstantial, that the enemies of our faith have declared that it must be regarded as a history rather than as a prophecy. It predicts almost every fact, and sets forth every doctrine connected with the person, the offices, and the work of Christ, as: the unbelief of the Jews, ver. 1; the reason of that unbelief, ver. 2; the sufferings and rejection of Christ, ver. 3; the cause of his sufferings, ver. 4, 5, 6; the patience of the Sufferer, ver. 7; the condemnation and death of Christ, ver. 8; his burial, ver. 9; his resurrection, ver. 10; his reward, ver. 11; and the reason of his reward in connection with the end of his death, ver. 12. All this was predicted by the prophet; and the apostle could tell how minutely it was fulfilled in the person and history of Jesus.

III. In regard to the nature of the change which was then wrought on the Ethiopian, and the practical results which flowed from it, I apprehend that it properly consisted in his believing that '*Jesus is the Christ;*' in so believing this as that he received and embraced him in all the fulness of his offices as the Lord's Anointed. For, on asking to be baptized – a request which plainly implies that he had been instructed in the nature and emblematic meaning of that sacred rite, and also felt that he needed to 'wash away his sins' – Philip said, 'If thou believest with all thine heart, thou mayest;'

and he answered and said, 'I believe that Jesus Christ is the Son of God.' This confession of faith, short and simple as it is, contains the sum and substance of all Gospel truth.

The immediate effect of his faith was a request that he might be baptized; and his baptism is at once a manifestation of his *faith*, and also a proof of his new obedience and submission to the *authority* of Christ. He was not ashamed to own, by this visible act, his attachment to Christ and the Gospel.

Being baptized, 'he went on his way rejoicing;' – he felt that the Gospel was glad tidings of great joy; from the instant when he believed it, it became the joy and the rejoicing of his heart; and, doubtless, 'the joy of the Lord was his strength,' fitting him for the right discharge of every commanded duty, and the patient endurance of every appointed trial, – so that he 'could run in the way of his commandments, when God had enlarged his heart.'

We learn from this interesting narrative that God is no respecter of persons, but that men of every nation, and colour, and clime, may become partakers of his grace; that a long preparatory work often precedes a sinner's conversion; that a conscientious and prayerful spirit is a hopeful symptom; that this may exist where as yet there is little light; that a sinner's circumstances, however unfavourable, are no bar to his progress, if only he seek and obtain the direction and blessing of God; that 'the truth as it is in Jesus' is the simple means of conversion; that the Gospel is glad tidings, and no sooner is it believed that the sinner *may 'go on his way rejoicing,'* for it is, capable of imparting immediate peace and joy in believing; that abundance of privileges may fail in working that change which may be brought about in more unfavourable circumstances, for the Ethiopian left Jerusalem unconverted, and was converted in a desert; that a diligent attention to the means of grace, accompanied with prayer, will sooner or later be crowned with a blessing; and yet, that an inquiring, prayerful, and exemplary man, may need to undergo a great spiritual change.

V. Cornelius: Acts 10

At the period of our Lord's advent, there existed amongst the Jews the same diversities of opinion and character as are found amongst ourselves at the present day, and the men to whom he preached were in very different states of preparation for the Gospel of the kingdom. There were Sadducees then, as there are sceptics now, who doubted or disbelieved the truth as it had been revealed by Moses and the prophets; there were Pharisees then, as there are formalists now, who rested in the form, whilst they denied the power of godliness; there were Pilates, who asked, 'What is truth?' and Gallios, who 'cared for none of these things.' But there were also not a few whose hearts the Lord had touched, and who waited, in faith and hope, for 'the consolation of Israel.' There were such men both among the Jews and Gentiles. Among the Jews we read of Zacharias and his wife Elizabeth, 'who were both righteous before God, walking in all the commandments and ordinances of the Lord blameless;' and Mary, the mother of Jesus, whose song breathes the spirit of genuine piety when she exclaimed, 'My soul doth magnify the Lord, and my spirit hath rejoiced in God my Saviour;' and Simeon, of whom it is said, that 'the same man was just and devout, waiting for the consolation of Israel: and the Holy Ghost was upon him;' and Anna the prophetess, 'a widow of about fourscore and four years, who departed not from the temple, but served God with fastings and prayers night and day, and spake of Christ to all them that looked for redemption in Jerusalem;' and Nathanael, of whom our Lord himself said, 'Behold an Israelite indeed, in whom is no guile!' And among the Gentiles, we read of the Ethiopian who came up to Jerusalem to worship, and on his return read in his chariot the Book of Isaiah the prophet; and of Cornelius, a Roman centurion, and a devout soldier who waited upon him, 'a devout man, and one that feared God with all his house, who gave much alms to the people, and prayed to God alway.' In these cases we have a most precious exemplification of the spiritual life which still existed in the bosom of the Jewish Church, and of the blessed fruits which had sprung from the faith of the Old Testament; and it is delightful to discover such instances of genuine piety in the retired walks of private life, at a time when their national character had been sadly deteriorated, and the scribes and rulers and Pharisees had made the commandment of God of none effect by their traditions. There was still amongst them a blessed remnant, a peculiar people, who cherished the faith and walked in the footsteps of faithful Abraham. And it is deeply interesting to mark that as they were prepared, on the one hand, by their spiritual acquaintance with the truth as it had been revealed in the Old Testament, for the reception of any other revelation which God might be pleased to make; so God was pleased to manifest the utmost care for them, and to give them the earliest and best opportunities of acquiring a knowledge of the truth as it is in Jesus, thereby fulfilling the law of his spiritual administration, 'To him that hath shall be given, and he shall have more abundantly, while from him that hath not shall be taken away that which he seemeth to have.'

Of this we have a very remarkable instance in the narrative which relates to the experience of Cornelius, at the time when he was made acquainted with the full truth of the Gospel, and a change was wrought upon him, which cannot, I think, be considered as a case of *conversion*, for he was already a devout believer, but as a case of *advancement*, or of *translation* from the lower form of the Jewish to the higher form of the Christian faith, but still in the same school and under the same teacher. This will become apparent, if we consider,

I. His state and character previous to the time when this change occurred. He was by birth a Gentile, by profession a soldier; but notwithstanding the disadvantages to which he was thus subjected, he had become a proselyte to the Jewish faith, and believed in and worshipped 'the one only, the living and true God.' His character is thus described: 'A devout man, and one that feared God with all his house, which gave much alms to the people, and prayed to God alway;' and again, 'A just man, and one that feareth God, and of good report among all the nation of the Jews.' I need not dwell on the proof which these words afford of his being a believer in the Jewish religion, and a worshipper of the true God. Suffice it to say, that such language is never applied in Scripture to any idolater or heathen; and that *his* was not a mere natural religion appears from its being incidentally mentioned that 'at the ninth hour of the day he was praying in his house,' the hour of evening sacrifice among the Jews, when such as were not present at the temple prayed at home, as we read, 'Peter and John went up together into the temple at the *hour of prayer*, being the ninth hour.' And as he conformed to the Jewish worship, so it is evident that his prayers were addressed to the God of Israel; and not only so, but that they were accepted of him, for the angel said to him, 'Thy prayers and thine alms are come up for a memorial before God,' whence we infer that he must have been a genuine believer and a justified man, since 'without faith it is impossible to please

God; for he that cometh to God must believe that he is, and that he is the rewarder of them that diligently seek him.' He was acquainted, then, with God's revealed truth, as it had been made known by Moses and the prophets, and had embraced it with a lively faith which led him to fast and pray, and to care for the religious instruction of his family. And loving God, he loved his neighbour also, for he 'gave much alms to the people;' nay, it would seem that he was not altogether ignorant of the Gospel itself, although he had not been fully instructed or firmly established in the belief of its truth, for when Peter came to him, he said, 'The word which God sent unto the children of Israel, preaching peace by Jesus Christ (he is Lord of all): that word *ye know*, which was published throughout all Judea, and began from Galilee, after the baptism which John preached.' We are to consider him, I apprehend, as a Gentile proselyte to the Jewish faith, who, without submitting to the rite of circumcision – for we learn that he was uncircumcised, from the objection to Peter's conduct which was afterwards founded on this consideration – did nevertheless embrace the faith of the Jewish Church, and worship the God of Israel, being encouraged, doubtless, by the gracious provision which had been made for the admission of strangers to a participation in its privileges (2 Kings 8. 41; Isa. 56. 6); and as a devout and conscientious man, who acted up to the light he had, and waited for more, listening to the reports which had reached him of the miracles and preaching of Jesus, but without having yet arrived at a clear apprehension or certain belief of the Gospel. And on the whole, he may be regarded as a believer, in the same sense in which Abraham was a believer, or the cloud of witnesses mentioned in the 11th of the Hebrews, who 'all died in faith, not having received the promises, but having seen them afar off, and were persuaded of them, and embraced them, and confessed that they were strangers and pilgrims on the earth;' and being a believer, he was justified and accepted, as they were, by faith in God's covenant promise; nay, as many were who, like himself, were not Jews, but sinners of the Gentiles, for there was a promise before the law was given, even the first promise, that 'the seed of the woman should bruise the serpent's head;' and that promise, with the accompanying rite of sacrifice which prefigured 'the Lamb slain from the foundation of the world,' afforded a sufficient object of faith, and a solid ground of hope, to many who had no natural connection with Abraham and his family. By this faith Melchizedek was justified, and Jethro the father-in-law of Moses, and Rahab before she had any interest in Israel; nay, Abraham himself, before he was circumcised; for, says the apostle, 'Faith was reckoned to Abraham for righteousness. How was it then reckoned? when he was in circumcision, or in uncircumcision? Not in circumcision, but in uncircumcision. And he received the sign of circum-

cision, a seal of the righteousness of the faith which he had yet being uncircumcised, that he might be the father of all them that believe, though
they be not circumcised, that righteousness might be imputed unto them
also; and the father of circumcision to them who are *not* of the circumcision
only, but who also walk in the steps of that faith of our father Abraham,
which he had being yet uncircumcised.' Such seems to have been the state
of Cornelius previous to the events which are recorded in the chapter before
us. But here a question may arise: If he was already a believer and a justified man, what necessity existed for any change such as is here described,
and especially for the employment of agency so various and so extraordinary as is said to have been put in motion for his instruction and improvement? Some have supposed that, had he died in his present state, he
must have perished,[1] founding mainly on an expression which occurs in
the following chapter, where Peter, rehearsing what had occurred, represents the angel as having said to Cornelius, 'Send men to Joppa, and call for
Simon, whose surname is Peter, who shall tell thee words whereby thou
and all thy house *shall be saved.*' Hence it has been inferred that he had not
yet acquired a saving knowledge of divine truth, nor entered on a state of
acceptance with God; but I apprehend the expression admits of being
understood in a sense which does not necessarily imply what is thus
ascribed to it, while the whole description which is given of his character
seems very plainly to imply the reverse.[2] The centurion, we believe, was
at that time in a state of *transition* from the Jewish to the Christian faith; and
the change which now occurred in his views ought to be regarded as his
advancement from an imperfect to a more perfect state, rather than as his
first conversion to God. He underwent precisely the same change which
was wrought on all the devout Jews who 'looked for redemption in
Jerusalem' and 'waited for the consolation of Israel,' when, having long
expected the promised Messiah, they were led to believe that Jesus was he.
That God would send a deliverer, was the subject of their faith as Jews;
that 'Jesus was the Christ,' became the subject of their faith as Christians.
Before he knew Christ, and while as ye under the influence of prejudice,
and saying, 'Can any good thing come out of Galilee?', Nathanael was 'an
Israelite indeed, in whom was no guile;' but when Jesus spoke to him, and
convinced him of his omniscient knowledge by a few simple words, he

---

[1] 'Cornelius had not, as yet, the knowledge of the Gospel of Jesus. He was not
even a Jew. He was a Gentile Roman, but had turned from the pagan idolatries to
pray to the true God. He was not, therefore, saved. Had he died in that state, he would
not have had salvation.' *Conversion*, J. K. Craig, vol. ii. p. 256.

[2] See Robert Haldane's *Evidences*, vol. ii. p. 429.

believed and exclaimed, 'Rabbi, thou art the Son of God; thou art the King of Israel.' Just such was the change which was wrought on Cornelius, the devout Gentile believer, and it was needful that such a change should be effected, for two *reasons*, one of which was personal to himself, the other of a more public nature. It was necessary for himself that he should now believe the truth as it is in Jesus; it was no longer true that God would send a deliverer – the Deliverer had already come; and from the time of his advent it became necessary to believe and acknowledge that 'Jesus is the Christ.' Had he died before Christ's advent, or even after his advent, but before he had any sufficient information on the subject, he might have been saved as Abraham was, and all the faithful children of Abraham were, by the faith of what God had promised to the fathers; but had he rejected Christ, or refused to believe in him, when he had been fully informed of all that he did and taught, his unbelief would have been fatal, not only because it rejected the Saviour, but also because it indicated the absence of that spirit of faith in the true meaning of the Old Testament itself, which, wherever it existed, was invariably found to embrace the Gospel when it was first proclaimed. There was an affinity betwixt the faith of a spiritual Jew or proselyte, and the faith of the New Testament, in virtue of which the one led on to the other, and found in it, not a new creed, but the completion, the perfecting of the old one. But the events which are recorded in this chapter were not designed exclusively, nor, perhaps, chiefly, for the personal benefit of Cornelius and his family; they were designed to subserve an end of the highest importance, and of a public nature, with reference to the Church at large; to make it manifest that the 'middle wall of partition,' which had long divided the Jews from the Gentiles, had been taken down; that in Christ 'there is neither Jew nor Greek, circumcision nor uncircumcision, bond nor free, but Christ is all and in all;' and that the Christian Church was to be truly catholic, as comprehensive of all nations and peoples and tongues, the Gentiles being admitted on an equal footing with the Jews to a participation of its holiest privileges, and a share in its highest hopes.

II. This leads me to consider the circumstances which accompanied, and the means which effected the change in the centurion's views and profession, when, from being a Jewish proselyte, he became a Christian convert. In the accompanying circumstances, many of which were miraculous, we have a beautiful example of the concurrence of various means towards the accomplishment of one end, such as affords a most interesting illustration of the working of God's providence. For one day at Cæsarea, about 75 miles from Jerusalem, a vision appeared to Cornelius, instructing him to send messengers to Joppa, and to call for one Simon, whose surname was Peter.

Next day, while the messengers were on their way, Peter went up to the house-top to pray, about the sixth hour, and he had the vision as it were of a great sheet descending from heaven, and containing all manner of beasts, accompanied with the command, 'Arise, Peter, kill and eat;' and when he objected, saying, 'Not so, Lord, for I have never eaten any thing common or unclean,' the voice answered, 'What God hath cleansed, that call not thou common:' this was done thrice, and the vessel was received up again into heaven. And while Peter doubted in himself what this vision which he had seen should mean, the messengers arrived, and furnished, unconsciously, a key for its explanation; for their words seem immediately to have suggested to his mind the true meaning of the vision, as appears from his language, when he said to Cornelius and his friends, 'Ye know how that it is an unlawful thing for a man that is a Jew to keep company or come unto one of another nation; but God hath showed me that I should not call any man common or unclean.' And when, after he declared the Gospel, 'the Holy Ghost fell on all them that heard the word,' so that 'they began to speak with tongues and magnify God,' the whole purpose of God in this series of visions was made clear, even that the Gentiles should be admitted, as well as the Jews, to the privileges and hopes of the Christian Church. All this was implied in the vision of the sheet which descended from heaven and contained all manner of four-footed beasts, for the distinction betwixt clean and unclean animals had been purposely adopted as a mark of separation betwixt the Jews and the Gentiles, as we learn from the law of Moses: 'I am the Lord your God, who have *separated* you from all other people. Ye shall *therefore* put difference between clean beasts and unclean, and between unclean fowls and clean: and ye shall not make your souls abominable by beast, or by fowl, or by any manner of living thing that creepeth on the ground, which I have separated from you as unclean. And ye shall be holy unto me: for I the Lord am holy, and have severed you from other people, that ye should be mine.' So long as the distinction subsisted betwixt the clean and the unclean beasts and fowls, a wall of partition interposed to divide and separate the Gentile from the Jew; but when the sheet descended, containing all manner of beasts, and creeping things, and fowls, and Peter was commanded to kill and eat – and when, in answer to his objection that 'he had never eaten any thing common or unclean,' he was told, 'What God hath cleansed, that call not thou common,' he was thereby significantly informed, not merely that the distinction of meats should now cease, but that the Old Testament dispensation was passing away, and that the separation betwixt Jew and Gentile, which that distinction marked and tended to perpetuate, was now to be completely and for ever abolished. And this great lesson was taught by a series of successive events, all distinct and independent of each other, but concurring by a most marvellous *coincidence* to the accomplishment of the same end, insomuch that the apostle's mind must have been as much impressed by the leadings of God's providence as by the express declaration of his will, with the belief of the great catholic truth, that the Christian Church was to comprehend both Jew and Gentile, and that they were all 'one in Christ.'

While these circumstances accompanied, and were subservient to the change which was wrought on his views and sentiments, the means by which it was properly effected was the truth declared by the apostle and applied by the Holy Spirit. The message which Peter delivered was in all respects suitable to his case. It contained (1) an unequivocal *recognition of Cornelius*, and other believing Gentiles, as belonging to the Church of God and accepted of Him. 'Then Peter opened his mouth, and said, Of a truth I perceive that God is no respecter of persons; but in every nation he that feareth him, and worketh righteousness, is accepted of him.' In these words the apostle clearly intimates the delightful truth, that the Church of God is catholic, and comprehends all believers, of whatever country, colour, or clime, – a truth which the Jews and the apostles themselves were slow to entertain, and which probably had first been carried home to the mind of Peter by the memorable incidents recorded in the chapter before us. Peter was employed on that occasion, and was the appointed agent in effecting a great change in the constitution of the Church, by the admission of Gentiles to the privilege of baptism; so that were the words of our Lord, when he said, 'Thou art Peter, and on this rock will I build my Church, and the gates of hell shall not prevail against her,' considered as having some reference to the person, as well as to the confession, of that apostle, we should find a sufficient fulfilment of the prediction in the fact, that Peter was actually employed to found the Catholic Church, and had thus a distinguished pre-eminence, although he could claim no primacy over the rest of the apostles. But however this may be, it is clear that Peter now understood and declared the great truth, that the middle wall of partition betwixt Jews and Gentiles was removed, and that 'in every nation he that feareth God, and worketh righteousness, is accepted of him.'

His words, however, on this memorable occasion have been grievously perverted; and *several false inferences* have been drawn from them. Some, considering Cornelius as a Gentile, and founding on his declared acceptance with God, have inferred the sufficiency of mere natural religion, and the in-difference or non-importance of all varieties of creeds, provided only they who profess them be sincere. This monstrous heresy, which prevails so extensively in the world, and which has sometimes been presented, with the fascinations of poetry, to the public mind – as when it is said,

'For modes of faith let graceless zealots fight,
He can't be wrong whose life is in the right'

– this grievous error is utterly repudiated by every Christian mind which
really believes the truth, and appreciates the value of the Gospel. The
Church of England does not hesitate to say, in her Articles, 'that they are to
be held accursed who presume to say, that every man shall be saved by the
law or sect which he professeth, so that he be diligent to frame his life
according to that law, and the light of nature;' and most assuredly, the
sentiment which is here so pointedly denounced derives no support or
countenance from the case of Cornelius. For the religion of Cornelius was
not derived solely, nor even chiefly, from the volume of Nature: it was
drawn from the revelation of God's truth in the Old Testament Scriptures,
with which he had become acquainted during his residence in Palestine, and
which had already converted him from the Gentile to the Jewish faith; and
so far from representing the knowledge and belief of the truth as a matter of
indifference, the narrative shows with what solicitude and care God
provided for the *further instruction* of Cornelius, with a view to his advancement, when he vouchsafed a series of supernatural visions, and employed
the ministry of Peter, and granted the gift of the Holy Ghost, in order that
the Jewish proselyte might become a Christian convert, a baptized professor of the Gospel. When, therefore, the apostle said, 'Of a truth I perceive
that God is no respecter of persons; but in every nation he that feareth him,
and worketh righteousness, is accepted of him,' he did not mean to intimate
that the privileges of salvation were extended indiscriminately to all men
without reference to their religious creed, as if they might be safe under any
form of natural religion, while they were ignorant of the Gospel; but simply
that these privileges, and the knowledge and faith with which they are
inseparably connected, were not confined to the nation of the Jews, but
extended to true converts from every nation under heaven.

Still less does the narrative afford any countenance to another erroneous
opinion which it has sometimes been employed to support, the opinion
that a *moral life* will render a man acceptable to God, independently of
religion; and that it matters little whether he be religious or no, provided
only his conduct be decent and exemplary. For whatever virtues are here
ascribed to Cornelius – his justice, his charity, and his social respectability –
were the fruits of religious principle, and inseparably combined with the
fear of God, and the faith of divine truth, and the habit of prayer; so that
those men of mere morality, who, from taste or education or the influence
of worldly prudence, or the example of others, maintain a decent exterior,
while they are utterly irreligious and live without prayer and without

God in the world, cannot justly found any hope of acceptance on the case of Cornelius, of whom it is said, that he was a devout or *godly man*, 'and one that feared God with all his house, and gave much alms to the people, and prayed to God alway.'

Nor does this narrative afford any countenance to the legal or self-righteous doctrine which represents the graces and virtues of a man's character as the ground of his acceptance with God. It is true that the angel refers to the devotion, and the alms, and the prayers of Cornelius, and declares 'that they had come up for a memorial before God,' just as we learn that, at the last day, the Judge will refer to the conduct of his believing people in feeding the hungry, and clothing the naked, as the proper fruit and evidence of their faith and love; but the sole ground of their acceptance is the redemption of Christ; and surely no one can imagine that the good qualities which are here ascribed to Cornelius were the meritorious cause of his salvation, when Peter was sent to speak to him as a sinner, and to tell him that, 'through Christ's name, whosoever believeth in him shall receive *remission of sins*.' The prayers and the alms of Cornelius are not referred to as being the grounds of his pardon, for that rested solely on the redemption of Christ, but as being the evidences of his faith in the promise of a Saviour; a faith which God graciously rewarded by making known to him the fulfilment of that promise in the person of Christ.

The message of Peter, while it contained an unequivocal recognition of Cornelius and other Gentile believers as belonging to the Church of God, presented also to his mind (2) *a summary of Gospel truth, accompanied with its appropriate evidence*, with the view of convincing him that 'what God had promised to the fathers,' he had so fulfilled in the person of Christ. The Gospel properly consists in the doctrine of Christ, in his person, offices, work, and reward; and all these points of Gospel truth are presented in the short but comprehensive statement of the apostle. He intimates the *personal dignity* of Christ: 'He is Lord of all;' his *humiliation*, as 'Jesus of Nazareth;' his *divine mission*, for 'God sent the word unto the children of Israel, preaching peace by Jesus Christ;' his *divine unction* with the Holy Ghost, whereby he became the Christ, the Lord's Anointed, for 'God anointed Jesus of Nazareth with the Holy Ghost, and with power;' his *holy life* and *beneficent ministry*, 'Who went about doing good, and healing all that were oppressed of the devil, for God was with him;' his *miraculous power*, 'For we are witnesses of all things which he did, both in the land of the Jews and in Jerusalem;' his ignominious and painful *death*, Whom they slew, and hanged on a tree;' his *resurrection* from the dead, and manifestation to his disciples, 'Him God raised up the third day, and showed him openly, not to all the people, but unto witnesses chosen before of God; even to us, who did eat and drink with him after he rose from the dead;' his *commission* to the apostles, 'He commanded us to preach unto the people, and to testify that it is he who was ordained of God to be the Judge of quick and dead;' and, finally, *the sum and substance of the Gospel*, the same Gospel which had been preached beforehand to Abraham, but was now more fully unfolded, 'To him gave all the prophets witness, that through his name whosoever believeth in him shall receive remission of sins.' Even this brief analysis, without any detailed exposition of Peter's address, may suffice to show how pregnant it is with all Gospel truth, and how admirably suitable to the case of Cornelius. He was a devout man, a proselyte to the Jewish faith, and one that waited for the consolation of Israel. He had even heard – for the apostle speaks of him as 'knowing' – the word which God sent unto the children of Israel, preaching peace by Jesus Christ; but probably he had not had an opportunity of satisfying himself as to the truth of the Gospel, and was waiting, in a prayerful spirit, for further instruction and clearer light. And while he waited and prayed, God sent this message, and prepared the way for it by those visions, first to himself and afterwards to Peter, which afford such an affecting proof of God's solicitude and care for every humble inquirer. And the message was in every respect suited to his case; for it made known to him the meaning and substance of the Gospel, of which it contains two brief but most comprehensive summaries, being described in the one as *God's proclamation of peace through Jesus Christ* (ver. 36), and in the other as a message which declares 'that through his name *whosoever believeth in him shall receive remission of sins;'* and, secondly, it made known to him the *evidence* by which the truth as it is in Jesus is certified as of divine and infallible authority; for he appeals to God's testimony, who 'anointed him with the Holy Ghost,' and who was with him in his mighty works; to the testimony of the apostles, who were eye-witnesses of his miracles, and conversed with him after his resurrection; and to the concurrent witness of ancient prophecy, for 'the testimony of Jesus is the spirit of prophecy.' And when this reference to the evidence which arises from God's testimony, and that of his inspired apostles and prophets, was immediately followed up by the descent of the Holy Ghost, insomuch that 'while Peter yet spake, the Holy Ghost fell on all them which heard the word; so that they of the circumcision which believed were astonished, as many as came with Peter, because that on the Gentiles also was poured out the gift of the Holy Ghost; for they heard them speak with tongues, and magnify God,' need we wonder that Cornelius at once embraced the Gospel, and entered, by baptism, into the Christian Church?

The Holy Spirit was the agent by whom Cornelius was convinced and established; partly by his miraculous gifts, which are no doubt intended in the narrative, and which afforded evidence on which his faith might securely rest; but partly, also, by his spiritual grace, accompanying the preaching of the Word, by which he was enabled to believe to the saving of his soul.

III. As to the nature of the change which was now wrought on the mind of Cornelius, and its practical results in his life and conversation, it properly consisted in his being enabled to believe that the Messiah whom God had promised to the fathers, and whom, as a believer in Old Testament prophecy, he had long expected, had actually come, and that Jesus of Nazareth was he. The whole of Peter's message is directed to the establishment of this great truth, that 'Jesus is the Christ;' and the cordial reception of that truth in its full Gospel import constituted the change which now passed on the mind of the devout centurion.

In the case of one who had previously been so conscientious, and whose whole character was consistent with his profession as a Jewish proselyte, there was no room for such a striking manifestation of the change which is wrought by conversion, as in the case of the Philippian gaoler, or even of Saul of Tarsus. But it was doubtless attended, even in his experience, with a very great and happy change; for not only is it said that 'he was baptized,' in token alike of his *faith* in Christ and his *submission* to Christ's command, but that he and his household *'glorified God.'*

We have here a beautiful exemplification of the way in which the providence of God works in different places, on the same plan, and for the same object. Simultaneously at Joppa and at Cæsarea God's agency was at work, and the coincidence or concurrence of events demonstrated the interposition of Him 'who is wonderful in counsel, and excellent in working.' We have also an interesting example of personal and family religion under the less perfect dispensation of the Old Testament, and one which may well put to shame many a professor enjoying far higher privileges amongst ourselves. Cornelius was a godly man, and he carried his religion into his family, caring for the souls of those who were committed to his care: 'he feared God with all his house,' 'he prayed in his house,' he had 'a devout soldier' for his servant, and he collected his whole household to listen to the apostle, saying, 'Now therefore are we all here present before God, to hear all things that are commanded thee of God.' Again, the case of Cornelius affords a memorable proof of the efficacy of prayer, and how much prayer is concerned in the advancement of believers, as well as in the conversion of sinners. Cornelius was praying when 'the man in bright clothing stood before him;' Peter was praying when the sheet descended from heaven; and the centurion's kinsfolk and friends were assembled for the same purpose when Peter arrived. But the great end of all the visions and events recorded in this chapter was to declare the abolition of all distinctions betwixt Jew and Gentile, so that both were alike welcome to share in the blessings of the Gospel, and that no man should now be called common or unclean. The instruction of Cornelius and his family, important as it was, was not the only, nor even the chief object of God in this wonderful interposition. It was designed to remove the prejudice which the Jews, and even the apostles themselves, still entertained against the Gentiles, and to open the door for their admission into the Christian Church. The narrative teaches us to cherish a *catholic spirit*, first, as it represents Cornelius as a true believer, although a Gentile by birth, and a Jewish proselyte by profession; and, secondly, as it shows that every one on whom the Holy Spirit is bestowed, be it in his miraculous gifts or in his renewing grace, is to be recognized and received as a member of the Church of Christ. 'Can any man forbid water that these should not be baptized, who have received the Holy Ghost as well as we?'

VI. Lydia : Acts 16.13-15

THERE is one important circumstance which was common to all those cases of conversion that are recorded in Scripture, and which well deserves our most serious consideration; I mean the direct operation of the Holy Spirit on the mind of every true convert to the Christian faith, in the way of applying the truth, which is ordinarily the means of conversion. The agency of the Spirit is specially referred to by our Lord himself, in one of the last and most affecting of those addresses which he delivered to his disciples before his death. And by comparing his words with other passages of Scripture, we learn that there were two very different ways in which the Spirit should act, or that there are two distinct modes of operation by which he carries into effect his great design. The one is external, and sensible; the other is internal, and spiritual. We read of 'the *manifestation* of the Spirit which is given to every man to profit withal;' and we read of the '*indwelling* of the Spirit in the hearts of true believers.' In other words, the dispensation of the Gospel is called the 'ministration of the Spirit,' for two distinct reasons; first, on account of miraculous gifts which were vouchsafed to the apostles and first converts; and, secondly, on account of the enlightening, converting, and sanctifying grace which rendered the Gospel effectual for their salvation. There is a wide difference betwixt the two. They differ in their nature, their use, and their effects; the one being an appropriate evidence, a divine attestation of the truth; the other, a direct operation on the soul, by which it is renewed and quickened, and turned from darkness to light, and from the power of Satan unto God. And not only are they widely different; we have reason to believe that they might be separated from each other. Such being the difference betwixt the miraculous gifts and the inward graces of the Spirit, it is a delightful truth that the latter and the more valuable of the two is the permanent inheritance of the Christian Church. His miraculous gifts were to cease when they had fulfilled their end by establishing the truth; but his office did not cease. Nor was his work completed when, by his descent on the day of Pentecost and his subsequent effusion at Cæsarea on the Gentiles, the promise of the Father was fulfilled, and the truth of the Gospel established. Considered as an evidence, the gift of the Spirit was decisive; but evidence is not enough, nor an inspired Bible, nor a faithful ministry. In every human heart there is a spirit of unbelief and enmity, and many a lofty imagination, which exalteth itself against the knowledge of God; which is not overcome by any amount of evidence, or by the mere force of truth, and can only be subdued by the inward grace of the Spirit; and hence we learn that it belongs to his office, and forms a part of his blessed work, at all times, to 'shine into our hearts,' 'to renew us in the spirit of our mind,' 'to quicken us into spiritual life,' 'to open our eyes,' and 'to turn us from darkness to light, and from the power of Satan unto God.'

The direct personal operation of the Spirit on the soul of every convert is beautifully illustrated by the case of Lydia. It is said of her, that while she listened to the preaching of the Word, '*the Lord opened her heart*, so that she attended unto the things which were spoken of Paul.'

I. In regard to her state and character before her conversion and baptism, the narrative, although extremely short, contains several intimations which throw a very interesting light on her case, and that of a large class in our own time who resemble her in the chief points of their character. It is intimated that, like the Roman centurion and the Ethiopian treasurer, she was a proselyte to the Jewish faith, and a believer in the one only, the living and the true God. By birth a Gentile, and a native of Thyatira, she had come to Philippi as a seller of purple; and although a stranger, she maintained in the city of her adoption, and amidst the idolatries which prevailed in it, a devout attachment to her religion, and continued in the worship of God. It is also intimated, I think, with sufficient clearness, that she was really devout, and imbued with a spirit of prayer; for not only did she observe the Sabbath, in conformity with the law of Moses, but, when probably no other opportunity was afforded of attending the ordinances of public worship, in a city where both the magistrates and the multitude seem to have been easily excited against any innovation in their public customs, she 'went out of the city by a river side, where prayer was wont to be made.' It is deeply interesting to mark, that, at the time of her conversion, this devout woman was attending a *prayer meeting*, in the open air, by the water side, along with a few other women who were in the habit, it would seem, of assembling together for this purpose, for it is said that 'they resorted thither;' and it is not less interesting to notice, that Paul and his companions did not reckon it beneath them to join that humble meeting, but, on the contrary, leaving the noise and tumult of the city, they sought out the little band of praying women, and sat down beside them, and spake to them the word of life. And while they were thus engaged in prayer and conference, 'the Lord opened the heart of Lydia,' a striking proof of the immediate efficacy of prayer. Without prayer we have no reason to look for a blessing. God may, indeed, and sometimes does surprise a prayerless sinner: he is sometimes found of them that sought him not, as in the case of the gaoler in this same city; and then the first effect of his change will be the same that the Lord marked in the case of Paul, when he said, 'Behold, he prayeth!' But although this may happen in manifestation of God's sovereignty and the riches of his undeserved mercy, there is no promise in the Bible except to prayer, and that promise is alike unlimited and sure: 'Ask, and ye shall receive; seek, and ye shall find; knock, and it shall be opened unto you. For *every one* that asketh receiveth; and he that seeketh findeth; and to him that knocketh it shall be opened.' 'If *any man* lack wisdom, let him ask of God, who giveth to all men liberally, and upbraideth not, and it shall be given him.'

It is implied, however, in the narrative, that while she was a proselyte to the Jewish faith, and a sincere worshipper of the true God, her heart was still *shut* or *closed* against the reception of the truth as it is in Jesus. It is said, 'the Lord opened her heart;' an expression which clearly implies that, devout as she was, her heart was in such a state, that, but for the gracious operation of the Spirit, it would have excluded the Gospel message. Such is the natural state of every heart; and by the heart, I mean, as is generally meant in Scripture, the whole moral nature of man, including alike his understanding, his conscience, his will, and his affections. In this comprehensive sense, the heart is closed against the reception of the truth, and every faculty presents an obstacle such as divine grace alone can remove. In reference to unregenerate men, it is expressly said that their *understandings* are shut against the light of the Gospel, insomuch that of the Jews, with the Old Testament in their hands, it is said, 'But their minds were blinded,' 'the veil was upon their hearts,' and 'if our Gospel be hid, it is hid to them that are lost: in whom the god of this world hath blinded the minds of them which believe not, lest the light of the glorious Gospel of Christ, who is the image of God, should shine unto them;' and 'the natural man,' universally, 'receiveth not the things of the Spirit of God, for they are foolishness unto him; neither can he know them, because they are spiritually discerned.' And so *the conscience* is 'seared as with a hot iron,' the 'very mind and conscience is defiled,' and '*the heart* is hardened; and thus there are many *bars* or *obstacles* which obstruct the entrance of the truth. There is the bar of *ignorance:* many 'hear the word,' but understand it not; and the wicked one takes away that which was sown; there is the bar of *unbelief*, which rejects the testimony of God; there is the bar of *enmity*, for 'the carnal mind is enmity against God; it is not subject to the law of God, neither indeed can be;' there is the bar of *presumption or pride:* 'The wicked, through the pride of his countenance, will not seek after God; God is not in all his thoughts;' there is the bar of *discouragement and despair:* 'Thou saidst there is no hope; for I have loved strangers, and after them will I go;' there is the bar of *unwillingness:* 'Ye will not come to me that ye might have life;' there is the bar of *worldly-mindedness:* 'The cares of the world, and the deceitfulness of riches, choke the word, and it becometh unfruitful;' there is the bar of *sloth:* 'A little more sleep, a little more slumber, a little folding of the hands to sleep;' there is the bar of *vicious passion and depraved habits,* any one bosom sin being enough to exclude the saving power of the truth: 'For this is the condemnation, that light hath come into the world, and that men have loved the darkness rather than the light, because their deeds are evil.' Under the influence of these and similar hindrances, the heart is closed against the admission of the truth, closed as really as are the eyes of the blind or the ears of the deaf; for, says our Lord himself, 'In them is fulfilled the prophecy of Esaias, which saith, By hearing ye shall hear, and shall not understand; and seeing ye shall see, and shall not perceive: for this people's heart is waxed gross, and their ears are dull of hearing, and their eyes they have closed; lest at any time they should see with their eyes, and hear with their ears, and should understand with their heart, and should be converted, and I should heal them;' and in the same light does he represent the state of our own hearts, when he now says to each of us, 'Behold, I stand at the door and knock: if any man will hear my voice, and will open the door, I will come in to him.'

But it may be asked: If Lydia was a sincere and devout worshipper of the true God, is it reasonable to suppose that her heart was thus shut against God's truth? I answer that, even in persons of true piety, there may be much remaining ignorance and many groundless prejudices, which, but for the enlightening grace of the Spirit, might prevent them from embracing the Gospel. This was remarkably exemplified in those '*devout and honourable women,* and the chief men of the city, whom the Jews stirred up, and who raised persecution against Paul and Barnabas, and expelled them out of their coasts, insomuch that the apostles shook off the dust of their feet against them;' and still more in the case of Paul himself, who was a Pharisee, and the son of a Pharisee, living according to the straitest sect of the law, yet his heart was barred, by invincible prejudices, against the truth, until it was removed on his way to Damascus. And so of Lydia. She, too, was devout; but her heart was *closed,* until it was opened by the Lord. And many professors, in modern times, resemble her in this, being conscientious and devout according to their light, but still ignorant or unbelieving, or imbued with strong prejudice,[1] in regard to the Gospel of Christ; just as Nathanael

[1] See John M'Laurin's Essay on 'Prejudices against the Gospel.'

himself, of whom our Lord said, 'Behold an Israelite indeed, in whom there is no guile,' was yet so far influenced by mere prejudice as to say, in answer to the first intimation he received of the Messiah, 'Can any good thing come out of Nazareth?' And if, in such cases, divine agency be needful to open the heart for the reception of the truth, how much more in the vast majority, who are utterly irreligious and unconcerned!

II. If we consider the means by which her conversion was effected, we shall find that here there was no miraculous accompaniment of any kind, but an example only of what takes place in the experience of every genuine convert. It is simply said, 'A certain woman heard us, whose heart the Lord opened, that she attended unto the things which were spoken of Paul.'

But this pregnant statement brings before us, in a state of beautiful combination, two things which are equally essential to a sinner's conversion: the first is, the *agency* of the Spirit; and the second is, the *instrumentality* of the Word. There was a direct personal operation of the Spirit on the heart of Lydia; he removed those obstacles which might otherwise have obstructed the admission of the truth. It was not Paul who effected this. Paul preached; but though inspired with supernatural wisdom, and endowed with miraculous powers, and especially with the gift of tongues, he says himself, 'Paul may plant, and Apollos water; but God giveth the increase. Who then is Paul, and who is Apollos, but ministers by whom ye believed, according as the Lord gave to every man!' God alone can open the heart. That change consisted in opening the understanding to discern the light of God's truth, the conscience to feel its convincing power, and the heart, to receive its sanctifying influence; and this belongs to the office of the Holy Ghost, whose *work is heart-work*, and consists of two parts, the opening of the Scriptures, and the opening of the mind, as we learn from the case of the disciples after his resurrection, of whom it is said in one place that they exclaimed, 'Did not our hearts burn within us while he talked with us by the way, and *opened unto us the Scriptures?*' and in another, 'Then *opened he their understanding*, that they might understand the Scriptures.'

But while the Lord only can open the heart, he employs the truth as the instrument of conversion to the careless, and of edification to the devout inquirer. The Spirit's agency does not supersede the use of the Word: on the contrary, the truth read or heard is still the wisdom of God, and the power of God, unto salvation. 'The Lord opened the heart of Lydia,' but he did so 'that she might *attend unto the things which were spoken of Paul.*' It is by the truth contained in the Word that this great change is wrought, that being the instrument which the Spirit of God renders effectual; and hence, while we are said to be 'born of the Spirit,' we are also said to be 'born not of corruptible seed, but of incorruptible, even by the Word of God, which liveth and abideth for ever;' and again, while the Spirit is revealed as the Sanctifier, our Lord himself prayed, in these memorable words, 'Sanctify them by thy truth; thy Word is truth.' And both are combined, both the agency of the Spirit and the instrumentality of the Word, in that comprehensive statement of the apostle, 'God hath from the beginning chosen you unto salvation through sanctification of the Spirit and belief of the truth.' Various similitudes are employed to represent the same thing; the Word is compared to a *fire* or *furnace*, in which His people are melted and tried, but the Lord sits as a refiner over it; and as a *hammer*, a powerful instrument, but inert in itself, and effectual only when applied by a powerful arm; and as a *sword*, 'the sword of the Spirit, which is the Word of God,' a sharp two-edged sword, but utterly powerless unless it be applied by the Spirit. So David's prayer combines a reference to both: '*Open thou* mine eyes, that I may see wonderful things *out of thy law.*'

III. The nature of Lydia's change, and the practical results which flowed from it, are briefly indicated; but enough is said to show, that she had that 'faith which worketh by love,' and in which properly consists 'the new creation;' for we read that she was *baptized*, thereby professing her faith in Christ, and her submission to his authority, and that, too, in a city where the professors of the Gospel were exposed to reproach and persecution; that, as soon as she was baptized, she besought the apostles, saying, 'If ye have judged me to be faithful to the Lord, come into my house, and abide there,' her faith working by *love* to Christ and to his ministering servants, and producing zeal for his cause and service, such as prompted her to make sacrifices for his name's sake; and if these principles of faith and love were really planted in her heart, they would unquestionably produce in her after-life all the 'peaceable fruits of righteousness.'

The case of Lydia suggests various practical lessons. It affords an example of the care with which God provided for the instruction of sincere inquirers in the Jewish Church. It shows, in a very striking light, the efficacy of prayer, as a means of spiritual advancement. It illustrates the necessity of a great spiritual change, even in the case of such as are regular in their attendance on ordinances, and conscientious according to their light. It affords a beautiful exemplification of the relative functions of the Word and Spirit in the work of conversion, and enforces the duty of combining diligence, in the use of means, with a spirit of dependence on the divine blessing. And it shows how different are the feelings of one 'whose heart the Lord has opened' towards his faithful ministers, and those of the ungodly multitude: – she constrained the apostles to reside in her house; they rose against them, and committed them to prison, making their feet fast in the stocks.

VII. Timothy: 2 Timothy 3.14, 15

IT appears from Scripture, that while many are converted after a long course of carelessness and sinful indulgence, others are trained up for God from their earliest years, and sanctified even from the womb. The experience of these two classes must necessarily be widely different; while, in whatever is essential to regeneration, it must be substantially the same in all. All men being by nature fallen and depraved, that which is 'born of the flesh being flesh,' and 'the carnal mind being' in every instance 'enmity against God,' a new spiritual birth is universally and indispensably necessary in order to a new spiritual life; and no man lives, however gentle his natural disposition, and however propitious his early education, of whom it may not be said, that except 'he be born again, he cannot see the kingdom of God.' Whenever that change occurs, and by whatever means it may be accomplished, it is substantially the same in all; it implies the enlightening, convincing, renewing, and sanctifying work of the Spirit, whereby the natural blindness is removed, and the natural enmity subdued, and the natural man becomes a *new creature*, in all his views and feelings, his desires and affections, his aims, and habits, and hopes. And we greatly err if we suppose that, in any one case, a good natural temperament, or a sound religious education, can of themselves introduce a fallen being into the spiritual kingdom of God, or supersede the grace and the agency of the Holy Spirit. That is spirit, and that only, which is born of the Spirit; and every soul that is really converted must have that experience which is common to all true believers, and which consists in conviction of sin, an apprehension of the mercy of God in Christ, a cordial compliance with the Gospel call, and a course of conflict and warfare with its own corruptions. But while some such change must be wrought on every one at the period of his conversion, it may be brought about in a variety of ways, which will occasion great diversity in the experience of different believers. Some, for instance, are permitted to grow up without any religious culture, being deprived of the inestimable privilege of a father's counsel and a mother's prayers, and surrounded instead with the noxious influences of a domestic circle where there is no fear of God, no form of religion, and nothing in the shape of example, except what is fitted to corrupt and contaminate. Thus neglected in early life, and inured to vice from their earliest years, they go forth into the world, not only unprepared to resist, but predisposed to comply with its temptations; and following the bent of their own evil passions, and falling in with the current of evil society, they may remain for years utterly careless of their souls, of God, and of eternity, and may be allowed to go on to great lengths in wickedness, till, by some providential dispensation, or by an awakening sermon, or even by the remorseful restlessness of their own consciences, they are brought under serious concern, and led to inquire, 'What must we do to be saved?' The case of such persons is illustrated by the experience of the dying malefactor and of the Philippian gaoler, who had both been careless, and one of them utterly flagitious in life; till by the awful circumstances in which they were placed, they were awakened, convinced, and converted to God. But while such cases do occur, and are sufficient to show that God's grace is alike free and sovereign, and able to soften the hardest heart, and to save even at the eleventh hour, there are others whose experience is widely different; they are the children of religious parents; they have enjoyed the inestimable advantages of Christian instruction, and the still more precious privilege of constant intercourse with a domestic circle where every influence is favourable to their moral culture, where example is combined with precept, and the tenderest affection with paternal authority, and the family meet around the domestic altar, to read God's Word, and to sing his praise, and to unite in social prayer; and every association, the more tender and the more enduring because formed in the morn of life, connects religion with the most endearing relations and the holiest charities of home. By such means, many grow up in those families which are nurseries for the Church of Christ, well instructed in the truths of the Gospel, impressed with a feeling of reverence for religious ordinances, and imbued with sentiments and dispositions which render them amiable and engaging in their manners, and which serve at least to preserve them from the grosser pollutions of the world; while in not a few, the precious seed sown in early life takes root in the heart, and grows up so *gradually* and *imperceptibly*, that they may not be conscious, at any one time, of any great or sudden change, such as was experienced by the dying thief and the poor gaoler, although really the work of grace is begun, and will be carried on to perfection. In such cases, it is manifest that we are not to expect precisely the same course of experience as is found in those who, after a life of sin, are suddenly awakened and changed. And of this class we have selected the case of Timothy as a very interesting and instructive example.

The account which is given of this eminent and devoted servant of God shows that his first serious impressions were derived from his religious education in early life, and from the pious care and example of his parents. The apostle tells us, that from 'a child he had known the holy Scriptures,' referring to his early instruction in the truths of the Old Testament, to which he had access, although his father was a Greek, through the pious care of his mother, who was a Jewess. For he is thus introduced to our notice: 'Then came Paul to Derbe and Lystra: and, behold, a certain disciple was there, named Timotheus, the son of a certain woman which was a Jewess, and believed; but his father was a Greek.' But what is of much more importance than her mere profession, she was a woman of sincere piety; and the same piety characterized other members of her family. For the apostle writing to Timothy, as 'his dearly beloved son,' says, 'I thank God when I call to remembrance the unfeigned faith that is in thee, which dwelt first in thy grandmother Lois and thy mother Eunice; and I am persuaded that in thee also.' Here is a beautiful example of domestic piety: the aged grandmother cherishing an unfeigned faith in the promise which God had given to the fathers, and waiting for the consolation of Israel; the mother cherishing the same hope, and gladly embracing the Gospel as soon as it was proclaimed to her, for she was not only a Jewish but a Christian believer; and the young man, taught from his earliest years to 'know the Scriptures, which were able to make him wise unto salvation,' and becoming, under Paul's ministry, a disciple in the school of Christ, and afterwards an eminent, zealous, and devoted minister of the everlasting Gospel. Being connected with a Greek by marriage, the pious Jewess had not, it would seem, insisted on the circumcision of her child; but she was not inattentive to his religious training; she instructed him in the knowledge of God's truth. And most amply was her motherly care repaid, when this child of many prayers became the companion of an apostle, and the honoured instrument of founding many churches, and winning many souls to Christ. The details of his experience are not recorded; but from the incidental intimations which are given in the course of the two epistles which were addressed to him, we may gather that his experience corresponded in substance with that of every other child of God. He must have been convinced of sin, so as to feel his need of a Saviour; he must have been enlightened in the knowledge of Christ, so as to perceive his all-sufficiency and suitableness; and he must have personally closed with Christ, receiving him as his Prophet to teach, as his Priest to reconcile, and as his Lord to govern him. All this is implied in his profession as a Christian, and especially as a Christian evangelist, since nothing short of this could have sufficed either for his own salvation or for the work of the ministry. And what secret conflicts, what inward struggles he endured, educated as he had been by pious parents, and instructed, too, by an inspired apostle, is sufficiently

[195]

evinced by the exhortation of Paul, where he speaks of his being engaged in a *warfare:* 'Fight the good fight of faith, lay hold on eternal life,' 'Hold fast the form of sound words which thou hast heard of me,' 'Continue thou in the things which thou hast learned and hast been assured of, knowing of whom thou hast learned them; and that from a child thou hast known the holy Scriptures, which are able to make thee wise unto salvation, through faith which is in Christ Jesus.'

The case of Timothy affords several useful lessons.

1. It shows that *little children* are capable subjects of divine grace. In the case of adults, the truth apprehended and believed is the instrumental means of conversion and sanctification; but before children are capable of knowing the truth, they are fit subjects of God's grace, as is evident from many passages of Scripture. We read of some who were sanctified from the womb: 'Now hear, O Jacob my servant; and Israel, whom I have chosen: Thus saith the Lord that made thee, and formed thee from the womb; I will pour my Spirit on thy seed, and my blessing upon thine offspring; and they shall spring up as among the grass, as willows by the water courses. One shall say, I am the Lord's; and another shall call himself by the name of Jacob; and another shall subscribe with his hand unto the Lord, and surname himself by the name of Israel.' 'Hearken unto me, O house of Jacob, and all the remnant of the house of Israel, which are borne by me from the belly, which are carried from the womb: and even to your old age I am he; and even to hoar hairs will I carry you: I have made and I will bear: even I will carry, and will deliver you.' It was by the Spirit that the Lord Christ was sanctified in his human nature, so that the angel spake of 'the holy thing that should be born of Mary;' and the prophet, of whom it is said that 'he was called from the womb, and formed from the womb to be his servant.' And when, during his personal ministry, 'there were brought to him little children, that he should put his hands on them and pray, and the disciples rebuked them,' Jesus said, 'Suffer little children, and forbid them not, to come unto me; for of such is the kingdom of heaven.' Nay, on another occasion, 'Jesus called a little child unto him, and set him in the midst of the disciples, and said, Verily I say unto you, Except ye be converted, and become as little children, ye shall not enter into the kingdom of heaven.' That little children are capable subjects of God's grace is implied in the provision that was made for their admission to the privileges of the covenant, first, by circumcision under the Old Testament, and, secondly, by baptism under the New; and this precious truth is our warrant and encouragement in prayer, when we remember those objects of our tenderest affections at the throne of grace, while as yet they are unable to pray for themselves.

2. We learn from the case of Timothy that a sound religious education in early life is often blessed as a means of saving conversion to God. The apostle traces Timothy's religion to this source: 'From a child thou hast known the holy Scriptures, which are able to make thee wise unto salvation.' His early acquaintance with the Bible was a great and precious privilege; for although, from the operation of other causes, Bible knowledge is sometimes unproductive of saving benefit, yet it is the instrument by which God works, and an instrument which is in itself at once absolutely perfect, and admirably adapted for the end which it is designed to serve. A great commendation is given to the Word, when it is said that 'it is able to make us wise unto salvation;' that 'it is profitable for doctrine, for reproof, for correction, and for instruction in righteousness;' and that it is sufficient 'to make the man of God perfect, thoroughly furnished unto all good works.' The Bible contains all the truth which is needful to be known for our salvation; considered simply as a means or instrument, it is absolutely perfect; and every parent who really believes in God's Word, and considers it as God's instrument for the salvation of sinners, must feel it to be his most sacred obligation, as well as his sweetest privilege, to impart to his immortal children a knowledge of its precious truths. He will remember that he has in his hands an instrument which God himself declares to be 'the sword of the Spirit,' that he has that truth which is emphatically described as 'the good seed;' and, with mingled feelings of awe, and gratitude, and hope, he will seek to apply that instrument to the heart of his child, and to sow that precious seed in his soul from his earliest years. Nor will he be content with giving a few formal lessons, or prescribing a few stated tasks; out of the 'abundance of his heart his mouth will speak,' and his conversation will be seasoned with God's truth, in those hours of affectionate and confiding converse when the hearts of his children are most open to receive 'the truth in love,' remembering God's words to his ancient people, 'These words, which I command thee this day, shall be in thine heart; and thou shalt teach them diligently unto thy children, and shalt talk of them when thou sittest in thine house, and when thou walkest by the way, and when thou liest down, and when thou risest up.' But neither formal instruction nor frequent conversation on divine truth will avail, unless they be combined with exemplary faith and piety on the part of parents. Children are quick to discern every, even the minutest indication of real character; and a great part of their education consists in those impressions which are made on their minds incidentally, and which are often imperceptibly deepened, by circumstances which escape the notice of their parents. True education is a course of *training*, not a system of lessons, but the formation of practical habits; and these depend far more on the spirit and conduct of a family than

on the tasks of the school: '*Train* up a child in the way he should go, and when he is old he will not depart from it.' This training implies much more than mere teaching; it is best promoted by the unfeigned faith and holy living of which the apostle speaks in the mother and grandmother of Timothy; and it is deeply interesting to mark how this eminent servant of God was prepared for his future labours by the quiet and unostentatious, but real piety of these women in the private walks of domestic life, and that the Holy Spirit himself, in preparing a record for the universal and permanent instruction of the Church, does not disdain to mention, in connection with the labours of an inspired evangelist, the unfeigned faith which dwelt first in his grandmother Lois, and afterwards in his mother Eunice; nor can we doubt that this is the reason why many an aged saint is spared, when their work on earth might seem to be finished, even that they may exhibit the power of God's grace and truth to the generation following, and leave the impress of their own characters on the tender minds of the children that are playing around them!

3. We learn from the case of Timothy that true religion is sometimes implanted in the soul of a child at a very early period, and continues to grow with his growth, and strengthen with his strength, although for a time his progress may appear to be almost imperceptible. Jesus himself said, 'The kingdom of heaven is like to a grain of mustard seed, which a man took and sowed in his field, which indeed is the least of all seeds; but when it is grown, it is the greatest among herbs, and becometh a tree, so that the birds of the air come and lodge in the branches thereof;' and again, 'The kingdom of heaven is like unto leaven, which a woman took and hid in three measures of meal, till the whole was leavened.' These parables are equally descriptive of the kingdom of God as it exists in the world, and of the kingdom of God in every single soul; grace grows and spreads, and that, too, imperceptibly, just as the mustard seed springs from the earth, and the leaven diffuses itself amongst meal. This is often the blessed effect of an early religious education; and although the good seed of the Word should not spring up so quickly as we could desire, yet, being incorruptible, we may cherish the hope that, sooner or later, it will be quickened, so as to produce the peaceable fruits of righteousness, long, it may be, after we have been gathered to our fathers.

In now addressing those who, like Timothy, have enjoyed the privilege of an early religious education, and who may still enjoy the society, or at least remember, with affectionate gratitude, the counsels and the prayers of their pious parents, I must not forget that they may yet belong to *two* very different classes. There may be some who, like Timothy, have not only known the Holy Scriptures from their youth, but have also that 'unfeigned faith which dwelt in him;' while there may be others who enjoyed like him the advantages of a religious education, and are, as yet at least, destitute of saving grace. No human being may be able to discriminate betwixt the two classes, so as to determine to which you individually belong; but I would affectionately remind you that there *are* two classes even amongst those who have received a religious education, and that it is of infinite moment that you should determine for yourselves whether you belong to the one or the other.

The apostle's exhortation is addressed to Timothy on the supposition that he was a true believer, and is applicable, in its original purpose, only to such as have, like him, been made wise unto salvation; but before applying it to such, I would address myself to all who have shared in the advantages of early religious instruction, and would affectionately remind you that you have much reason for gratitude, and, at the same time, for a very deep sense of your responsibility, on account of the privileges which you have enjoyed. Even should the instruction which you have received, and the example which you have been privileged to witness, fail in leading you to saving conversion, be assured that they are in their own nature privileges of great value, and that they will form an element in your last account. You will stand at the judgment-seat on a very different footing from that of the poor *outcasts* who live in the wretched streets and lanes of our city, and will be reckoned with for the use of your Bibles, and your closets, and your family worship, and all your other means of grace; for it is the equitable law of God's kingdom, that 'to whomsoever much has been given, of him shall the more be required.' Impressed, as I trust you are, with this solemn reflection, and with a sense of God's distinguishing goodness to you, permit me further to remind you, that as there are many advantages, so there are also some peculiar dangers in your case; and of these I shall only mention, first of all, the tendency, of which you may perhaps be conscious, to take too readily for granted that you are religious, merely because you are a member of a religious family, and have been from your youth accustomed to religious observances, forgetting that religion is, with every soul of man, a personal matter, and that it has its seat in the heart; secondly, the danger of your mistaking the natural and common fruits of a religious education for thorough conversion to God. Your knowledge, your amiable dispositions, your gentle manners, your correct habits, your attendance on ordinances – all these and many more may be nothing else than 'the form of godliness, while you are destitute of its power;' and, thirdly, the danger of your supposing that because you know a great deal more than others, you have no need for further inquiry, and may give your thoughts to other studies, and your time to other pursuits. These temptations are peculiarly incident to you, and while I warn you against them, I would point out a few symptoms by which you may discover the real state of your heart. Are you conscious of a sincere desire Godwards, such a desire as leads you to pray for yourselves in secret, as well as to join with your families in prayer? Do you, in your private, and family, and public prayers, do you really seek after God, and offer up the desires of your heart to him? Are you convinced of sin, and have you discovered that 'the heart is deceitful above all things, and desperately wicked?'; and, under a sense of sin, are you seeking to be cleansed by the blood of Christ, and to be purified by the grace of his Holy Spirit? If thus concerned for the salvation of your souls, you are seeking it in the way of God's appointment, and making conscience of duty, then 'wait upon the Lord, and be of good courage, and he will strengthen your heart; wait, I say, upon the Lord.' To you the apostle's exhortation may be addressed, when he says to Timothy, 'Continue thou in the things which thou hast learned, and hast been assured of, knowing of whom thou hast learned them, and that from a child thou hast known the Holy Scriptures.' *Continue, i.e.*, 'hold fast the beginning of your confidence, be not turned away from the hope of the Gospel, but continue in these things;' nay, 'meditate upon these things; give thyself wholly to them, that thy profiting may appear to all.' Paul deemed it necessary to address such exhortations to Timothy, his dearly beloved son, of whose unfeigned faith he had no doubt, and to whom he gave that honourable testimony, 'Ye know the proof of him, that, as a son with the father, he hath served with me in the Gospel.' And if, notwithstanding, Paul be so urgent in exhorting him to flee youthful lusts, to avoid the snares and temptations of the world, to watch over his own spirit, and to maintain a constant warfare with sin – oh! is not this an affecting proof that you too require to be strengthened, and stirred up, and animated in the path of duty? His exhortation specially points to the careful and continued use of the *means of grace;* and if these were needful for Timothy, how much more for you?

But if there be any who have enjoyed the advantages of a religious education, and who are yet unable to discover in themselves any of those hopeful symptoms which I have described; if they cannot honestly say that they have ever made the salvation of their souls a matter of personal concern, that they have ever sought after God, either in the retirement of their closets, or in the season of domestic worship, or that they are now resting on Christ's atonement, and desirous of the Spirit's grace; if, on the contrary, they begin to be conscious of a repugnance to the strict views of religion in which they were brought up, of a disposition to cherish slighter thoughts of sin and to extenuate its guilt, or of a tendency to be weary of a religious life, and to long after greater license and gaiety than their father's house affords; if they are seldom or never found on their knees, or with their Bibles in their hand, and yet flatter themselves that there may be some easier road to heaven than their fathers trod before them – oh! let me beseech them, now, and before they advance one step in that way which appears to them so attractive, to pause, and *choose such a course* as they will be content to live and die in; and to remember, while they make their choice, that heaven or hell is involved in it!

VIII. Conversions at Pentecost: Acts 2

THE nature, method, and results of true scriptural conversion may be illustrated by the striking narrative which is given of the events that occurred at Jerusalem on the day of Pentecost. These events were in many respects extraordinary; they were accompanied with miraculous interposition, they produced a powerful impression on the public mind, and they resulted in the sudden and simultaneous conversion of many thousand souls; yet, in other respects, they correspond exactly with the usual methods of God's procedure in the conversion of individual sinners, and may be improved, as affording an instructive example of the great change which may be still wrought by the faithful preaching of the Gospel, when it is applied by the power of his Spirit.

I. In regard to the *previous state* of the three thousand souls who were converted on this occasion, there is reason to believe that they belonged to *two* distinct classes, – the first including devout persons who were religious according to the light which they had previously enjoyed; and the second including, perhaps, a still larger number of irreligious men who had rejected and persecuted the Saviour, and were chargeable with the guilt of instigating or consenting to his death. The distinction which I draw betwixt these two classes is founded on those parts of the narrative on the one hand, which declare that among the assembled multitude 'there were dwelling at Jerusalem, *devout men* out of every nation under heaven;' and on the other hand, on those parts of Peter's sermon in which he directly charges on those whom he addressed the guilt of the Lord's blood: – 'Him, being delivered by the determinate counsel of God, *ye* have taken, and by wicked hands have crucified and slain,' – 'God hath made that same Jesus, whom *ye* have crucified, both Lord and Christ.' So that here we have a *variety of characters*. Among the 'devout men' who were assembled at Jerusalem for the celebration of a great religious festival, there might be some intelligent and godly Jews or proselytes, who, like Cornelius, 'feared God, and gave much alms to the people, and prayed to God alway;' some others, who, like the Ethiopian treasurer, were ignorant but sincere; while, perhaps there were not a few, who, like the devout women at Antioch, were filled with Jewish prejudices, and with an intolerant zeal which might lead them to take part in persecuting Christ and his humble followers. And among the mixed multitude who listened to Peter's sermon, there were probably men of every different shade of character, some who had been active agents in the crucifixion of the Lord, others who had been mere spectators of it, and who, according to their several habits of thought and feeling, were so differently affected by the miraculous manifestation of the Spirit, that while some were impressed and affected by it, others treated it with mockery and scorn. How many belonging to each of these various classes were converted, we have no means of ascertaining; but it is plain that not a few then underwent this great change who were chargeable with the guilt of the Saviour's blood: for when Peter pressed this charge on their consciences, they 'were pricked to the heart,' a clear proof that they were self-convicted and self-condemned.

II. If we now consider the circumstances which accompanied, and the means which effected their conversion, we shall find that it is of considerable practical importance to distinguish betwixt these two things, and to assign to each the place which properly belongs to it. The circumstances of this case were, in some respects, extraordinary and peculiar, and such as have no parallel in the usual experience of the Christian Church; and the *means* which contributed more or less directly to the result which is here recorded were some of them preparatory, others immediate and direct.

This great awakening of souls was preceded by *fervent and united prayer*. This was an important preparatory means, a means which, in accordance with the faithful promise of God, engaged almighty power on the side of the preachers of the Gospel. The apostles had been commanded by the Lord, immediately before his ascension to glory, to wait at Jerusalem until they should receive the promise of the Father; and when they returned to the city from Mount Olivet, 'they went up into an upper room, where abode both Peter, and James, and John, and Andrew, Philip, and Thomas, Bartholomew, and Matthew, James the son of Alpheus, and Simon Zelotes, and Judas the brother of James. These all continued with one accord in *prayer and supplication*, with the women, and Mary the mother of Jesus, and with his brethren.' The number of the disciples at this time was about one hundred and twenty; these all continued to meet for prayer; and so, 'when the day of Pentecost was fully come, they were all with one accord in one place,' when the promise of the Father was suddenly fulfilled by an outpouring of the Holy Ghost.

Mark here how prayer preceded the most remarkable awakening of souls that ever occurred in the Church of God; nay, how it stood connected with the miraculous gifts of the Spirit. It was after frequent united prayer, and it was when they were again assembled for the same purpose, that 'they were all filled with the Holy Ghost, and began to speak with other tongues, as the Spirit gave them utterance.' It is worthy of remark, too, that the Lord had given them an express *promise*, which left no doubt as to the communication of the Spirit's gifts; for not only had he said, before his crucifixion, 'I will pray the Father, and he shall give you another Comforter, that he may abide with you for ever; even the Spirit of truth;' but again, after his resurrection from the dead, and immediately before his ascension to glory, he said, 'Behold, I send the promise of my Father upon you: but tarry ye in the city of Jerusalem, until ye be endued with power from on high.' 'And being assembled together with them, he commanded them that they should not depart from Jerusalem, but wait for the promise of the Father, which, saith he, ye have heard of me.' 'Ye shall receive power, after that the Holy Ghost is come upon you: and ye shall be witnesses unto me, both in Jerusalem, and in all Judea, and in Samaria, and unto the uttermost part of the earth.' The Lord's promise, then, was express; but his promise did not supersede their *prayer;* on the contrary, the former was the ground and reason of the latter, according to the saying of the prophet, 'I the Lord have spoken it, and I will do it. Thus saith the Lord God, I will yet for this be inquired of by the house of Israel, to do it for them.'

Great things are still promised in answer to believing prayer. For not only have we the general promise, 'Ask, and ye shall receive; seek and ye shall find; knock, and it shall be opened unto you,' but specially, in regard to the Holy Spirit, we have that precious assurance, 'If ye, being evil, know how to give good gifts unto your children; how much more shall your Father in heaven give the Holy Spirit to them that ask him?' And a peculiar blessing is annexed to *united* social prayer; for, 'I say unto you, that if two of you shall agree on earth as touching any thing that they shall ask, it shall be done for them of my Father which is in heaven. For where two or three are gathered together in my name, there am I in the midst of them.' Let these gracious promises be an encouragement to fervent, persevering prayer; and let us, with holy importunity, never hold our peace day nor night. 'Ye that make mention of the Lord, keep not silence, and give him no rest, till he establish, and till he make Jerusalem a praise in the earth.'

In answer to believing prayer, the primitive disciples received the *miraculous gifts* of the Holy Spirit, which were also a *preparatory means* in leading to the great work of conversion which was soon afterwards accomplished. These gifts were, in various respects, fitted to prepare the way for that glorious work. They served at once to strengthen the faith of the disciples, as they were a manifest fulfilment of the Lord's word of promise, to qualify them for declaring the Gospel message to men of various nations then assembled at Jerusalem, as they conferred a power of speaking to them in their own languages, and to afford ample evidence to others of God's interposition, as they were, in their own nature, clearly and undeniably miraculous. We have already seen that the gift of the Holy Spirit was the crowning evidence of the divine mission of the Saviour: it was purposely reserved, and expressly promised, as the divinely appointed proof of his ascension and exaltation to the right hand of God, of the acceptance of his finished work, and of its efficacy in procuring those gifts for men which he died to purchase, and was exalted to bestow. And we may well admire the wisdom of God in providing this crowning proof of the divine mission of the Saviour, and manifesting it at that particular time. For not only did it strengthen the faith of the apostles, and qualify them for declaring the Gospel in various languages,[1] but being sent during one of the great annual festivals of the Jews, it made known the truth, and its divine evidence, to multitudes who were then collected at Jerusalem, and who, on their return to their respective homes, carried with them the seed of the Word, and scattered it everywhere throughout the world; for there were among them 'Parthians, and Medes, and Elamites, and the dwellers in Mesopotamia, and in Judea, and Cappadocia, in Pontus, and Asia, Phrygia, and Pamphylia, in Egypt, and in the parts of Libya about Cyrene, and strangers of Rome, Jews and proselytes, Cretes and Arabians.'

Such were the *preparatory means* which led to the great work of conversion on the day of Pentecost – united social prayer on the part of the disciples or Church of Christ, and a miraculous effusion of the Holy Ghost in the gift of tongues.

But you will carefully observe that the conversions which are here recorded are not ascribed solely, or even chiefly, to the miraculous and extraordinary circumstances by which they were preceded; otherwise, they would afford no ground to expect similar conversions in these modern times, when the gift of tongues has ceased. The miraculous dispensation of the Spirit was a powerful preparatory means; but the direct and immediate means of conversion in this, as in every other case, was the preaching of Gospel truth, applied to the heart and conscience by the Holy Ghost. The gift of tongues served an important purpose in preparing the way for the free proclamation of the Gospel on the part of the apostles, and for the believing reception of it on the part of the people; for it enabled the apostles

---

[1] I take for granted that the words are to be understood in their natural and obvious meaning. Dr. Neander of Berlin has attempted to show, as it appears to me without success, that the apostles did not speak in other languages than their own, but spoke in their own language with such ecstasy and power that others could understand them. – Neander's *History of the First Planting of the Christian Church*, vol. i. p. 15.

to speak, and the people to hear, the Gospel in various languages, so as that it could be clearly understood, and intelligently believed. It was fitted also to excite their interest, and to awaken their attention to the Gospel message, inasmuch as the gift of tongues evinced the miraculous interposition of God; and it afforded sufficient evidence to authenticate the truth, and to establish the divine commission of the apostles. But further than this it went not: it was not of itself the means of converting the soul: that change could then be wrought by no other means than those which are still effectual for the same end; I mean the truths of the Gospel, applied with power by the Spirit of God. You will observe, that no conversion followed immediately on the miraculous gift of tongues. The effect of that wonderful manifestation was that all wondered, some doubted, others mocked; but none were converted till the glorious Gospel was proclaimed.

There were, in fact, *three* successive stages in the experience of those who were converted on the day of Pentecost; and as many distinct results of the various means which were brought to bear upon them. First of all, before any discourse was addressed to them, the whole multitude were called to witness the *miraculous gift of tongues;* and this produced, as its appropriate effect, in some, a sense of awe and wonder, and in others mockery and scorn; it set the minds of both classes to work, but the one in the way of anxious inquiry, the other in the way of sceptical explanation; for the immediate result of this miraculous dispensation is described, when it is said, 'And they were all amazed, and were in doubt, saying one to another, What meaneth this? Others, mocking, said, These men are full of new wine.' They were not converted; they were not even convinced by the miracle; but their attention was arrested by means of it.

Then followed, secondly, a *work of conviction*, which was wrought by the first part of Peter's sermon, in which he established, by incontrovertible proof, the great truth that Jesus is the Christ; and this effect is described, when it is said, 'Now when they heard this, they were *pricked* in their heart, and said unto Peter, and to the rest of the apostles, Men and brethren, what shall we do?' Here we see the gift of the Spirit, considered as the fruit and manifestation of Christ's exaltation to glory, producing in the minds of unbelievers a deep conviction of sin: according to his own intimation to the apostles; 'When he is come, he will reprove,' or convince, 'the world of sin', 'of sin, because they believe not on me.' Still their conversion was not complete; they were as yet only undergoing the preparatory discipline of conviction, and imbued with a spirit of thoughtful inquiry; but then followed,

Thirdly, *The work of real conversion*, by which they were enabled and persuaded to embrace Christ for salvation: and which was effected instrumentally by the second part of Peter's address, in which he declared the Gospel message, and exhorted them to close with it, by the gracious assurance that, guilty as they were, they were welcome to come to Christ for life. 'Then said Peter unto them, Repent, and be baptized every one of you for the remission of sins, and ye shall receive the gift of the Holy Ghost. For the promise is unto you and to your children, and to all that are afar off, even as many as the Lord our God shall call.' So that, on the day of Pentecost, it was the *Gospel* chiefly, and not the miracle, which led to the great work of conversion, by which three thousand souls were added to the Church of such as should be saved.

The direct means, then, of this great work of conversion, was *Peter's sermon*, in which he unfolded the Gospel message, and pressed it home on their hearts and consciences, with demonstration of the Spirit and power.

Let us briefly consider the scope and substance of this remarkable discourse. It divides itself into two parts. In the first, Peter does not disdain to remove a prejudice from the minds of his hearers, which might have disinclined them to receive the message he was about to deliver; and, accordingly, he begins by referring calmly to the accusation which 'mockers' had raised against the apostles, as if they were intoxicated or unduly excited. He then refers to a passage in the prophecy of Joel, which predicted an outpouring of the Spirit of God, in virtue of which many should prophesy, before 'the great and notable day of the Lord;' and represents the events which they now witnessed as the visible fulfilment of that prediction. He proceeds fearlessly to *preach Christ crucified;* he declares that Jesus of Nazareth was a man approved of God among them, by miracles, and wonders, and signs, which God did by him in the midst of them, appealing to their own knowledge, as affording ample confirmation of his testimony; he then charges home upon them the guilt of having taken, and by wicked hands crucified and slain him, appealing to their own consciences, as sufficient to convict them of this flagrant sin; he then declares his resurrection from the dead, both as predicted by the Psalmist, and as testified by the apostles, who were all witnesses that God had raised him up; and finally, he declares his *exaltation* by the right hand of God, not his ascension merely, but his glorification, in token of God's acceptance, and in preparation for his great reward; for he represents the gift of the Holy Ghost as having been received from the Father as a pledge of his approbation, and as having been dispensed by the Son in the exercise of his royal power as a Prince and Saviour; a gift which made it manifest, that He who once hung on the cross was now seated on the throne; and that he occupied that throne by virtue of *His* authority who said to him, 'Sit thou at my right hand, until I make thy foes thy footstool.' Thus Peter narrates the leading facts of the Lord's personal history: beginning at Nazareth, he traces him through his public ministry to the cross, from the cross to the grave, and from the grave to the throne of heaven; and the one purport and design of the whole of his discourse is just to establish, on the ground of its proper evidence, and to impress on their minds, that one great but simple truth, which is stated on the 36th verse, as the sum and substance of his present testimony, – 'Therefore let all the house of Israel know assuredly, that God hath made that same Jesus, whom ye have crucified, BOTH LORD AND CHRIST.' The great object of the first part of Peter's discourse, then, was to show that '*Jesus is the Christ;*' in other words, that the same Jesus who was born at Bethlehem, brought up in Nazareth, and crucified on Calvary, was the Messiah who had been promised to the fathers; and that he was, as his name imports, God's anointed One: his anointed Prophet, to declare his mind and will; his anointed Priest, to make reconciliation for the people; and his anointed Lord and King, whom they were bound to obey. This one truth, if established, was sufficient to demonstrate their guilt in having crucified the Lord of glory, and to change all the views and feelings with which they had heretofore regarded him; for if Jesus was the Christ, then they had been guilty of rebellion against God when they put him to death! and how could they be safe, if *He* were now on the throne?

The immediate effect that was produced on their minds by the first part of Peter's sermon, was a conviction of *their guilt and danger*, a conviction which is here described as deeply painful and penetrating, when it is said, 'They were pricked in their hearts;' and under the influence of this conviction they uttered that serious question, 'Men and brethren, what shall we do?' They might have begun to think that all was over with them, that their case was utterly hopeless, that having crucified the Lord of glory, there remained nothing for them 'but a certain fearful looking for of judgment and fiery indignation:' their language bespeaks bewilderment, if not despair: they speak as men who know not to what hand to turn themselves, or what they could do. But oh! mark the freeness of the Gospel: having thus prepared them to receive the gracious message, having established the fact that Jesus is the Christ of God, and thereby awakened a sense of guilt and danger, and prompted a spirit of earnest inquiry, Peter at once, and without any qualification or reserve, unfolds the glad tidings of a full and free salvation: he excepts none; he excludes none; he exhorts all; he encourages all; for this is the glorious message which he was commissioned to deliver, 'Repent, and be baptized every one of you in the name of Jesus Christ for the remission of sins, and ye shall receive the gift of the Holy Ghost. For the promise is unto you, and to your children, and to all that are afar off, even as many as the Lord our God shall call.'

This is emphatically *the Gospel*, the Gospel in all its fulness and in all its freeness. It proceeds on a supposition of their guilt and danger, and addresses them as sinners, but, at the same time, and to these same sinners, it proclaims the *remission of sins;* nay, the remission of sins through that very blood by which their hands were stained, and which now lay heavy on their consciences. They are exhorted to be *baptized*, in token of their being washed by that blood which might seem, like the blood of Abel, to call for Heaven's vengeance against them; but this was 'the blood of sprinkling, which speaketh better things than the blood of Abel,' and here God, instead of saying, 'What hast thou done? the voice of thy brother's blood crieth unto me from the ground,' commissions his ministering servant to preach that very blood for the remission of sins! True, it was their sin that they had shed this blood; and Peter charges them with it, when he says, 'Him, being delivered by the determinate counsel and foreknowledge of God, ye have taken, and by *wicked* hands have crucified and slain;' but mark, it was the very blood which they had sinfully shed whereby they were to obtain the remission of that and of every other sin, for this 'was the blood of the new testament, shed for many, for the remission of sins.' It was their sin that they crucified the Lord; yet his crucifixion was the means of their salvation. And the same truth is applicable to ourselves; for be it remembered, our guilt was the real cause of the Saviour's sufferings, our sins were the nails which suspended him to the accursed tree. He who knew no sin was made sin for us; he was wounded for our transgressions, he was bruised for our iniquities; and as without the shedding of blood there could be no remission, so by the blood of Jesus the sins which caused his death are freely forgiven: for now, in consequence of that stupendous atonement, God can be the just God and yet the Saviour; the sin has been expiated, and the sinner may be saved. This is the Gospel message; and it was the will of Him who died on the cross 'that repentance and remission of sins should be preached in his name among all nations, beginning at Jerusalem.'

The sum and substance of the Gospel is repentance and remission of sins, remission of sins through the *name of Jesus;* and the perfect freeness of it is beautifully illustrated by the narrative of what occurred on the day of Pentecost, viewed in connection with our Lord's command, that this doctrine should be preached among all nations, *beginning at Jerusalem*. Beginning at Jerusalem!, the city of his murderers, the same city whose streets had but recently resounded with the cry, 'Crucify him! crucify him!', the city that had called forth his tears when he wept over it, and said, 'O Jerusalem, Jerusalem, thou that killest the prophets, and stonest them that are sent unto thee, how often would I have gathered thy children, as a hen gathereth her chickens under her wings, but ye would not!' – 'Oh that thou hadst known, even thou in this thy day, the things which belong to thy peace! but now they are hid from thine eyes,' the city, which, besides being washed with his tears, was now stained by his blood; that same city, guilty, devoted as it was, was yet to receive the first announcement of the remission of sins, and the Lord's command was fulfilled on the day of Pentecost, when Peter freely proclaimed repentance and the remission of sins even to the very men whom he charged as the murderers of his Lord. To them, without exception and without reserve, he proclaimed a full and free salvation; and in this one fact we have a conclusive proof of the perfect freeness of the Gospel, for where is the man now under the Christian ministry whose case is worse than that of the thousands who then received the joyful sound? Viewing it in this light, John Bunyan, the able author of the 'Pilgrim's Progress,' makes a felicitous and powerful application of this part of the Gospel narrative, to remove all the doubts and scruples of those who think themselves too guilty to be saved, or who do not sufficiently understand the perfect freeness of this salvation. He supposes one of those whom Peter addressed, exclaiming, But I was one of those who plotted to take away his life: is there hope for me? Another, But I was one of those who bare false witness against him: is there grace for me? A third, But I was one of those that cried out, 'Crucify him! crucify him!' can there be hope for me? A fourth, But I was one of those that did spit in his face, when he stood before his accusers, and I mocked him when in anguish he hung bleeding on the tree: is there hope for me? A fifth, But I was one who gave him vinegar to drink: is there hope for me? And when, in reply, Peter proclaims, 'Repent, and be baptized EVERY ONE OF YOU for the remission of sins, and ye shall receive the Holy Ghost; for the promise is unto you, and to your children,' – Bunyan thus applies it to the conscience of every sinner: 'Wherefore, sinner, be ruled by me in this matter; feign not thyself another man, if thou hast been a vile sinner. Go in thine own colours to Jesus Christ. Put thyself amongst the most vile, and let him alone to put thee among the children. Thou art, as it were, called by name, to come for mercy. Thou man of Jerusalem, hearken to the call, – say, Stand aside, devil! Christ calls me. Stand away, unbelief! Christ calls me. Stand away, all my discouraging apprehensions! for my Saviour calls me to receive mercy.' 'Christ, as he sits on the throne of grace, pointeth ever the heads of thousands directly to such a man, and says, *Come*, – wherefore, since he says Come, let the angels make a lane, and all men make room, that the Jerusalem sinner may come to Christ for mercy!'

But while the free remission of sins through the blood of Christ was the salvation which Peter proclaimed, it was a salvation which stood connected

with an entire change of mind and heart; and hence the offer of a free
forgiveness is combined with an exhortation to 'Repent, and be baptized.'
Repentance means properly a *change of mind*, and implies faith in the truth
which they had formerly rejected, but which they were now called to
receive; sorrow for their sin in crucifying the Lord of glory; and a cheerful
surrender of themselves to his authority, now that they were convinced of
his exaltation. It might seem to be an unreasonable thing in Peter to call
upon them to *repent*, when this implied so great a change of mind and heart,
a change so far surpassing the power of unaided nature. Was it not written
that 'The carnal mind is enmity against God,' that 'The natural man
receiveth not the things of the Spirit of God, for they are foolishness to him;
neither can he know them, because they are spiritually discerned,' and
'That no man can call Jesus Lord, but by the Holy Ghost?' And what was
there in his words that could overcome that enmity, or cure this blindness,
or impart power to repent and believe? Peter was not deterred by any
consideration of this kind: he preached boldly, 'Repent, and be baptized,'
and afterwards, 'Repent, and be converted,' simply because he knew that
his word, weak in itself, might be made mighty through God to the pulling
down of strongholds. For while such was the substance of Peter's sermon,
which was the instrumental means of the great work of conversion on the
day of Pentecost, it must never be forgotten that the truth thus declared
was rendered effectual by the accompanying grace of the Holy Spirit. I
speak not at present of the gift of tongues, or of any other of the miraculous
manifestations of the Spirit's power, but of his inward grace, exerted on the
minds, the consciences, and the hearts of the hearers, whereby 'their eyes
were opened, and they were turned from darkness to light, and from the
power of Satan unto God.' It is true that Peter was an inspired apostle; it is
also true that the Gospel which he preached was in every respect suited as an
instrument for effecting the conversion of souls; nay, it is equally true that
his words were accompanied with such a manifest interposition of divine
power as was plainly miraculous; but all this would not have accomplished
the work, had the inward enlightening and regenerating grace of the Spirit
been withheld. It is the solemn testimony of another apostle, himself an
inspired man, and endowed with the gift of tongues and the power of
working miracles, that 'Paul may plant, and Apollos water, but God giveth
the increase. Who then is Paul, and who is Apollos, but ministers by whom
ye believed, as the *Lord* gave to every man?' If any believed, it was because
'it was given to them on the behalf of Christ to believe on his name,' for
'faith is the gift of God;' and if any repented, it was because their hearts
were softened and changed by Him who is 'exalted as a Prince and Saviour,
to give *repentance* and the remission of sins.'

There are two very different operations of the Spirit of God which are distinctly mentioned in the New Testament, the one external, the other internal, the one temporary, the other permanent, the one peculiar to a few, the other common to all in every age who are savingly converted to God. The first consists in those gifts of prophecy, or tongues, or miracles, which were the appropriate evidences of God's interposition, but which were not in themselves either the sure means or the invariable symptoms of salvation; the second consists in those inward graces of faith, repentance, love, peace, and joy, which constitute the elements of a new spiritual life in the soul.

It follows that there must have been on the day of Pentecost another operation of the Holy Ghost, besides the miraculous gift of tongues, even a direct operation on the soul of every convert, applying the truth with power to his heart and conscience, subduing his will, and bringing him into captivity to the obedience of Christ. The effect of the miraculous dispensation corresponded with the impression which is now produced on the public mind by the reading of the Scriptures: many are impressed and half convinced, who are not savingly converted; and in both cases an *internal work of the Spirit* is essentially necessary to give efficacy to his outward teaching by the Word, or his outward testimony by miracles and signs. Thousands probably left the streets of Jerusalem on that memorable occasion, awestruck and astonished by what they had seen and heard, but still unconvinced and unconverted; and the three thousand who believed were enabled and persuaded to do so by the effectual grace of the Spirit of God. So is it at the present time. We still live under a dispensation which is emphatically called the 'ministration of the Spirit;' and although his visible testimony by signs and miracles is no longer vouchsafed, we have in our hand his written testimony, even the Word, which is the Spirit's witness to Christ; but that Word, although replete with proofs of the Spirit's teaching, will not avail for our conversion any more than the gift of tongues availed on the day of Pentecost for the conversion of all who witnessed it, unless it be accompanied with that inward and effectual operation by which the three thousand were added to the Church of the living God. But this enlightening, convincing, and sanctifying grace of the Spirit is the permanent privilege of the Christian Church; and 'while miracles have ceased, and tongues have failed,' we are still privileged to expect that 'God will give the Spirit to them that ask him;' and surely the Word, now completed, and the Spirit, always promised, may yet accomplish as great a work in the experience of modern believers as was wrought on the day of Pentecost by the first preaching of the Gospel in the streets of Jerusalem.

III. We now proceed to consider the *result* of this great work, as it is described in the short but significant account which is here given of the numbers who were converted, and the subsequent life and conduct of the converts.

In regard to the *numbers* who were converted on this memorable occasion, it is said, 'Then they that gladly received the word were baptized: and the same day there were added unto them about three thousand souls.' Here is a remarkable and precious proof of the efficacy of the Gospel ministry when it is accompanied with the grace of the Spirit – three thousand souls converted suddenly by one sermon, and that, too, from amongst a multitude who were chargeable with crucifying the Lord of glory, and in a city which was already doomed to righteous destruction! There is much in this wonderful event that is fitted to encourage the hope and to animate the zeal of the Christian Church, in prosecuting the arduous, and, with reference to mere human power, the impracticable work of the world's conversion; for here we see how soon and how suddenly the most virulent opposition may be disarmed, and the most sceptical indifference broken up, by the exercise of that divine power which can change the hearts of men, and convert the boldest gainsayers into humble disciples, the fiercest enemies into the most devoted friends of the Gospel. That divine power still exists, and will be put forth for the conviction of the world, and the increase and edification of the Church, in answer to believing prayer; and this is the sheet-anchor of our hope, the sole ground of our confident expectation, that sooner or later the whole earth shall be full of the knowledge of the Lord, and that all the kingdoms of the world shall become the kingdom of our God and of his Christ. The conversion of three thousand souls by one sermon, on the day of Pentecost, is only an example of what may yet be accomplished by the preaching of the Gospel, when 'a nation may be born in a day;' and the suddenness and magnitude of that work, accomplished as it was in circumstances so unfavourable, and on subjects so unpromising, should rebuke the incredulity with which we are too apt to regard any general awakening or remarkable revival amongst ourselves.

Perhaps it may be thought that we are not entitled to expect the same or similar results from the preaching of the Gospel in modern times. It may seem that, as the age of miracles is past, and as we are now left to the ministry of uninspired men, it would be unreasonable, if not presumptuous, to anticipate any such remarkable success as attended the preaching of the apostles on the day of Pentecost. But why? Is not the Gospel still mighty through God? Is not the Spirit of God a permanent agent in the Christian Church? And was it not by the Word and Spirit that the three thousand were converted at Pentecost? It is true, there was a miraculous gift of tongues; but it was not the miracle, it was the truth applied to the heart by the Spirit, which effected the great and sudden change. The miracle made them *wonder*, the miracle prompted some to *mock*, saying, 'These men are full of new wine;' but it was the truth that pricked their hearts, and led them to inquire, 'Men and brethren, what must we do?' and it was the truth which converted them, when they 'gladly received the word;' so that the real cause of their conversion was the gracious internal operation of the Spirit, whereby 'he opened their eyes, and turned them from darkness to light, and from the power of Satan unto God.' And that same agency which was put forth on the day of Pentecost is continued with the Christian Church, and is in fact exerted in its enlightening, convincing, and saving power, on the mind and heart of every sinner who is, or ever will be, converted and saved. And if, in the primitive Church, the Spirit was pleased to exert his agency in various ways, sometimes calling individuals singly, and adding them one by one to the fellowship of the Church, as in the case of Lydia, and Paul, and the gaoler at Philippi; and at other times awakening a multitude at once, as in the case of the three thousand on the day of Pentecost, it is not unreasonable to expect that there may be a similar diversity in the mode of his operation in modern times, and that if he be pleased ordinarily to bless a stated ministry for the gradual gathering in of his sheep, he may occasionally, when it seems meet to his infinite wisdom, effect a more sudden and general awakening.

The sudden and simultaneous conversion of many souls, and the daily and gradual increase of the Church by successive single additions to their number, are *both* mentioned in the narrative; for after recording the conversion of the three thousand, it is said, 'And the Lord added to the Church *daily* such as should be saved.'

But in considering the *result* of this memorable work of grace, we must take into view not merely the numbers who were converted, but also the subsequent life and habits of the converts. They underwent a complete and permanent change of mind and heart, a change so great that they might well be called 'new creatures, in whom old things had passed away, and all things had become new;' for, in the short but comprehensive narrative before us, several expressions occur which will be found, when considered attentively, to exhibit a beautiful exemplification of the nature and magnitude of that change, and the peaceable fruits of righteousness which invariably spring from it.

Their change properly consisted in their believing 'the truth as it is in Jesus;' for it is said that after Peter's sermon, 'they that gladly received his word were baptized,' clearly intimating that faith in the divine testimony concerning Christ was the turning point of their conversion, and their qualification for being recognized and admitted as members of the Christian Church. Formerly they were unbelievers, – they had rejected, condemned, and crucified the Lord of glory; because, through blind ignorance, and inveterate prejudice, they refused to receive him as 'the Messiah that had been promised to the fathers,' and therefore concluded, that as a deceiver of the people he was 'worthy of death;' but now, convinced by the apostle's testimony, and the concurrent attestation of God in the miraculous gift of tongues, they believed that the 'same Jesus whom they had crucified was both LORD and CHRIST,' and, instructed in the gracious message which he had commissioned his apostles to proclaim, even the message of 'repentance and remission of sin,' they gladly received it as the very Gospel of their salvation, and glad tidings of great joy, thereby evincing their deep conviction of sin and danger, and, at the same time, their self-application of the Gospel, as a message sent from God unto them. And by this simple faith they entered on a new spiritual state, for 'whoso believeth that Jesus is the Christ,' and a Christ to him, 'is born of God.'

But this faith was productive of much fruit: it was not the inert speculative faith of which the Apostle James speaks when he says, 'It is dead, being alone;' nor was their gladness in receiving the word like the evanescent excitement of those 'who hear the word, and anon with joy receive it, but have no root in themselves, and dure only for a while.' On the contrary, the good seed of the Word, well rooted in their hearts, sprang up and produced fruit in their lives; for they 'continued steadfastly in the apostles' doctrine and fellowship, and in breaking of bread, and in prayers,' – and 'continuing daily with one accord in the temple, and breaking bread from house to house, did eat their meat with gladness and singleness of heart, praising God, and having favour with all the people.'

The *continuance* of their religious impressions, the constancy of their profession, and their perseverance and advancement in the Christian course, are here specially mentioned, along with their diligent use of all the means of grace, as marks of the genuine nature of that change which they had so suddenly experienced; and this should be seriously considered by all, but especially by those who are conscious of having been occasionally impressed by divine truth, and who may be able to remember some seasons when they were deeply affected by it, while, notwithstanding, there is no evidence of a permanent change, and no symptom of growing advancement. Of the three classes of unproductive hearers mentioned by our Lord himself, two are represented as experiencing some transitory and evanescent change of feeling; for 'he that received the seed into stony places' is represented as 'hearing the word, and anon with joy receiving it; but having no root in himself, he dureth for a while; and when tribulation or persecution ariseth because of the word, by and by he is offended.' And he also that received seed among the thorns is represented as 'hearing the word; but the care of this world, and the deceitfulness of riches, choke the word, and he becometh unfruitful.' Occasional impressions and transitory emotions are not enough; many have perished in their sins who were often and deeply impressed, and the Lord himself has forewarned us that he, and he only, 'that endureth to the end shall be saved.' This is the first feature of genuine conversion which is here represented to us, I mean the permanent and abiding power of religious principle in the heart.

Another feature of their case is the public profession which they made of their faith in Christ, and obedience to him, by submitting to be baptized in his name. This profession they made in very trying circumstances; for not only did their baptism amount to a confession that the same Jesus whom they had crucified as a malefactor was indeed the Lord of glory, and a virtual acknowledgment of their own guilt, and the guilt of their rulers in condemning him to death, but it pledged them to the maintenance and defence of his cause in a city where there were many scoffers, and at a time when they had reason to apprehend the most bitter opposition and trial. Yet in the very streets of Jerusalem which had resounded with the fearful cry, Crucify him, crucify him!, a cry which their voices had helped to raise, they now consent to be publicly baptized in his name; and this consideration also deserves to be seriously weighed by those who are prevented by shame or fear from avouching Christ as their Lord, along with his own solemn declaration, 'Whosoever shall be ashamed of me, and of my words, in this adulterous and sinful generation, of him also shall the Son of man be ashamed, when he cometh in the glory of his Father, with the holy angels.'

Another interesting feature of their character, is their steady desire for instruction, and their regular attendance on ordinances. In the case of young converts, especially when their conversion has been suddenly effected, and accompanied with remarkable manifestations of divine power, there has sometimes been observed a presumptuous neglect of the ordinary means of grace, and a disrelish for the common exercises of Christian worship; and this, whether it proceeds from undue excitement or from spiritual pride, is alike injurious to their own peace, and to the comfort of their fellow-disciples. How different the spirit and conduct of the primitive disciples, converted as they had been by the preaching of inspired apostles, and in circumstances which evinced the signal interposition of God! They neither felt as if they had no more need of instruction, nor as if they were independent of the common ordinances of the Church: 'They continued steadfastly in the apostles' doctrine and fellowship, and in breaking of

bread, and in prayers,' uniting with all who professed the same faith, and
sharing with them in the usual exercises by which the glory of God was
promoted and the edification of the Church advanced. They continued
'in the apostles' doctrine,' listening to their instructions, and adhering to the
faith as it was taught by them; and 'in the apostles' fellowship,' not
separating themselves, but preserving the unity of the Spirit in the bond of
peace; 'in breaking of bread,' uniting with their fellow-disciples in the
celebration of the Lord's Supper, and in the secret and social exercise of
prayer and praise.

Another interesting feature of their case is the spirit of brotherly love and
mutual charity which then prevailed in the Church at Jerusalem. Faith
worketh by love, love being the sum of God's law and the substance of
all acceptable obedience. And most beautifully is the operation of faith in
producing a spirit of love exemplified in the case before us. It is said, 'And
all that believed were together, and had all things common, and sold their
possessions and goods, and parted them to all men, as every man had need.'
There was no law to this effect: it was the spontaneous fruit of their love to
Christ and to each other, prompted probably by the consideration that
many among them were strangers at Jerusalem, and needed the accom-
modations and supplies which their wealthier brethren could afford. The
apostles never sought to abrogate the right of property, or to inculcate the
duty of having all things in common, as has sometimes been supposed, and
more recently maintained by a class of men calling themselves Socialists,
who maintain that the three cardinal evils of society in modern times are
the belief in a God, the institution of marriage, and the right of private
property; and who propose to abolish and sweep them all away, in order to
introduce a new social, a *new moral* world, in which religion shall be
exchanged for Atheism, and marriage for indiscriminate licence, and all
personal rights for a community of goods. These horrible principles, fast
spreading, we fear, amongst the neglected and uneducated poor, and
undermining the foundations of our oldest and most revered institutions,
are so flagrantly opposed to the truths of the Bible that, so long as the Bible
is believed, they must be repudiated and condemned. But, anxious to avail
themselves of any seeming support which they may draw from the sacred
volume, some have not hesitated to represent that part of their system
which consists in the abolition of private property and the institution of a
community of goods, as being exemplified in the case of the primitive
Christians, who, after the day of Pentecost, 'had all things common, and
sold their possessions and goods, and parted them to all men, as every man
had need.' But that the apostles did not mean to abrogate the rights of property is clear, from its being expressly said that they *sold* their goods,

thereby conveying to others the right which they had previously possessed; and that they were not constrained by any imperative rule to part with them even for this purpose appears from the case of Ananias and Sapphira, to whom Peter said, 'Why hath Satan filled thine heart to lie to the Holy Ghost, and to keep back part of the price of the land? Whiles it remained, was it not thine own? and after it was sold, was it not in *thine own power?*' clearly intimating that there was no such community of goods among them as is now contended for, and no constraint on the exercise of their charity. But this only shows the more clearly the fervour and the strength of that disinterested love which prompted them, of their own accord, to sacrifice their wealth for the support and comfort of their poorer brethren, and exhibits to us a beautiful example of self-denying charity, which it were well for us to imitate; so that now, as then, the world might be constrained to say, 'Behold these Christians, how they love one another!' But why was there so much love in the infant Church at Jerusalem? Our Lord explains the reason, when, speaking of the 'woman that was a sinner from the city, who stood at his feet behind him weeping, and began to wash his feet with tears, and did wipe them with the hair of her head, and kissed his feet, and anointed them with ointment,' he said, 'Her sins, which are many, are forgiven; for she loved much: but to whom little is forgiven, the same loveth little.' The three thousand who were converted on the day of Pentecost were chargeable with the great sin of crucifying the Son of God: they had much forgiven them; and, according to the principle explained by the Lord, they *loved* much, there being on such instance of human love recorded in the whole Bible as that of the Church at Jerusalem, which was composed of men stained with the blood of Jesus, and by that same blood washed from their sins!

Another feature in their case was the consistency of their conduct and the beauty of their example, which produced a deep impression on the public mind, and one that was, in no small degree, favourable to the cause of the Gospel. 'And they, continuing daily with one accord in the temple, and breaking bread from house to house, did eat their meat with gladness and singleness of heart, praising God, and having favour with all the people. And the Lord added to the church daily such as should be saved.' We are here taught to consider their consistent, and cheerful, and devoted conduct, as a means of conciliating the favour of the people, and promoting the success of the Gospel itself; and their mutual concord and happy fellowship together, are specially noticed as conducive to this effect. Oh! would to God that we enjoyed the same concord, and were imbued with the same spirit, and that all the sincere disciples of Christ could live together in unity; then might we hope that our faith and love, and catholic union, would produce a favourable impression on the public mind. Not that the world's enmity would be destroyed; for, notwithstanding the favour with which the primitive Church was for a time regarded, that enmity soon broke out in open persecution, and it is impossible to conciliate the world until the world is itself converted: but the absence of all strife and divisions, and the prevalence of love and peace in the Church itself, would give it a favourable opportunity of directing its whole energies to the conversion of the world; while the exhibition of all Christian graces on the part of Christ's people would make its own impression on the mind of every spectator; for thus it was at the first: 'fear came upon every soul;' and 'they had favour with all the people;' 'and the Lord added to the church daily such as should be saved.'

IX. Revivals: Acts 2.17, 18

THE greatest work that is going on in the world is that of the conversion of sinners, and the edification of saints.

Sometimes this work proceeds slowly and silently under the stated ministry of the Word, one after another being secretly impressed with the power of divine truth, and taken under the teaching of God's Spirit, and 'built up in faith, and holiness, and comfort, unto eternal life.' At other times, it is accomplished in a more extraordinary and remarkable way, vast numbers being brought suddenly under the power of divine truth, and exhibiting in a striking manner the effects of divine grace.

We have been so much accustomed to look to the more slow and quiet and gradual method of maintaining and extending the kingdom of Christ, that we are apt to be startled, and even to listen with some degree of incredulous surprise, when we hear of any sudden and general work of the Spirit of God; nay, we cease even to expect and to pray for any more remarkable or more rapid change in the state of the Church and world than what is usually observed under a regular ministry.

But 'God's ways are not as our ways, neither are his thoughts as our thoughts;' and often, in the history of his Church, has he been pleased for wise reasons to manifest his grace and power in a very extraordinary and remarkable manner; partly to awaken and arouse a slumbering Church; partly also to alarm and convince gainsayers; and, most of all, to teach them at once the sovereignty and the power of that grace which they are too prone to despise.

When any real revival of the power of true religion takes place in any country, however local and temporary, provided only that some immortal souls are thereby savingly converted, we have reason to know that such an event, however it may be ridiculed by the world, is the occasion of joy to the angels in the upper sanctuary, and also of unmingled satisfaction to the Redeemer himself. If we have any thing of the same spirit, such an event will be an occasion of joy to ourselves, and is fitted, indeed, in many ways, to confirm our wavering faith, to animate our flagging zeal, to add energy to our lukewarm prayers, and strength to our languid hopes. Wherever God's power and glory are remarkably displayed, it is alike the duty and the privilege of his Church to behold and adore it; and surely, if it 'be the ground of much rejoicing among the angels before the throne, it should also engage the praises of the Christian brotherhood on earth.'

The Bible speaks of 'times of refreshing from the presence of the Lord', seasons of remarkable revival which should occur long after the days of the apostles; and it records several memorable examples which occurred both under the Old and the New Testament dispensations; to which we may briefly advert, with the view of showing that such revivals are expressly recognized in the Word of God.

It is probable that when it is said of those who lived in the days of Seth, 'Then began men to call upon the name of the Lord,' there is an allusion to some general revival of religion which occurred before the deluge. But we have a more particular account of a very general and remarkable revival in the times of Joshua. Of the whole generation which entered with him into the promised land, we read: 'The people served the Lord all the days of Joshua, and all the days of the elders that outlived Joshua, who had seen all the great works of the Lord, that he did for Israel.' But when 'all that generation were gathered unto their fathers, there arose another generation after them, which knew not the Lord, nor yet the works which he had done for Israel: and the children of Israel did evil in the sight of the Lord.' Several circumstances are recorded in the sacred narrative, which show that under the ministry of Joshua there was a very deep spirit of earnest religion among the people, and that it exerted a wide and extensive influence. The nation acted as one man, and in a spirit of devoted piety, when 'the whole congregation of the children of Israel assembled together at Shiloh, and set up the tabernacle of the congregation there; and the land was subdued before them.' Again, when 'all Israel, and their elders, and officers, and judges stood on this side the ark and on that side,' while 'Joshua read all the words of the law, the blessings and cursings, according to all that is written in the book of the law; there was not a word of all that Moses commanded which Joshua read not before all the congregation of Israel, with the women and the little ones, and the strangers that were conversant among them;' and so when 'all Israel stoned Achan with stones, and burned him with fire, for his trespass in the accursed thing;' and when 'the whole congregation of the children of Israel gathered themselves together to Shiloh,' to go up to war against the two tribes and a half, on the first suspicion of their falling into idolatry. Such a general and lively zeal on behalf of God's service indicates a deep and prevailing sense of religion; and it is interesting to reflect on the means by which this had been produced. We are told that the Israelites who came out of Egypt with Moses were a stiff-necked and rebellious people; but none of these, excepting Joshua and Caleb, entered into the promised land: they all died in the wilderness; and it was their children – children born and bred in the wilderness – who afterwards exhibited so much of the power of religion on their hearts; and their religious earnestness and zeal may be ascribed to three things: first, that they had seen the wonderful works of the Lord, the miracles which he wrought in the wilderness, and the remarkable fulfilment of his word; secondly, that, from their earliest years, they had received a *wilderness education*, – being trained from their childhood in hardships and trials, which taught them their entire dependence on God, and the duty of an absolute submission to his sovereign will; thirdly, that they had heard the reading of God's law, and were acquainted with its glorious truths. These were suitable and appropriate means; but the experience of their fathers shows, that of themselves, neither the hardships nor the miracles of the wilderness would have produced true religion; that depends on the *blessing of the Spirit of God.*

Another remarkable season of the revival of true religion occurs in the history of the Kings. When Shaphan read the book of the law before Josiah, 'It came to pass, when the king had heard the words of the book of the law, that he rent his clothes. And the king commanded the priests and scribes, and other officers, Go ye, inquire of the Lord for me, and for the people, and for all Judah, concerning the words of this book that is found: for great is the wrath of the Lord that is kindled against us, because our fathers have not hearkened unto the words of this book, to do according unto all that which is written concerning us.' The king's concern for his people was now remarkably displayed: he knew that they were exposed to God's wrath, and dreaded the judgments with which they were threatened. And forthwith 'he sent and gathered unto him all the elders of Judah and of Jerusalem. And the king went up into the house of the Lord, and all the men of Judah, and all the inhabitants of Jerusalem with him, and the priests, and the prophets, and all the people, both small and great: and he read in their ears all the words of the book of the covenant which was found in the house of the Lord. And the king stood by a pillar, and made a covenant before the Lord, to walk after the Lord, and to keep his commandments, and his testimonies, and his statutes, with all their heart, and all their soul, to perform the words of this covenant that were written in this book. And all the people stood to the covenant.' Then followed a great national reformation; as we read, in the sequel of the same chapter, the vessels that had been made for Baal and the host of heaven were burnt; idolatrous priests were suppressed; the houses of the Sodomites were broken down; Topheth, in which children were made to pass through the fire to Molech, was defiled; the horses and chariots which had been given to the service of the Sun were taken away or destroyed; the idolatrous altars of the kings of Judah were overthrown; the high places which Solomon had built were not spared; the images were broken in pieces, and the groves cut down; Jeroboam's altar at Bethel was overturned; the offending priests were cut off, according to the national law; – and then there followed a great convocation, a solemn general assembly to keep the Passover, of which it is said, 'Surely there was not holden such a passover, from the days of the judges that judged Israel, nor in all the days of the kings of Israel, nor of the kings of Judah.' And of Josiah himself it is said, 'Like unto him was there no king before him, that turned unto the Lord with all his heart, and with all his soul, and with all his might, according to all the law of Moses; neither after him arose there any like him.'

Some other similar instances of a revival of the power of religion among the people of Israel might be mentioned: such as that which took place under king Asa, and that also under king Hezekiah; and the remarkable change that was wrought on the hearts of the captives at Babylon, and by which they were prepared for their restoration to their own land, a change which occurred chiefly amongst the younger Jews who were left, since their fathers had died in captivity, just as formerly the young generation were impressed in the wilderness, and of which Ezra says, 'Now for a little space grace hath been showed from the Lord our God, to leave us a remnant to escape, and to give us a nail in his holy place; that our God may lighten our eyes, and give us a little reviving in our bondage.' And there are many passages in the Old Testament (Psal. 35; 102. 13–22) which are beautifully descriptive of the spiritual revivals which occurred from time to time under the Jewish dispensation.

In many other passages of the Old Testament (Isa. 52. 7; 54. 1–5; Ezek. 36. 25; Hos. 14. 4; Joel 2. 28) we find predictions of great and general revivals of religion, which should occur under the new and better dispensation to which the faith of the Jewish Church looked forward. And accordingly, in the New Testament, we read the authentic account of the most remarkable revival of true religion that has ever occurred in the history of the world. It was as it were 'life from the dead.' A new impulse was then given to the world, the force of which is felt, and its effects witnessed, at the present day. It was not a new religion that was then introduced, but a completion of that which had been revealed from the beginning, the visible fulfilment of God's word of promise, and a clearer manifestation of his grace and truth. Amidst the general defection of the Jewish Church and nation, there were some hidden ones who cherished a sincere and devoted piety, and waited for the hope and consolation of Israel; and these were revived and refreshed by the ministry of John the Baptist, and still more by the manifestation of the Son of God. Multitudes of careless sinners were converted; and although the work might have seemed to be suspended by the crucifixion of the Lord of glory, that event only prepared the way for a more remarkable outpouring of the Spirit of God, and a more general awakening among the nations. Jews and Gentiles, men of all nations and of various languages, were suddenly arrested, convinced, converted, and became Christian missionaries to spread the glorious Gospel over the whole world. No sooner had the Spirit of God descended in his miraculous gifts on the apostles, than he descended also in his saving grace on their hearers, insomuch that on the day of Pentecost, three thousand souls were converted by a single sermon. Oh! let those who doubt the power of God's Word and Spirit, or who are conscious of a latent jealousy and distrust respecting any remarkable and sudden work of conversion, consider that case which stands recorded in the Word of God, and let them listen to the question of the prophet: 'Oh! thou that art named the house of Jacob, is the Spirit of the Lord straitened?'; 'Is his hand shortened, that it cannot save? is his ear heavy, that it cannot hear?' Nor is the great work of conversion on the day of Pentecost a solitary instance in the New Testament; great multitudes believed in other places – the Lord 'added to the Church daily such as should be saved;' and in Athens, and Rome, and Corinth; in Galatia, Asia, Cappadocia, and Bithynia; in places the most rude, and the most refined, the preaching of the apostles was mighty through God, and was felt to be the power of God and the wisdom of God unto salvation. Follow one of the apostles through the various scenes of his labours; trace his course on the deep, and his journeys by land; suppose yourself to be a companion of Paul, and a witness of the scenes which he saw, of the converts whom he gathered, and the churches which he founded, and which long existed as monuments and memorials of his successful labours; and say, could you then doubt that the preaching of the Gospel, accompanied by the power of the Spirit, is sufficient to revolutionize the world, to overturn the kingdom of darkness, and to erect on its ruins that kingdom of God which consists in righteousness, and peace, and joy in the Holy Ghost?

While such was the experience of the Church of God, both under the Old and the New Testament dispensations, it remains to inquire how far we are entitled to expect the same, or similar results, from the preaching of the Gospel in modern times. It might seem that, being far removed from the age of miracles, and being left, in so far as the use of means is concerned, to depend on the mere preaching of the Word, it would be unreasonable, if not presumptuous, in us to anticipate any such remarkable success as attended the preaching of the apostles on the day of Pentecost. Yet there are some weighty considerations applicable to this question which may serve to abate the supposed improbability of such an expectation. In the first place, there are many prophecies which predict, many promises which insure, the progressive advancement and the ultimate universality of the Gospel: 'Ask of me,' says the Father to his beloved Son, 'and I will give thee the heathen for thine heritage, and the uttermost parts of the earth for thy possession.' 'In thee, and in thy seed,' said he to Abraham, 'shall all the families of the earth be blessed.' 'There shall be an handful of corn in the earth upon the top of the mountains; the fruit thereof shall shake like Lebanon: and they of the city shall flourish like grass of the earth. His name shall endure for ever: his name shall be continued as long as the sun: and men shall be blessed in him: all nations shall call him blessed.' 'The earth shall be filled with the knowledge of the Lord, as the waters cover the sea.' 'For I would not, brethren, that ye should be ignorant of this mystery, lest ye should be wise in your own conceits, that blindness in part is happened to Israel, until the fulness of the Gentiles be come in. And so all Israel shall be saved; as it is written, There shall come out of Zion the Deliverer, and shall turn away ungodliness from Jacob.' These passages, which declare the progressive advancement, and insure the ultimate universality of the Gospel, imply that the work of conversion is to be carried on in the Church of Christ, a work which is to be accomplished instrumentally by the preaching of the Gospel, applied with power to the heart and conscience by the direct operation of the Holy Ghost. Every soul that is successively added to the Church of such as shall be saved, must be enlightened, convinced, subdued, and converted, by precisely the same agency which was put forth on the day of Pentecost. If the Gospel, even when it was declared by inspired men, and accompanied with the signs of God's miraculous interposition, depended, for its converting power and its saving efficacy, on the grace of that divine Spirit who 'divideth to every man severally as he will,' how much more now, when it is proclaimed by men alike destitute of the light of inspiration and the power of miracles?

That the gracious operation of the Spirit of God was to be continued with the Christian Church, and to be effectual to the end of time for the conversion of sinners and the sanctification of his people, is matter both of prediction and of promise. Many are apt to suppose that, because the miraculous gifts of tongues and healing and prophecy have long since ceased in the Christian Church, the agency of the Spirit of God has been discontinued, forgetting that what is in reality the most valuable part of the Spirit's work is permanent, and will be carried on till the end of time. The work of conversion, by which sinners are turned from darkness to light, and the work of sanctification, by which they are gradually prepared for glory, are as much the fruit of the Spirit as was the inspiration of the

[225]

apostles: and these must be continued, until the whole company of the redeemed shall have been gathered in from among all people, and tongues, and nations. So far from having discontinued his gracious agency, the Spirit of God is at work in every congregation, in every soul that is deriving spiritual benefit from his Word; and we live in these latter times under a dispensation which is emphatically 'the ministration of the Spirit.' Before the miraculous gifts of the Spirit were bestowed on the day of Pentecost, his agency, as the Sanctifier of God's people was felt in the Church, and acknowledged by the sacred writers of the Old Testament. And surely, if He was known in his enlightening and sanctifying influence by the Old Testament Church, it cannot be supposed that the Church under a new and better dispensation will be deprived of his gracious presence; especially when we find that one of the greatest blessings that was predicted and promised to the Church in later times was an out-pouring of the Holy Spirit. Referring to New Testament times, Isaiah says, 'The palaces shall be forsaken,' 'until the Spirit be poured out upon us from on high;' and Joel, 'I will pour out my Spirit upon all flesh;' which is expressly applied to the New Testament Church in the Acts of the Apostles: and, accordingly, the sacred writers in all their epistles refer to the ordinary gracious work of the Spirit as a matter of experience with every true believer, even with such as had no miraculous gifts. It was their prayer for all believers, that 'the communion of the Holy Ghost,' not less than 'the grace of the Lord Jesus Christ and the love of God,' should be with them all; nay, it is solemnly declared that every one that should be converted to the end of time must be converted by the Spirit; that every soul that should be born again, should be born of the Spirit: and to say, then, that the gracious operations of the Spirit of God have ceased in the Christian Church were virtually to declare that the work of conversion is finished, that the gate of heaven is now closed, that not one soul can now be added to the Church of such as shall be saved; for it is clear, that 'except a man be born again he cannot enter into the kingdom of God; and it is equally clear, that if he be born again, he must be 'born of the Spirit.'

The renewing and sanctifying agency of the Spirit of God, then, has not ceased in the Christian Church; nor will it ever cease until the last convert has been won, the last penitent restored. The continued agency of the Spirit of God in the Church, under the present dispensation, which is emphatically called 'the ministration of the Spirit,' is a doctrine which teaches us to expect great results from the faithful preaching of the Gospel, and is, in fact, the sheet-anchor of the Gospel ministry, their sole en-couragement to persevere in the otherwise hopeless effort to evangelize and regenerate the world. Take away the grace of the Holy Spirit, expunge those passages from the Bible which contain the promise of his enlightening, renewing and converting grace, and then you leave us with none but natural means to accomplish a supernatural work; you leave us, by our mere persuasion and importunity, to convert enmity into love, to quicken the dead to life, to raise a fallen world to heaven, then, indeed, our hopes were deluded, our expectations visionary, our aims abortive; but leave with us the promise which God has given; grant that the Gospel is an instrument in his hands, and that the Holy Spirit is the ever living and ever active Teacher and Sanctifier of souls, then, in the strength of this truth, we can face all difficulties and rise above all discouragement; and stand unmoved amidst the mockery of the world; and preach the Gospel with confidence of ultimate success, both to Greek and barbarian, to savage and to civilized men; for the Gospel is adapted to every human heart, and the Spirit of God has power to make it effectual, and the promise stands on record for ever, 'He will give the Spirit to them that ask him.'

It being admitted, then, that the real and active agency of the Spirit of God for the conversion of souls may reasonably be expected in the Christian Church, the only question which remains to be considered is, whether that divine Agent will always act in one uniform method, quietly and gradually extending the kingdom of Christ by the successive conversion of individual sinners, as he is wont for the most part to do: or whether he may not, for wise reasons, and in the exercise of that sovereignty which belongs to him, act occasionally in a more extraordinary and remarkable way, turning multitudes at once, and perhaps suddenly, from darkness to light, and bringing about a general revival of the power of religion in particular places and congregations? In other words, may we reasonably believe and expect that the Spirit of God will occasionally produce a remarkable religious revival?

That we may proceed to the calm and impartial consideration of this question, it may be useful, first of all, to obviate and remove some prejudices which might either prevent us from entertaining it at all, or unfit us for deciding it aright.

It is of great importance to form a clear and definite idea of what is meant by a revival of religion. It properly consists in these two things: – a general impartation of new life, and vigour, and power, to those who are already of the number of God's people; and a remarkable awakening and conversion of souls who have hitherto been careless and unbelieving: in other words, it consists in new spiritual life imparted to the dead, and in new spiritual health imparted to the living.

A revival properly consists in one or both of these two things – a revived state of religion among the members of the Church, and the increase of their number by the addition of souls converted to God. Can it be doubted by any professing Christian, either that such a revival is possible, or that it is desirable? Why, what is the end of the Gospel ministry? what the great design of our Sabbaths and our sanctuaries? what the purport of all Gospel promises in reference to the kingdom of grace? Is it not that such souls as have heretofore been 'dead in trespasses and sins' may be quickened into spiritual life? and that such souls as have already been quickened into life may grow in spiritual health and vigour, and be revived and restored when they have fallen into declension and decay? Do we not all pray for these things? And is it not our privilege to expect, that for these things our prayers will be heard and answered?

The simultaneous conversion of many souls, and the increasing power of true religion in the hearts of God's people, are the constituent elements of a religious revival; and these two effects of the Spirit's grace, while they may be wrought separately, are nevertheless found, when they are wrought together, to exert a powerful reciprocal influence on each other. Sometimes, under a Gospel ministry, the faith, and love, and zeal of a Christian Church are revived and strengthened, without being immediately accompanied with any remarkable awakening of careless sinners; at other times, many successive conversions are wrought one after another, while the general tone of Christian piety is not observably raised or strengthened: but when at one and the same time believers are invigorated with new strength, and many careless sinners are converted, there is a powerful reciprocal influence exerted on each by the experience of the other. Decaying and backsliding Christians are aroused and reclaimed, when they see God's power exerted in the conversion of sinners; they feel that there is a reality and a vital energy in God's truth, that Christ lives and reigns, that the Spirit is still present with the Church; and they are excited to greater earnestness in prayer, to greater devotedness of heart, to greater holiness of life; while their reawakened zeal and their fervent prayers fit them for exerting a holier influence over others, and may be the means of adding many to the Church of such as shall be saved. Thus it was on the day of Pentecost. On that remarkable occasion it is recorded that 'fear came upon every soul;' and the result was that 'the Lord added to the Church daily such as should be saved.'

It is of great practical importance to observe that the work of the Spirit on the soul of *every individual convert* is substantially the same with that which takes place, but only on a more extended scale, in a general revival of religion. When *many* are suddenly arrested and convinced, when conversions take place in large numbers, and are attended with remarkable circumstances, the work of the Spirit attracts more of public attention and produces a larger measure of excitement; but substantially it is the self-same work, which has often been carried on in silence in the secret chamber, in the retired recesses of the heart; when one poor sinner in a congregation has been singled out from a multitude of careless professors, and made the subject of a saving change. It matters not whether a man passes from death unto life in solitude or in society, whether he ventures alone to the mercy-seat, or is accompanied thither by a multitude of earnest suppliants, whether the light of heaven shines in upon his soul, leaving others in darkness, or shines at the same time into the hearts of thousands more. The same change which was wrought on the three thousand converts of Pentecost passed also on the spirit of Lydia, when she worshipped with a few other women by the river side; and on the spirit of the Philippian gaoler, when he stood alone with the apostles. One may be converted at a time, or many; but the work of conversion is the same in all. Every soul, in a general revival, must be enlightened by divine truth, and awakened to concern about its salvation, and melted into godly sorrow, for sin, and stirred up to lay hold on Christ and his free salvation, and imbued with new views, new affections, new desires, new tastes, new hopes, new habits; in a word, every such soul as passes from death unto life, in a season of general awakening, must pass through the same general experience, which on other occasions is realized by the solitary inquirer, when, in his secret chamber, he thinks and repents and believes and prays and enters into peace with God. No one, therefore, who has experienced that great change in his own soul, who has known what it is to be awakened to concern about his own salvation, who has wept and prayed in secret, and earnestly read his Bible, and has drunk in the precious truths of the Gospel, ought to feel any jealousy concerning a general revival of true religion: on the contrary, he should regard it with such feelings as befit the occasion, the feeling of hope and expectation that some great good will be accomplished; the feeling of gratitude and joy, that new manifestations and proofs of the Saviour's power are vouchsafed; and the feeling of solemn awe, arising from the thought that God is interposing, that immortal souls are being born again, and that these souls are now undergoing all that solemn conviction, and feeling all those anxious fears, and impressed with all those awful views of God and judgment and eternity, which he himself had experienced when he first repented and wept and prayed and wrestled for his own salvation.

The Holy Spirit is not limited to any one mode of operation in the execution of his glorious work; and his sovereignty ought ever to be remembered when we are considering a subject of this nature. It has, unfortunately, been too much overlooked, when, on the one hand, some have insisted, as we think with undue partiality and confidence, on a general and remarkable revival, as being in itself the best manifestation of the Spirit's grace, and as being, in all cases, a matter of promise to believing prayer; and when, on the other hand, not a few have looked to the quiet and gradual success of the Gospel ministry, to the exclusion, or at least disparagement, of any more sudden and remarkable work of grace. The former have given a too exclusive preference to what is extraordinary and striking; while the latter have fallen into the opposite error, of preferring what is more usual and quiet. We think it were better to admit of both methods of conversion, and to leave the choice to the sovereign wisdom and grace of the Spirit. It is equally possible for him to convert souls successively or simultaneously; and in adopting either course doubtless he has wise ends in view. We have no sympathy with those who, overlooking the steady progress of the great work of conversion under a stated ministry, make no account of the multitudes who are added, one by one, to the Church of the living God, merely because their conversion has not been attended with the outward manifestations of a great religious revival; nor can we agree with them in thinking that the Church has any sure warrant to expect that the Spirit will be bestowed, in every instance, in that particular way. But as little have we any sympathy with those who, rejecting all revivals as unscriptural delusions, profess to look exclusively to the gradual progress of divine truth, and the slow advance of individual conversion under a stated ministry. Both methods, the simultaneous and the successive conversion of souls, are equally within the power of the Spirit; and there may exist wise reasons why, in certain cases, the first should be chosen, while, in other cases, the second is preferred.

Several important purposes may be promoted by the sudden and simultaneous conversion of many souls, and the concurrent revival of Christian congregations, which either could not be attained at all, or not to the same extent, by the more ordinary and gradual progress of the Gospel. A season of general awakening affords, both to believers and unbelievers, a new and very impressive proof of the reality and power of the Spirit's grace; it strengthens the faith and enlarges the hopes of God's people; it awakens those nominal professors who are at ease in Zion, and it alarms and arouses the consciences of the irreligious multitude. For when many are suddenly arrested by the power of the Spirit, and turned from the error of their ways, and made to break off their sins by repentance, and are seen flying to Christ like doves to their windows, the mind of every spectator must be impressed with a sense of the reality and importance of religion, and the most ungodly for a time will tremble.

Such a season of revival may be designed to manifest in an extraordinary way, the continued presence and the active agency of the Holy Spirit, to demonstrate the faithfulness of God in fulfilling the promises of his Word, to evince the efficacy of believing prayer, to teach the Church the weakness of human instruments, and the true source of all spiritual power, to quicken her faith and hope, when, through manifold trials and increasing difficulties, she might be ready to faint and be discouraged, as if the task of regenerating the world were left to be accomplished by inadequate resources, to stir her up to greater efforts in a spirit of lively faith and humble dependence, and to afford new evidence to succeeding generations that Christ is the exalted Head of the Church, and that all power is still given to him in heaven and on earth. These are some of the important practical lessons which may be taught by such seasons of revival in the Church, lessons which might be deduced from the more ordinary operations of the Spirit under the regular ministry of the Word, but which are more prominently presented, and more impressively enforced, when, in the exercise of his adorable sovereignty, the Spirit of God, instead of descending like '*dew* on the grass,' comes like '*showers* which water the earth,' or like '*floods* on the dry ground.' And if these or similar ends may be promoted by such means, who will say that they may not be employed by Him who is 'wonderful in counsel, and excellent in working,' and of whom it is written, 'There are diversities of gifts, but the same Spirit. And there are differences of administrations, but the same Lord. And there are diversities of operations, but it is the same God which worketh all in all.' 'All these worketh that one and the self-same Spirit, dividing to every man severally as he will?'

That such seasons of general religious revival as occurred at the feast of Pentecost were to be expected in subsequent times appears from those promises of Scripture which relate to 'times of refreshing from the presence of the Lord,' which ensure the continued presence of Christ and his Spirit with the Church in all ages, and which declare that 'when the enemy shall come in like a flood, the Spirit of the Lord shall lift up a standard against him.' And that such seasons of revival *have* occurred at intervals along the whole line of the Church's history is a fact which is amply confirmed by historical evidence, and sufficient to obviate any prejudice arising from the idea that such an event is novel or unprecedented.

The history of the collective Church resembles the experience of individual believers in many respects, and chiefly in this, that in both there occur seasons of growth and decay, of progress and declension, each bearing a resemblance to the course of nature with its spring and winter, its seed-time and harvest.

Thus in the great Reformation of the sixteenth century, a reformation in the outward state of the Church, which had its source and spring in a revival of religion in the hearts of a few chosen men, when simultaneously in Germany, and Switzerland, and Britain, the Holy Spirit said, 'Let there be light; and there was light.' 'As in spring time the breath of life is felt from the sea-shore to the mountain-top, so the Spirit of God was now melting the ice of a long winter in every part of Christendom, and clothing with verdure and flowers the most secluded valleys, and the most steep and barren rocks. Germany did not communicate the light of truth to Switzerland, Switzerland to France, France to England – all these lands received it from God, just as no one region transmits the light to another, but the same orb of splendour dispenses it direct to the earth. Raised far above men, Christ, the day-star from on high, was at the period of the Reformation as at the first introduction of the Gospel, the divine source whence came the light of the world. One and the same doctrine suddenly established itself in the sixteenth century at the domestic hearths and in the places of worship of nations the most distant and dissimilar. It was because the same Spirit was everywhere present, producing the same faith.'[1]

A series of *local revivals*, on a more partial and limited scale, have occurred since the great general revival at the era of the Reformation.

From 1623 to 1641 there occurred a very remarkable revival of true religion in the province of Ulster, in Ireland, which was the germ of that Presbyterian Church which continues to bless that province to the present time. The inhabitants of Ulster were settlers drawn from England and Scotland, and planted there as a colony by King James. At first they were men of reckless and dissolute character, and 'ripe for a great manifestation either of judgment or of mercy.'[1] In God's good providence, some able and zealous ministers of the Gospel, being oppressed in Scotland and England, took refuge in Ireland, and amongst them the eminent Blair, and Livingstone, and Welsh; and such a remarkable blessing accompanied their preaching, that not only were many souls converted, but pure Gospel Churches were planted, and a Gospel discipline introduced. Not a few of the higher ranks were converted; and it is a memorable fact that the greatest success attended the preaching, not of the ablest and most prudent ministers, but of one whose gifts were weak, who knew little more than the terrors of the law, and who was 'a man, it is said, who would never have been chosen by a wise assembly of ministers, nor sent to begin a reformation in the land. Yet this was the Lord's choice, that all men might see that it was not by power, nor by might, nor by man's wisdom, but by my Spirit, saith the Lord.'

[1] D'Aubigné, *The History of the Reformation of the Sixteenth Century*, ii. 347.
[2] Reid's *History of the Synod of Ulster*.

In 1625 a remarkable revival of religion occurred in the parish of Stewarton, chiefly through the instrumentality of the David Dickson, minister of Irvine. He had but recently before been driven from his church by the Court of High Commission, and banished to the north of Scotland; but being restored in 1623, he was greatly blessed in his ordinary ministry, and having instituted a weekly lecture on the market-day, with a view to the benefit of those coming in from the country, he was enabled to cast the precious seed far and wide, so that it took deep root, and produced an abundant harvest, especially in the parish of Stewarton, where the 'revival spread from house to house for many miles along the valley.' Sometimes there would be upwards of an hundred waiting to converse with him in the manse after the lecture; and a complete change was wrought in the hearts and habits of a great number. This is attested, not only by the venerable minister himself, but also by some eminent characters, such as Professor Blair, Principal Boyd, Lady Eglinton, Lady Robertland, and others, who visited the scene and shared in the services.

In 1630 a very extraordinary revival occurred at the Kirk of Shotts, in Lanarkshire. A number of ministers, then suffering under the persecution of the civil power, assisted at the dispensation of the Supper; and such was the interest felt in the solemn service, that the people expressed a desire to have a sermon on the Monday after the feast. John Livingstone, then a preacher of the Gospel, and chaplain to the Countess of Wigton, was requested to officiate; but 'when he was alone in the fields in the morning, there came upon him such a misgiving, under a sense of unworthiness and unfitness to speak before so many aged and worthy ministers, and eminent experienced Christians, that he was thinking of stealing away, and was just about to lose sight of the kirk, when these words, 'Was I ever a barren wilderness, or a land of darkness,' were brought into his mind with such an overcoming power as constrained him to think it his duty to return and comply with the call to preach. He preached accordingly, from Ezekiel 26. 25: 'Then will I sprinkle clean water upon you,' &c.; and with such power, through the accompanying grace of the Spirit, 'that about five hundred persons were converted, principally by means of this sermon.' This great revival was afterwards described as 'the sowing of a seed through Clydesdale, so as many of the most eminent Christians in that country could date either their conversion or some remarkable confirmation from it.'

In 1638, the same year in which was held the celebrated Assembly at Glasgow, there commenced a general revival of true religion in the Church of Scotland, which has left its precious fruits as an inheritance to the present times, a revival not confined to particular districts, but extending over the whole Church, and influencing her judicatories as well as her congregations.

In 1734, a remarkable revival occurred in Northampton, and many other towns in New England, North America, under the ministry of such men as President Edwards and David Brainerd: whose faithful narratives contain not only an authentic statement of facts, but many rich and instructive observations suggested by experience and observation.

In 1742, many parishes in Scotland were visited with times of refreshing. The parish of Cambuslang, near Glasgow, then under the pastoral charge of William McCulloch, was one of the first to be visited. After he had preached for about a year on the nature and necessity of regeneration, he was requested by about ninety heads of families to give them a weekly lecture. Prayer-meetings were formed; and one after another, and at length fifty in the same day, came to him in distress of mind. After this, such was their thirst for the Word of God, that he had to provide them a sermon almost daily; and before the arrival of George Whitefield three hundred souls had been converted. When that eminent servant of God preached at the dispensation of the sacrament soon after, there were present about twenty-four ministers, and from thirty to forty thousand souls. Three thousand communicated at the tables, many of them from a great distance, who carried with them to their several homes a savour of good things; and not fewer than four hundred, belonging to the parish, were enrolled in the minister's lists as having been converted in that year.

In the same year, the parish of Kilsyth, then under the pastoral care of James Robe, who had laboured for thirty years without any remarkable success, was visited first of all with violent fever, and afterwards with famine, without any salutary effect. The minister was much discouraged, but betook himself to prayer, and soon some symptoms of growing seriousness appeared, which rapidly ripened into a great spiritual revival. Sometimes thirty, sometimes forty were awakened in a week; in all there were about three hundred, whose subsequent life attested the sincerity of their conversion.

In the same year, we have authentic accounts of the sudden and simultaneous revival of religion in many other parishes – as in Baldernoch, where there was at the time no stated minister, but many were awakened through the labours of a pious schoolmaster – in Campsie, in Calder, in Kirkintilloch, in Cumbernauld, in Gargunnoch, and also in St Ninians, and in Muthil.

In 1794, a remarkable revival of religion occurred in various parishes of Wales, chiefly through the instrumentality of Thomas Charles of Bala. As early as 1649, soon after the Westminster Assembly, commissioners had been appointed by Parliament to supply the religious destitution of that neglected country; and one hundred and fifty pious ministers were planted in its various counties, and good schoolmasters appointed in every market-town, besides thirty preachers who were appointed to itinerate from place to place. Several eminent ministers were afterwards raised up, such as Hugh Owen, Thomas Gouge, Griffith Jones, Howel Harris, Daniel Rowlands, who successively devoted themselves to the cultivation of the same interesting field, and often with great success. Whitefield testifies that the people thought nothing of coming twenty miles to hear a sermon, and that thousands were savingly impressed. Thomas Charles of Bala was himself one of the fruits of Daniel Rowlands' ministry; and he devoted himself with the like zeal to the prosecution of the same glorious work. He instituted schools in every part of his wide circuit; and thousands, both old and young, received the Word with joy, while a general re-formation was effected even among the careless and unconverted.

In 1798, a remarkable revival of true religion occurred in the parish of Moulin, then under the pastoral charge of Alexander Stewart, after-wards one of the ministers of the Canongate. In the interesting account which he has left of this event, he ingenuously confesses that he was himself ignorant of divine truth, at least in its saving power, for several years after he was ordained to the holy ministry; and that he was much perplexed when some persons, under concern for their souls, applied to him for advice. At length, through the writings of Newton and Scott, and the conversation and preaching of Charles Simeon of Cambridge, who visited him in 1796, he was brought to a knowledge of the truth, and immediately declaring what he had learned, a great impression was made on the minds of the people, insomuch that many nominal professors abstained of their own accord from going forward to the Lord's table. Seldom a week passed without one, two, or three persons being brought under deep concern, till he could count seventy souls as his 'crown of joy and rejoicing.'

In 1812, a great revival occurred in the island of Arran, under the ministry of the Rev. Mr M'Bride, which was accompanied with much excitement, and what the world will call extravagance, but which resulted in the conversion of between two and three hundred souls. And in the same year, another occurred in the island of Skye, which is in many respects extraordinary. Religion appeared to be wellnigh dead. Among several thousand persons, there were found only five or six New Testaments, and they had few advantages under the ministry. An itinerant preacher appeared, and laboured for some time amongst them, attracting consider-able audiences, but without any apparent success, till a poor blind fiddler was converted, and raised up as a mighty agent in the great work. One of

[235]

the ministers soon followed, and at length the revival spread, until several hundreds were added to the Church of such as should be saved.

In 1824, a revival occurred under very different circumstances, in the parish of Uig, in the island of Lewis, under the pastoral care of Alexander M'Leod. The first visible symptom of it was a rapid decrease in the number of communicants; but nine thousand people flocked from all quarters to hear the Word, and to witness the service in which they would not partake. Multitudes were converted, and a general spirit of prayer poured out from on high. And this interesting revival has continued steadily to grown down to the present time.

I have not adverted to many revivals reported to have taken place more recently in America, nor to those which have gladdened our hearts in our own day, and in our own land, but have confined myself to the authentic narrative of cases whose fruits and effects we have had time to test and ascertain. And I think the cases which have been enumerated are sufficient to show that such revivals are not novelties in the history of the Church, and ought not, therefore, to be regarded with those feelings of jealousy and suspicion which novelties in religion are so apt to awaken.

PART III

The Work of the Spirit
in the Edification of His People

I. The Work of the Spirit as the Spirit of Holiness

THE general work of the Spirit of God consists of two parts – the regeneration of sinners, and the edification of his people. Under the latter, several special operations of his grace are included, which are distinctly mentioned in sacred Scripture, and which may be considered separately, as examples of the connection which subsists betwixt his grace and all our duties, and as evidences of the love and wisdom with which his blessed agency is adapted to all the wants and weaknesses of our nature. It is an animating and consoling thought, that the promised grace of the Spirit has respect to every duty which we can be called to discharge, and to every change that can possibly occur in the condition, the temptations, and the trials of his people; for whether we be called to fight against our corruptions – the Spirit is our sanctifier; or to endure affliction – the Spirit is our comforter; or to choose the path of duty in times of perplexity – the Spirit is our guide; or to engage in prayer – the Spirit is the Spirit of grace and supplication; or to cultivate any one of the graces of the Christian character – they are all 'the fruits of the Spirit;' so that whatever may be our duty, and however formidable the difficulties by which we are surrounded, we can look up to God on the warrant of his own Word, for the aid of that 'good Spirit' who has promised 'to help our infirmities,' and who says to each of his people, 'I will never leave thee nor forsake thee,' 'My grace is sufficient for thee, I will perfect my strength in weakness,' 'As thy day is, so shall thy strength be,' 'Wait on the Lord, and be of good courage, and he will strengthen thine heart; wait, I say, upon the Lord.'

Sanctification is the work of the Spirit; and the commencement of it in the soul is to be dated from the time of a sinner's conversion. Until he is converted, he is 'dead in trespasses and sins;' for, says the apostle to the Ephesian converts, 'You hath he quickened, who were dead in trespasses and sins; wherein in time past ye walked according to the course of this world, according to the prince of the power of the air, the spirit which now worketh in the children of disobedience. Among whom also we all had our conversation in times past in the lusts of our flesh, fulfilling the desires of the flesh and of the mind; and were by nature the children of wrath even as others.' And again, to Titus, 'For we ourselves also were sometimes foolish, disobedient, deceived, serving divers lusts and pleasures, living in malice and envy, hateful and hating one another. But after that the kindness and love of God our Saviour toward man appeared, not by works of righteousness which we have done, but according to his mercy he saved us, by the washing of regeneration and renewing of the Holy Ghost; which he shed on us abundantly through Jesus Christ our Lord.' At the time of a sinner's conversion, spiritual life is imparted to his soul; he who was dead is quickened; he rises with Christ to newness of life; he is born again; he is 'God's workmanship, created anew in Christ Jesus unto good works.'

This great change is often preceded, as we have seen, by a preparatory work of conviction and instruction, and is always followed, as we shall now see, by a progressive course of sanctification; but it properly consists in his closing with Christ in the Gospel, by the deliberate assent of his understanding in an act of faith, and the decisive consent of his will in an act of choice. At the instant when a sinner, duly instructed in the truth, and impressed with a sense of his guilt and danger, flees to Christ for refuge, and embraces him as his own Saviour in all the fulness of his offices; at that instant he passes from 'death unto life,' and becomes a partaker of all the privileges of the children of God. That we might understand the nature, the reality, and the magnitude of this blessed change, God has been pleased to record many examples of it in Scripture, which serve the double purpose of teaching us, both what is essentially involved in all cases of genuine conversion, and also the varieties of individual experience which may exist notwithstanding. In reviewing the cases of the Philippian Gaoler, and the dying Malefactor; of Lydia, Cornelius, and Paul; of Timothy, the Ethiopian Treasurer, and the three thousand who were converted on the day of Pentecost, we are enabled to see that, while there were great diversities of individual experience among them, both in respect to their previous character, and the manner and circumstances of their conversion itself, yet there was a *radical change* that was common to all, and which properly consisted in their being brought under the power of 'the truth as it is in Jesus,' while it was followed in every instance by a life of new, and cheerful, and devoted obedience.

When the apostle says, 'If we *live* in the Spirit, let us also *walk* in the Spirit' (Gal. 5. 25), his words are addressed to those who have undergone this great change; and they refer, not to the work of the Spirit in the conversion of a sinner, which has been already illustrated, but *to the continued work of the Spirit in the progressive and growing sanctification of the believer after he has been born again*. And in directing your thoughts to this interesting subject, it may be useful, first of all, to illustrate some important truths which are implied in this exhortation, and then to explain and apply the exhortation itself.

I. It implies that *a new birth* will invariably be followed by a *new life*, and, conversely, that *a new life* necessarily presupposes a *new birth*, so that regeneration and sanctification are inseparably conjoined. In other words, a renewed heart will be followed by practical reformation, and a holy life can only spring from an inward change of heart. Regeneration is the spring, sanctification is the stream; if we live in the Spirit, we shall also walk in the Spirit; but we cannot walk spiritually unless we be spiritually alive.

This important truth is clearly taught by our Lord, as will appear at once from a comparison of two passages, in which he presents it in each of these aspects. In the first (Matt. 7. 16–20), he says, 'Ye shall know them by their fruits. Do men gather grapes of thorns, or figs of thistles? Even so every good tree bringeth forth good fruit; but a corrupt tree bringeth forth evil fruit. A good tree cannot bring forth evil fruit, neither can a corrupt tree bring forth good fruit. Every tree that bringeth not forth good fruit is hewn down and cast into the fire. Wherefore by their *fruits* ye shall know them.' Here we are taught that the nature of the tree may be judged of by the quality of its fruit; and that wherever spiritual life exists in the heart, it will manifest its presence there by bringing forth the peaceable fruits of righteousness in the life; so that utter barrenness is a proof of spiritual death, according to His own words, 'Every branch in me that beareth not fruit he taketh away'; 'Behold these three years I come seeking fruit on this fig-tree, and find none: cut it down; why cumbereth it the ground?' But, seeing that there may often be many outward semblances of holiness where there is no inward change of heart, our Lord teaches us in another passage (Matt. 12. 33), that the quality of the fruit depends on the nature of the tree; in other words, that there cannot be a spiritual life without a living principle within. 'Either,' says he, 'make the tree good, and his fruit good: or else make the tree corrupt, and his fruit corrupt: for the tree is known by his fruit. O generation of vipers, how can ye, being evil, speak good things? for out of the abundance of the heart the mouth speaketh. A good man out of the good treasure of the heart bringeth forth good things: and an evil man out of the evil treasure bringeth forth evil things.' And, in the 6th chapter of Matthew's Gospel, he gives three distinct instances of the way in which actions, apparently good and moral, may be vitiated by the depraved state of the heart: he mentions *almsgiving*, *prayer*, and *fasting*, and declares that if they proceed from an unhallowed principle or improper motive, they are not acceptable in the sight of God.

It is equally clear, then, that every sinner who has been quickened by the Spirit will also walk in the Spirit; and also, that a holy life, such as the

Christian leads, must be preceded by a new spiritual birth. If he be alive, he will walk; but if he would walk, he must be made alive. And the *inseparable connection* which subsists between a new birth and a new life, or betwixt regeneration by the Spirit and a progressive course of sanctification, is well worthy of our serious consideration, because it serves to guard us against *two widely different errors* which, it is to be feared, are too prevalent at the present day. The first is of an Antinomian complexion; and consists, not, perhaps, in the positive disbelief or denial of the duty which is incumbent on Christians, but in the practical forgetfulness or habitual neglect of those considerations which should lead them to maintain a close and conscientious walk with God, and often results in their 'turning the grace of God into licentiousness,' as if they were at liberty to 'continue in sin because grace abounds.' Perhaps the most common and fatal form which this dangerous error assumes in modern times is the presumptuous confidence with which some professing Christians will venture to do what their consciences condemn, or, at least, what they can with great difficulty reconcile even to *their* ideas of duty, with the latent feeling, that if they sin, they have only to repent at some future time to ensure their forgiveness, a feeling which, wherever it exists, evinces an utter ignorance of the nature and source of genuine repentance, and an awful want of fear and reverence for God. But to every man who is conscious of any tendency to continue in the indulgence of known sin, or to relax his diligence in the work of a growing sanctification, may it not be said, If you *walk not* in the Spirit, what evidence have you that you *live* in the Spirit? Is it not alike the command and the promise of Christ's Gospel; 'Let not sin, therefore, reign in your mortal body,' for 'sin shall not have dominion over you; for ye are not under the law, but under grace. What then? Shall we sin, because we are not under the law, but under grace? God forbid.' 'How shall we that are dead to sin live any longer therein?'

But if a new life will invariably follow the new birth, it is equally certain that there can be *no real holiness of life without a thorough change of heart*. And this truth also, which is implied in the apostle's words, stands directly opposed to another error of a different kind; I mean the error of those who are mere formalists, and who suppose that if their life be regular and decent, and above all, if they abound in the outward acts of apparent morality, they need give themselves little concern about any spiritual change. Augustine was wont to say that the very virtues of such men were only 'splendid sins;' and our Lord sanctions the same sentiment, when, referring to the *alms*, and *prayer*, *and fasting*, which were done from an impure and unhallowed motive, he declares that, however applauded by men, they were utterly unacceptable to God. Nay, I will venture to say, that every man's conscience will decide in the same way: it estimates the morality of an action by the motive from which it springs. Suppose you see an individual relieving the wants of a poor brother; you immediately approve of an act by which the sufferer's wants are relieved; but suppose you could look in on that man's heart, and found no *love* there, and no touch of human sympathy, but in its stead, a lust of praise, or a desire of vain-glorious applause, I ask whether, on the instant, the vicious motive would not, even in your estimation, demoralize and desecrate the whole character of his conduct? And so is it with ourselves in our relation to God. He looks in upon the heart; and the heart must be renewed before the life can be reformed according to his will. If it be true that 'without holiness no man shall see the Lord,' it is equally true that we can only become holy by being 'renewed in the spirit of our mind.'

II. It is further implied in the apostle's words, that not only *the commencement, but the continuance also of spiritual life in the soul, depends on the gracious operation of the Spirit of God.* As the great initial change by which we pass from death unto life is wrought by him, so is the succeeding course of our progressive sanctification; and as he brings us into the way, he must conduct us, from first to last, by the constant communication of his wisdom to direct, of his grace to animate, and of his strength to sustain us. We are made alive by the Spirit, and we are enabled to walk by the same Spirit. At the time of conversion, he may implant a gracious principle in the heart; but that principle is not self-sustained, nor does it derive its nourishment from the soil in which it is planted, but is fed from his secret springs. The liveliest Christian would soon decay were the Spirit's grace withdrawn: he has no stability and no strength of his own; and there would be neither growth nor fruitfulness, but for those constant supplies which he receives of all needful grace from the fulness that is in Christ.

Accordingly, various expressions are used in Scripture to intimate the constant operation, and the abiding presence, and the intimate fellowship of the Spirit with his people. Sometimes they are represented as being *in him* – 'If we live *in* the Spirit, let us walk *in* the Spirit' – an expression which, whatever else may be implied in it, plainly intimates a constant dependence on their part, and a continued care on his. And at other times he is represented as *being in them*, as when our Lord said, 'I will pray the Father, and he shall give you another Comforter, that he may abide with you for ever; even the Spirit of truth; whom the world cannot receive, because it seeth him not, neither knoweth him; but ye know him; for he *dwelleth with you*, and shall be *in you:*' and the apostle: 'What! know ye not that your body is the temple of the Holy Ghost which is in you, which ye have of God?' And both expressions occur in the same verse (Rom. 8.

9), 'Ye are not in the flesh, but *in the Spirit*, if so be that the Spirit of God dwell *in you*.'

The consideration of the continued presence and constant operation of the Spirit of God in the soul of every true believer is fitted at once to encourage and animate him in the path of holy obedience, and to impress him with an awful sense of reverence and godly fear. It is a strong consolation, and a cheering ground of confidence and hope, that amidst all the corruptions with which he is called to contend, and the innumerable temptations by which he is assailed, he is not left to depend on his own wisdom and strength, but may ask, in believing prayer, the supplies of the Spirit of all grace, and rest on the promise, 'My grace is sufficient for thee; I will perfect my strength in weakness.' And when the believer is most sensible of his infirmity and corruptions, he is only the better able to appreciate the value of this promise, and to say with the apostle, 'When I am weak, then am I strong.' But if it be fitted to cheer and animate the believer in his warfare, by giving him the hope of final victory, it is also unspeakably solemn: it may well fill him with holy awe to think that the Spirit of God is at all times present with his soul, watching over its progress or declension, its growth or decay; that by cherishing unholy thoughts or desires, he may 'grieve the Spirit,' and even provoke him, for a time, to withdraw; and when he reads the solemn appeal, 'Know ye not that ye are the temple of God, and that the Spirit of God dwelleth in you? if any man defile the temple of God, him shall God destroy,' how forcibly should he feel the motive which is urged in the apostle's exhortation, 'Work out your own salvation with *fear and trembling; for it is God that worketh in you* to will and to do of his good pleasure.'

III. When the apostle says, 'If we live in the Spirit, let us also walk in the Spirit,' his words, while they contain a doctrinal truth, prescribe also *a practical duty;* and that duty is inculcated by a motive derived from the consideration of our having been quickened into life by the Spirit of God. It is as if he had said: If we have been born again, let the new birth be followed by a new life; let our walk correspond with our past experience and our present profession. There is much even in this general view of the apostle's meaning that may well humble us in the very dust for our past negligence, and at the same time incite us to greater diligence in future: for every one who professes to be a Christian must be considered as one who has been 'born again,' and in whom the 'Spirit of God dwells;' and if this be implied in our profession, oh! how deeply should we be affected by the thought of our many miscarriages, our frequent declensions and decays, and the strength of our remaining corruptions; and how ardently should we desire that, in time to come, we may walk more worthy of the vocation wherewith we have been called, and become altogether such as God's Spirit would have us to be!

But more particularly, this walking in the Spirit consists in *the habitual exercise of faith in Christ,* that faith by which we are united to him, so as to receive out of his fulness even grace for grace. Christ is made of God unto us sanctification, as well as redemption; and it is by faith in him that our sanctification is advanced; for, says the apostle, 'I am crucified with Christ; nevertheless I live; yet not I, but Christ liveth in me; and the life which I now live in the flesh, I live by the faith of the Son of God, who loved me, and gave himself for me.' And this corresponds with His own language to the disciples, 'Abide in me, and I in you. As the branch cannot bear fruit of itself, except it abide in the vine; no more can ye, except ye abide in me. I am the vine, ye are the branches: he that abideth in me and I in him, the same bringeth forth much fruit: for without (or, out of) me ye can do nothing. If a man abide not in me, he is cast forth as a branch, and is withered; and men gather them, and cast them into the fire, and they are burned.' Now, 'we abide in Christ' when 'his word abideth in us.' It is by faith that we are first united to Christ, and it is by the continued exercise of the same faith that our union with him is maintained, and that we derive from him, as a branch draws sap from the vine, the nourishment which makes us fruitful. It was 'the truth as it is in Jesus' that was the means of our conversion, and it is the same truth that is the instrument of our progressive sanctification; for Christ's prayer for his disciples, even when he spoke of the promise of the Spirit, was, 'Sanctify them through thy truth; thy word is truth.' And the truth here spoken of is not solely, nor even chiefly, the *truth contained in the law,* although that is useful, as affording a perfect rule and authoritative directory for the conduct of life, but it is especially the *truth contained in the Gospel;* for that affords the most constraining motives to a life of new obedience; and what 'the law cannot do, seeing that it is weak through the flesh,' the Gospel can accomplish, because it is, in the hand of the Spirit, an effectual means of sanctification. We are not only justified, we are sanctified also by the truth as it is in Jesus; and they who are jealous of the doctrine of free grace, because of its supposed tendency to relax the obligations of holiness, betray a lamentable ignorance at once of the scheme of revealed truth, and the actual experience of all believers. Man's method of sanctification is by the law, God's method of sanctification is by the Gospel; the former is by works, the latter is by faith, unto works.

The walking in the Spirit which is here enjoined consists further in *maintaining a constant conflict with indwelling sin,* and seeking to crucify the flesh, with its corruptions and lusts. I need not say – for your own experience must convince you – that regeneartion does not destroy sin in the soul: it dethrones sin; it breaks its power; but it does not extirpate or expel it from the heart; it is still there; not as a tyrant, but as a traitor, ever ready to deceive and seduce, and then most likely to succeed when we are least sensible of its presence, and least watchful against its wiles. Even in the bosom of the child of God there is many a 'root of bitterness,' which, springing up, may trouble and defile him; there is a 'sin which doth so easily beset him'; there is 'a law in his members warring against the law of his mind, and bringing him into captivity to the law of sin and of death.' The whole course of his sanctification is a ceaseless warfare, which will never terminate until the body is dissolved in death. Now the steady maintenance of this arduous and protracted conflict is included in 'his walking in the Spirit,' and can only be successful in this way; for, says the apostle, 'Walk in the Spirit, and ye shall not fulfil the lust of the flesh. For the flesh lusteth against the Spirit, and the Spirit against the flesh: and these are contrary the one to the other: so that ye cannot do the things that ye would. But if ye be led by the Spirit, ye are not under the law.' By the *flesh* in this context, we are to understand all our sinful propensities and passions, whether such as belong properly to the body, or such as have their seat in the soul; for, in enumerating the works of the flesh, he mentions 'adultery, fornication, uncleanness, lasciviousness, idolatry, witchcraft, hatred, variance, emulations, wrath, strife, seditions, heresies, envyings, murders, drunkenness, revellings, and such like;' and, in reference to these, he says, 'They that are Christ's have crucified the flesh with the affections and lusts.' The use of the word *flesh*, however, seems to intimate that our evil passions derive much of their virulence and strength from our connection with these 'vile bodies,' whose appetites we are so prone to indulge, and for whose comfort we are so anxious to provide: and if so, we may do well to remember the example of the apostle, who said, 'I keep under my body, and bring it into subjection, lest having preached the Gospel to others, I should myself be a castaway.' And the use, again, of such terms as '*mortify* and *crucify* the flesh,' implies that we are called to a very painful task, and to the exercise of much self-denial; but this is involved in our profession and inseparable from it; for our Lord thus forewarned his disciples, 'If any man will come after me, let him deny himself, and take up his cross, and follow me.'

Again, this walking in the Spirit consists in maintaining a *spiritual frame of mind*, by having our thoughts much engaged with spiritual truth, and our affections set on spiritual objects, and all our faculties employed in spiritual services. That this spiritual frame of mind is included in the duty appears from the statement of the apostle in another place, 'For they that are after the flesh *do mind* the things of the flesh: but they that are after the Spirit the things of the Spirit. For to be carnally minded is death; but to be spiritually minded is life and peace.' To walk in the Spirit clearly implies that we should be *spiritually minded;*[1] and this gracious habit mainly consists in our thoughts being much occupied with divine truth, and our affections and desires being set, not on the things which are seen and temporal, but on those things which are unseen and eternal. The real state of our hearts may be determined by the prevailing bent of our thoughts, affections, and desires; for if these be mainly occupied with the world, and naturally and instinctively point to some earthly good, then we have reason to fear that we are still walking after the flesh, and not after the Spirit; but if they are chiefly set on things spiritual and divine; if not only in the hour of prayer, but at other times, they recur to God, and Christ, and heaven, and dwell on these subjects with complacency and satisfaction, or at least with earnestness; then we have reason to hope that we may be of the number of those who have been quickened into spiritual life, of which the first and surest symptom is the appetite and desire for spiritual nourishment and food. And he who is thus spiritually minded is said to 'walk in the Spirit,' not only because it is the Spirit which quickened him at the first, but also because it is the Spirit which continues to sustain his spiritual life, keeping alive his appetite for spiritual food, directing his thoughts to spiritual things, and exciting his affections for spiritual objects. This he does by means of the *truth;* and hence the same truth which is declared to be the germ of the new birth – by which we are 'born again, not of corruptible seed, but of incorruptible, even by the Word of God, which liveth and abideth for ever' – that same truth is also the aliment by which the Spirit nourishes his people; for, 'as new born babes, they desire the sincere milk of the Word, that they may grow thereby.' And so the same Word which cleanses the sinner at first – for we read of 'the washing of water by the Word' – is also the means of his growing sanctification; for 'now ye are clean through the word which I have spoken unto you.'

Walking in the Spirit consists further in our habitually seeking to cultivate and exercise all the graces of the Christian life, by bringing forth abundantly the *peaceable fruits of righteousness*. These are expressly said to be, in every believer, 'the fruit of the Spirit;' for, says the apostle, 'The fruit of the Spirit is love, joy, peace, long-suffering, gentleness, goodness, faith, meekness, temperance;' and again, 'The fruit of the Spirit is in all goodness, and righteousness, and truth.'

Without attempting to illustrate each of those elements of the Christian character, I may observe in general, that when combined, as they always are,

---

[1] See John Owen on *Spiritual Mindedness*.

although in different degrees and proportions, in the experience of believers, they are to be regarded as the first lineaments of that divine image which was lost at the fall, and which it is the great design of the Spirit to restore, while they are at the same time a source of the purest and most permanent happiness. Love to God as our Father, to Christ as our best benefactor, and to his people as brethren; joy and peace, springing from the Gospel; the joy which the world can neither give nor take away; the very peace of God which passeth all understanding; long-suffering and gentleness, springing from that love which 'beareth all things, believeth all things, hopeth all things, endureth all things;' goodness, which rejoiceth not in iniquity, but rejoiceth in the truth; faith, which believes God, and trusts in his faithful promise; meekness, which is not overcome of evil, but overcomes evil with good; and temperance, which restrains indulgence within the limits of duty; these are the elements of the Christian character; and they are as conducive to our true happiness as they are opposed to our natural dispositions.

But especially, let us realize the thought, that these graces are, one and all, the *fruits of the Spirit;* they are not the spontaneous products of our corrupted nature, nor even the forced nurslings of our own culture and industry; they are the 'beauties of holiness,' with which the Spirit of God adorns 'the new creature', and by which he prepares him for the society and services of heaven. If, then, we feel ourselves deficient in any one or more of these graces, we should not depend on our own strength; but, while we are diligent in the use of every appointed means, we should pray for the Spirit.

It is a very serious truth, that each of us must be walking either after the flesh or after the Spirit; and that according as we pursue the one course or the other, we are proceeding, with the swiftness of time itself, towards heaven or hell. Our personal interest in all the privileges and promises of the Gospel depends on our choice betwixt these two; for, speaking of those who are interested in the Gospel, the apostle describes them in these words: 'There is now no condemnation to them which are in Christ Jesus; who *walk* not after the flesh, but after the Spirit;' for 'as many as are led by the Spirit of God, they are the sons of God.' But he adds, 'If any man have not the Spirit of Christ, he is none of his.' 'So then they that are in the flesh cannot please God.' 'If ye live after the flesh, ye shall die.' The apostle urges this solemn truth even on the attention of those to whom he wrote, although they were professing Christians; partly because there are, in every visible church, some mere nominal professors, who need to be awakened to a sense of their real condition; and partly also, because it is salutary for believers themselves to be reminded of the wide difference which subsists betwixt the Church and the world, and of the holy jealousy with which they should watch over their own souls. 'Wherefore work out your own salvation with fear and trembling; for it is God that worketh in you both to will and to do of his good pleasure.'

II. The Work of the Spirit as the Spirit of Adoption

THE Spirit of God not only sanctifies his people, but he *imparts a new character to their obedience*. They 'run in the way of his commandments, when he has enlarged their hearts;' and this he does as the Spirit of adoption. 'For ye have not received the spirit of bondage again to fear; but ye have received the Spirit of adoption, whereby we cry, Abba, Father. The Spirit itself beareth witness with our spirit, that we are the children of God: and if children, then heirs; helrs of God, and joint heirs with Christ.' – (Rom. 8. 15–17). When the apostle says, 'Ye have not received the spirit of bondage again to fear,' the word '*again*' implies that at some former period there did exist amongst God's people that spirit of bondage unto fear which is here contrasted with the spirit of adoption, and that they had even received it from God himself. There is reason to believe that the apostle refers, in the first instance, to the difference between the two great dispensations of divine truth, or to the contrast which is elsewhere so strikingly marked betwixt the law and the Gospel. The widely different characters of these dispensations are described, when in one place it is said, 'The law was given by Moses; but grace and truth came by Jesus Christ;' and in another, where we read of 'the two covenants, the one from Mount Sinai, which gendereth to *bondage:* the other from Jerusalem, which is above, and is *free;*' the law being alike fitted in its own nature, and designed in the purpose of God, to generate a spirit of bondage, to shut men up to the faith that was still to be revealed, and to place them, as it were, under tutors and governors, until the time appointed of the Father. 'Even so we,' adds the apostle, 'when we were children, were in bondage unto the elements or rudiments of the world. But when the fulness of the time was come, God sent forth his Son, made of a woman, made under the law, to redeem them that were under the law, that we might receive the adoption of sons.' In so far as the law given by Moses was a republication of the covenant of works, it had no power to give peace to the sinner's conscience, and no tendency to liberate him from the bondage of his fears. On the contrary, it was fitted and designed to convince him of his guilt and danger, to impress him with an awful sense of God's unchangeable rectitude and justice, and to teach him, that 'by the works of the law shall no flesh be justified.' It was, in fact, a ministration of *death*, a ministration of *condemnation;* and the bondage of the law preceded, and tended to prepare the way for, the glorious liberty wherewith Christ makes his people free.

But while the apostle's words may be understood as referring, in the first instance, to the difference betwixt the two great dispensations of the law and the Gospel, they may be considered also as descriptive of *two corresponding stages in the experience of every believer.* There is a remarkable resemblance in this respect betwixt the course of God's dispensations to the Church at large, and the methods of his dealing with each individual in particular; for just as, in the history of the Church, the first covenant, which gendered unto bondage, preceded the fulness of Gospel liberty in Christ, so, in the experience of private Christians, there is often, in the first instance, a spirit of bondage unto fear, before they receive the Spirit of adoption, whereby they cry, Abba, Father. Many a soul is kept in bondage for a time, before it is brought into the liberty of a child of God. I refer not to the bondage of *sin*, of which the apostle speaks when he says of the ungodly, 'While they promise them liberty, they themselves are the servants of corruption; for of whom a man is overcome, of the same is he brought in bondage;' and again, 'That they may recover themselves out of the snare of the devil, who are taken captive by him at his will.' This is indeed the natural condition of all men, and there is no tyranny more absolute and no bondage more severe; but it is a servitude which lamentable experience declares to be perfectly compatible with the *utmost carelessness*, and its unhappy victims, so far from suffering under the spirit of bondage *unto fear*, have often no apprehension of their danger, and no desire to escape from their misery, but cling to the chains by which they are bound. They *are* slaves but they know it not, slaves to their sin, and in bondage to their lusts; but, following 'the sight of their own eyes, and the desire of their own hearts,' they love their bondage, and even glory in their shame. But I speak not of the bondage of *sin*, but of the bondage of the *law*, not of the yoke of natural corruption, but of the galling yoke of convictions produced in the conscience by the Word and Spirit of God: such convictions as were felt by the Philippian gaoler, when, from being a careless sinner, he became a convinced and anxious inquirer, and called for a light, and sprang in, and came trembling, and fell down before Paul and Silas, and said, 'Sirs, what must I do to be saved?'; and by the dying thief on the cross, when, under strong impressions of God's justice, he said to his fellow-sufferer, 'Dost thou not *fear* God, seeing thou art in the same condemnation? and we indeed justly, for we receive the due reward of our deeds;' and by the three thousand on the day of Pentecost, who, when they heard Peter's sermon, 'were pricked in their heart, and said unto Peter and the rest of the apostles, Men and brethren, what shall we do?' When the law of God is applied to the sinner's conscience; when he is enabled to understand its spirituality and extent, as reaching even to the thoughts and intents of the heart; when he is impressed with a sense of his own sinfulness in particular, its aggravated guilt, and its awful demerit; and when, applying to himself God's threatenings, he is made to feel as if God were saying to him, 'Thou art the man' – then he will learn from his own experience what is meant by 'the spirit of bondage unto fear;' and the sudden change which is thus wrought in all his views and feelings will enable him to understand what the apostle felt, when he said, 'I was alive without the law once; but when the commandment came, sin revived, and I died.' The right apprehension of God's law, and the serious application of it to a man's conscience, cannot fail to awaken convictions of guilt, and these, again, are always accompanied with fear and terror, for 'the law worketh wrath;' and its fearful curse will be felt either as a heavy burden oppressing the conscience, or as a grievous bondage from which no human power can effect his deliverance. This has been the bitter experience of many an anxious inquirer at the commencement of his course: he has been so deeply convinced of sin, and so much impressed with a sense of divine wrath, that he can have no difficulty in understanding what is meant by the *spirit of bondage. God has been a terror to him*, so that, like Job, he was ready to say, 'The arrows of the Almighty are within me, the poison whereof drinketh up my spirit; the terrors of God do set themselves in array against me;' or like David, 'I remembered God, and was troubled; I complained, and my spirit was overwhelmed.' And the prospects of his soul, and especially the thought of death, and judgment, and eternity, have been unspeakably dreadful, insomuch that 'through fear of death he was subject to bondage.'

This spirit of bondage unto fear is the effect of the law, and the utmost that the mere law can accomplish: it 'gendereth unto bondage;' it awakens fear, and may occasion deep distress; but it has no capacity or fitness for pacifying the conscience, or ensuring the salvation of a sinner. God is pleased to use the law as an instrument of *conviction*, turning up, as with a plough-share, the fallow ground of nature, and thereby preparing it for the reception of the good seed; and this preparatory work is of great practical use, and, indeed, of absolute and indispensable necessity, in order to saving conversion. When the apostle says, therefore, 'Ye have *not* received the spirit of bondage again to fear,' his words are to be understood as intimating, not that sinners are now exempt from this preparatory discipline, or that it is no longer used under the Gospel, but that another and better spirit is the proper fruit of the new dispensation under which we have been placed, and ought to be found in the heart of every believer. I refer to 'the Spirit of adoption, whereby we cry, Abba, Father.'

II. The spirit of bondage unto fear, which is produced by the law applied to the conscience, can only be exchanged for 'the Spirit of adoption' by our believing the Gospel. When the sinner, awakened out of the lethargy of nature, and convinced in his conscience, or pricked in his heart, begins to inquire. 'What must I do to be saved?', he is in a hopeful state of preparation for receiving the Gospel; and if, under the teaching of the Spirit, he is enabled to understand the message of peace which God has sent from the upper sanctuary; if he is taught to apprehend the nature of the scheme of grace, the design and object of the Saviour's work, the value and the efficacy of his death as an atonement for sin, the all-sufficiency of Christ as one who is able to save unto the very uttermost, and the richness and free-ness of his grace as it is expressed and declared in the free and universal calls and invitations of the Gospel; and if, especially, he be enabled to apply the truth to his own case, so as to feel that the Gospel, which is glad tidings to all, is a Gospel to him, and that Jesus, who is the Christ of God, is a Christ to his own soul – then, on the instant when he understands and believes the Gospel message, and appropriates it to himself, may the spirit of bondage be displaced by the spirit of adoption in his heart, and he may enter at once on the glorious liberty wherewith Christ makes his people free. For it is simply *by faith*, simply by believing what God speaks to him in the Word, that the convinced sinner becomes a converted man; and there is enough in Christ's Gospel to produce and sustain a spirit of adoption in his heart, even were he the very chief of sinners. The reason why we remain so long under the bondage of legal fears is, not that the Gospel is inadequate to remove them or insufficient to produce a spirit of adoption, but because there is either some defect or error in our apprehension of the truth, or some lurking spirit of unbelief concerning it, or some remaining unwillingness to close with it. If we would only believe, we should see the salvation of God. If the most disconsolate sinner would only look out of himself to Christ, and behold him as the Lamb of God that taketh away the sin of the world, and, opening his mind to the full impression of the truth, would receive it as a faithful saying, and worthy of all acceptation, that Christ came into the world to save sinners; that Christ speaks to him individually in the Gospel, and offers him a free salvation, and calls, and invites, and beseeches, and commands him to accept of it; that he who died on the cross is now on the throne, a Saviour mighty to save; and that God is revealed no longer as the Lawgiver, Judge, and Avenger, but as God in Christ reconcil-ing ('the Lord God merciful and gracious, forgiving iniquity, and trans-gression, and sin'), oh! then might the most anxious inquirer that ever

smarted under the yoke of bondage pass at once into a state of perfect freedom, and exchange all his misgivings, and forebodings, and fears, for peace
and joy in believing – that peace which passeth all understanding, and that
joy which is unspeakable and full of glory.

For by faith in the Gospel he comes at once into a *new state and relation to
God*. Formerly he was a child of disobedience, a child of wrath even as
others; now he is, by adoption, a son; and if a son, then an heir, an heir of
God, and a joint heir with Christ. This change in his relation to God is
necessarily antecedent to the witness of the Spirit by which it is declared
and confirmed; and it is because we *are sons* that God sends forth the Spirit
of his Son into our hearts, crying, 'Abba, Father.' And this filial relation is
constituted by faith; for on the instant that a sinner believes the Gospel, he is
adopted into God's family, and becomes a partaker of all the privileges of
his children. His whole relation to God is changed, so that to him may be
addressed the language of the apostle, "Wherefore thou art no more a
servant, but a son; and if a son, then an heir of God through Christ.'
Adoption is a most precious privilege; it brings us into a new and most
endearing relation to God; it makes us the children and the heirs of him
who graciously condescends to call himself our Father in heaven; and as it is
bestowed, like every other privilege of his grace, through the mediation of
his own Son, it confers an infallible security by making us 'joint heirs with
Christ,' heirs not in our own right, but in the right of him who is God's
only begotten and well-beloved Son. And this precious privilege, which
brings us now under the paternal protection of God, and gives us a sure
interest in all the promises of the Gospel, is attained simply by believing;
for there is enough in the message of the Gospel to warrant even the very
chief of sinners in drawing nigh unto God as a forgiving Father; and as soon
as that message is clearly understood and cordially believed, we may enter
at once on the state and condition of children.

But this change in *his relation* to God will be accompanied with a corresponding change in his *views and feelings* towards him; he will now regard
him as his Father; his state being changed, his spirit will be changed also;
and he will be conscious of a new frame of mind, which is here called 'the
spirit of adoption, whereby he cries, Abba, Father.' This childlike disposition can only be produced by the truth as it is in Jesus, received in the
exercise of a simple faith, and applied with power by the Spirit of all grace;
and the *spirit of adoption springs as naturally from the Spirit's work in applying
the Gospel, as the spirit of bondage from the Spirit's work in applying the law*. It
belongs to the office of the Holy Spirit to unfold to the believer the unsearchable riches of Christ, to open up the freeness of his grace, and the
fulness of Gospel privilege which belongs to his people; 'for,' says our

Lord, 'he shall glorify me: he shall receive of mine, and shall show it unto you;' – and the apostle, 'Eye hath not seen, nor ear heard, neither have entered into the heart of man the things which God hath prepared for them that love him; but God hath revealed them unto us by his Spirit.' 'Now we have received, not the spirit of the world, but the Spirit which is of God, *that we might know the things which are freely given* to us of God.'

The work of the Spirit in applying the Gospel for the comfort and establishment of believers, considered as the children of God, consists of two parts, which, although they may be intimately connected and mutually related with each other, are nevertheless capable of being distinguished, and are mentioned separately by the apostle. For two distinct effects of his operation are referred to, when we read in the 15th verse of 'the *spirit of adoption*, whereby we cry, Abba, Father;' and in the 16th, *of the witness of the Spirit*, whereby he assures us that we are the children of God. The one denotes the childlike disposition which characterizes every true believer; the other, the assurance of their sonship, which is a higher attainment than the former, but one that is not always enjoyed, even by those who manifest much of the spirit of filial reverence, submission, and love. Some latent feeling of hope, some secret trust and confidence, is indeed necessarily implied in the spirit of adoption, by which the believer cries, 'Abba, Father;' and he may really be drawing near to God with the confidence of sonship, while, from some remaining darkness or defect in his faith, he may shrink from using the strong language of assurance, and dare not say in so many words that 'the Spirit beareth witness with his spirit that he is a child of God.' But if he has believed the Gospel at all, if he has been enabled to understand the Gospel message, and to apply it to his own soul, he must have experienced a great and a growing change in all his views, and feelings, and dispositions towards God; he must have been liberated in some measure from the spirit of bondage, and imbued with the spirit of adoption; and wherever this new spirit exists, it is in itself a proof of sonship, and in its growing strength and habitual exercise, it may lay the foundation of that full assurance of hope which is produced in the mind of a believer when 'the Spirit beareth witness with his spirit that he is one of the children of God.'

That we may understand the nature of this childlike frame of mind, and the new character which it imparts to the believer's obedience, it may be observed,

1. That the spirit of adoption implies reverence and godly fear, such as is due to God's infinite and adorable perfections, but excludes that slavish dread and terror which a conviction of guilt is apt to inspire. We read in Scripture of two kinds of *fear*, the one of which belongs to the spirit of

bondage, the other to the spirit of adoption. They are usually distinguished, in the writings of divines, by the name of *filial* and *slavish* fear, the latter being the fear with which a slave regards his taskmaster, the former the fear with which a son regards his father. You can have no difficulty in distinguishing betwixt the two, or in seeing that while the one is excluded by faith in the Gospel, the other may be only deepened and confirmed by it. The fear which springs from a spirit of bondage arises from the terrible apprehension of God as an avenger, and is apt to exasperate our natural enmity, to widen our separation from God, and to excite distrust, dislike, and aversion; and this unhappy frame of mind it is one of the great objects of the Gospel to change, by removing the ground of our apprehensions, and proclaiming a message of reconciliation. But even where the Gospel message has been so clearly understood and so sincerely embraced that it has destroyed the spirit of bondage, and brought the soul into the conscious enjoyment of that liberty which belongs to the children of God, it does not remove, on the contrary it deepens, that filial fear, which it becomes us, as children, to cherish towards such a being as God is, even when he is regarded as our Father in heaven, a fear which properly consists in reverence, and expresses itself in the language of humble adoration, and produces a circumspect and watchful habit, such as is described when the apostle says to believers themselves, 'Be not high minded, but fear,'; 'work out your own salvation with fear and trembling;' and 'pass the time of your sojourning here in fear.' This reverential fear is not the fruit of guilt or mere conviction of conscience, nor is it confined to the bosoms of sinners; it is felt and cherished by the angels and seraphim of heaven, when they veil their feet and their faces with their wings, and cry one to another, 'Holy, holy, holy, Lord God of hosts;' it was felt by all the saints of old who were admitted to near converse with God, or who witnessed any remarkable manifestation of his divine perfections; as Elijah, when he covered his face with his mantle; and Moses when he said, 'I exceedingly fear and quake;' and the beloved disciple, when he 'fell at his feet as dead.' It is indeed an essential and permanent part of true religion, both on earth and in heaven; for it will never cease to be true, that 'great fear is due unto the Lord in the meeting of his saints, and that he is to be had in reverence of all them that approach him.' The spirit of adoption, then, although it delivers us from the spirit of bondage, and the slavish dread which devils feel, of whom it is said that 'they believe and tremble,' has no tendency to cherish an undue familiarity with God, or to relieve our minds from that salutary awe and godly fear which is the very beginning of wisdom. On the contrary, the same Gospel which releases us from the yoke of slavish terror, by revealing the grace and mercy of God to sinners, is fitted to deepen even our deepest thoughts of the holiness and justice, the truth and the majesty of God, insomuch that no believer can contemplate the cross of Christ without feeling a solemn sense of awe on his spirit, and entering into the meaning of the Psalmist's words, 'There is *forgiveness* with God, that he may be *feared*.'

2. The spirit of adoption implies a lively sense of gratitude, and a principle of supreme love to God, such as a child feels towards a forgiving and affectionate father; and excludes that sullen discontent and that resentful opposition which the spirit of bondage is apt to inspire. Slavish fear, a fear arising merely from convictions of conscience and the prospect of judgment, naturally tends to increase our aversion to God, and to inflame our natural enmity; and whether it evinces itself in violent opposition, as in the case of Herod, who feared John, and afterwards cast him into prison, or in dark and dreadful despair, as in the case of Judas, when under the influence of remorse he went and hanged himself, it has no power to attract or reconcile the sinner to his Judge. But 'what the law could not do, in that it was weak through the flesh, God sending his own Son in the likeness of sinful flesh, and for sin condemned sin in the flesh; that the righteousness of the law might be fulfilled in us, who walk not after the flesh, but after the Spirit.' The Gospel, as a message of love, is fitted to inspire the sinner with gratitude; and wherever it exists, faith works by love, by love to God for the benefits which he has conferred, for the compassion and mercy which he has exercised, and for all the adorable perfections of his divine nature which he has displayed in the scheme and work of redemption; and this *love*, engendered by the glad tidings of salvation through Christ, utterly excludes the slavish anxieties and terrors which belong to the spirit of bondage; for, says the apostle, 'There is no fear in love; but perfect love casteth out fear: because fear hath torment. He that feareth is not made perfect in love.' But 'we love him, because he first loved us.' Who can describe the feelings of a convinced sinner when he is first enabled to look up to God as a forgiving Father, and to hear, as it were, from his own lips, the gracious words, 'Son! be of good cheer, thy sins are forgiven thee!' Just such as were the feelings of the poor prodigal, when, after his wayward and weary sojourn in a strange land, where, professing himself to be free, he inwardly felt that he was the slave of his own passions, and in 'the spirit of bondage' preferred, even when he was in want, to go into a field, and fill his belly with the husks which the swine did eat, rather than return to his father's house; yet remembering his father's love, his heart relented, and he said, 'I will go to my father,' but still in the spirit of bondage added, 'Make me as one of thy hired servants'. He came, 'and when his father saw him afar off, he ran and fell upon his neck, and kissed him, and said, This my son which was dead is alive again, was lost and is found; bring out the fairest

robe for him, and kill the fatted calf;' oh! just such, if we can conceive them, are the feelings of a sinner, when the spirit of bondage unto fear is displaced by the spirit of adoption, 'whereby he cries, Abba, Father.'

3. The spirit of adoption implies a warm brotherly love towards all who are members of God's family, a new affection corresponding to the new relation into which we have been introduced, and bearing some proportion to the sacred and endearing ties by which, as Christians, we are connected with one another. The spirit of adoption points directly to God, and consists in supreme love to him; but it necessarily implies also love to the brethren, for, says the apostle, 'Every one that loveth him that begat, loveth him also that is begotten of him,' – 'If a man say, I love God, and hateth his brother, he is a liar; for he that loveth not his brother whom he hath seen, how can he love God whom he hath not seen? and this commandment have we from him, that he who loveth God love his brother also.' The intimate connection which subsists betwixt the two – I mean betwixt love to God as our Father, and to one another as brethren – is abundantly proved by the experience of our own hearts, as well as by the express testimony of the Word: for if, on the one hand, we experience at any season an enlargement of affection towards God; if we taste most sweetly, and see most clearly, that the Lord is gracious, and have much liberty and comfort in crying to him, 'Abba, Father;' then also shall we feel a corresponding love to all his people, a disposition to forgive as we hope to be forgiven, and a desire to do good unto all men as we have opportunity, but especially unto them that are of the household of faith. And if, on the other hand, we allow our spirits at any time to be ruffled by strife and contention; if, in the heat of undue excitement, we begin to think or to speak harshly of one another, and allow the sun to go down upon our wrath; we shall feel in the very hour of prayer how fatal this unhallowed spirit is to comfortable fellowship with God, how it fetters our freedom and embitters our feelings; and even when we seek to cry, 'Abba, Father,' in the spirit of adoption, it infuses into our souls all the discomfort and anxiety of the old spirit of bondage. Hence our Lord's command to his disciples, 'If thou bring thy gift to the altar, and there rememberest that thy brother hath ought against thee, leave there thy gift before the altar, and go thy way; first be reconciled to thy brother, and then come and offer thy gift;' and the exhortation of the apostle, 'Let all bitterness, and wrath, and anger, and clamour, and evil speaking, be put away from you, with all malice; and be ye kind one to another, tender-hearted, forgiving one another, even as God, for Christ's sake, hath forgiven you. Be ye, therefore, followers of God, as *dear children, and walk in love.*'

4. The spirit of adoption implies a disposition to hold fellowship and

communion with God as our Father, and with his children as our brethren in Christ.

The spirit of adoption prompts the believer to hold communion with God; for it is by this spirit that he cries, 'Abba, Father.' And as it leads him to be much engaged in prayer, so it gives a new character to his devotions; they are no longer the expression of an anxious and fearful heart, but the outpourings of a spirit confiding in a father's wisdom, rejoicing in a father's love, and committing itself to a father's care. So long as he was under the spirit of bondage, prayer, instead of being a sweet and refreshing privilege, was felt to be a task, or used only as a form; his petitions were dictated by fear more than by faith, and he felt rather as a criminal speaking to his judge, or as a slave deprecating his master's wrath, than as a *child* communing with his father. But now, adopted into God's family, and reconciled through the blood of Christ, he feels a confidence in drawing near to God, such as a child has in speaking to a wise and affectionate parent, and which is only the more tender and deeply rooted in his heart, because he has been a rebellious child, and is now forgiven. The very recollection of his sins, when combined with a sense of God's pardoning mercy, will fill his heart to overflowing with love, and gratitude, and joy; and while he is deeply humbled, and ready to acknowledge that he is 'no more worthy to be called a son,' yet knowing that his adoption was an act of sovereign grace, and that it was vouchsafed, not on account of his own righteousness, but solely through the righteousness of Christ and the redemption of his cross, 'he can *come boldly to the throne*, that he may obtain mercy, and find grace to help him in every time of need.' And in doing so, he is encouraged by the relation in which God stands to him as his Father in heaven; and by the recollection of those gracious assurances which are founded on this relation in the Word; he remembers the words of Christ himself: 'But thou, when thou prayest, enter into thy closet; and when thou hast shut thy door, pray to *thy Father* which is in secret; and thy Father, which seeth in secret, shall reward thee openly;' '*Your Father* knoweth what things ye have need of before ye ask him;' and, 'If ye, being evil, know how to give good gifts unto your children, how much more shall *your Father in heaven* give good things to them that ask him.' There is a rich fountain of encouragement to prayer in the idea that God is our *Father;* for it assures us that even our weakness and infirmities, nay, our very sins and shortcomings, may not exclude us from his notice and regard: on the contrary, 'Even as a father pitieth his children, so the Lord pitieth them that fear him;' and this is his own promise: 'I will spare them, even as a man spareth his own son that serveth him.' If such be the relation in which we stand to God, and such the feelings with which he regards us, then, when we draw near to him in the spirit of adoption, we need not be cast down or discouraged by a sense of our weakness and infirmities: for just as a father's heart is touched by the weakness of his child, so that the child is never more tenderly dealt with than when he is sick and faint;[1] and just as a father's arm is all the more ready to be stretched forth for his child's support, when, sensible of its own weakness, it clings to him with fear lest it should fall; nay, just as a father's sympathy and love are sure to be called forth when an obedient son seeks to serve him, and grieves that he cannot serve him better, and are never more sincerely or deeply felt than when, in the exercise of a wise discipline, he chastens and rebukes the child of his love; just so God, as our Father in heaven, or rather much more, seeing that his love is infinite and unchangeable, will regard the weaknesses and wants, the infirmities and imperfections of his children. For hear his own gracious words, 'Can a woman forget her sucking child, that she should not have compassion on the son of her womb? yea, they may forget, yet will I not forget thee.' 'Is Ephraim my dear son? is he a pleasant child? for since I spake against him, I do earnestly remember him still: therefore my bowels are troubled for him: I will surely have mercy upon him, saith the Lord.' With such views of God, and of his relation to him as a Father, the believer's communion with him is sweet: he feels in prayer very much as a child does when he speaks to a father both able and willing to help him; and having liberty of access at all times, and frequent occasion, as well as the richest encouragement, to pour out his heart and to spread out his case before him, he acquires a growing desire for his fellowship, and prayer comes to be his constant habit and his sweetest privilege: he is 'careful for nothing, but in every thing by prayer and supplication, with thanksgiving, he makes his requests known unto God; and the very peace of God, which passeth all understanding, shall keep his heart and mind through Christ Jesus.'

And just as the filial love which he bears to God as his Father is associated with a fraternal love to all his people, so the communion which he enjoys with God will ever be accompanied with the desire to hold communion also with all in every place who belong to the same family, who share in his privileges, and partake of his spirit, and cherish his hopes, as children of the same Father, and expectants of the same inheritance. It is the counsel of God to all his children, 'See that ye fall not out by the way,' 'love as brethren, be pitiful, be courteous;' and in token of their common relation and their mutual love, God is pleased to make them sit down at the same table, and to unite in commemorating the riches of redeeming grace, while, by partaking of the sacred symbols, they profess the same faith, and are fed with the 'children's bread.' It is in 'the spirit of adoption' that every com-

[1] Robert Bolton, p. 247.

municant should approach the table; not in the spirit of bondage, as if it were a task, or a gloomy and uncomfortable service; but in the spirit of adoption, crying, 'Abba, Father:' for the sacred symbols represent the broken body and the shed blood of the Saviour, through which we obtain liberty of access, and may come boldly to the throne of grace; they point to 'the new and living way which he hath consecrated for us through the veil, that is to say, his flesh:' and when we are called on to partake of them together, in an act of solemn social worship, we should feel towards each other as *brethren*, as children of the same Father, seated around the same table, all sharing more or less in the infirmities and weaknesses which still cleave to his children on earth, but sharing also in the same precious privileges, partaking of the same spiritual food, and cherishing the same everlasting hopes.

5. The spirit of adoption implies a disposition *to trust in God* for the time to come, just as a child confides in the wisdom, and faithfulness, and care of a wise and affectionate father. If we have been delivered from the spirit of bondage unto fear, and if we have been enabled to draw near to God, through Christ, as our reconciled and forgiving Father, then we have ample reason to cherish an unshaken confidence in his unchangeable love, and to commit our future way unto the Lord, in the assurance that 'he will bring it to pass.' The prospects even of a child of God in this world may, indeed, be often dark and threatening; the future may seem to the eye of sense to afford much cause for anxiety and apprehension; and in musing over it, the believer may sometimes be conscious of many painful misgivings and dark forebodings of heart. Even when he has been on the mount of communion, and has been ready to exclaim, 'It is good for us to be here,' the thought may have occurred to him that he must soon descend again into the world, to be harassed once more by its business, and beset by its temptations, and exposed to all the dangers, and difficulties, and trials which must be his portion in the vale of tears; and he may occasionally feel a tendency to cherish the sad apprehension that possibly, after all the privileges he has enjoyed and all the professions he has made, he may fall short of the rest which remaineth for the people of God, and may make shipwreck of faith and of a good conscience, by yielding to those adverse influences which he cannot avoid, and which he is so unequal to resist and overcome. At all events, he must lay his account with *many trials;* and he is perhaps afraid to face, and disposed to shrink from them. The spirit of bondage which is unto fear can give no relief, and afford no comfort in such a case; on the contrary, it is ever ready to brood over all the varieties of possible evil, and to convert future danger into present distress, and even to magnify, by its own distorted vision, the difficulties which lie before us: but the spirit of

adoption may give relief; not, indeed, by exempting us from trials, still less by making us indifferent or insensible to them, but by enabling and disposing us to commit *our case into God's hands*, in compliance with his own declaration, 'Cast thy burden upon the Lord, and he shall sustain thee.' For just as a little child looks to the wisdom, and confides in the care of an affectionate father, and when he ventures out into the world feels all the more secure when he knows that a father's foresight has arranged his plans, and a father's eye is still watching over his progress, just so the believer, looking up to God as his Father in heaven, and knowing that nothing can happen to him without His permission or appointment, that He is ever present to observe, and almighty to sustain, and unerring to direct him; and that he has pledged his faithful word of promise, saying, 'I will never leave thee, nor forsake thee,' 'as thy day is, so shall thy strength be,' 'my grace is sufficient for thee,' 'I will perfect my strength in weakness,' and 'all things shall work together for good to them that love God' – the believer, I say, is able to say with the apostle, in the spirit of childlike confidence, 'Therefore may we boldly say, The Lord is my helper, I will not *fear;*' and with the psalmist, 'The Lord is my shepherd, I shall not *want.*'

6. The spirit of adoption implies a spirit of cheerful *obedience* and *submission* to God's will, of obedience to his will as it is revealed in the Word, and of submission to his will as it is displayed by the dispensations of his providence.

An obligation to *obedience* is necessarily involved in the relation of sonship, and wherever that relation really exists, and is associated with the corresponding spirit of adoption, it will lead to the unreserved, unconditional, and cheerful observance of every part of God's revealed will. For 'a son honoureth his father, and a servant his master: if, then, I be a father, where is mine honour? and if I be a master, where is my fear?' If you have aught of the spirit of adoption, it will be 'your meat and your drink to do the will of your Father in heaven;' your language will be, 'Father, not my will, but thine be done;' 'Our Father which art in heaven, thy will be done on earth, even as it is done in heaven.' And this being your sincere desire, you will be solicitous, in the first instance, to ascertain in every case what is the *will of God*, by carefully consulting the law which he has written on the tablets of your hearts, and the clearer law which he has revealed in the pages of his Word; and when you have ascertained his will, you will obey it at all hazards, suffering neither the temptations of the world, nor the lusts of your own hearts, nor the sophistry by which your passions would beguile and mislead your conscience, nor any considerations of interest or expediency, to deter or seduce you from following that straight path of duty in which God commands you to walk. For being God's children, the opinions of men and the gain of the whole world will be as nothing to you in comparison with the slightest intimation of his will. And the spirit of adoption will give a *new character* to your obedience; it will be no longer the reluctant and half extorted service of a slave, but the willing, and cheerful, and devoted homage of a son submitting to his father's guidance, not of constraint, but willingly, and devoted to his service because he delights to do him honour. This is the characteristic difference betwixt the legal obedience of fear, and the evangelical obedience of love. And just as love is a more kindly and generous principle of action, so the obedience that flows from it will be at once more unreserved in its extent and more cheerful in its nature, pleasant to him who renders, and acceptable to him to whom it is paid. Such is the obedience which God, as a Father, expects from all his children; but oh! if an unreserved and cheerful compliance with his will be the test of sonship, if the spirit of adoption must reconcile us to all his commands, and engage us in a life of holy obedience, what shall we say of those who, bearing the Christian name, and appearing amongst the children at his table, are nevertheless living in the habitual neglect or violation of his law; communicants who come to his table, saying, 'Abba, Father!' and as often as they pray, call him 'Our Father which art in heaven;' yet, when they go back to the world, 'return like a dog to his vomit, or like a sow that is washed to her wallowing in the mire?' Are there none bearing the Christian name among us, who are conscious that their practice ill accords with their profession as children of God? I speak not of the infirmities and shortcomings with which every Christian is chargeable; but of that wilful and habitual opposition, in some respect or other, to God's will, which is utterly inconsistent with the spirit of filial reverence and love. Can he be a child of God, who, when God commands him to sanctify the Sabbath, profanes it by worldly business or vain amusements; or when God commands him to be sober and temperate, gives himself to rioting and drunkenness; or when God enjoins purity of heart and life, lives in uncleanness and licentious pleasure; or when God prescribes the path of honour and integrity prefers the crooked paths of dishonesty and deceit? It cannot be: and they who, presuming on their Gospel liberty, dare to live in the habitual neglect or violation of any part of God's will, must bear to be reminded, that if the spirit of adoption gives a new character to our obedience, it is not in the way of relaxing it or bringing it down to the standard of the world's opinions and habits, but by *raising* it, and infusing into it new life and strength, and making it at once more cheerful, more unreserved, and more devoted than before; and that if, 'where the Spirit of the Lord is, there is liberty,' it is not the liberty of those who turn the grace of God into licentiousness, or 'who continue in sin because grace abounds, but the liberty of men 'who run in the way of his commandments, when God has enlarged their hearts;' and who feel the force of the apostle's exhortation, 'Brethren, ye have been called unto liberty; only use not liberty for an occasion to the flesh;' as 'free, and not using your liberty for a cloak of maliciousness, but as the servants of God.'

The spirit of adoption, while it implies a disposition to obey God's will as it is revealed in his Word, will manifest itself also in the way of quiet and resigned *submission* to his will as it is displayed in the dispensations of his providence. These dispensations may often be afflictive; and they may serve to try the faith and patience of his people, insomuch that they may sometimes be in heaviness through manifold temptations. But the spirit of adoption will lead them to regard all these trials, however numerous and severe and protracted they may be, as the *discipline* of a Father's hand; and they will bow before the rod, and kiss it, even when it smites them. Knowing that nothing happens by chance, and that every thing in their lot is ordained by unerring wisdom and infinite love, and will be overruled for God's glory and their own good; and remembering the gracious words, 'Whom the Lord loveth he chasteneth, and scourgeth every son whom he receiveth;' they will not only lay their account with trials, but feel it to be alike their duty and their privilege to resign themselves into the Lord's hands, saying, 'It is the Lord, let him do as seemeth good in his sight.' And who does not see that the spirit of adoption gives a new character to our submission, and imparts a sweetness to our very trials? The spirit of bondage may produce a sullen and reluctant submission, such as a man would yield to inevitable necessity, or to overwhelming power; but the spirit of adoption, whereby we cry 'Abba, Father,' views every trial as a Father's chastisement, and connects it with a Father's love; and responds to the apostle's touching appeal: 'We have had fathers of our flesh who corrected us, and we gave them reverence; shall we not much rather be in subjection unto the Father of spirits, and live?'

7. The spirit of adoption is associated with inward *peace, and comfort, and hope;* which, although they may be disturbed and interrupted by the operation of other causes, are its proper and natural fruit, and which springing up, and growing by degrees, may issue in the *full assurance* of sonship. The spirit of adoption is essentially, in its own nature, a peaceful and happy frame of mind. Every thing, within and around, above and beneath, present and future, temporal and eternal, assumes a new aspect when we can call God our Father. Even the beauties of nature, always lovely, acquire a fresh loveliness to the Christian, when he can look abroad over its sublime mountains and smiling landscapes, and say, 'My Father made them all;' and so the events of providence, the unfoldings of that mighty scheme

which embraces all our interests and hopes, appear in a new light to the believer, when he can say, 'My Father rules them all.'

But more especially, *the vast scheme of grace and redemption* appears in a new light, when, in the spirit of adoption, he can look to the Author of that scheme as his Father, once offended but now reconciled; and to what God has already done for him as a pledge of what he is still willing to do, an earnest of the fulfilment of all his promises. For 'if God spared not his own Son, but delivered him up to the death for us all; much more will he, with him, also freely give us all things.' 'I am persuaded that neither death, nor life, nor angels, nor principalities, nor powers, nor things present, nor things to come, shall be able to separate us from the love of God which is in Christ Jesus our Lord.'

The spirit of adoption, implying, as it does, a sense of God's love, and faith in his covenant promises, must necessarily be accompanied with some measure of hope; and although that hope may be too weak to admit of our using the strong language of *assurance* in regard either to our present state or our everlasting prospects, it may be sufficient to sustain and animate and encourage us in our Christian course. A childlike disposition of mind, including trust and resignation, and a contrite and tender spirit, may exist where, through remaining darkness or occasional weakness, a believer may be unable to use that language; but as this filial spirit is matured, it may grow up to the full assurance of hope, being in itself at once an *evidence* of our sonship, and an *earnest* of our future inheritance; for the Holy Spirit of promise is itself the earnest of our inheritance, and the first-fruits of the Spirit are a pledge of a glorious harvest: and this may explain the *difference*, as well as the *connection* which subsists betwixt the spirit of adoption, whereby we cry, 'Abba, Father,' and the witness of the Spirit, of which we read in the succeeding verse, by which 'He witnesseth with our spirits that we are the children of God; and if children, then heirs, heirs of God, and joint heirs with Jesus Christ.'

There are two different classes, whose experience may be the *same* in so far as the absence of all sensible comfort is concerned, but is so different in other respects, that we must carefully discriminate betwixt them in offering, as we now propose to do, a few observations for their direction and relief.

There may be some who are sensible that they have never, at any time, been enabled to look to God with other feelings than those of terror and aversion; that his holy character, and righteous law, and awful government have invariably filled them with apprehension and alarm; and that they have obtained relief from these distressing feelings only when they succeeded for a time in banishing the thought of God and death and eternity from their minds, or in cherishing such conceptions of his perfections and purposes as they knew to be at variance with the revelation of his character and will in the Word, but which were felt to be more in accordance with their own wishes, and indispensable to their inward peace. Such persons may be assured, that, as often as their habitual carelessness has been disturbed by occasional convictions of conscience, or awakening glimpses of the truth, they have experienced what is meant by the apostle when he speaks of the spirit of bondage unto fear; and if there be any who are labouring under the burden of guilt, and groaning under the bondage of fear, while they are sensible of no relief, and even ignorant of the remedy which is provided for them in the Gospel, I would affectionately remind them that there is much in their present condition which is fitted alike to suggest a solemn warning and to impart a rich encouragement. There is something unspeakably solemn in the thought that these *convictions* – these *fears* and *misgivings*, of which they are conscious – have all been awakened by God's law applied to their consciences by the Holy Ghost; and that their present experience may be the first-fruit of the Spirit's operation, to whom it belongs 'to reprove the world of sin.' And considering them in this light, I would say nothing to allay their convictions, or to remove their fears, or to rebuke their misgivings, as if they were either extravagant or unfounded. On the contrary, believing that they are the proper fruits of the law when applied to a sinner's conscience, and that, so far from being too intense, they fall far short of what the real state of the case warrants and requires, I would seek to deepen even your deepest convictions of guilt, and to impress you with the thought that your danger is really greater than your fears. But while we dare not offer you relief from your present bondage, by relaxing the fetters, or lowering the demands, or tampering with the curse of God's righteous and unchangeable law, we can point to a way in which you may exchange your bondage for perfect freedom without any violation of God's law, without any disparagement of His character, without any dishonour to His government, without any denial, either of your own sin, or of His eternal justice. Look from the Law to the Gospel, from the curse to the cross, from Sinai, with its thunderings and lightnings, to Calvary, where the lawgiver became the law-fulfiller, and the end of that law for righteousness to every one that believeth. Look, even now, under all your legal terrors, to Christ, as the Lamb of God that taketh away the sins of the world; and to God in Christ, reconciling the world to himself, and not imputing unto men their trespasses; and on the instant when you apprehend the great truth, that, just as God is, and guilty as you feel yourselves to be, God can be, through Christ's propitiation, the just God and yet the Saviour, on that instant you may pass from a state of bondage into the liberty of a child, and feel that a new spirit is given to you, even the spirit of adoption, whereby you may cry, 'Abba, Father.' And that you may be encouraged to avail yourselves of this gracious deliverance, remember, I beseech you, that while the calls and invitations of the Gospel are alike universal and free, so that they belong to sinners as such, and to all sinners without exception; yet, as if with a special view to your own case, they are often particularly addressed to such as are labouring under the spirit of bondage unto fear (not that careless and fearless sinners are excluded, because all are invited, even the wicked and the unrighteous), but to meet the difficulties, and fears, and scruples, of convinced and awakened sinners, they are mentioned as it were by name: – 'Come unto me, all ye that labour, and are heavy laden, and I will give you rest'; 'Ho, every one that thirsteth, come ye to the waters'; 'Whosoever is athirst, let him come, and take of the water of life freely.'

But there is another class, very different from the former, who may be labouring under a spirit which, if not the same, is yet nearly akin to the spirit of bondage unto fear. I mean *the spirit of heaviness*, through manifold temptations, to which many of God's people themselves are subject, and which is often associated with, and apt to engender doubts and fears as to their safety, misgivings as to their interest in Christ and their participation in the privileges of sonship. Such persons have experienced, in former times, the liberty and enlargement of heart which the Gospel imparts, and have known what it is to be translated out of darkness into God's marvellous light, and to look up to God, with childlike confidence, as a reconciled Father. But now they are visited again with a spirit of heaviness, arising from a sense of shortcoming, or from a season of declension, or from the withdrawment of the light of God's countenance: and this spirit of heaviness may, like the spirit of bondage, be accompanied with many distressing misgivings and fears; so that, in their present state, they may have no comfort, and no childlike confidence in looking up to God, and no freedom to say, 'Abba, Father.' To such I would affectionately say, in *the way of warning*, Your present experience is a very solemn call to search and try your ways; to consider what may be the occasion of God's controversy with you; to humble yourselves on account of your sins and shortcomings, your neglected privileges, your abused mercies, your broken resolutions and vows; and to make full and frank confession before God, just as a child should do when he has offended an affectionate father. But I would also say, in *the way of encouragement*, that you are not to regard your present experience, dark and distressing as you may feel it to be, as affording, of itself, any evidence that you do not belong to the number of God's children.

You may be apt to imagine that it would not be thus with you if you had obtained the privilege of sonship; but be assured, no trial has befallen you which has not been common to God's children in all ages of the Church: for Peter speaks of God's children, when he says, that 'now, for a season, if need be, they are in heaviness through manifold temptations;' and we have the recorded examples of holy David, who said, 'I remembered God, and was troubled: I complained, and my spirit was overwhelmed;' and of Heman: 'Lord, why castest thou off my soul? why hidest thou thy face from me? I am afflicted and ready to die from my youth up; while I suffer thy terrors, I am distracted;' and of Job: 'The arrows of the Almighty are within me, the poison whereof drinketh up my spirit; the terrors of the Lord do set themselves in array against me;' and of Jonah: 'I said, I am cast out of thy sight, yet will I look again toward thy holy temple;' and of the Lord Jesus himself, who exclaimed on the cross, in words which breathe at once a spirit of heaviness and of childlike faith, '*My* God, *my* God, why hast thou forsaken me?' And finally, in *the way of direction*, You must obtain relief from your present distresses and fears by the exercise of the same simple faith by which you first entered into peace; you must look out of yourselves to Christ, and, forsaking the law, find refuge in the gospel; you must repair anew to the fountain which God has opened for sin and for uncleanness, and cast yourselves on the mercy and faithfulness of a covenant-keeping God; and be assured, that, sooner or later – for you must *wait* the Lord's time – he who has taken you into the wilderness will speak comfortably unto you; the cloud which now intercepts from you the light of his countenance will be dispersed; and you will yet go on your way *rejoicing*, – and cry, in the spirit of adoption, 'Abba, Father.'

III. The Work of the Spirit as the Spirit of Prayer

IN the Scriptures a special operation of the Spirit is mentioned, by which he aids his people in the exercise of *prayer;* and it is spoken of as one that is common to all believers, and permanent through all ages of the Church. This cheering truth is implied in God's promise of old, 'I will pour upon the house of David, and the inhabitants of Jerusalem, *the Spirit of grace and of supplications;*' and it is implied also in the declared duty of all believers, which is described in the apostle's exhortation, 'Praying always with all prayer and supplication in *the Spirit.*' But the most emphatic testimony on the subject is contained in the words of the apostle (Rom. viii. 26), 'Likewise the Spirit also helpeth our infirmities; for we know not what we should pray for as we ought; but the Spirit itself maketh intercession for us with groanings that cannot be uttered.' That the Spirit of God does in some way 'make intercession for the saints,' is abundantly evident from these passages; but it may be useful to inquire, first, In what sense this is to be understood, or in what way the Spirit acts as a Spirit of grace and supplication; and secondly, What lessons, whether of warning, direction, or encouragement, may be deduced from the doctrine of his agency in prayer.

I. In explanation of this doctrine, it is not to be understood as importing that the Holy Spirit makes intercession for us in his own person, or that he directly addresses his prayer to the Father on our behalf. Christ, as Mediator, prayed for his disciples while he was yet on earth, and he still makes continual intercession for them in heaven, by appearing in the presence of God for them; but the Holy Spirit is never represented in Scripture as interceding in the same way, either by offering up his own personal request, or by appearing for us at the throne. He does intercede, however, in another way, by 'dwelling in us' as 'the Spirit of grace and supplication,' disposing and enabling us to pray for ourselves. He is the Spirit of supplication, just as he is the Spirit of faith, and repentance, and hope. He is the author of these spiritual graces, the source whence they flow, and by which they are continually sustained. Yet they exist in the believer, and are exercised by him, so as to form part of his own personal character; and just so the Spirit is said to make intercession for us, when he stirs us up to intercede for ourselves, and gives us grace to desire and to ask what blessings we severally require. That this is the sense in which the doctrine is to be understood appears from several expressions, which imply that, by the Spirit's grace, believers are taught and enabled to offer up their own supplications at the throne; for, first of all, it is not the Spirit considered as a distinct person of the Godhead that is said to intercede, but 'the Spirit *that dwelleth in you,*' even the Spirit of adoption, whereby *we* cry, 'Abba, Father'. And, secondly, it is expressly said, that the *Spirit helpeth our infirmities;* for we know not what we should pray for as we ought – our *own* prayers being directly referred to, and his interposition designed to remove those hindrances, and supply those defects *in us,* which would otherwise impair or interrupt our communion with God: – and thirdly, it is added, that 'he maketh intercession for us with *groanings* which cannot be uttered;' an expression which cannot be applied personally to the Spirit, but is aptly descriptive of that moral earnestness and deep concern which he awakens in *our own hearts;* and accordingly it is added, 'He that searcheth *the hearts* knoweth the mind of the Spirit.' These various expressions are sufficient to show, that, by the intercession of the Spirit, we are to understand the earnest supplication and prayer which we are disposed and enabled, by his grace, to offer up at the throne.

If any one doubt the *necessity* of the Spirit's aid in the exercise of prayer, there is enough in the words of the apostle to convince him of his error; for even an inspired man, classing himself along with other believers, says, 'The Spirit also helpeth our infirmities; for WE know not what we should pray for as we ought.' This humbling confession of our own infirmity and ignorance, and of our simple dependence on the grace and strength of the Spirit, is, indeed, much at variance with the natural feelings of the human heart, which is prone to self-sufficiency and presumptuous confidence in its own unaided powers; but there is reason to fear that those who have never felt their need of the Spirit's grace in the exercise of prayer have either never prayed at all, or if they have observed the outward form, are still strangers to its spiritual nature, as the greatest work, the highest and holiest service of the soul, by which it holds communion with God, in the exercise of those graces of faith, and love, and hope, which are all inspired and sustained by the Holy Spirit. The careless and presumptuous sinner, or the cold and formal professor, may be conscious of no difficulty in prayer which cannot be overcome by the power of his own natural faculties: he may content himself with a repetition of a form of words, such as his memory can easily retain and recall, and caring for no further communion with God than what may be implied in the occasional or regular use of that form, he is not sensible of any infirmity such as calls for the aid of the Spirit. But not such are the feelings of any true believer, for never is he more sensible of his own infirmity, and of his absolute dependence on the Spirit's grace, than when he seeks, in the hour of prayer, to spread his case before the Lord, and to hold communion and fellowship with him as his Father in heaven. Having some idea, however inadequate, of the greatness and majesty of God; and some sense, however feeble, of the spirituality of his service; knowing that 'God is a Spirit, and that they that worship him must worship him in spirit and in truth;' but conscious at the same time of much remaining darkness, of the corruptions which still cleave to him, and of the manifold distractions to which his mind is subject, even in the most solemn exercises, he knows what those 'infirmities' are of which the apostle speaks, and will be ready to join with him in the humbling confession, 'We know not what things we should pray for as we ought.' His own experience teaches him that the spirit of prayer is not the natural and spontaneous product of his own heart; that it was implanted there, and that it must be continually sustained by grace from on high; and long after he has been enabled to come with comfort to the throne of grace, and to pour out his heart with much of the peace which a spirit of adoption imparts, he may be reminded, by the variations of his own experience, that he must be dependent, from first to last, on the Spirit's grace for all his earnestness and all his enjoyment in prayer. Oh! what believer has not occasionally felt his own utter emptiness, and the barrenness even of this precious privilege, when, left to himself, he attempted to pray, while the spirit of prayer was withheld! You may have retired at your usual hour to your closets, and fallen upon your knees, and used even your accustomed words; but you felt that your affections were cold, your desires languid, and your whole heart straitened and oppressed. You strove once more to renew your request, and with greater urgency than before; but in spite of all your efforts your thoughts began to wander even in God's immediate presence; and as you rose from your knees, you were ready to exclaim, 'Oh that it were with me as in months past! Oh, that I knew where I might find him! that I might come even to his seat! I would order my cause before him, and fill my mouth with arguments.' On such occasions you complain of unbelief, of a wandering mind, of a hard and insensible heart; and these complaints are frequently heard amongst God's people, for I believe that he often visits them with such experiences for the very purpose of impressing them with a humbling sense of their own *infirmity*, and reminding them of their dependence on the Spirit for the right use and enjoyment of all the means of grace.

The grace of the Holy Ghost, then, is indispensable, if we would maintain the spirit and enjoy the exercise of prayer; but we must ever remember, that in this, as in every other part of his work, he acts by the use of means, and in a way that is wisely adapted to the rational and moral nature with which we are endowed. He acts upon us, not as mere machines, but as moral agents; and by various considerations and motives, he teaches and disposes us to pray. Every part of his work as the Spirit of grace has a tendency to prepare us for this exercise; for whether he act as a reprover, convincing us of sin, – or as a sanctifier, subduing our corruptions, or as a comforter, giving us peace and joy in believing, or as a teacher, enlarging our views of divine truth, and confirming our faith in it, all the operations of his grace are subservient more or less directly to the exercise of prayer. But that we may have a clear and distinct idea of the Spirit's agency as 'the Spirit of grace and supplication,' it may be observed more particularly, that—

1. He enables us for prayer, by disclosing to us our *necessities and wants, our sins and shortcomings*, so as to impress us with a deep sense of our absolute dependence on God. This is intimated when it is said, 'The Spirit also helpeth our infirmities; for we know not *what we should pay for* as we ought.' Self-ignorance is a great hindrance to fervent prayer. We are not duly sensible of our wants, and hence we have no earnest desire for those supplies of grace which we really need: we are apt to say with the Laodiceans, 'I am rich and increased with goods, and have need of nothing;' not knowing that 'we are wretched, and miserable, and poor, and blind, and naked.'

Our prayers have respect either to our temporal or our spiritual wants, and with reference to both we need the enlightening and directing grace of the Spirit. In respect to our temporal wants, it might seem that we could have little difficulty in understanding them, and in praying for what things we need; but I apprehend every experienced believer will be ready to acknowledge his ignorance on this subject, and to confess that he often knows not what is really good for him. Every condition of life has its peculiar snares, and temptations, and trials; and one of the most precious fruits of the Spirit is a disposition to resign ourselves to the will of God, and to pray for temporal blessings only in so far as they may be consistent with, or conducive to, our spiritual welfare. This resigned and spiritual frame of mind is beautifully expressed in the prayer of Agur: 'Give me neither poverty nor riches: feed me with food convenient for me: lest I be full, and deny thee, and say, Who is the Lord? or lest I be poor, and steal, and take the name of my God in vain.' This is so far from being the natural disposition of our hearts, that the apostle represents the very opposite spirit as prevailing among professing Christians, and breathing in their very prayers: 'Ye ask and receive not, because ye ask amiss, that ye may consume it on your lusts.'

In reference, again, to our spiritual wants, we are often lamentably ignorant of their nature and extent; and they who have paid most attention to the state of their hearts will be the first to feel how much they need the grace of the Spirit to direct them to a discovery of their sins. Thus David exclaims, 'Who can understand his errors? cleanse thou me from secret faults;' 'Search me, O God, and know my heart: try me, and know my thoughts: and see if there be any wicked way in me, and lead me in the way everlasting.' Nothing is more necessary to prayer than to know the 'plague of our hearts.'

2. The Holy Spirit, besides disclosing to us our wants, our weaknesses, and our sins, makes known *the rich provision of all needful grace* which is treasured up in Christ; and this is as useful for our direction and encouragement as the discovery of our necessities is for awakening our desires, since it is, in a great measure, owing to our ignorance or unbelief in regard to the rich provision of the Gospel, that we 'know not what we should pray for as we ought.' The Holy Spirit makes known to the believer, in all their fulness and variety, the inestimable blessings of redemption; for 'he takes of the things of Christ, and shows them unto us;' and he is sent that we may 'know the things which are freely given to us of God.'

A clear discovery of the rich and glorious privileges which Christ has purchased for his people, is at once a means of direction and a source of encouragement in prayer: when they are placed before us in all their variety and extent, we feel how much we need them, how suitable they are to our real wants, and how infinitely precious and desirable in themselves. Pardon, repentance, holiness, peace of conscience, eternal life – when these and similar blessings are vividly conceived of as having been purchased by the Saviour for his people, and offered to all without exception in the Gospel, we see what we should pray for; and we feel also that we have a free right and warrant to pray for them, infinitely great and precious though they be. Ignorance of the gracious provisions of the Gospel, or a dim and indistinct apprehension, either of the nature of these blessings, or of the method by which they were provided, or of the terms on which they are offered, is a great hindrance to prayer; but prayer becomes free and lively in proportion as we are taught by the Spirit to know the things which are *freely* given to us of God.' These are great blessings, and when we pray for them we may well feel that we make a great request of God; but when we know that they are all treasured up for us in the fulness that is in Christ, and that they are freely tendered to us in the Gospel, 'we come boldly to the throne of grace, that we may obtain mercy, and find grace to help in every time of need.'

3. The Holy Spirit assists us in prayer, by working in us such *dispositions and desires* as make us to seek for those supplies of grace which we need, with earnest, importunate, and persevering supplication: 'As the hart panteth after the water brooks, so panteth my soul after thee, O God. My soul thirsteth for God, for the living God: when shall I come and appear before God?'

Naturally we have no such disposition or desire. The carnal mind, which is enmity against God, is naturally averse from those spiritual blessings of which it stands in need. True, it is desirous of exemption from pain and punishment and danger; but whatever is spiritual is obnoxious to its taste, insomuch that were an unrenewed mind supposed (if we may suppose a case which is never realized in actual experience) to be sensible, on the one hand, of its sin and misery and danger, and enabled to perceive, on the other, the number and variety of the blessings which have been purchased and offered by Christ; it would, if left to follow its own inclination without the restraining and renewing grace of the Spirit, refuse to accept God's great salvation!

The awakening of spiritual desire in the heart is the work of God's Spirit; and that desire must be kept alive by his continued agency: 'Blessed are they that hunger and thirst after righteousness; for they shall be filled.' This new disposition or desire makes prayer natural, easy, and delightful to the people of God. Just as a natural man hungers and thirsts for food and drink, so the renewed man hungers and thirsts after righteousness. He has a new spiritual appetite, which naturally and spontaneously seeks its proper spiritual aliment. And hence those commands and observances which are a burden and bondage to mere formalists are an easy yoke to every living Christian.

4. The Holy Spirit helps us in prayer by strengthening and exciting into lively exercise *those spiritual graces* which are essentially implied in communion with God. Prayer properly consists in the exercise of these graces: it is not the mere utterance of words, nor is it even the mere expression of natural feeling; it is an exercise of repentance, of faith, of love, of trust and delight in God; of repentance, which is expressed in the language of confession; of faith, for he that cometh to God must believe that he is the rewarder of them that 'diligently seek him;' of love, for we call him 'Abba, Father,' 'our Father which art in heaven;' of trust, for we commit our case into his hands; and of delight, for the promise is, 'Delight thyself in the Lord, and he will give thee the desires of thine heart.' These graces are not only presupposed or implied in prayer, but prayer properly consists in the lively exercise of them, insomuch, that where these graces are awanting, there is no prayer, whatever forms may be observed, and whatever words employed. Now let it be remembered, that all these graces are the fruits of the Spirit, that they are at first implanted, and must ever afterwards be nourished, by the Spirit, and you will perceive at once how the Spirit may assist us in prayer simply by strengthening and exciting into lively exercise all the gracious affections of the soul. By this means he gives us freedom and comfort in prayer: for where these graces are absent, prayer is a mere form; where they are weak, prayer is cold and languid;

but where they abound, prayer is the soul's communion with God.

5. The Spirit aids us in this exercise, by helping our infirmities, when he either removes *the hindrances* to prayer, or stirs us up to watch against them, and to rise above them.

There are many hindrances to prayer, some of them external, arising from the body, or the world, others of them internal, arising from the state of our own hearts. Of the latter, I may mention ignorance, unbelief, indifference, despondency, and such like; which are removed by the Holy Spirit, as he is the enlightener, the sanctifier, and the comforter of God's people: and of the former, bodily infirmities, the cares and business of life, the dissipating influence of society, and such like, from which the Spirit promises no exemption to any of his people, but which he strengthens them to resist, and enables them to overcome. But if we would overcome these *hindrances* to prayer, we must avail ourselves of those *helps* which the Spirit of God has provided for us, remembering that he acts in the use of ordinary means, and that his grace is to be sought in the way of duty.

II. Many lessons might be deduced from the doctrine of the Spirit's agency as 'the Spirit of grace and supplication,' applicable alike for our warning, our direction, and our encouragement in prayer.

We learn from it that prayer is a very solemn exercise, an exercise in which we not only hold direct converse with God whom we address, but in which God also holds converse with us by the operation of his Spirit in our hearts; and as this reflection is fitted to rebuke and humble us on account of the carelessness with which we have too often approached his throne, so it should warn us against the guilt and danger of calling on his name without some suitable feelings of reverence and godly fear.

We learn from it that prayer is an exercise far beyond our natural power, and demands the exercise of *graces* which can only be imparted by the Spirit of God; and this reflection, again, should direct us to look to the Spirit of all grace, and to implore his aid, as often as we come to the throne.

We learn from it that God has made the most ample provision for our being restored to his communion and fellowship: for not only is he revealed as the hearer and the answerer of prayer, sitting on the throne of grace, and waiting to be gracious; and not only is Christ revealed as our advocate and intercessor, standing beside the throne, and ready to present our requests, perfumed with the incense of his own merits; but lest, when all outward impediments were removed, there might still remain some hindrance in our own hearts, the Holy Spirit is also revealed as 'the Spirit of grace and supplication,' 'who intercedeth for the saints according to the will of God'; and as this precious truth should encourage us to ask his grace to help our infirmities, so should it inspire the hope of an answer in peace; for every prayer that is prompted by the Spirit is a pledge of its own fulfilment, seeing that 'God who searcheth the hearts knoweth what is the mind of the Spirit, because he maketh intercession for the saints according to the will of God.' And although we should feel as if we were at a loss for words to express our desires to God, even this should not discourage us; the *desire* of the heart is prayer, although it should find no fit utterance; for Moses' heart spake only, when God said, 'Wherefore criest thou unto me;' and Hannah's, when 'she spake in her heart;' her lips moved, but her voice was not heard, yet without words 'she poured out her heart before the Lord;' and the very want of suitable expressions may only show that the Spirit is making intercession for us 'with groanings that *cannot be uttered.*'

But while we are warned, and directed, and encouraged by this precious truth, we must habitually bear in mind that the Spirit's grace is to be sought in the path of duty; that his influence is not designed to supersede but to stimulate our industry; and that if we would overcome the *hindrances* which prevent or mar our communion with God, we must diligently avail ourselves of the *helps* which he has provided for our use. Where prayer is prevented or abridged by any necessary cause, and especially by bodily infirmity, the words of Christ himself show that he will make every reasonable allowance for our weakness: for on that memorable night, when he was in an agony in the garden, and when his soul was exceeding sorrowful, even unto death, and his sweat was as it were great drops of blood falling to the ground, his disciples, whom he commanded to watch, began to sleep; he gently rebuked them, saying, 'What! couldest thou not watch one hour?' and exhorted them, 'Watch and pray, lest ye enter into temptation;' yet no sooner was the warning uttered, than he himself suggested their excuse, 'The spirit truly is willing, but the flesh is weak.' But there are other hindrances to prayer, for which no such allowance can be made, and which we must watch against and overcome in the use of every appointed means, if we would expect the blessing of the Spirit. Our bodily infirmities themselves, when they proceed, as they often do, from sloth and self-indulgence, and from the fulness of a pampered appetite, are reasons for deep self-humiliation, when they mar our communion with God; and we should watch unto prayer, and even fast, if need be, remembering the apostle's words, 'I keep under my body, and bring it into subjection, lest by any means, having preached the Gospel to others, I should myself be cast away.' And in like manner, the necessary business of life must be attended to; but the absorbing cares, the idle amusements, the mere vanities of the world, which so often abridge the time and destroy the comfort of prayer, should be watchfully guarded against, and steadily resisted, if we would enjoy the communion of the Spirit in our fellowship with God.

IV. The Work of the Spirit as the Comforter

OUR blessed Lord intimated to his disciples before his departure, that he would not leave them desolate, or orphans, but would send them the Holy Spirit, that he might abide with them for ever; and he spake of the Spirit as a *paraclete* (an expression which has been translated in our version – a *comforter*, but which admits of being rendered – an *advocate*, or *monitor*), whose office it should be to plead the cause and to secure the welfare of his people in various ways, by helping their infirmities, guiding them into all truth, strengthening them against the assaults of temptation, sustaining them under the pressure of trial, and aiding them in the exercise of prayer. It is the less necessary to dwell on the mere meaning of that expression, because unquestionably in other places the Spirit is represented as executing the office of a comforter; as when the apostle says, 'Now the God of hope fill you with all peace and joy in believing, that ye may abound in hope through the power of the Holy Ghost.' (Rom. 15. 13). The peace and joy, and hope, which are here mentioned, are the constituent elements of that comfort which God has provided for his people; and elsewhere they are severally described as being of inestimable value, fruits alike sweet and precious of the riches of his grace: for this peace is called 'the very peace of God, which passeth all understanding;' and this joy is said to be 'a joy unspeakable and full of glory;' and this hope is 'a living, a lively hope, an anchor to the soul both sure and steadfast, entering into that which is within the veil.'

It may be useful to direct your thoughts to the source of this comfort; to the method in which it is bestowed; to the various degrees in which it may be enjoyed; and to the duty which is implied in the apostle's prayer, of seeking 'to be filled with all peace and joy in believing, and to abound in hope.'

I. With reference to the source of this comfort, it is important to remark, that the peace and joy and hope in which it consists are severally ascribed in Scripture to each of the three persons in the Godhead, and represented as flowing to us out of the various offices which they execute under the covenant of redemption. *God himself is the author of this comfort*, the inexhaustible fountain of his goodness being the source whence it proceeds; but it is not as the God of nature and providence, the Creator, Preserver, and Governor of the world; it is as the God of grace and redemption, that he imparts it to his people. It is to God in his covenant relation as God in Christ – the Reconciler and the Saviour of the guilty, that the apostle refers, when he speaks of him as 'the God of hope,' and as 'the God of patience and consolation;' and more expressly still in another place, where he says, 'Blessed be God, even the Father of our Lord Jesus Christ, the Father of mercies and the God of all comfort; who comforteth us in all our tribulation, that we may be able to comfort them which are in any trouble by the comfort wherewith we ourselves are comforted of God.' As God is the author of this comfort, so it comes to us in and through Christ, as the Mediator of the new covenant. He was sent 'to preach peace to them that were afar off, and to them that were near.' He is himself 'our peace,' as he is 'the propitiation for our sins;' for 'being justified by faith, we have peace with God through our Lord Jesus Christ; by whom also we have access by faith into this grace wherein we stand, and rejoice in hope of the glory of God.' Christ is 'the Prince of peace,' and his Word is the 'gospel of peace;' and he was sent at once to procure and to proclaim that reconciliation on which our peace and joy and hope depend: 'He hath anointed me to preach good tidings to the meek; he hath sent me to bind up the brokenhearted,' 'to comfort all that mourn; to appoint unto them that mourn in Zion, to give unto them beauty for ashes, the oil of joy for mourning, and the garment of praise for the spirit of heaviness.' And, accordingly, both the Father and the Son are conjoined in the apostle's prayer: 'Now our Lord Jesus Christ himself, and God, even our Father, which hath loved us, and given us everlasting consolation and good hope through grace, comfort your hearts and stablish you in every good word and work.' But this comfort, flowing from God himself as its source, and through Christ the Mediator of the new covenant as the channel by which it is conveyed to us, is applied to our hearts by the gracious agency and inward operation of the Holy Spirit. The apostle prays for the Roman converts that they might be 'filled with all peace and joy in believing, and abound in hope through the power of the Holy Ghost;' and of the primitive believers we read, that they 'walked in the fear of the Lord, and in the *comfort of the Holy Ghost.*'

The Spirit's love as a Comforter is manifested in various ways. For, *first,* It was the Spirit with which Christ himself was anointed, and by which he was qualified, in respect of his human nature, for the execution of his great design: 'The Spirit of the Lord God is upon me, for he hath anointed me to preach;' *secondly,* It was the *Spirit* who dictated the whole of that message of grace and mercy which is contained in the gospel, for 'holy men of God spake as they were moved by the Holy Ghost;' and to him, there-fore, is to be gratefully ascribed every consolation which the Gospel im-parts, and every hope which it inspires; – and *thirdly*, It is the Spirit who, by his continued agency in the Church, and his internal operation on the minds of believers, enables them to understand the gracious inport, and to feel the blessed influence of the gospel; so that they are 'filled with all peace and joy in believing, and abound in hope through the power of the Holy Ghost.'

Such is the view which is given in Scripture of the source or origin of the comfort that is here spoken of; it is ascribed to each of the three persons of the Godhead, and represented as flowing to us out of the various offices which they fulfil under the covenant of redemption. And, by this view, two reflections are suggested, which may be briefly noticed. The first is, How *gracious* and *lovely* is the aspect in which God's character is presented, when each person in the Godhead is declared to be so much interested, not only in the safety, but in the comfort and happiness of his people: and the second is, How sweet and comfortable is the dispensation under which we are placed, seeing that it is alike fitted and designed to *fill us with all peace and joy* in believing, so that we may abound in hope through the power of the Spirit of God. If, then, the Father be the very God of peace, the Father of mercies, and the God of all comfort; and if his beloved Son be the Prince of peace; and if the Holy Spirit be the Comforter, the Spirit of all grace and consolation; and if the Gospel be indeed, as its very name imports, glad tidings of great joy: it follows, that however from the operation of *other* causes, such as the remaining darkness of their understandings, or the un-subdued corruption of their hearts, or the weakness of their faith, or the strength of their temptations, or the number and weight of their trials, God's people may sometimes have their peace disturbed, yet, in its native tendency and proper effect, the Gospel is fitted to produce and sustain 'a peace which passeth all understanding,' and 'a joy which is unspeakable and full of glory.' And if any of his people are 'for a season in heaviness through manifold temptations,' 'walking in darkness, and having no light,' they may rest assured that their want of present comfort arises from no defect in Christ's Gospel, and still less from any indifference to their real welfare on the part of God;' on the contrary, God is 'the comforter of those who are cast down;' and it is only 'if need be,' and with a view to their ultimate good, that he subjects them for a season to this sore discipline, taking them, as it were, for a little time into the wilderness, that he may there speak com-fortably unto them.

II. Having seen that God in Christ is the inexhaustible source of that comfort which is imparted to his people by the agency of the Spirit, it will be of considerable practical importance to consider the means and method by which the Holy Spirit fulfils this precious and endearing part of his work.

It were a dangerous error to suppose that the Spirit comforts his people, by infusing peace and joy and hope into their hearts without the use of the ordinary means of grace, or separate and apart from his other fruits and operations as their teacher and sanctifier. He acts in this, as in every other part of his work, in a way that is consistent with the laws, and adapted to the necessities, of our moral nature. And his work is not *divided;* its various parts may be distinctly considered, but they never exist separately from each other; they constitute one grand work by which our happiness is secured while our holiness is advanced.

The Spirit comforts his people by *means of the truth revealed in his Word,* enabling them to understand its import, to feel its power, and especially to apply it, in the exercise of an appropriating faith, to the case of their own souls. That the Gospel, or the truth contained in the Gospel, is the instrumental means by which the Spirit comforts his people, appears from the apostle's prayer above quoted, for he prays that they might be 'filled with all peace and joy *in believing;*' and from his language in another place, 'For whatsoever things were written aforetime were written for our learning, that we through patience and *comfort of the Scriptures* might have hope.' David, too, refers to the same means of consolation, when he says, 'This is my comfort in mine affliction; for thy *Word* hath quickened me.'

He begins to impart this comfort at the very time of a sinner's conversion; for no sinner is converted until he is so far enlightened in the knowledge of Christ as a Saviour, and persuaded of the certainty and freeness of the Gospel, as to feel that he may, as a sinner, guilty and helpless as he is in himself, venture, on a scriptural warrant, to put his own personal trust in Christ, and to draw near to God through him, in the humble hope that 'whosoever cometh shall in no wise be cast out;' and there is enough in these, the simplest elements of Gospel truth, to impart immediate relief and comfort to the sinner's heart, insomuch that, like the Ethiopian treasurer, he may from that hour 'go on his way rejoicing.' For the Gospel of Christ is really a *Gospel* – good news, glad tidings of great joy, addressed as it is, not to the innocent, but to the guilty, and affording, as it does, to every man that is a sinner, and just because he is a sinner, a divine warrant to return unto the Lord, in the assurance that he will have mercy upon him, even to our God, who will abundantly pardon. But while, from the beginning of his Christian course, the believer may taste and see that the Lord is gracious, and may experience that measure of peace and joy and hope which the simplest elements of divine truth, when rightly apprehended and really believed, are fitted to inspire, his comfort, like every other fruit of the Spirit, admits of growth and increase, and is advanced in proportion as he acquires larger and clearer views of the truth as it is in Jesus. The believer's comfort is often, for a time, weak and fluctuating, just because his views of divine truth are dim and indistinct; but as these become, under the teaching of the Spirit, more clear and comprehensive, his comfort also becomes more settled and stable. Every new view which he obtains of the character of God, as it is displayed in the cross of Christ; every new proof of his wisdom and justice and love in the work of redemption, and especially in his dealings towards his own soul; every fresh experience of the power of God's truth, must increase that comfort, which even his first faint glimpse of these things imparted to his heart; and it is in this way, and especially by enlightening him more fully in the knowledge of Christ, that the Spirit comforts his people, as we learn from that remarkable prayer of the apostle: 'For this cause I bow my knees unto the Father of our Lord Jesus Christ, of whom the whole family in heaven and earth is named, that he would grant you, according to the riches of his glory, to be strengthened with might by his Spirit in the inner man; that Christ may dwell in your hearts by faith; that ye, being rooted and grounded in love, may be able to comprehend with all saints what is the breadth, and length, and depth, and height; and to know the love of Christ, which passeth knowledge, that ye might be filled with all the fulness of God.' Mark here (1) That even true converts, genuine believers in Christ, are as yet comparatively ignorant of the *boundless love of Christ.* (2) That they must be strengthened with might by the Spirit in the inner man, in order to form any suitable conception of it. (3) That a knowledge of Christ's love is slowly and gradually acquired in the course of Christian experience; for Christ must *dwell in our hearts by faith,* and we must be *rooted and grounded in love,* in order to comprehend it. (4) That, after all, they never can exhaust a subject which is in itself inexhaustible: it has a height and a depth in it 'which passeth knowledge.' And, (5) To *know Christ's love,* as the Spirit only can make us know it, is the means of a comfort as full as it is sweet: it is to 'be filled with all the fulness of God.' In this manner the Spirit comforts his people, by disclosing to them the fulness that is in Christ, and the freeness with which his privileges are bestowed; for 'we have received,' says the apostle, 'not the spirit of the world, but the Spirit which is of God; that we might know the things which are freely given to us of God.'

It is of great practical importance to remember that all genuine evangelical comfort has its ground and warrant in the revealed truth of God; for then it is not delusive and groundless, like the false security of those who say, 'Peace, peace, while there is no peace,' but it is stable, and sound, and permanent, in proportion to the strength of the ground on which it rests.

Again, the Holy Spirit provides for the comfort of his people *by sancti-fying them*. We read of two kinds of rest which Christ proposes to us in the Gospel; and these two are not only inseparably conjoined in Scripture, but will be found, in experience, to be very intimately connected. The first is the *rest of justification or pardon*, of which Christ speaks when, addressing the guilty sinner laden with the burden of his sins, he says, 'Come unto me, all ye that labour and are heavy laden, and I will give you rest;' He will take the burden of guilt away; He will abundantly pardon. But the second is the *rest of sanctification*, 'Take my yoke upon you, and learn of me; for I am meek and lowly in heart; and ye shall find rest unto your souls. For my yoke is easy, and my burden is light.'

This comfort arises from the subjugation of our unholy passions, and the substitution in their room of the gracious fruits of the Spirit; which are essentially, in their own nature, as peaceful as they are lovely, and not only conducive to our happiness, but its constituent elements. It is only necessary to enumerate them, and to contrast them with their opposites, to see that in their own nature, and apart from all arbitrary rewards or punishments, they are essentially and inherently blissful. Mark the contrast, as it is drawn by the apostle: 'The works of the flesh are manifest, which are these: Adultery, fornication, uncleanness, lasciviousness, idolatry, witchcraft, hatred, variance, emulations, wrath, strife, seditions, heresies, envyings, murders, drunkness, revellings, and such like.' 'But the fruit of the Spirit is love, joy, peace, long-suffering, gentleness, goodness, faith, meek-ness, temperance: against such there is no law. And they that are Christ's have crucified the flesh with the affections and lusts.' The mere enumeration of these opposite qualities of character should be sufficient to convince you that the graces of the Spirit are fitted, in their own nature, to minister to your comfort; and we have the Lord's own assurance that every beatitude stands connected with one or other of these graces, when he says, 'Blessed are the poor in spirit: for theirs is the kingdom of heaven. Blessed are they that mourn: for they shall be comforted. Blessed are the meek: for they shall inherit the earth. Blessed are they which do hunger and thirst after righteousness: for they shall be filled. Blessed are the merciful: for they shall obtain mercy. Blessed are the pure in heart: for they shall see God.'

The Spirit comforts us, then, by carrying on the great work of sancti-fication; but it is no part of his office to comfort us 'in *our sins;*' and it is still true, as it ever was, that the wicked are as a raging sea, when it cannot rest; for 'there is no peace, saith my God, to the wicked.'

Again, the Spirit comforts his people by disclosing to them, and enabling them to discern *such marks and evidences of a work of grace in their hearts*, as may afford a comfortable assurance of their sonship, and awaken a cheering hope of future glory. 'The Spirit itself beareth witness with our spirits that we are the children of God; and if children, then heirs, heirs of God, and joint heirs with Christ.' Here, too, the Spirit acts as our Comforter, not by making known our election with an audible voice, or revealing any thing that may not be gathered from the Word, when viewed in connection with our own experience, but simply by producing his gracious fruits, and then enabling us to discern them as so many scriptural marks and evidences of our conversion. For it is the presence of the Spirit in our hearts, evinced by the change which his power produces there, which is the witness or evidence of our sonship: 'Hereby we know that we dwell in God; because he has given us of his Spirit;' and 'he that hath wrought us for the self-same thing is God, who also has given to us the *earnest* of his Spirit;' and 'ye are sealed with the Holy Spirit of promise, which is the earnest of our inheritance, until the redemption of the purchased possession.'

I need not say that it is no part of the Spirit's work as a Comforter to exempt his people from trials; on the contrary, they seem to be subjected to afflictions at once more numerous and severe than are those of the men of this world; for, in addition to disease, and bereavement, and disappointment, which they share in common with others, they are exposed to trials which are peculiar to themselves: some inward, arising from the exercise of their own minds, the warfare in which they are engaged, the discipline to which, if need be, they are subjected, for their trial, and humiliation, and establishment; and others outward, arising from the obloquy and opposition, the ridicule or persecution of the world. But here is the mystery of their peace: it is peace in the midst of trouble, joy in the midst of sorrow. 'In the world,' says the Saviour, 'ye shall have tribulation; but be of good cheer, I have overcome the world;' and hence the apostle could say, 'We are troubled on every side, yet not distressed; we are perplexed, but not in despair; persecuted, but not forsaken; cast down, but not destroyed.'

III. The comfort of which we have spoken, arising from our views of God's truth, the sanctification of our nature, and the inward witness of the Spirit, may exist in various degrees, according to the greater or less extent of our spiritual attainments; and this is intimated to us, as well as the duty of seeking for a large measure of evangelical comfort, in the apostle's prayer, 'The God of hope *fill* you with all peace and joy in believing; that ye may abound in hope, through the power of the Holy Ghost.'

From the manner in which this prayer is expressed, we may learn that there is an intimate and mutual relation betwixt the constituent elements of which the Christian's comfort is composed; that there must first be present peace and joy in believing, before we can experience a lively hope which respects our future prospects; as it will invariably be found that there is no real hope of eternal life *hereafter*, until we are enabled so to believe the Gospel as to enjoy some measure of peace *now*. Those, therefore, who complain of the want of confidence, should be directed in the first instance to those simple elements of Gospel truth which are fitted to give immediate relief and comfort to the sinner; and those, again, who have experienced some small measure of peace, and have been enabled occasionally to look forward with something like hope to the future, should be encouraged to seek after larger measures of these blissful feelings; so that, 'being filled with *all* peace and joy in believing, they may *abound* in hope through the power of the Holy Ghost.' This is alike their duty and their privilege: it is their duty, since God himself requires them 'to give all diligence to make their calling and election sure;' and it is their privilege, for this abundant consolation, and this good hope through grace, are declared to be attainable; and every believer will acknowledge that they are most desirable. And He who is revealed as 'the Father of mercies, and the God of all comfort,' is not unwilling to give the Spirit to them that ask him; nor is the Spirit unwilling to impart his consolations, for he is 'the good Spirit', 'the Spirit of all grace,' who is 'grieved' when his consolations are slighted, and ever ready to 'bind up the broken-hearted, to comfort all that mourn.'

But while we are encouraged by these considerations to expect and seek for a larger measure of peace and joy and hope than we have yet experienced, we must ever remember that they are to be sought for in the *way of duty*, and in the use of the ordinary means of grace. It is, *first*, by *faith* by believing the testimony of God in the Gospel; and, *secondly*, by 'diligence in duty,' giving all diligence to make our calling and election sure; and, *thirdly*, by prayer for ourselves and for others; – it is by these and similar means that we may expect to realize what the apostle supplicated on behalf of his converts, when he prayed for them, 'The God of hope fill you with all peace and joy in believing; that ye may abound in hope, through the power of the Holy Ghost.'

And now, on a calm and comprehensive review of all that has been said concerning the Work of the Holy Spirit, both in the conversion of sinners, and in the edification of His people, how appropriate to the case of every reader, whatever may be his character, are these prayers of David:

'Create in me a clean heart, O God; and renew a right spirit within me. Cast me not away from thy presence; and take not thy Holy Spirit from me. Restore unto me the joy of thy salvation; and uphold me by thy free Spirit.' 'Teach me to do thy will; for thou art my God: thy Spirit is good; lead me into the land of uprightness.'